MAN-DEVIL

Man-Devil

THE MIND AND TIMES OF BERNARD MANDEVILLE, THE WICKEDEST MAN IN EUROPE

John Callanan

PRINCETON UNIVERSITY PRESS

PRINCETON & OXFORD

Published by Princeton University Press
41 William Street, Princeton, New Jersey 08540
99 Banbury Road, Oxford OX2 6JX

press.princeton.edu

ISBN 978-0-691-16544-8
ISBN (e-book) 978-0-691-26498-1

British Library Cataloguing-in-Publication Data is available

Editorial: Ben Tate and Josh Drake
Production Editorial: Jenny Wolkowicki
Jacket design: Ben Higgins
Production: Danielle Amatucci
Publicity: Alyssa Sanford and Charlotte Coyne
Copyeditor: Maia Vaswani

Jacket image: Grafissimo / iStock

This book has been composed in Miller

Printed in the United States of America

10 9 8 7 6 5 4 3 2 1

For Becky

CONTENTS

Introduction

AT THE BEGINNING OF the eighteenth century the Dutch doctor Bernard Mandeville put forward an idea that appalled and
scandalized the society of his adopted English homeland: that
human beings are merely animals. Far from being elevated, rational
creatures, we are in fact all greedy, self-interested, lazy, and deceiv-
ing, and live our lives according to mere rules of convenience.
What's more, Mandeville claimed that these base passions and
desires are the glue that holds our prosperous societies together.
Mandeville was not surprised to be met with fierce opposition,
for embedded within his theory of the human being was the crucial belief that we are animals who are in deep denial of our animal nature.

Mandeville published *The Fable of the Bees* in 1714, and if his
name is still remembered today, it is for this. This notorious work
is a humorous little tale of a hive full of greedy and licentious bees
that, through a sudden act of God, is rid of all vice, from the hum-
blest workers right up to the queen herself. Overnight the whole
of bee society changes and now engages in only virtuous activity,
and within a matter of days all the carefully maintained economic
structures of the hive spectacularly collapse. Without crime, there
is no need to employ a police force, or a construction industry for
prisons; without gluttony, there is no need for medical treatment
for overindulgence, or for health fads or quack cures; without
deception and conniving there is no need for arbitration to settle
legal disputes, so lawyers find themselves suddenly useless; without

vanity, there is simply no fashion industry. It was the vices of the bees, it turns out, that had been keeping the little hive abuzz.

Readers knew of course that the work was intended as a direct analysis of London's modern commercial society, and for this Mandeville was denounced as a champion for vice. He always denied the charge, adopting the pose of a wounded and haughty moralist who was merely bemoaning the sad state of the human species. Few thought him sincere in these denials. In reality, Mandeville had come to his controversial view of human nature while a student and never veered from it, right up until his final mature works. He was deeply committed to the truth of this idea, but he also found it highly amusing. He revelled in the fact that it is such an unflattering and paradoxical picture of the human creature. For this reason, he set out his thoughts not in a series of scientific or philosophical works, reasoning carefully and seriously from first principles. Instead, Mandeville wrote poems, fables, satires, and dialogues, all meant to entertain, and to shock, but ultimately to coax the reader around to his way of thinking. He expected to be rejected, so committed himself early on to a literary persona that was alternately crude, sly, amused, offensive, ironic, and, above all, elusive.

Despite the irreverent tone of *The Fable of the Bees,* and the uproar that ensued, it turned Mandeville into one of the most influential thinkers of the eighteenth century. Within a few years, his infamy had spread not just in England but throughout France and Germany, and later America also. His writings influenced the subjects of philosophy, literature, and politics, and also the newly emerging disciplines of economics, sociology, and anthropology. He would later be cited appreciatively by figures as diverse as Marx, Darwin, Hayek, and Keynes. Philosophers such as Hume, Smith, Rousseau, and others disavowed Mandeville, while in the same breath they took up his ideas and integrated them into their own more well-known works.[1]

The fact that *The Fable of the Bees* would also become an important text in future analyses of free-market capitalism has led many to include Mandeville as one of the founding figures of economic thought. But Mandeville is not primarily an economist at all, and he would hardly recognize himself in the description. Mandeville is first and foremost a theorist of human nature, a proto-anthropologist, and his economic theories are only a special application of his more general theory of human behaviour. In the seventeenth and eighteenth centuries the breakdown of religious authority and the advent of the scientific revolution inaugurated a new approach to our ethical concerns. Instead of looking to the mind of God for guidance on how to live, various thinkers recommended that we should simply live in accordance and harmony with our own nature. But this then merely raised another question: just what is human nature? This would be perhaps the most hotly contested philosophical question of the eighteenth century, and Mandeville set that debate running with an answer no one could bring themselves to accept.

This work is about *The Fable of the Bees*, its theory of human nature, and its role in Mandeville's thought. It will also aim to position the man himself in his proper place in European intellectual history. There is no attempt made here to write a biography of Bernard Mandeville. We in fact know very little about the details of his life from contemporaries, and hardly any correspondence survives.[2] We have no decent images of him, no good idea even of what he may have looked like. This work will aim instead to give the reader a sense of Mandeville's mind through his writings. Only a thinker of Mandeville's character, and in possession of his rich intellectual heritage, could have written a book quite like the *Fable*. I will also answer the question of just how and why the *Fable* attracted such notoriety in its day—and, I hope, in so doing give a sense of a fascinating and unique cultural moment in London in the first quarter of the eighteenth century.

In what follows, I'll set the crucial aspects of his intellectual character into sharper relief. These include Mandeville's medical background, which provides the origin of his conception of the human being and its ailments; the broad cultural anxiety regarding wealth creation that had marked Dutch culture in the seventeenth century and was only just emerging in England in the early eighteenth; his successful medical practice in London and his first-hand observation of the complex interplay among the physical, psychological, and societal factors that determine well-being; his medical treatment of women and his acute analyses of their vulnerability in society; his particular literary sensibility and his uncanny grasp of the psychology of the reader; his keen understanding of the unprecedented political situation in England at the time, where the interests of Whigs and Tories, court and country, Protestant and Catholic, businessman and aristocrat, vied in increasingly complex combinations; and above all, his philosophical inheritance from figures such as Erasmus, Montaigne, Spinoza, Bayle, La Rochefoucauld, and many others. I have chosen epigrams from La Rochefoucauld to begin these chapters, each expressing a central plank in Mandeville's own thinking.

Mandeville was deeply embedded in a particular kind of sceptical humanism. His writings did not serve just as a conduit for that tradition, however—they adopted it and adapted it, combining it with his own radical theory of human beings' strange animal nature. Mandeville's life was reflected through his writings. They reveal a man perfectly suited to analyse and satirize the emerging phenomenon of modern society, to reveal the gap between its self-image and its reality.

CHAPTER ONE

'The Wickedest Cleverest Book in the English Language'

Propriety is the least of all laws, and the one most often obeyed.

—LA ROCHEFOUCAULD, *MAXIMS*, 5:447

ON 8 JULY 1723 A book was put on trial. The Grand Jury of Middlesex County Court was presented with a work that corrupted public morals to such an extent that it might 'debauch the nation'. Bernard Mandeville's *The Fable of the Bees* was said to recognize no evidence of God's influence or providence in the world; it attacked all the decent institutions of society—politicians were derided, the clergy were slandered, and universities mocked; and, most offensive of all, it attempted to 'run down religion and virtue as prejudicial to society, and detrimental to the state . . . and to recommend luxury, avarice, pride, and all kind of vices, as being necessary to public welfare'.[1] The book claimed that vice ought to be pursued because the immoral activities of individuals can generate an overall economic benefit for society as a whole. Vice was not only necessary but desirable. Like Milton's Lucifer, its author seemed to declare: evil, be thou my good.[2]

The *Fable* that was published in 1723 comprised a poem, *The Grumbling Hive*, alongside a series of expansive 'remarks', each nominally dedicated to explicating the meaning of some line of the poem, but in reality a series of philosophical reflections on everything from sexual mores to the social function of fashion. It concluded with some brief essays on the nature of virtue, society, and the recent popular phenomenon of schools for the poor set up by charitable donation. This wasn't the first edition of the book. It had originally appeared nearly a decade earlier in 1714. In fact, its central claim, expressed poetically in an extended piece of doggerel verse, had first appeared in print as *The Grumbling Hive* as early as 1705. Bernard de Mandeville (he later dropped the 'de'), a Dutch doctor who had migrated to England in the 1690s, had set out to establish both a medical practice and a literary reputation. While his medical practice had done reasonably well, his writings had initially failed to attract any attention at all. This time it was different. The grand jury declared that Mandeville's work promoted a 'general libertinism', one that had 'a direct tendency to propagate infidelity, and consequently to the corruption of all morals'.[3] Thanks to the Middlesex County Court, and nearly a quarter of a century after his immigration to Great Britain, Bernard Mandeville had arrived.

The central idea of the *Fable* was that private individual indulgence in traditional vices—such as drunkenness and gluttony, the squandering of energy in leisure activities, the conspicuous consumption of luxury goods, and acquisitive materialism in general—is a crucial part of any dynamic large-scale economy. Were one to eliminate these elements from an economy then that economy would stagnate, to the detriment of everyone. There was a 'paradox' at the centre of modern life, one that had to be acknowledged and tolerated. This paradox formed the subtitle of the *Fable—Private Vices, Public Benefits*.

The story of *The Grumbling Hive: or, Knaves Turn'd Honest*, the poem that begins the *Fable*, is one of a prosperous beehive populated by rich but vice-riddled bees. Despite living lives of depraved indulgence, the bees find themselves in a state of peculiar dissatisfaction, perpetually 'grumbling' about the behaviour of those who seem to have achieved the greatest success. This envy begins to manifest in entirely hypocritical moral condemnation of one another, and soon cries of 'Damn the Cheats,' 'The Land must sink for all its Fraud,' and 'Good Gods, had we but Honesty!' become a constant refrain in the hive. Eventually their god Jove—more in irritation than beneficence—grants their wish and rids the beehive of all immoral behaviour overnight. All the bees are now virtuous and good—the knaves have been turned honest.

The consequences are not quite what the bellowing moralists had anticipated, however. It turns out that the presence of the bees' vices had been the very thing that made the hive so flourishing. Now the 'least thing was not done amiss': for example, there is no rule breaking in business that requires arbitration:

> The Bar was silent from that day;
> For now the willing debtors pay,
> Even that's by creditors forgot;
> Who quitted them that had it not.[4]

In this reformed beehive everyone pays their debts, and if misfortune means that they are unable to do so, then the spirit of charity intervenes to wipe the debt clean. The problem is not just that certain dealings are now run honestly, however; it is that all the industries that are associated with the regulation and correction of moral wrongdoing are now redundant. Once the last wrongdoers have been taken care of, the business of crime and punishment is otiose, and all the honest trades contingently connected with the maintenance of prisons and prison services are decimated:

> Justice hanged some, set others free;
> And after gaol delivery,
> Her presence being no more required,
> With all her train and pomp retired.
> First marched some smiths with locks and grates,
> Fetters, and doors with iron plates;
> Next gaolers, turnkeys, and assistants,
> Before the goddess, at some distance.[5]

It is a similar story for all the industries that are sustained by the bees' vanity, by their love of social one-upmanship, and demonstrations of wealth, culture, and power. The property market collapses, as does the interior design trade as a whole, since no one now wishes to construct grand houses, adorned with frescoes and

sculptures. There are no more commissions for the most fashionable artists to produce portraits of esteemed ancestors in classical
dress:

> The price of land and houses falls;
> Miraculous palaces, whose walls,
> Like those of Thebes, where raised by play,
> Are to be let; while the once gay,
> Well-seated household gods would be
> More pleased to expire in flames than see
> The mean inscription on the door
> Smile at the lofty ones they bore.
> The building trade is quite destroyed,
> Artificers are not employed;
> No limner for his art is famed,
> Stone-cutters, carvers are not named.[6]

The reduction in conspicuous consumption extends down from the
highest echelons of society to the newly emerging bourgeoisie. Now
the latter's taste for coffee, sugar, silk, and every other imported
product is disdained. Instead, people learn to make do with the dull
local produce, finding themselves perfectly content to shun the luxurious pleasures for which they had once lived. The very lifeblood
of foreign trade has disappeared:

> As pride and luxury decrease,
> So by degrees they leave the seas,
> Not merchants now, but companies,
> Remove whole manufactories,
> All arts and crafts neglected lie,
> Content, the bane of industry.[7]

The Grumbling Hive concludes with disaster for the beehive. Now
that glorious military ventures are frowned upon and the bees'
standing army has been stood down, the hive begins to look vulnerable to its enemies. It comes under sustained attack, and in the
ensuing wars is almost completely destroyed. In the end only a few
bees are still alive—those that have been toughened by a new character that 'counted ease itself a vice'. In the poem's final couplet, we
discover that the few poor remaining bees have had to regroup and

find a new home, living now with only their sense of moral superiority to warm them:

> They flew into a hollow tree,
> Blessed with content and honesty.[8]

Mandeville's poem, with its clever interplay between prosperity and vice, touched upon a particularly sensitive spot in the public consciousness of the time. At the beginning of the eighteenth century England was undergoing cultural and political changes that might not seem entirely unfamiliar today. London could justifiably claim to be the financial centre of the global economy, and the relatively new economic phenomenon of market speculation had led to an explosion of commercial activity. It also began the process of creating a new economic class. The generation of wealth was decreasingly tied to land ownership, and therefore no longer decisively dominated by the aristocratic class. One could now make one's fortune in the city, and with that possibility came another: that of a radical shift of political influence from the country landowner to moneyed men and city merchants.[9]

The opportunities generated by this shift brought with them new anxieties, and the moral implications of this new economic reality were a matter of constant debate. For some, the possible negative consequences had already been borne out by one of the first real financial crises created purely by market speculation—the South Sea Bubble. Politicians on all sides were eager to decry the event and to point out the corrupting influence of the possibility of rapidly gained capital. Many advocated a culture of disciplined austerity as the path to both private virtue and secure public finances. The commercial class might have defended the new prosperity as something that could be channelled into improvements for human welfare, and could even provide the means of eliminating the short-term increases in vice that may arise from this fast wealth. This more hopeful attitude claimed that modern commerce might be the source of the solution to its own problems.

The *Fable* addressed head-on this question of the relationship between economics and morality. But it gave an answer that no one wanted to hear. On the one hand, it agreed that increased commercial activity would bring about benefits for society. However, it would not—in fact, *could not*—do so by eliminating individual vice. According to this book, it was individual vice that generated the increased commercial activity in the first place, vice being an ineliminable part of what we have now come to think of as the whole modern capitalist project.[10] It is in the nature of that same project to prey upon the frailties of human beings' desires—and it is the indulgence and indeed the stimulation of those desires that generates increased economic activity. What is more, having sold people the indulgence of vice, one need not worry about the individual problems this causes, because one could simply sell yet more cures and treatments: medicines and health spas for our overindulgences, the latest fashions for our insecurities over social status. Mandeville laid bare the reality of modern economic life—that it functioned to perpetuate itself in endless cycles of stimulating our desires and soothing their consequences. One could not use increased prosperity as a means of eliminating vice, because it was vice that made the world go round.

Mandeville would ultimately escape any formal punishment, but the presentment to the Middlesex County Court initiated a barrage of outrage against both the *Fable* and Mandeville himself. Critics found various grounds for protest. Three weeks after the presentment, on 27 July, a letter appeared in the *British Journal* signed under the pseudonym 'Theophilus Philo-Britannus' (the writer thereby self-identifying as a lover both of God and of Britain). The letter claimed that 'this profligate author of the *Fable* . . . has taken upon him to tear up the very foundations of moral virtue, and establish vice in its room'. On 28 September, Robert Burrow, chaplain to the bishop of London, preached in a sermon to the Lord Mayor of London in the Guildhall Chapel against those 'men, who strike at the *foundations* of *virtue* and *morality*; and who labour to sink the *dignity* of human nature extremely low'.[11] William Law, the priest who would become known for his religious work *A Serious Call to a Devout and Holy Life* (1729) claimed in his 'Remarks on the *Fable of the Bees*' that Mandeville would 'dare . . . affirm in praise of immorality' and dismissed Mandeville for (among other things) his self-avowed 'low' style:

> These are the chief doctrines, which with more than fanatic zeal you recommend to your readers; and if lewd stories, profane observations, loose jests, and haughty assertions, might pass for arguments, few people would be able to dispute with you.[12]

Mandeville, Law concludes, was an 'advocate for moral vices' and wanted to give human beings the 'privileges of brutality'. There is no doubt that some of the opposition concerned just *how* Mandeville wrote. Mandeville set out to offend, and it could be said that he made offence a skill. One can find on almost any page an outrageous claim uttered with a casual simplicity, and a jocular matter-of-factness. He revels in a plain and self-described 'low' manner of expression. In the 'remarks' that follow *The Grumbling Hive*, Mandeville's commentary on the hypocrisy of regulated gender norms is expressed in typical style:

> *Miss* is scarce three years old, but she is spoke to every day to hide her leg, and rebuked in good earnest if she shows it; while *little master* at the same age is bid to take up his coats and piss like a man.[13]

The attacks continued to arrive over the following months and years. In 1724, the Anglican priest Richard Fiddes published *A General Treatise of Morality*, which, he said, was written to oppose that recent writer who, in his 'free, easy and lively manner', fools the reading public and 'directly attacks the moral distinction of good and evil'.[14] Fortunately, Fiddes claimed, the author's theory, which is 'offensive to Christianity', should be disregarded, since 'it is not very intelligible and withall imperfect'.[15] Mandeville's writings, specifically with regard to the implication that morals are mere cultural constructions, gave 'great occasion of offence'.[16] Fiddes concludes his attack with fawning praise for the grand jury:

> Both will be preserved as perpetual standing monuments, to show, that how numerous so ever the advocates of irreligion and vice, at present, are; or how considerable so ever they may affect to be thought, on account of their friends or adherents: Yet still we have persons of character and merit, in authority, who know how to express a pious and just resentment, at any open dishonour done to God, to their prince, and to their country.[17]

In the same year, the writer and dramatist John Dennis published *Vice and Luxury Publick Mischiefs*. Mandeville, Dennis claimed, 'made an open attack on the public virtue and the public spirit of Great Britain'. Dennis put an interesting and overtly political slant on his critique. The *Fable*, and similar publications, put the hard-won British tradition of individual liberty from tyrannical monarchs at risk. Works of this kind should not be allowed to circulate, since 'if we should ever have a prince, who should be weak enough to become an infidel, by the delusion of these free-thinking authors, the main obstacle to arbitrary power would be removed'.[18] For Dennis, the very existence of Mandeville was proof of the degradation of British society caused by the unchecked publication of those 'free-thinking' writings that advocated atheism and licentiousness. While there have in the past been authors whose positions perhaps opened the door for excusing occasional vice, he claimed, Mandeville was an author who openly and boldly advocated in vice's favour; 'to show the utmost profligacy of the times which we live in, vice and luxury have found a champion and defender, which they never did before'.[19]

An Enquiry whether a General Practice of Virtue Tends to the Wealth or Poverty, Benefit or Disadvantage of a People, published anonymously in 1725 (though attributed to the little-known George Bluet), marked out the *Fable's* particular offence as its attack on the concept of virtue. The paradox of private vices being public benefits seems to imply that there are actions that can be morally wrong in a private context which are nevertheless justifiable if we take the broader public context into account. This seemed to undermine the very idea of inherently moral action, action that is right in every possible context. While numerous writers before Mandeville had argued that actions carried out in the name of virtue might in fact be covers for vice, Mandeville was now attacking the *very idea* of morality. More than this, he was claiming that any attempt to be virtuous could in fact be harmful to the public good, since 'it is not only that most things are not virtue, which the world take for such, but the thing itself, we are told, is ridiculous in theory, and mischievous in practice'.[20]

Mandeville of course denied that the *Fable* was written to 'debauch the nation'. He declared that his motive for writing the *Fable* was solely that of 'the reader's diversion'[21]—humorous entertainment for the type of gentleman who had sufficient time and means to reflect on its contents. Yet Mandeville knew that he was presenting to that gentleman a set of new and thoroughly modern questions: Was it possible to be morally good in a commercial capitalist society? Is the very idea of virtue out of place in the market?

Isn't greed just a straightforward *good* for the modern individual, who is now as much a consumer as they are a citizen? That modern individual has been the subject of attack ever since, from Anthony Trollope's Melmotte in *The Way We Live Now* ('Gentlemen, it is your duty to make yourself rich!') to Oliver Stone's Gordon Gekko in *Wall Street* ('The point is, ladies and gentlemen, that greed, for lack of a better word, is good. Greed is right, greed works').

Mandeville's critics were forthcoming as to what *they* supposed to be the motives behind his writing such a monstrous work. Fiddes had snidely conceded that the most that could be granted to Mandeville is that 'human nature is very corrupt, and that he is no stranger to the corrupt state of it'.[22] This kind of ad hominem attack, where it is implied that the *Fable* could have been written only as a justification for Mandeville's own immoral lifestyle, would be a constant refrain in the work's reception. George Walker, a curate at Twickenham, sermonized in 1728 that the only plausible motive for advocating such a philosophy was to support one's own licentious disposition. Mandeville was one of those who 'generally undervalue what is good, because they have followed the practice of the contrary'.[23] William Hendley, another curate and a strong advocate of the charity schools attacked in the *Fable*, wrote that Mandeville's 'hellish design' was clearly prompted by his anti-religiosity, 'the destruction of the Christian religion and the promotion of the kingdom of Satan'.[24] 'Theophilus Philo-Britannus' had raised the same charge:

> This much may be said at present, that those have abundantly shown their spirit of opposition to sacred things, who have not only inveighed against the national profession and exercise of religion; and endeavoured, with bitterness and dexterity, to render it odious and contemptible, but are solicitous to hinder multitudes of the natives of this island from having the very seeds of religion sown among them with advantage.[25]

Others, though, proposed simpler motives—later there would emerge a popular, though entirely groundless, accusation that London distillers had employed Mandeville's pen, and that he was little more than a hack for the gin trade.[26]

On 9 March 1728, the *London Evening Post* reported a stunning new turn of events. It described how, perhaps as a result of the relentless denunciations, Mandeville had had a dramatic change of heart:

> On Friday evening . . . a gentleman well dressed appeared at the bon-fire before St. James's Gate, who declared himself the author of a book, entitled The Fable of the Bees: And that he was sorry for writing the same . . . and pronounced these words: I commit my book to the flames: And threw it in accordingly.[27]

The report was a prank, probably made by one Alexander Innes. Mandeville, as he would himself amusedly report later, made no such denunciation of his own work. That same year, Innes fraudulently published a work in his own name entitled *Arete-Logica, or, An Enquiry into the Original of Moral Virtue*. The actual author was the philosopher Archibald Campbell, and Innes later had to confess his outrageous plagiarism. Innes added a long preface of his own where—marvellously untouched by any sense of irony—he railed against the immorality advocated by the author of *The Fable of the Bees*. The preface is written as an open letter to Mandeville and upbraids him for the 'rude clamour you have raised against moral virtue and the dignity of *human nature* in your Fable of the Bees', which he asserted 'proceeds from your not being acquainted with one or the other'.[28] Mandeville's writings are read, Innes claimed, only because they are offensive and scandalous. Were they not, the paper they were written on would be reused, and would more often be found 'in the hands of pastry-cooks, and tobacconists, than in booksellers' shops or gentlemen's libraries'.[29] Innes is as much disturbed by the low-class readership for Mandeville's writings as he is by their content.

A letter by 'Anglicanus' to the journal the *Craftsman* in 1731 adopted a similarly anxious approach. It claimed that even if Mandeville's analysis were correct, the more important thing was that these thoughts did not escape into the public domain, since they could serve only to validate the already unsavoury habits of the common folk:

> Whatever truths may be found within that book, or whatever might be the *author's* design, the publication of such doctrines amongst the common people of a country, already too much debauched and corrupted, is

certainly prejudicial to the interest of society in general, and therefore cannot be justified.[30]

In 1732, an anonymous tract called *The Character of the Times Delineated* claimed that the kingdom's tolerance of immorality was entirely unprecedented in the whole of history, even among non-Christian cultures:

> We discover not only *common* vices and immoralities surpassing any age or nation that we read of, and the very heathens, who knew not God, but every species of vice *improved* to so monstrous a size, so daring and bare-faced, as *publicly* to triumph in our streets, and to bid defiance to the laws of both God and man.[31]

The author leaves us in no doubt as to who he believed to be the high priest of this new religion of immorality. In the following couplet he compares Mandeville to the Antichrist. God's son was made incarnate to rescue humanity from sin; now the devil had become incarnate to push us back into sin once more:

> And, if GOD-MAN Vice to abolish came,
> Who Vice Commends, MAN-DEVIL be his Name.[32]

'Mandevil' was a common misspelling of 'Mandeville' in any case, but the pun was irresistible. As Mandeville's reputation grew, more eminent literary figures took the opportunity to oppose him. Jonathan Swift's *Miscellanies* (1733) included his 'A True and Faithful Narrative . . .', a satire detailing the behaviour of the people of London in the days before their anticipated annihilation from a comet striking the earth. He wrote that while before it had been 'groundlessly reported' that 'Dr Mandevil' had publicly burned his own book, Swift could now confirm that Mandeville *really had* renounced his entire views, again at Saint James's Gate.[33] Clearly Swift had noted the previous prank by Innes, as well as Mandeville's denial, so he now sought to irritate Mandeville by falsely reporting a second recantation.[34]

In the following decades, Mandeville's reputation became solidified in the consciousness of those concerned with the literary and political culture of the times. The philosopher Francis Hutcheson published several works targeting Mandeville specifically. The Irish philosopher Bishop George Berkeley devoted a chapter of his dialogue *Alciphron* to opposing Mandeville. Another bishop, William Warburton, wrote in *The Divine Legation* (1737) that Mandeville's proposal was an 'execrable paradox'.[35] With Warburton's encouragement, Alexander Pope immortalized Mandeville (along with the radical dissenter Thomas Morgan) in the last edition of *The Dunciad* in 1742. Lauding their passing—Mandeville had died in 1733—Pope wrote that thankfully 'Morgan and Mandevil could prate no more.'[36] In Henry Fielding's *Amelia*, published in 1751, the Mandevillean references to self-interest and society—merely implicit previously in *Tom Jones* (1749)—were now stated outright. In *Amelia* Miss Matthews evinces scepticism at the very words 'virtue' and 'religion': 'I look upon the two words you mention, to serve as cloaks under which hypocrisy may be better enabled to cheat the world. I have been of that opinion ever since I read that charming fellow *Mandevil*.'[37] Her interlocutor is scandalized, since in his view 'Mandevil' has 'represented human nature as a picture of deformity'—at which point Miss Matthews quickly retracts her admiration.[38] By the middle of the eighteenth century everyone knew Mandeville's name as a byword for immorality. *The Fable of the Bees* was publicly burned—in reality, finally—by the Paris hangman when translated into French in 1740.[39]

The intensity of the opposition to Mandeville and his ability to aggravate right-minded individuals are phenomena in need of some explanation. A clue can be found in the journal of Methodist founder John Wesley: 'I looked over a celebrated book, The Fable of the Bees. Till now I imagined there had never appeared in the world such a book as the works of Machiavelli. But de Mandeville goes far beyond it.'[40] Niccolò Machiavelli was a devil, but at least he had recommended immorality only for princes as a means of holding on to power. Mandeville recommended immorality for all. He maintained three claims: firstly, that human beings are fundamentally driven by their own self-interest (or 'self-love'); secondly, that individuals' self-interested and frequently vicious actions can bring about positive economic benefits for society at large; thirdly, that vice flourishes in a prosperous modern economy. So stated, none of these claims were new. The political philosopher Thomas Hobbes had notoriously affirmed human beings' fundamentally self-interested nature. The thought had also been a mainstay of the theories of the French *moralistes*, such as La Rochefoucauld, Bruyère, and Abbadie. Machiavelli himself had held that the vicious activities by a willing prince could bring about positive effects for the state that he ruled; and the notion that modern urban economies were hotbeds of vice was as old as urban economies themselves. Wesley's comment, though, captured the specific aspect of Mandeville's thesis that had so outraged his contemporaries:

> The Italian only recommends a few vices, as useful to some particular men and on some particular occasions. But the Englishman loves and cordially recommends vice of every kind; not only as useful now and then, but as absolutely necessary at all times for all communities![41]

Wesley perceived that Mandeville did not believe modern urban societies just happened to have evolved to be environments where vice flourishes. Instead, he was arguing for a conceptual link between economic prosperity and individual immorality. For every vice indulged in by a private individual there might be some corresponding benefit to the public. Mandeville argued that the conceptual connection was so tight that the abolition of vice from society would necessarily end prosperity within that society. This was seen as the most heinous aspect of Mandeville's thought. Whereas self-love had been traditionally viewed as the source of society's problems, Mandeville recast self-love as the source of society's success.

Mandeville's public response to his many critics seems to have been decidedly facetious—he certainly wasn't going to spoil the fun now with recantations or apologies for over-egged satire. His protestations that the *Fable* was in fact a work of the 'strictest morality' were rarely believed, and understandably so.[42] He added a 'Vindication' of the *Fable* in the next edition, reprinting a letter to the *London Journal* where he expresses shock and confusion that anyone could have so misread him. His aim was never to recommend vice, merely to point out that it cannot be eradicated from the human species: 'I am far from encouraging vice, and should think it an unspeakable felicity for a state, if the sin of uncleanness could be utterly banished from it; but I am afraid it is impossible.'[43] Mandeville again states that the *Fable* 'is a book of severe and exalted morality'—after all, it is his keen sense of the standards for moral probity that have revealed to him how rarely they are met in practice. Little can be said with absolute certainty about his sincere private views, as we have no personal writings wherein he confesses his true position. It is highly likely, however, that his reaction to the hatred and abuse directed at him would have been one of sheer delight. By the time of the outcry, he had toiled for two decades in literary obscurity, and if he was unable to achieve the fame of the contemporary greats to which he aspired, he was happy to settle for infamy. The *Fable* aimed to shock—in fact, one could say that Mandeville was a pioneer of the literary succès de scandale.

Samuel Johnson was one of the many writers alive to Mandeville's satisfaction in his own black reputation. His biographical note to Pope's *Dunciad* describes Mandeville as follows:

> This writer, who prided himself in the reputation of an immoral philosopher, was author of a famous book called the Fable of the Bees; written to prove that moral virtue is the invention of knaves, and Christian virtue the imposition of fools; and that vice is necessary, and alone sufficient to render society flourishing and happy.[44]

Despite his notoriety, some writers even began to use Mandeville's theme for their own satirical purposes. The Irish writer Matthew Pilkington's *An Infallible Scheme to Pay the Publick Debt of Ireland in Six Months* (1732) employed the *Fable*'s subtitle when he argued that what was needed was a further taxation system on swearing, fornication, and so on, concluding that 'there can be no other method half so good as mine, to make *Private Vices Publick Benefits*'.[45] It was perhaps only after Mandeville's death in 1732 and after the scandal of the *Fable* had subsided that some felt more free to express their appreciation of the richness of his writings. The diarist Crabb Robinson wrote that the work was the 'wickedest cleverest book ever written'.[46] Samuel Johnson himself told Boswell that he held the *Fable* in high regard, and that it had 'opened my views into real life very much'.[47] Voltaire took to Mandeville's thought, reporting it back to Enlightenment France and endorsing Mandeville's insistence on the importance of luxury to society in his poem *Le Mondain*. The physicist and philosopher Émilie du Châtelet, introduced to Mandeville's work by Voltaire, clandestinely prepared a translation of the *Fable*, and declared that Mandeville 'could be called the Montaigne of the English if it were not for the fact that [Mandeville] has more method and healthier ideas about things'.[48] The philosopher and historian David Hume, in his *Treatise on Human Nature* (1738), included Mandeville as one of the essential forerunners in the development of the 'science of man'—the empirical study of human nature viewed as the fundamental aim of the Enlightenment project.[49] The father of modern economics, Adam Smith—despite discussing Mandeville's views in a chapter he entitled 'Of Licentious Systems' in his *Theory of Moral Sentiments* (1759)—was enormously indebted to Mandeville's mode of thought.[50] In particular, both the notions of the 'division of labour' and Smith's account of the 'invisible hand' in *The Wealth of Nations* (1776) have a source in *The Fable of the Bees*. Jean-Jacques Rousseau's fame initially rested on his *First* and *Second Discourses* (1750 and 1755, respectively), both of which critically engage with Mandeville's opinions regarding virtue and commercial prosperity, as well as the natural passions of the human species. By the end of the eighteenth century, the German philosopher Immanuel Kant could without controversy list Mandeville in the *Critique of Practical Reason* (1788) as one of the key figures in the history of ethics.[51]

This is just to mention the influence Mandeville had upon his own century—he has also been read seriously by some of the later thinkers who formed our understanding of the world today. Charles Darwin read the *Fable*. Karl Marx read the *Fable* (and commented that 'Mandeville was of course infinitely bolder and more honest than the philistine apologists of bourgeois society').[52] John Maynard Keynes treated Mandeville as a key figure in his *General Theory of Employment, Interest, and Money* (1936). Keynes's great opponent, F. A. Hayek, similarly marked out Mandeville in one of the 'Master Minds' lectures in 1966. Mandeville's position regarding the laissez-faire economic doctrine has been debated ever since.[53] The anthropologist Louis Dumont argued that Mandeville's theories mark a crucial stage in the development of Western individualism.[54] It has even been argued that the founding father of sociology is not Émile Durkheim but Bernard Mandeville.[55]

Undoubtedly, no history of economic thought is complete without a discussion of *The Fable of the Bees*.[56]

Clearly, therefore, as well as asking what made Mandeville's work so offensive, we should also ask why it nevertheless emerged as one of the most influential theories of human nature and society of the eighteenth century. The answer concerns the distinction between Mandeville's method and his theory, between the form and content of his writing, especially in the later sections of the *Fable* that deal with modern mores and the hypocrisy that runs through them. Mandeville approached his subject matter—the nature of human beings and their society—in a manner quite unlike anyone before him. He did not proceed from a stipulated definition of the human being, setting down the rules of society a priori, or by sermonizing upon God's plan for humanity. Instead, Mandeville adopted the method of a social anthropologist. The introduction to the *Fable* begins with a complaint: 'One of the greatest reasons why so few people understand themselves, is, that most writers are always teaching men what they should be, and hardly ever trouble their heads with telling them what they really are.'[57]

We may naturally think that understanding ourselves involves firstly an examination of how human beings ought to behave, and what it is to be a *good* human being. But for Mandeville our first question should not be such an ethically loaded one. We must observe the human being just as it is in its current form, in society as it has evolved and as it continues to evolve. Mandeville analysed human beings' behaviour, noted the small details of their interactions, and characterized the complex psychological processes at play in daily social interaction. Far from eschewing the mundane, Mandeville turned precisely to the quotidian aspects of human existence as the place where the most profound parts of human nature are on display, if we only care to look. Moreover, he proposed the simple causal mechanisms of social conditioning and reinforcement as the source for some of the most complex aspects of our interactions with one another. Mandeville's method for uncovering human nature brought that study down to earth in a way that was liberatory for his successors. It is this type of inquiry—naturalistic, historical, sociological—that surely led Hume to include Mandeville on his list of those philosophers (such as Locke and Shaftesbury) who had begun the great project of the 'science of man'. Every field of inquiry, Hume held, but perhaps especially the field of morals, must be conditional upon a prior investigation into the character and limits of human nature.[58]

But despite this ground-breaking approach, those who initially emulated Mandeville's method were reasonably hesitant to mention his name in association with it. This was due to Mandeville's forthright commitment to debunking the pretensions of the species he was studying. A central theoretical claim of all his writings is that the human species is illegitimately elevated above other animals, that we are deceived as to the extent and power of our own rationality, and that our moral codes are little more than fig leaves for our true self-interested motivations. None of this could be accepted by right-minded theorists in the eighteenth or even nineteenth century. Mandeville's anthropological approach could be adopted only if his name was denounced in the same breath— Hume, Smith, and Rousseau all opposed Mandeville, while each in his own way continued his project.

Mandeville's picture of humanity was formed first-hand in his practice as a physician: he saw what human beings were like literally under their skin. He worked with the poor and the rich alike. He observed the new phenomenon of commercial society, the capacity for individuals to spring from poverty to wealth and back down again. He saw the rules that people claimed to behave by, and then their actual behaviour (behaviour for which they occasionally had to visit Mandeville to seek medical treatment). He observed the role of women in society, the hazardous nature of their situation, and the precariousness of their social existence, as well as the arbitrary and punitive character of sexual mores. Remarkably, Mandeville saw these cruel realities as being reinforced by the emergence of romantic literature, with its conventional repackaging of feminine virtue sold to and eagerly consumed by the new fashionable reading public.

All of this—this gamut of humanity—Mandeville observed and satirized. He was the perfectly right man to say the perfectly improper thing.[59] Mandeville's opening complaint—that human beings struggle to accept what they really are—sets the agenda for everything that follows in the *Fable*. He thinks that as a species we have a natural and powerful tendency towards self-deception. We are not who we like to think we are. The aim of the *Fable* is to enable at least some human beings—the small portion of society that constituted his readership—to understand their own species a little better. Mandeville introduced an idea that had no term yet, that of false consciousness. His message was that the whole of modern society was premised on a confabulated self-image, one that it worked hard to perpetuate. Mandeville's aim was to show society to itself.

CHAPTER TWO

Pride and Animal Spirits

It seems that nature, which has so wisely arranged the organs of our body
for our happiness, has also given us pride to spare us the pain of knowing
our deficiencies.

—LA ROCHEFOUCAULD, *MAXIMS*, 5:36

EVERY ASPECT OF Mandeville's scandalous theories—expressed in writings that will be explored more fully in the subsequent chapters—is premised upon a particular theory of human nature. His accounts of modern sexual relations, morality, politics, economics, and sociology all prioritize the influence of human beings' corporeal nature. In particular, Mandeville invites us to consider the subtle ways in which the biology of human bodies interacts with and influences our mental lives and conscious behaviour. Moreover, he claims that we are standardly unaware that this is happening, and that what is normally attributed to 'reason' or 'intellect' is in fact properly attributed to the more animalistic side of our being. In fact, Mandeville thinks that what we call our 'rationality' is better thought of as a figment of our imagination, an image of humanity that we present to ourselves precisely in order to disguise the distasteful reality of our animalistic nature. This theory was formed in the context of his training as a medical physician, and a proper examination of these early influences is essential for understanding the rest of Mandeville's subsequent writings.

Crucial also to that context, we will see, was a hotly contested philosophical and theological debate on the nature of the human animal, how it is similar to and how it is different from other animals, and what this meant for consideration of the human being's immortal soul. These questions form part of the background to Mandeville's major piece of medical writing, *A Treatise of the Hypochondriack and Hysterick Diseases in Three Dialogues*, first published in 1711. In this work we in fact find many of the core elements of Mandeville's thinking, elements that would constitute the notorious picture of human behaviour presented just a few years later in the first edition of the *Fable* in 1714. Mandeville revised the *Treatise* significantly in 1730, when his new-found infamy afforded him the opportunity to republish this work. He was no doubt appreciative of the greater potential readership that the scandal of the *Fable* in the 1720s would have brought him, and it is clear that the *Treatise* was a work he hoped would cement his reputation. The *Treatise* is, moreover, the work in which Mandeville reveals the most about himself.[1]

Bernard de Mandeville was born on 15 November 1670 in Dordrecht, and baptized in Rotterdam. He was born into a relatively privileged family—his father, Michael de Mandeville, was an established and well-regarded Rotterdam physician (as his father before him had been). Mandeville clearly held his father in high regard, since he entered into the family profession, and even pursued the same medical specialization concerning digestive and stomach illnesses. Mandeville would even praise his father's expertise in the *Treatise*. Arguably, though, it would be not his father's medical profession but his political and social status that would exert the more significant influence on the direction of Bernard's life. Mandeville senior was an alderman (or councilman) in the neighbouring jurisdiction and was a senior member of the Rotterdam militia, as well as being appointed 'city physician' and an administrator of the municipal hospital.[2] The Mandevilles were clearly a family of some social significance in Rotterdam at the time.

Bernard was entered into a local school that had recently been transformed by the arrival of French Protestant intellectuals escaping the persecution of Louis XIV. In 1685 Louis had revoked the Edict of Nantes, which had previously allowed French Protestants to practise without persecution. One of the intellectuals now fleeing the resumption of religious intolerance was Pierre Bayle. Bayle, a Huguenot theologian and philosopher, would prove to be one of the most influential and important thinkers of the seventeenth and eighteenth centuries. He arrived only in the last year of Mandeville's time at the school, but would subsequently become the central figure in his intellectual development. Bayle began his monumental *Critical and Historical Dictionary* in the late 1690s, and Mandeville would repeatedly make use of it (in fact whole parts of Mandeville's *Free Thoughts on Religion* (1720) are by his own admission straight borrowings from Bayle).[3] Bayle's *Dictionary* was widely known and respected in its own time, and was translated into English in 1709. While we don't know whether young Mandeville was taught by Bayle himself, it is certainly the case that Mandeville saw himself as having a special advantage from his familiarity with Bayle's thought and saw himself as in effect introducing many of its themes to English readers for the first time when he migrated there sometime in the 1690s.

The *Dictionary* is a remarkable literary production, ostensibly covering major figures and concepts from the history of ideas (entered under headings of individuals such as 'Machiavelli' and 'Spinoza'). Yet, within the work, Bayle discourses on a range of theological and philosophical issues, displaying his own immense erudition. These issues are usually further examined in a series of lettered footnotes within each entry that engage in curious digressions, side discussions, and meanderings, the point of which is not always immediately obvious. Bayle himself remains an elusive figure, and his comments on philosophical and theological tangles have been interpreted both as pious conscientiousness and as sceptical scorn.[4] Mandeville would deliberately echo Bayle's literary conceit when composing the *Fable*, attaching a series of lettered 'Remarks' to the poem *The Grumbling Hive*, wherein he would expound in an amused and digressive manner on some particular line. The influence of Bayle upon Mandeville's intellectual development should not be underestimated.

The education that Mandeville received at the school would have been first class, and it appears that he took advantage of the opportunities offered to him. The first known writing we have from Mandeville is a kind of valedictorian's speech, entitled *De Medicina Oratio Scholastica*,[5] written when he was fifteen and graduating from the school. It signalled his intention to engage in a medical career and extolled its virtues. A picture of Mandeville that emerges is that of a young man with a precocious intelligence and a valuable education, steeped in classical writings as well as contemporary Protestant theology and philosophy. More pertinently, it would have been impossible for him to acquire this learning without understanding it in the contemporary context of the competing movements of religious persecution and the importance of toleration.

Mandeville also developed into a young man who had first-hand experience of the rough realities of political life. In 1693 a catastrophe occurred—Mandeville's father was banished from Rotterdam. This was the result of events that came to be known as the 'Costerman Riots'.[6] Essentially, it was an example of the occasional eruptions of resentful violence directed at those responsible for gathering taxes for different products, a task that was outsourced by the government to private 'tax farmers'. One night a group of Rotterdam militiamen carrying a cask of wine—intended for their own refreshment while they were on duty—were stopped by the agents of a wine tax farmer. The cask had not had its excise duty paid, and an argument broke out. A scuffle ensued, swords were drawn, and a tax agent was killed. One militiaman, Costerman, confessed to the act. The cause of the riot was not Costerman's crime but rather his punishment for it. The local bailiff, Van Zuijlen, himself a government representative already notorious for his greed and corruption, pushed for the harshest possible sentence, that of execution. Militiamen were generally well regarded by the public—taxmen less so—and now one was to be executed for killing one of the least popular members of society. What is more, a rumour that Costerman was innocent of the charges had begun to circulate. It seemed to many that political power would protect the taxation racket and execute an innocent man. The execution nevertheless took place in public, and Costerman was decapitated by sword. Perhaps young Mandeville even witnessed it. The following day, a crowd arrived at the tax farmer's house and ransacked it. Tensions remained high and the central government in The Hague even sent troops to Rotterdam, who nevertheless could not prevent another crowd from ransacking Van Zuijlen's own house two weeks later. In response to the situation, the city administration sacked Van Zuijlen from his office.

It was widely reported in the local press that both Michael de Mandeville and his twenty-year-old son, Bernard, had been deeply involved in the disturbances. In fact, it seems that they were key in stirring up discontent against Van Zuijlen. It was claimed that the young Bernard had written a lampoon of Van Zuijlen and had it posted up in the local exchange, leading to scuffles between the public and the soldiers who tried to tear it down. Bernard (if it was indeed he) had written that Van Zuijlen was a 'money-grubbing tyrant', a 'spawn of hell' who had 'raped the law'. The Mandevilles' claims may well have been justified. However, it could also have been an attempt by Michael and Bernard to oust Van Zuijlen in favour of a bailiff from whom they might reap political and financial advantages in the future. It is unclear in this tale as to who is motivated by public virtue and who by private interest.

The attacks on Van Zuijlen were successful, but only temporarily. The city government had dismissed him from office, but his original appointment was due to the patronage of the Dutch leader, or *stadholder*, William III. His dismissal was a challenge to William's authority, and William intervened in the case, ensuring that Van Zuijlen was acquitted and reinstated into his office in 1692. Once he was back in power, Van Zuijlen promptly banished Michael de Mandeville and others from Rotterdam. The victory for Van Zuijlen marked a reassertion of authoritarian rule in the city. Toleration also seemed to be on the wane in Rotterdam. Pierre Bayle, for instance, would eventually lose his position in the school, not least as a result of sustained attacks on Bayle's theological views by his reactionary colleague Pierre Jurieu. Bernard Mandeville left Rotterdam to finish his medical studies, never to return. Whether this was a matter of necessity due to the now-inhospitable environment or self-exile is difficult to determine. It was without doubt a disaster for the Mandeville family. Bernard might have been expecting a somewhat predictable future for himself in the form of a rise through the medical, political, and social cliques of Rotterdam. Instead, not only was that path closed now to him, he was a persona non grata in his own city.

Mandeville returned to his studies at the illustrious medical university of Leiden, fifteen miles north of Rotterdam. As part of his education, he completed two medical writings, *De brutorum operationibus* (1689) and *De chylosi vitiata* (1691). The latter work outlined Mandeville's own preferred medical theory regarding the operation of the stomach and digestive system. The rudiments of the theory are that the stomach is lined with nerves, and that these nerves are hollow tubes through which 'animal spirits' flow. The stomach system requires a regular flow of these spirits, and too much or too little can lead to a wide variety of bodily disorders. Just what these 'animal spirits' really are is left quite mysterious, as Mandeville himself would later acknowledge. Although the theory of animal spirits and the workings of the digestive system are central to the *Treatise*, it is arguably the other work written at Leiden that would prove the more important for Mandeville's intellectual formation. His dissertation, *De brutorum operationibus* (The operations of animals), written at the age of nineteen, ostensibly does not concern the treatment of human beings at all, but rather the minds of non-human animals.[7]

Perhaps surprisingly, this was a tense topic to focus upon, one that held ramifications for early modern science, theology, and philosophy. The core questions are straightforward: do animals think and reason as we humans do, or are we the only species truly possessed of rational capacities? More generally, what kind of consciousness do animals possess? Do they see and hear the world in the same ways we do? Do they feel sensations in the same way we do? Even at this early stage of his thinking, Mandeville was already drawn to the question of what, if anything, distinguishes human beings from other creatures. His stated answer to that question was very much in keeping with the expected academic orthodoxy, which at the time followed the thought of the rationalist philosopher René Descartes. Mandeville's supervisor at Leiden was Burchard de Volder, a renowned follower of the Cartesian line.

Descartes had argued, on perfectly reasonable philosophical grounds, it must be said, that since animals lack the peculiarly self-conscious minds that humans possess, their entire consciousness must be radically different from our own. In fact, Descartes seemed to insist that they lacked anything that we would recognize as consciousness at all. While Mandeville's university writings concurred with Descartes's view, his answers to this and other questions in his later writings would be anything but orthodox. In fact, Mandeville's opposition to Descartes, expressed as soon as he could write outside of the constrictions of academic institutions, would form the backbone of his theorizing on human nature in all his later work. Simple observation suggests to us that animal behaviour has all the marks of consciousness—the dog shows excitement at the return of its owner; the cat shows irritation with being stroked too roughly—and something must have gone terribly wrong with the way we are investigating animals (and humans) if we have let philosophical theory contradict what is evident to a child's eyes.

Everything in Mandeville's thought can be traced back to his claim that human beings are merely another species of animal. Mandeville's education was Dutch, but the key thinkers in his intellectual development were French, especially the French philosopher Michel de Montaigne, who set many of the terms of the debate regarding animals in the early modern period. In his *Essays* (1580) Montaigne had argued for continuity between human and animal minds. The difference between the two was merely one of degree rather than of kind. Some of the more notable points are made in his famous chapter 'An Apology for Raymond Sebond'. For Montaigne, the essential weakness of human beings as a species—our 'maladie naturelle et originelle'—is the quality of pride. Pride was the original sin of Lucifer and ours also. Pride manifests itself especially in terms of our unwillingness to accept that this world with all its imperfections, injustices, and routine humiliations might nevertheless be our proper station:

> The natural, original distemper of Man is presumption. Man is the most blighted and frail of all creatures and, moreover, the most given to pride. This creature knows and sees that he is lodged down here, among the mire and shit of the world, bound and nailed to the deadest, most stagnant part of the universe, in the lowest story of the building, the farthest from the vault of heaven; his characteristics place him in the . . . lowest category of animate creatures.[8]

The low condition of human beings' bodily existence might be something they could bear were it not for the one other strange distinguishing characteristic they possess, the ability to think. The capacity for thought is—among other things—the ability to detach oneself from one's current predicament, to project one's mind into different places and times, to imagine what it would be like to be otherwise than the way one is. If we lacked this capacity for thought we would be able to bear our hardships a little more easily, as other animals seem to do. Human beings have the double misfortune of having both the capacity to feel suffering and the capacity to think about the very fact that they are feeling suffering, an activity which brings a further suffering in itself.

On the other hand, thinking involves a capacity to remove oneself in one's imagination from those sufferings, and it is in this ability that Montaigne perceives the seeds of man's prideful status. Removing one's mind from the present circumstances provides a kind of freedom from bodily hardship and also a sort of power, since 'in thought, he sets himself above the circle of the moon, bringing the very heavens under his feet'.[9] It is at this very point that, Montaigne complains, pride begins to do its work. It drives humans to exaggerate and prioritize their capacity for thought as the pre-eminent feature of the species, since by so doing they can claim that it is the ability to position themselves above terrestrial suffering that reflects their true nature. Furthermore, pride drives the human being to claim that it is thought itself that marks our special status among God's created living beings, and that 'the vanity of this same thought makes him equal himself to God; attribute to himself God's mode of being; pick himself out and set himself apart from the mass of other creatures.'[10] We decide that it must be this rational and discursive ability that reflects our divine heritage, such that in the act of abstract thinking we are doing no less than realizing our own exalted status as God's children.

Montaigne is not of this view. For him, the capacity for thought is unique to human beings, but it is more of a curse than a gift:

> Granted that, of all the animals, Man alone has freedom to think and such unruly ways of doing so that he can imagine things which are and things which are not, imagine his wishes, or the false and the true! But he has to pay a high price for this advantage—and he has little cause to boast about it, since it is the chief source of the woes which beset him: sin, sickness, irresolution, confusion and despair.[11]

Montaigne's accusation is that in order to achieve our aim of identifying more closely with a higher being we actively strive to distinguish ourselves from creatures that are obviously similar to us in many ways, and instead classify them as different and 'lower'. We mischaracterize animals as a radically different 'other' for the purpose of establishing a more secure sense of our own identity. This is the true motivation for the vehemence with which the task of distinguishing human beings from animals is pursued.

Montaigne then proceeds to cast doubt on our ability to provide a theoretical basis for the distinction between human and animal minds. In interpreting all behaviour, he claims, we should simply reason 'from similar effects . . . that there are similar causes'. Thus, if the observable effects—the behaviour of animals—are similar to those of human beings' behaviour, and if we hold that rationality is what drives human behaviour, then we should surely also conclude that animals possess some degree of rationality. He uses the memorable example of a fox testing a frozen river to see if it is in fact solid and capable of being crossed.[12] Its behaviour—that of approaching the river tentatively, bringing its head down to check whether the river water has its usual sound and movement, running onto the ice briefly before retreating, and so on—is all best explained by saying that the fox is *reasoning* in exactly the same way we do in such situations. Obviously, and as many philosophers of the time pointed out, the fox does not reason explicitly or self-consciously in language, as we do. The absence of a capacity for linguistic expression, however, does not indicate the absence of rationality per se—the fox's behaviour is surely appropriately characterized in terms of a kind of hypothesis testing, prediction of effects from causes, and so on. One might choose to say that rationality and language use are just one and the same thing, but this would seem to be an ad hoc move, designed simply to stipulate that the thing that best characterizes *human* reasoning is what we have decided *we* will call 'rationality'. Montaigne claims that 'we should admit that animals employ the same method and the same reasoning as ourselves when we do anything'.[13] The goal of this is not to represent human beings in a negative light. Rather, Montaigne sees the move as a corrective one, presenting human beings at their proper level, so as to counteract their innate propensity to fraudulently exalt their own species: 'I have gone into all this to emphasise similarities with things human, so bringing

Man into conformity with the majority of creatures. We are neither above them nor below them.'[14]

Descartes's rationalist philosophy is by contrast firmly enmeshed in a theological world view in which human beings are in fact creatures of a special higher order. It is perhaps unsurprising then that it is Montaigne who is the immediate target of Descartes's defence of human rationality, and the reason for the latter's vehement denial that animals have any higher representational capacities resembling those of humans. Descartes holds that Montaigne's views represent both an intellectual and moral failing and that 'after the error of those who deny God ... there is none that leads weak minds further from the straight path of virtue than that of imagining that the souls of the beasts are of the same nature with ours'.[15] Descartes's rhetorical grouping of atheism along with the denial of a strict demarcation between human and animal minds is suggestive, though not uncommon. To give a single example, Thomas More's famous work *Utopia* (1516) described how the inhabitants of Utopia allowed for a diverse range of religious belief systems, so long as they each retained the core theological element of belief in the afterlife:

> Thus they believe that after this life vices will be punished and virtue rewarded. Anyone who denies this proposition they consider not even one of the human race, since he has degraded the sublimity of his own soul to the base level of a beast's wretched body.[16]

To deny that human beings have a special kind of soul is to raise the possibility that there is nothing beyond their animal bodies that might continue into the afterlife. Part of the importance of distinguishing the two types of beings then is not just the scientific endeavour of explaining the similarities and differences between animal and human behaviour but that of isolating the appropriately exclusive theological status for human beings.

One of Descartes's arguments, outlined in his letter to the Marquis of Newcastle in 1646, is that the behaviour of animals that Montaigne claimed is evidence of their possession of rational capacities is equally well explained by the claim that animals are merely guided by *non*-rational forces. Beasts, unlike us, are only ever moved by their bodily feelings, their 'passions'. The behaviours that might appear to be rationally guided 'are only movements of

their fear, their hope, or their joy, in such a way that they can perform them without any thought'.[17] In this way Descartes tries to
argue with Montaigne on his own terms, by claiming that if we
are truly reasoning from observed effects to hypothesized causes,
then we should advance the simplest hypothesis possible. If animal
behaviour can be explained by the attribution of simple *feeling*-like
responses rather than proper thought, then we should do so, and it
is unnecessary to attribute rationality to them as well. Descartes's
only real concession in the letter is to acknowledge that there is a
strong physiological continuity with regard to the cognitive make-
up of some animals and that of the human being:

> The most one can say is that although animals do not act in any way
> that assures us they think, since the organs of their bodies are not very
> different from ours, it can be conjectured that there is some thought
> attached to those organs, such as we experience in ours, although theirs
> is much less perfect.[18]

Descartes denies that this is a worrisome piece of evidence in favour
of animal minds, however. His reasoning does not concern claims
about physiology but is instead theological:

> To this I have nothing to reply, except that, if they thought as we do, they
> would have an immortal soul as we do. But that is not probable, since
> there is no reason to believe this of some animals without believing it of
> all of them, and there are some too imperfect for us to be able to believe
> this of them, like the oysters, sponges, etc.[19]

This is the corollary worry to that of Thomas More regarding animal
minds and human souls. More had worried that if we are classified
too closely to other animals then, since animals do not have immortal
souls, there would be grounds for doubting that we humans had
them either. On the other hand, one could also argue in the opposite direction: if we are classified too closely to other animals, and
if one wanted to insist that we obviously do possess immortal souls,
this gives grounds for thinking that other animals have them too.
There is a slippery slope argument: if one attributes souls to higher
animals, then one must do so to lower animals too, and eventually
to all animate beings. The risk is of overpopulating heaven not only
with lions, tigers, and bears but even with sponges, plankton, and

amoebae. The consequence would be that the goal of identifying human beings as having a special place in God's creation would be no less undermined than had our possession of immortal souls been denied altogether, since the afterlife begins to look much like the current one in terms of its members. Descartes cannot accept this consequence. He claims that since lower animals simply do not have immortal souls that will proceed to an afterlife, and since lower animals are classified together with higher ones, then there is no reason to hold that *any* animals possess thinking souls. Therefore, no animal—apart from the human being—possesses that special capacity belonging to immortal souls: the capacity of thought and rational consciousness. Descartes's approach goes much further than to deny animals rationality. Not only do they lack a rational soul, he claims, animals even lack lower conscious states. They are in fact incapable of even having the true conscious feelings or sensations that we humans possess. When animals are experiencing 'passions' they are not experiencing them in the way that human beings do. Rather, animals are like automata, machines that simply respond to causal stimuli in certain complex ways, but without any representations entering their consciousness, since there is no consciousness comparable to a human being's there at all. Descartes's attitude to the brutes was itself brutal—he is known to have used this theory to justify his own practice of vivisection on animals.

The philosopher and theologian Pierre Gassendi opposed Descartes on the nature of animal minds in the Fifth Set of Objections to Descartes's *Meditations on First Philosophy* (1641). There Gassendi argues that 'although man is the foremost of the animals, he still belongs to the class of animals'.[20] Inspired by Epicurus and Lucretius and seeking to integrate their insights into a Christian context, Gassendi himself believes that humans are superior to animals in that the former have a 'rational soul' while the latter possess a mere 'sensitive soul'. Moreover, he thinks that the sensitive soul of animals allows for some kind of intelligence. This kind of soul is composed of matter and is perishable, while the human being's rational soul is not made of matter and is immortal. Gassendi does not think that Descartes has done enough to show that there is something special and sui generis about the human soul:

To prove that your nature is different (that is, incorporeal, as you maintain), you ought to produce some operation which is of a quite different kind from those which the brutes perform—one which takes place outside the brain, or at least independently of the brain; and this you do not do.[21]

For Gassendi, it is clear that although animals 'lack human reason . . . they do not lack their own kind of reason'. Who is to stipulate that, just because animal minds do not involve some of the features of human rationality (such as self-consciousness, sophisticated language use, etc.), the type of behaviour they manifest isn't rational at all? Gassendi echoes Descartes's opponent Montaigne when he claims that 'although they do not reason so perfectly or about as many subjects as man, they still reason, and the difference seems to be merely one of degree'.[22] This idea—that a form of rationality might be in present in the natural world—would radically influence Mandeville's way of looking at things.

Gassendi perceived that the topic of animal minds goes to the core of Descartes's theological aspirations for his philosophy. Animal consciousness is linked with the kind of cognitive operations that take place in a material body, such as a brain, and when that material body perishes, so does the soul or mind that relates to it. The idea that a special operation of consciousness—namely, thinking—is attached not to a material brain but to an immaterial soul is crucial, since here there opens up the possibility that this immaterial soul might also be an immortal soul that continues to exist after the material body it inhabits perishes. If one cannot find a specific and special difference for human consciousness that distinguishes it from animal consciousness, then it is possible that thought itself is just something that material stuff does (and will cease to do when that material stuff is no more). Admittedly, it is no easy thing to explain how 'thinking matter' is even possible, but this difficulty doesn't entirely help the Cartesian, since it is not easy to explain how an *im*material soul that thinks might be possible either.

The young Mandeville would have been intimately familiar with the various positions of Montaigne, Descartes, and Gassendi. Yet the most influential account of the problem of animal minds came from a fourth Frenchman, the teacher at his school, Pierre Bayle. In the 'Rorarius' entry in his *Dictionary*, Bayle plays with Descartes's arguments in an ingenious and disruptive way. One of the standard moves of the Cartesian camp is to claim that the behaviour of animals, while superficially resembling the behaviour of creatures with rational minds such as ourselves, is in fact quite different. According to this theory, while it can *seem* to the untutored eye that an animal is engaged in reasoning—such as pausing to reflect, predicting an outcome, and choosing a preferred strategy for action—in fact none of these things are really happening inside the animal's mind at all. All that are happening are low-level cognitive responses that have developed to mimic rational behaviour.

Bayle points out the danger with this kind of argumentative manoeuvre. The worry is not the claim that apparent rational behaviour can be mimicked by sophisticated non-rational responses. On the contrary, the worry is this if this is a plausible account as to what is happening in the minds of animals then it might work for *human beings* also. Perhaps this is in fact all that is really going on when *we* are engaged in that process we call 'thinking'? It could as well be that underneath our apparently rational activity there is just some mechanical operation going on of which we are unaware. As Bayle mischievously points out, this Cartesian explanation of apparently rational behaviour is just a bit *too* good. It threatens to explain away *our* rationality as a merely illusory phenomenon and show that we too are creatures possessing nothing more than Gassendi's 'sensitive soul', creatures whose behaviour only *appears* to be that of rational beings. Even worse, perhaps we are only those sophisticated automatons Descartes accused the animals of being (a possibility that would be later seriously taken up by La Mettrie in his *Man a Machine* (1748)). Yet long before La Mettrie, as we shall see, Mandeville explored the same thought. In the *Fable*, he pushes the thought that human beings' ostensibly rational behaviour might in fact be nothing more than a prolonged exercise in self-deception, the self-glorification of what is in truth nothing more than the pushes and pulls of sensations, passions, and desires.

Ostensibly pious, it is unclear what Bayle's own true feelings were in this matter. It is impossible to ignore the sardonic tone in his commentary when he notes the theological advantages of the Cartesian position. Another of the traditional worries within Christian theology is explaining why an omnipotent and omnibenevolent being would allow the existence of pain at all in this terrestrial life. One possible response is that the existence of pain is a kind of punishment for our sinfulness. Yet it would seem obvious that there are many cases where human beings suffer without having even the opportunity to commit sin, such as in the case of young infants' illness and death. The doctrine of original sin, whereby all human beings inherit sinfulness from Adam as their essential existential condition, is a way of explaining why even those who suffer before committing any wrongs may nevertheless be suffering on account of their sinfulness. This account might be thought harsh in itself, but it also has a further problem in that it doesn't seem to allow any room to explain the pain and suffering of animals. Animals surely don't have souls such as ours, and certainly do not seem to be beings born with original sin, yet they too seem to suffer pain and death. The issue of animal suffering thus seems to press again the question of why a benevolent God would create beings who have the capacity to feel pain even though they lack the capacity to reason about good and evil, to choose freely actions that might allow them to be responsible for their actions, atone for their sins, and so on. If one accepts the Cartesian account of animal minds, Bayle notes, one has a neat (if again quite brutal) technical solution to the problem. If animals in fact lack the very capacity to suffer, if their apparent suffering behaviour is just that—merely *apparent* suffering—then God has not in fact allowed them to suffer. If they have no sensitive souls, and no real consciousness, there is no real pain either—even if the animal that one is vivisecting appears to be in extreme distress.[23]

Descartes's approach offers a handy fix to the theological worry of God's benevolence. Yet there is surely something deeply disturbing about Descartes's willingness to rationalize into a complete denial that something as obvious as animal suffering, something anyone with two eyes can routinely observe, is not really happening. The cognitive dissonance involved is such that it must have some powerful mechanism behind it. The grounds for such beliefs, as Mandeville will later claim in the *Fable*, are neither scientific nor philosophical, nor even exclusively theological. Instead he will follow Montaigne's original insight that they derive from a deep-seated drive within human beings to rationalize to themselves that they are a special kind of being. Mandeville will characterize human beings as a species that needed to domesticate itself in order to get along, and that created self-serving narratives to fuel the project. It is also clear that opposing Descartes on animal minds can align one with those also opposed to the theological motives behind Descartes's position. It is no exaggeration to say that one who denied the fundamental difference between humans and other animals was often supposed to maintain atheistical leanings. Mandeville too will court controversy by showing how much a role religious belief plays in the process of self-deception.

Mandeville's reading of Bayle could also have been instructive for the development of his medical thought. The theory of the correct treatment for human beings' ailments interweaved with these philosophical and theological issues about the nature of human and non-human animals, of how humans' souls interacted with their bodies, and so on. Mandeville's own medical theories are ultimately born from disputes of a quite different nature. Bayle admits to relying at times upon the writings of the English physician Thomas Willis. Willis's *Two Discourses concerning the Souls of Brutes* (1672) operates with the same distinction Gassendi had drawn between rational and sensitive souls and claimed that only humans possessed the former. The purpose of his work, though, is to determine the actual constitution and operations of the sensitive soul that he thought we also share with animals. Willis had evocatively described how the sensitive soul is constituted by an immensely complex nervous system, made up of minuscule nerves which transport within them even more minuscule particles, invisible to human observation, which flow throughout various parts of the body:

> [These particles are] variously employed in the offices of the others; but of these, those which are chiefly subtle, as it were beams of light sent from a flame, are, as it were distilled into the brain. . . . These most subtle particles are called the animal spirits, and first of all entering the cortical substances of those parts, and from thence flowing into the *Meditullia* or middle parts of either of them, and into the oblong and spinal marrow, and further into all the nerves and nervous fibres, dispersed through the whole body, constitute the other and more noble part of the corporeal soul, commonly called the sensitive . . . [24]

Willis's picture is one of the human body as a holistic machine, run through with a nervous system that functions as an exchange market whose currency is the flow of animal spirits. They run from nerve endings inside bones through intestines and organs and up to the brain itself. Since the brain is what the majority of the nerves are connected to, Willis has the sensitive soul located there:

> especially because it plainly appears, that the Offices of the Interior
> Motions, and Senses, as well as the Exterior, are acted by the help of
> the animal Spirits, ordained within certain and distinct Paths, or as it
> were small little pipes.[25]

In all these theories Willis had been following the broad empiricist approach of his teacher, the philosopher and physician John Locke. One of the features of Locke's empiricism was a kind of caution with regard to the extent of human knowledge. For all its impressiveness, we cannot assume that human reason is always able to reveal the fundamental explanations for things. On the contrary, Locke assumed that our cognitive faculties simply lack this capacity. Just as Montaigne seemed to want to limit the pretences of human reason so as to render us humble about our species, Locke thought that the proper scientific method involved a strict humility about what human reason can know. In his classic work of philosophy, the *Essay concerning Human Understanding* (1689), Locke had written that the notions that 'we can attain to by our faculties' are in fact 'very disproportionate to things themselves'.[26] Gassendi had also suggested that our ability to peer into the inner recesses of reality and perceive the fundamental essences of things is far more limited than we would like to think. For Gassendi and Locke it was important not to 'perplex our selves and others with disputes about things, to which our understandings are not suited'.[27] Willis's theories of the animal soul were based on the hypotheses that one might reasonably formulate after careful observation of animals' anatomies and behaviour, though he would be hesitant to claim that he had thereby unlocked the secrets of nature.

One of Locke's close friends was Thomas Sydenham, who came to be one of the most renowned and influential physicians of the seventeenth century. After the rarefied theories of Leiden, it would be the Englishman Sydenham's focus on physical processes in the treatment of mental disturbance that would be revelatory for the down-to-earth Mandeville. Sydenham also adopts the theory of animal spirits and claims that many illnesses could be explained in terms of their flow, whether in producing an overabundance of animal spirits in one area of the human system or in depleting them in another. In his well-known *Epistolary Dissertation* (1682), Sydenham expounds on how this theory explained the common and peculiar ailments generally known as 'hypochondria' and 'hysteria'. Hypochondria was understood not in its current colloquial form as a disposition to imagine or invent illnesses (though it could certainly include this as a symptom). It was rather a broader term intended to catch a range of negative mental phenomena including anxiety, irritability, lethargy, melancholy, paranoia, and depression. It became so well known as a catchall for various forms of lowness of spirit that it was referred to as 'the Hyp' (or 'the Hypo'). Hysteria involved many of the same symptoms, though in this case applied only to women. Indeed, Mandeville, adopting the theories of Sydenham and others, claims that they are in fact exactly the same condition only distinguished by the gender of the patient.

The essential question for seventeenth- and eighteenth-century physicians concerned the identification of the physical causes of these conditions. They were generally assumed to be linked to a huge range of physical ailments, such as stomach ache, indigestion, flatulence, loss of appetite, reduced sex drive, and so on. The connection between mental well-being and intestinal health was always assumed to be a close one (the condition was thought to be differently manifested in women owing to the added complication of being related to illnesses of the uterus). We are now very far from Descartes's rational soul. For Sydenham, hypochondria and hysteria are fundamentally caused by 'a disorder . . . of the animal spirits'.[28] The theory of animal spirits was well positioned to explain the nature of the phenomena, since it proposed a holistic connection between the minuscule 'pipes' that connected the stomach lining with those that ran to the brain and elsewhere in the nervous system. It would be central to such a theory that overburdening the use of animal spirits in one area of the human system might provoke a depletion of them in another area. To take a simple case, overeating might demand hard digestive work to be undertaken that might subsequently redirect the animal spirits away from their other functions and then could generate the symptoms of lethargy, and so on. Importantly, though, causation could run in the opposite direction also—a lethargic or lazy attitude might incline a patient to engage in fewer of the activities that account for a normal distribution of the animal spirits and as such provoke new physical symptoms. This feature of the condition makes treatment of the case a curiously nuanced affair, since while there is in some sense always a simple practical solution involved, it often requires a sensitivity to how environmental and psychological factors can impact the otherwise straightforward physical aspects of the condition.

Among the simple fixes Sydenham recommends for the purpose of getting the spirits moving—one that Mandeville the medic would return to again and again in his writings—is physical activity. Such activity could help recirculate the spirits where they had become moribund. Sydenham particularly recommends riding, saying that 'nothing so cherishes and strengthens the blood and spirits, as riding on horseback, long distances, every day'.[29] The reason he prefers riding is that it is a type of activity where the bouncing and straining of the abdominal muscles entailed that 'all the exercise falls upon the lower belly', where, he thought, so many of the problems lay. Sydenham's claim that it is the lack of physical activity that allows for the degeneration of the spirits also brings other social factors into play in considering both the causes and the treatments of the conditions. He suggests that the large group of women privileged enough to be raised to be genteel and to shun arduous physical labour were particularly vulnerable to the condition, as were men who devoted themselves to a more sedate lifestyle:

> As to females, if we except those who lead a hard and hardy life, there is rarely one who is wholly free from them—and females, be it remembered, form one half of the adults of the world. Then, again, such male subjects as lead a sedentary or studious life, and grow pale over their books and papers, are similarly affected.[30]

It was for this reason that melancholy and depression associated with hypochondria came to be known as the 'disease of the learned'. Frequently Mandeville turns to this trope, diagnosing this or that ailment as effectively the result of too much free time spent thinking.

A final crucial source of inspiration for Mandeville, alongside Willis and Sydenham, was the physician Giorgio Baglivi. In particular, Baglivi's *The Practice of Physick* (1704) was a direct influence upon many of the views expressed by Mandeville in the latter's *Treatise*. Baglivi's writing is polemical—it concerns itself not just with actual diagnoses or cures of particular illnesses, but also with the problems attached to the theoretical foundations of medical practice itself. Baglivi shares Locke's empiricist outlook, one that Locke in turn had inherited from the philosopher Francis Bacon. Both of them had warned against the presumption of thinking one can know the deep essence of the natural world. Baglivi agrees that 'nature is its own master, and lies more extended than to be confined within certain bounds prescribed by our scanty reason'.[31] He complains that the key fault is physicians' tendency to retreat into idle speculation—so much easier than the hard graft of empirical investigation—when searching for an explanation. Baglivi has a wonderfully frank and simple explanation about our inherent disposition to dubious theorizing in medicine, which is that 'men give more credit to the useless comments of their own brains, than to observation and the cautions of nature'.[32] That they do so is determined by nothing more than convenience, since obtaining knowledge of nature is, as Bacon and Locke had insisted, a very difficult task. The only appropriate recourse is to what nature will grant us access to through observation:

> And indeed while I consider that nature is not subject to our control, and that she performs her motions in so occult a manner, that they can never be so easily traced as by observation, and reason retaining to observation; and on the other hand, that men talk of her as it were at pleasure by a certain impulse of the mind.[33]

The observation of nature is difficult since, as Heraclitus put it, 'nature loves to hide'. Baglivi focuses on the role of the human will more than that of the intellect, however. We are confronted with a stark difference when we engage in observation versus theorizing. Observing is premised on the fact that nature simply does not obey our will and confronts us with mysterious and unpredictable events. Theorizing is by contrast marked by that unfettered freedom that Montaigne had suggested characterized human thinking in general—one can summon up a theory from one's armchair on a whim, if one only has the capacity and the spare time to do so. Those who might engage in abstract theorizing might be motivated by two very different reasons. On the one hand, they might just be naturally inclined to abstract reasoning; on the other, they might be lazy. Those who prefer to get results quickly and with the minimum of effort will naturally prefer the method of understanding nature that does not require them to get out of their armchair to do so. As Montaigne warned, we have a vested interest in prioritizing the importance of our rational faculty.

Baglivi expands by listing a series of 'obstacles' to the improvement of the practice of medicine. The first obstacle he mentions concerns the tribalism of traditional medical schools and the derision they pour upon one another. The cause of the animosity is again related to the question of the true motivation of physicians, which he claims has too often been the desire for renown rather than the pursuit of truth. Fame in one's area is more easily attained by attacking an opponent's theory than by doing actual fieldwork in that science. Instead of attempting to attend to the nature of things by close observation, they have instead embarked on the bold task of simply stipulating what nature is according to their own theories:

> The desire of vain glory, has in all ages put physicians rather upon the forming of sects, than the daily discovery of new phenomena, to illustrate and confirm the history of diseases. Thus they've moulded the nature of things at pleasure; and almost overturned it with their undigested meditations.[34]

The second obstacle Baglivi notes is that of the adoption of 'false idols', specifically in the tendency to take something that has worked on some occasions as a panacea for any illness whatsoever. This tendency is one of the practical quick fixes that Baglivi thinks is inimical to proper medical practice. A further temptation is the use of similes or reasoning from analogy (which always impresses so long as it ignores subtle important differences between concrete cases); the attempt to back up one's theory with more support from classical medical texts rather than with empirical testing; and,

perhaps most of all, the 'pernicious custom of making systems'[35]—
the urge to construct rational edifices that aim to present a medical
theory of everything.

Mandeville, never afraid to borrow from others, repeats all of
these complaints in the *Treatise*. Most notable perhaps is Baglivi's
scepticism with regard to the use of mathematics in medicine,
presented in the same subtle way that Mandeville will do in the
Treatise. While he has nothing against the use of mathematics per
se, Baglivi opposes the notion that it is the key to understanding
medical issues. Mathematics is the paradigm example of a priori
reasoning, the discovery of truths independently of experience and
by the power of the mind alone. Baglivi and Mandeville are suspicious of the idea that appeals to mathematics can help solve *anything* about a particular patient's ills. The more general complaint
concerns the projection of standards and concepts from other
sciences onto medicine without justification. The motivation for
this projection echoes Baglivi's early complaints: theorists project
a preferred theory simply because it is their preferred theory. The
practice of medicine is simply not like the practice of mathematics,
and securing a medical result involves both different approaches
and different standards than those involved in securing a result in
mathematics. In overemphasizing the influence of mathematics,
physicians are accused of indulging their own intellectual whims
instead of carefully following the teachings of nature herself.[36]

It is perhaps the influence of Baglivi's anthropological observations of the foibles of medical practitioners that is most on display
in Mandeville's medical work. In his second medical submission
at Leiden, Mandeville had presented an account of the elements
that go into digestion and the maladies that are associated with
it. Moreover, in that work he made explicit reference to the role
of animal spirits. When it turned to actual practice it is perhaps
unsurprising that Mandeville made hypochondria and hysteria his
medical specialism. Mandeville settled in London around 1698,
and it seems quickly set up a practice. In the *Treatise*, Mandeville
describes how he 'brings himself onto the stage' in the form of a
character called Philopirio. His description of Philopirio there is
usually thought to reveal biographical information about Mandeville himself:

Philopirio is a foreigner and a physician, who, after he had finished his studies and taken his degree beyond-sea, was come to London to learn the language; in which having happened to take great delight, and in the meantime found the country and the manners of it agreeable to his humour, he has now been many years and is like to end his days in England.[37]

Given what is known about his role in the Costerman riots, this is a rather selective presentation of Mandeville's motivations for travelling to England. He no doubt did find an enthusiasm for the English language, people, and culture; however, he surely initially found himself looking to London because his previous prescribed future as an influential member of the modern professional and political elite in Rotterdam was in tatters. Instead, he had to forge a new future for himself. His reading of Montaigne and Bayle equipped him with the intellectual resources to seek naturalistic accounts of human behaviour that avoided theological dogmas and the privileging of human excellence. His empiricist and sceptical outlook set him on a direct collision course with his rationalist teachers, one that inclined him to find physical bases for what might at first appear to be exclusively rational mental phenomena. For Mandeville, diagnosing the ailments of the human animal required cutting through fraudulent theoretical edifices with careful observation. But Mandeville was an innovator here too—his model of observation was not simply that of looking at a patient's physical symptoms but of listening to them and conversing with them too, and engaging with the human subject with all their complications and contradictions.

CHAPTER THREE

The Anatomy
of Hypochondria

*To know things well, we must know the details; and as they are almost
infinite, our knowledge is always superficial and imperfect.*

—LA ROCHEFOUCAULD, *MAXIMS*, 5:106

ALTHOUGH MANDEVILLE EARNED HIS living in London as a medical practitioner, it is clear that he did not see himself as limited
to this field. His statement that he was enticed to England by the
language must be at least part of the story—by 1704 Mandeville
had begun publishing in a variety of literary forms: translations of
French fables, poetry, political pamphlets, and satirical dialogues
regarding contemporary society. Despite it being the published
work that would cement his fame, the work that meant most to
Mandeville personally was not in fact *The Fable of the Bees*. Rather,
it was an earlier book that would merge these medical and literary ambitions. In 1711, having practised for perhaps nearly twenty
years, Mandeville published the first edition of his major medical investigation. Its full title is not exactly pithy: *A Treatise of the
Hypochondriack and Hysterick Passions, Vulgarly Call'd the Hypo
in Men and Vapours in Women, in which the Symptoms, Causes
and Cure of Those Diseases Are Set Forth after a Method Entirely
New. The Whole Interspersed with Instructive Discourses on the
Real Art of Physick Itself; and Entertaining Remarks on the Real*

*Practice of Physicians and Apothecaries: Very Useful to All, Who
Have the Misfortune to Stand in Need of Either. In Three Dialogues.*
Mandeville was obviously extremely proud of this work, since once
his notoriety was secured he took the opportunity to publish an
extended edition in 1730, which he re-titled (somewhat more suc-
cinctly) *A Treatise of the Hypochondriack and Hysterick Diseases
in Three Dialogues.*[1]

The original title is instructive, however. On the one hand it is
obviously an advertisement for those who suffer from the mentioned conditions and want to educate as well as cure themselves.
The reader is promised some levity in the form of remarks on what
it is that doctors and drug merchants are 'really' up to. But the work
also proposes to offer an analysis of the whole of medical practice
itself (the 'real art of physick', as he puts it, echoing Baglivi). While
it is directed primarily at potential patients, ('having a mind to publish my sentiments concerning the distempers to which I had more
particularly applied myself for some years')[2] it was also clearly
intended to be read by other physicians, here in the land of his medical heroes Willis and Sydenham. Mandeville's explanation of his
approach is also telling. The standard method of presentation of
medical treatises is to provide long lists of symptoms and even longer lists of medicines to apply in different combinations. He claims
that 'impatience is one of the surest symptoms' of one suffering
from hypochondria or hysteria, and as such the book must be tai-
lored to accommodate a reader who is motivated to read the work—
that is, an actual sufferer of one of the illnesses in question. So the
work must be interesting enough to hold the attention of a reader
who might be distracted from reading about a condition by the very
fact that they are suffering from that condition. Already there is on
display a sly self-awareness of the complex relationships between
doctor and patient, writer and reader, relations that emerge as crucial to Mandeville's medical method.

The work is both a Baglivian polemic and a piece of advertising.
Mandeville begins the polemical tone in the preface and starts on
a theme that will become familiar to his readers. The key failing of
human beings, the one that is 'inseparable' from human nature, is
that one identified by Montaigne: pride. It is pride that led Adam
astray in the garden of Eden, he points out, and pride that stops

human beings from progressing any further after that initial fall. Pride is manifested everywhere, Mandeville claims, especially in the failings of the modern physician. He mixes Montaigne and Baglivi here to present his analysis of just what is wrong with the current state of 'physick':

> 'Tis pride that makes the physician abandon the solid observation of never-erring nature, to take up with the loose conjectures of his own wandering invention, that the world may admire the fertility of his brain.[3]

Mandeville adds a new twist to the theory, claiming that pride is equally evident on the patient's side of the relationship, since it is this that 'makes him in love with the reasoning physician, to have an opportunity of showing the depth of his own penetration'.[4] Pride and the crucial need for the esteem of others are the covert driving forces behind much of the social dynamic in which illnesses are treated. Locke's empiricism entailed humility about what the human mind can grasp about the world, but too often such humility is cast aside as a result of what Mandeville refers to as human beings' worship of the 'idol' of their own rationality. In the preface, he complains again that it is the vice of pride that precludes philosophers from admitting that there is a limit to their intellects, and that they 'won't allow that it is possible [that] nature should have recesses beyond the reach of their sagacity, and reckon the injurious assertion an affront to human understanding'.[5]

It is an interesting beginning to a treatise on medicine. Mandeville begins not at the level of the identification of symptoms of illnesses, nor with a postulation of their root causes, let alone with a general theory of how human health is determined. Instead he begins with a consideration of the sociological and psychological power dynamic in the doctor–patient relationship. He makes two simple and entirely plausible observations. Firstly, it is vital to the self-esteem of the physician that they present an image (both to themselves and to their patients) of a learned and authoritative figure. Secondly, that it is vital to the self-esteem of the patient that they portray an image of themselves as intelligent enough to understand the theories and diagnoses being offered. When the physician offers a diagnosis, there is at least a nominal attempt at communicating their knowledge—the implicature of the conversation is that the physician is saying something that they expect the patient to understand. However, in order to justify their own position in society, the physician is inclined to adopt theories that are *not* easy to understand. Were the physician's theories plain and simple to grasp, then ordinary people could treat themselves and render the physician's services obsolete. Thus, while there is on the surface an honest intention to communicate one's theory to the patient, under the surface the motivations are more complicated. It is vital to the economy of medical practice that the patient cannot help themselves and that the demand for outside expertise is constantly stimulated.

Things are no less complicated on the patient's side. On first being offered an obscure theoretical diagnosis by the physician— those 'loose conjectures of his own wandering invention'—the patient's immediate response is, unsurprisingly, that of a failure of understanding. After all, the theory is merely one dreamed up by the physician. However, although the rational response would be to request clarification or even to issue a challenge to it, the social and psychological forces at play are far too powerful to allow such behaviour. The patient grasps with an equal immediacy that the theory has been communicated in the expectation (so it seems to the patient) of it being understood. Facing embarrassment, the patient smiles and nods. Following Baglivi again, Mandeville writes especially amusingly of the fondness physicians have for similes.[6] If the physician is of a high social class, if they can roll off some Latin, if they can condescend to 'explain' the illness by appeal to some familiar analogy or metaphor, they can win over the ordinary patient, who feels intelligent in grasping the device:

> The witty philosopher, who can so exactly tell you which way the world was made, that one would think he must have had a hand in it, in his talk cures all diseases by hypothesis, and frigthens away the gout with a fine simile, but when he comes to practice oftener reasons a trifling distemper into a consumption.[7]

This, Mandeville implies, is in large part the operation of medical practice. A patient will endure illness happily if they think that they are receiving the best treatment from the most knowledgeable experts, irrespective of whether their symptoms are being alleviated or not. This also produces two responses: firstly, the patient is intellectually flattered that the physician presumed that they *would* understand the theory; secondly the patient now is deeply concerned at the thought of the social embarrassment at confessing any lack of understanding. Together these forces combine to elicit not just acceptance of the theory but also—overcompensating desperately now—enthusiastic support for the theory just presented. The doctor and patient eagerly collude to give and receive a theory regarding whatever ailment the patient has. This powerful psychological relationship already disposes the patient towards a positive outcome, which can have its own positive effect. This effect, however, takes place at one step removed from any facts about how the patient is feeling or what course of action would actually help improve their physical condition. It is a bold, contrarian, and deliberately controversial claim that Mandeville is proposing from the outset: the majority of medical diagnoses are bunk; the reason for their propagation and acceptance in the marketplace of the doctor's office has nothing to do with their effectiveness or even their coherence; positive results are as likely to be what we would now recognize as placebo effects generated from the mere event of consulting with a doctor and receiving a confident diagnosis and prognosis.

The *Treatise* is clearly an unusual and innovative work, not least with regard to its literary form. It is written as a dialogue involving three main characters. Misomedon ('hater of doctors') is a relatively comfortable gentleman who has suffered from various symptoms related to hypochondria for many years. Mandeville describes him in the preface:

> Misomedon is a man of learning, who whilst he had his health was of a gay, even temper, and a friendly open disposition; but having long laboured under the hypochondriack passion is now much altered for the worse, and [has] become peevish, fickle, censorious and mistrustful.[8]

The dialogue is set in Misomedon's home. The first dialogue involves him listing both his complaints and the history of the treatments he has received for them to Philopirio ('lover of experience')—that is, Mandeville himself. The second dialogue involves Philopirio making his case to the highly sceptical Misomedon for his chosen type of medical treatment and for his theory of medical practice in general. The third dialogue concludes with further discussion including detail of the actual particular recommendations for Misomedon and for his wife, Polytheca, who enters the discussion to note her own symptoms of hysteria—and to argue with her husband. There is also reflection upon the couple's teenage daughter who also suffers from hysteria, though she herself does not appear in the dialogue. Mandeville's pragmatic aim here was to include a cast that might cover possible patients of different ages and genders. Misomedon's condition is an exaggerated one, composed of an aggregate of different problems. Mandeville claims that the characters are based upon his own experience, and that the exaggerated conditions of the patients are merely the accumulated symptoms of a variety of people he has treated during his time in London.

Misomedon claims right from the start that he has sent for Philopirio despite being certain he will not be cured from his illness by whatever Philopirio recommends. Misomedon is seeking Philopirio's opinion more out of curiosity, and perhaps even from a desire to see his own jaded conclusions regarding the inefficacy of physicians further confirmed. The first dialogue is nearly a monologue as we hear Misomedon's medical life story. Throughout Misomedon's tale, Philopirio displays patience and expresses enthusiasm in hearing even the smallest details. Misomedon's life has in effect been that of a gentleman of leisure. Having studied at Oxford and been left a handy income upon his father's death, he gives himself up to a life of pleasure in London and subsequently travels abroad for a few years on the standard grand tour. He returns and marries, upon which he finally grasps the seriousness of the debts he has incurred over the preceding years. Misomedon tries to bring his lifestyle within the bounds of his income, though his finances remain perilous until another relative dies and leaves him an even more substantial fortune. Misomedon also inherits a prodigious library and discovers in himself an appetite for reading the classics. His relationship with his wife has always been a happy and passionate one, and Misomedon describes his life as a contented one 'inter venerem et musas' (between love and study).[9]

Misomedon's illness begins in his mid-thirties with heartburn and trapped wind, and the indigestion becomes gradually more serious over time. He eventually consults a physician, who informs him that the cause is a 'hot' liver and a 'cold' stomach. The recommendation—citing the eminent classical source of Galen—is in the first instance that of bleeding and purging, followed by three weeks in Epsom to drink the high-quality water. Misomedon reports that he 'admired the profundity of the venerable old gentleman's skill' and that he 'gave him a handsome fee, and thanked him for his advice'.[10] The effect of following the advice is disastrous, as Misomedon is laid low with stomach pains, faintness, and incapacitating weakness. The condition continues until Misomedon happens to meet another gentleman lodging at the same house who, upon seeing Misomedon's condition and gathering details of the treatment, angrily denounces it as nonsense and chicanery. The gentleman immediately gets Misomedon to drink some hot seasoned claret and eat some toast, and Misomedon is very soon restored. He regains his appetite and most of his strength, and returns to London.

Gradually, however, his symptoms return. Misomedon tries to ignore them since, as he puts it, by now he 'was as much afraid of physick, as a child of being whipped'.[11] He eventually relents and consults with a new highly regarded London physician. This physician confirms the criticism of the gentleman from Epsom, who ridiculed the idea that the heat of the stomach had anything to do with such illnesses. Instead he claimed, it was the 'menstruum'—a substance emanating through the pores that had been allowed to ferment in the nervous system—that was the cause of it. The recommended cure this time is that of emetics. They work at first, but the symptoms return as soon as the taking of emetics ceases. Worse still, the effect of the emetics itself gradually diminishes. Misomedon by now has become 'very melancholic'. On top of this, his relationship with the new doctor deteriorates steadily:

> When neither his former prescriptions, nor the various changes he made in them could ease me, and his plausible reasons for altering them were quite exhausted, I perceived that he grew perfectly weary of me. I could not but seldom see him, when he came he was always in haste, and all the comfort I got from him was that he either found some fault with my diet or manner of living; or else charged me with

omitting what he had ordered, till at last being conscious that I had never been more regular or observant, I told him my thoughts; at which pretending to be offended he took the opportunity of picking a quarrel, and left me in a pet.[12]

Mandeville's comic retelling invites the reader to raise a sceptical eyebrow at Misomedon's account here—although it is quite possible that the criticisms of the ineffective doctor are well founded, one can easily imagine the poor man being constantly harangued by an indefatigable Misomedon, who is by this point clearly unafraid to express his opinion on the quality of his treatment. Since this physician refuses now to see Misomedon, he goes to see 'two or three more' but does not follow their advice, since it invariably involves just more bleeding or purging. At this point, Misomedon resolves to treat himself, going over his previous prescriptions and judging in consultation with a local apothecary what mixture of potions might suit his condition best.

During his time of various treatments Misomedon has started to use his classical education to take an intellectual interest in the theoretical foundations of medicine, but by now his hopes are not to cure himself, only that he 'might at least enter into the fallacies of so treacherous and insignificant an art'.[13] Having now read everything there is to read on the subject, Misomedon contends that all he has learnt about medicine is that he knows 'it to be a deceitful art, that is never to be relied on'.[14] Given the vast differences between the various systems, given the suspicious venom with which each school pours scorn on the other, and given the hubris with which each school claims to have isolated the one true key to health and the removal of illness, Misomedon asserts that:

We may conclude that the art of physick is no more to be depended upon than that of astrology, and that even the learned professors of the first have rendered themselves neither less ridiculous nor more beneficial to the public than the ignorant pretenders to the latter.[15]

Unfortunately, Misomedon's autodidacticism fails to produce better results for his own condition. As he enters his forties he continues to suffer from the familiar stomach pains and wind, but he now also suffers from vertigo and dizziness, shooting pains in his

back, constipation followed by diarrhoea followed by more constipation, and much more. Unsurprisingly perhaps, Misomedon also
develops mental and emotional problems: he suffers from night-
mares, or else from an insomnia characterized by 'tossing whole
nights in a thousand fears or anxieties'. During his waking hours
his mental health deteriorates and occasionally 'strange roving
thoughts would slide through my brain, and wild as well as ridiculous fancies stole upon me'.[16] Then, Misomedon encountered a
spontaneous and inexplicable improvement from this low point
that allowed him to return somewhat to normal life. His condition
remains, however, and he has intermittent occasions of deteriora-
tion and improvement, inexplicable and unpredictable, and which
he simply has come to accept. He is now, at the time of consulting
Philopirio, fifty-six years old and a cynical but regular imbiber of
a variety of apothecaries' recommendations, having lost all hope of
serious recovery and all faith in the practice of medicine itself.

The effect of all this on the reader is one of oscillation between
sympathy and scorn. Misomedon's tale will be painfully familiar
to anyone who has suffered from a chronic illness and desperately
sought different cures over the years, or who has been tempted to
self-diagnosis after extensive internet research. He angrily relates
the history of his treatment, as he moved between physicians,
encountering one false dawn after another. Misomedon moves from
advice to advice like a cork buffeted on the waves of authority and
theory. As each new treatment reduced in efficacy, he reflects back
on what seemed so hopeful about it initially. He concludes that the
most effective treatment he received was the psychological boost
from the compellingly confident rhetoric of each new physician he
consulted. Every time, the new physician convincingly disparaged
the previous one's theory, proclaimed it bunk and hocus-pocus, and
then offered a new, simple, and commonsensical alternative. Each
one, though, proved as ineffective as the last. At the same time,
one recognizes here both a genuine sufferer and a hypochondriac
in the more modern sense of the term. Misomedon is annoyingly
obsessed with his own condition. He is frequently boring and pre-
tentious, endlessly expressing himself in Latin proverbs or turns of
phrase (many culled from Erasmus's *Adages*). As reading goes it is
a little tedious, since Misomedon himself is a little tedious, though

also occasionally funny in hearing him describe his own ridiculous bouncing from one quack to another. This effect upon the reader is deliberate: Philip Hilton, in his impressive study of the *Treatise*, points out that:

> One of the functions of the tone is to mime a symptom attributed to the hypochondriac in order to present the reader with the chance to observe these symptoms of the disease first hand. Mandeville clearly wanted the prose style itself to convey something of the symptoms that afflicted Misomedon.[17]

It is at this point in the first dialogue that we first hear properly from Mandeville's representative Philopirio, who so far has spoken only to encourage Misomedon to unencumber himself of his medical history. When Philopirio does now offer an opinion, it is to issue near complete agreement with Misomedon about the benighted state of the profession. If anything, he goes further than Misomedon himself in critiquing his contemporaries. Philopirio claims that it is the prideful and self-regarding character of physicians that is the root cause of the evil. Mandeville has Philopirio explain why it is that the medical profession has become so populated with this type of self-regarding individual. One of the remarkable aspects of the *Treatise* is that it is simultaneously the presentation of a 'method entirely new' for treating these conditions, and also an inquiry into what we might think of as the sociology of medical practice. Under the latter heading, Mandeville is interested in the question of why doctors propound the theories they do. His answers to these questions are not edifying. Rarely, he claims, is it the case that a young doctor commits to a particular school or method of medical practice because of clinical evidence. In reality, what motivates young doctors is the securing of a safe career, and establishing themselves in society with a profession that gains high social esteem, not to mention financial reward.

Mandeville does not deny that the simple aim of caring for others might be among the motives that drive would-be medical practitioners. His opposition is to the notion that such virtuous motives might be all there is at play in the choice of career. In a remark that anticipates his later writings, Mandeville asserts that he cannot understand why one must attribute a pure and uncorrupted motive of moral virtue to an individual for their actions to be worthwhile. Is it really so bad, he asks, if the motives for helping others are mixed, and always involve in their concoction some reward for oneself? Is it not better that the author freely and openly confesses to some self-interested motive on top of the desire to help others? Mandeville admits as much in defending his own writing of the *Treatise*:

> If a regular physician writing of a distemper, the cure of which he particularly professes after a manner never attempted yet be a *quack*, because besides his design of being instructive and doing good to others, he has likewise an aim of making himself more known by it than he was before, then I am one.[18]

He is also deeply suspicious of any claim where the pursuit of medicine is made on purely altruistic grounds, and without any claim to self-interest:

> The common good and benefit of mankind are stalking horses, made use of by every body, and generally most talked of by those that least regard them. But the men of sense of our clear-sighted age are wiser than to expect such flights of self-denying virtue from their fellow creatures.[19]

Mandeville's scepticism is not based on the idea that we never have others' interests in mind—it is rather directed against the idea that we can have *only* the interests of others in mind and simultaneously purge ourselves of any consideration of self-interest. It is just this model of pure self-denial as a necessary requirement of concern for others that Mandeville opposes. Given that he thinks that pure self-sacrifice is an unrealistic virtue to attribute to human beings, his suspicion regarding the moral rhetoric is more understandable. Pure pursuit of the 'common good' and an undiluted love for one's fellow human beings are implausible motives for ordinary individuals, and so there must be some other covert reasons for why some like to preach these high standards. Whenever someone attests to the admirable motive of the benefit of mankind, Mandeville thinks, one's ears should immediately prick up. Moralistic talk should instead immediately prompt an investigation into what that person's *real* motive is, and without fail what one will find will be something far lower than pure love of one's fellow creatures.

In the first dialogue Philopirio considers the type of person who would become a physician, as well as the kind of education they would receive.[20] There is a very basic type of medical training that someone who has had a solid classical education, involving Greek and especially Latin, a spattering of philosophy and logic, and practice in memorization, can accrue. This allows the person to learn how to use a technical term associated with some standard symptoms, and likewise a couple of standard treatment options for that illness. This shallow kind of quick general practice has its place, but it cannot be the core of medicine, Mandeville thinks. His point here is that this is the *easiest* form of medical practice, since it is the form of knowledge that someone from a classically educated and relatively privileged social class can master. The temptation for such practitioners is to claim that this is the *standard* form of medical practice. Of course, the motive for this assertion is not a rational one but is rather an attempt by those with vested career interests to provide an ad hoc legitimation for their own skill set. Classical medical training is defended because the costs for entry into the profession are exclusive, in that they are class based, but also low in terms of actual effort and expense.

Mandeville's view is that true medicine properly involves a lot of hard and unpleasant—not to mention dull—work. Medicine, under this conception, is not the thing one would devote one's life to if one wanted a life of ease, wealth, fame, and renown:

> If you are not extraordinary in any of the branches I have named, rather than that you should spend your time before the squalid beds of poor patients, and bear with the unsavoury smells of a crowded hospital, show yourself a scholar, write a poem, either a good one, or a long one; compose a Latin oration . . . [21]

Other ways to get ahead include penning high-minded but implausible Latin treatises on obscure topics; marrying into a family of physicians; getting into good graces with the apothecaries and promising them a lot of business; becoming a 'rigid party man' and forming political connections; or being an eminently sociable man and 'drink[ing] yourself into practice'.[22] Mandeville offers no critique of these pathways to success—he is satisfied merely to point out that they exist.

A central claim of the *Treatise* is that the proper practice of medicine is a time-intensive activity, owing to the individuality of the patient: each one bears a wide range of specific characteristics, which in turn depend on facts about their particular physiology, temperament, family history, employment, social class, physical environment, and so on. This range of factors raises the possibility that there are likely to be as many atypical symptoms of a possible condition as there are typical symptoms. If one is wedded to a certain general theory then the only way to make any kind of diagnosis is by selectively attending to some of those symptoms and disregarding others. The trick is to avoid the temptation to squeeze the patient in under whatever diagnosis a doctor might be inclined to make. Instead, what a physician has to do is simply spend long hours observing the patient, noting the differences as much as the similarities between this case and others. The proper diagnosis and the proper prescription of a course of action will in most cases be one that is tailor-made, as individual as the patients themselves: "Tis observation, plain observation, without decanting or reasoning upon it, that makes the art; and all, who neglecting this main point have strove to embellish it with the fruits of their brain, have but cramped and confounded it.'[23] There is nothing wrong per se with the practice of forming generalizations, Mandeville says, but where one goes wrong is in using them as anything other than a starting point for one's medical inquiries. At all times, one should grant priority to the patient's observed symptoms. If they contradict the generalization, then one should not try to explain away the awkward symptom so as to hold on to one's initial theory. Rather, one has to modify or even reject one's own theory. Mandeville's point is that human beings are constitutionally disposed to hold on to their preferred theories even in the face of opposing evidence, or in the face of that theory's lack of explanatory power, since too often commitment to that theory is the physician's meal ticket.

Mandeville asserts that the ancient physicians—those who practised before even Galen and others came to fame—refused to speculate with abstruse theories and instead formed their opinions upon the accumulation of masses of observational data:

The eminent physicians were honest painstaking drudges, that watch-
ing almost day and night by their patients bedsides, stuck close to
observations, and minded nothing, but how to cure those that were
committed to their care, without a thought of pleasing any other way.[24]

Several problems soon emerged with this approach. Firstly, it is
hard vocational work for the employee. Secondly, it is expensive
labour for the employer. A third problem is that the practice of
medicine, properly performed, really consisted of a very particular-
ized activity, whereby the practitioner formed their judgments on
the back of thousands of micro-observations, and made predictions
that were based on evidence that was too fine-grained and subtle to
explain clearly in a simple general theory:

This made physic a very austere study, as well as mysterious to all the
world besides; and consequently the reason of what was done to
the sick was as unintelligible to the most subtle philosopher, as it was
to the greatest clown.[25]

The original physicians must have seemed like mystics or gurus,
unable to express the nature of their insights into the human condition. This profession could not last as long as it was possible for an
enterprising individual to propound a more general and more communicable medical theory. The ability to theorize gave the physician a way to avoid doing the hard labour of bedside care, and gave
the patient something to understand while undergoing treatment.
Gradually the observation-heavy and difficult-to-convey method
fell out of favour, so that would-be physicians could both practise
medicine and afford themselves an easy lifestyle.

Mandeville expands on his theory of how diagnoses ought
to work with a remarkable example, one that reveals his radical
approach not just to medical thinking but to the very nature of
human thought itself. Philopirio mentions to Misomedon that he
has noticed a Van Dyck painting in Misomedon's parlour. He cannot give any evidence at all for why he knows that it is an original
and not a copy, but he is absolutely certain that it is an original. His
familiarity with the artist is based on thousands of visual observations over decades, the accumulation of which has given him a
kind of knack for distinguishing copies from genuine examples.

However, his ability to translate this know-how into words and to communicate how he knows what he knows to another person lags far behind.[26] Because we possess such know-how and yet, for all that, are unable to articulate exactly what it is that we are basing our judgment upon, we attribute these things to instinct, gut feeling, or even lucky guesses.

In Mandeville's mind, what is in fact occurring is that large amounts of small observations, data gathered over years by the medical specialist, have enabled them to make snap judgments that are both highly sophisticated and highly reliable. The physician observes skin pallor, breath, eye colour, posture, and dozens of other physical symptoms without even recognizing that they are doing it. Their response to what they are seeing occurs without the individual themselves being able to give an explicit reason for how they know the things they know. But this inability to give intellectual expression to their knowledge is not grounds for suspicion; on the contrary, Mandeville claims that this is a common feature of knowledge built up from long experience. For Mandeville, the proper practice of medicine reveals the truth in Montaigne's complaints about our attitudes towards the human mind. The thing we think of as our most distinctive cognitive capacity—the ability to reason, to articulate our thoughts in language, to think clearly and explicitly—is for Mandeville a red herring. The truly reliable human knowledge is that which stems from the thousands of tiny observations of which we are ourselves usually entirely unaware. We are, just as Montaigne had insisted, doing something much closer to what other animals do when they think. If it is reasoning that is happening, it is the reasoning of Gassendi's 'sensitive soul' and not Descartes's 'res cogitans', the immaterial thinking soul.

What is more, we have a tendency to attribute the knowledge to the wrong faculty. If we have come to know something we assume that the knowledge has come about through our higher ability for abstract reasoning. However, what is really going on, Mandeville implies, is that some subconscious and perhaps even *non*-rational impulse to accept something has *already* happened, unbeknown to ourselves. These basic responses—those that we plausibly share in common with other animals—are the real drivers of human behaviour. The explicit self-conscious framing of our thoughts in language is not an occasion of us really deciding anything—rather it is us explaining to ourselves the decisions that we have already made at the non-intellectual level. Reason does not do anything in the human being on this conception; rather, as Harold Cook puts it, Mandeville holds that 'what we think of as "reason" is post-hoc rationalizing about our experience'.[27]

Mandeville could not have travelled farther from his earlier supposed sympathies with Descartes. It is the basic capacity for sensory experience that is at the core of the original form of medical practice. For these reasons there arose in the market the opportunity to present a competitor model of medical practice, one based on general theories of the human being, full of definitions and notions of different humours and types of bile, which could be endlessly presented in different permutations so as to afford an explanation of everything, without offering an explanation of anything. The competitor model had the virtue of *appearing rational* in the sense of being easily expressible, communicable, and teachable. But these features of rationality are simply not relevant for understanding the messy reality of the human being.

All this might lead one to think that Mandeville is opposed to theorizing of any sort with regard to the operations of the body. As he points out in the preface, though, he is not an 'enemy of reason' and does not oppose reasoning or theorizing *überhaupt*.[28] He believes in what is now called abductive reasoning, the formation of explanatory hypotheses that *might* account for certain experienced data, but he resists a certain model of diagnostic reasoning, one that a physician could deduce logically from their armchair so long as they had a description of the symptoms, without recourse to experience and without consideration of the data provided by close and long observation of the patient themselves. He holds that if human beings are to be rational then they must give rationality its proper place in the human animal. The human tendency is always to exaggerate and promote the rational side of our existence beyond its actual station. Our desire to think of ourselves as rational is so strong that we strive to manifest behaviour that, whilst not rational, at least has some of the trappings of rationality—that is, abstruse definitions and difficult theories. These terms really refer to nothing:

'Tis certainly pride, that makes us so fond of the idol reason, but it is an
unaccountable dotage, that we should hug it so close, as to let it slip and
still continue the same love to the shadow and bare appearance of it.[29]

Our desire to appear rational is one of the least rational aspects of
the human being. To be truly rational is to put reason in its place
and to recognize it as less dominant in our behaviour than we
would like to think.

As the second dialogue opens, Misomedon is so cheered by
Philopirio's patience and his lively conversation that they are going
through books together in Misomedon's study. Much of the discussion here is given over to examination of the various theories on
offer from physicians—such as Willis and others—that correspond
to some of the treatment Misomedon received over his life. The
discussion is somewhat laboured, though this is because it serves
a double function. Firstly, it is an opportunity for Mandeville to
present *his* learning and his criticisms of the medical tradition
to the reader. Secondly, it serves a strategic purpose within the
narrative of the text, because Misomedon has taken an interest in
his own condition and desires nothing more than good intellectual conversation on the theories behind his own ailments. Part of
Philopirio's treatment is indulgence of the individual patient being
treated, and as such the long discussion of medical theories in fact
constitutes part of Misomedon's own medical care.

A characteristic feature of Mandeville's writing, clearly on display in the *Treatise*, is his willingness to engage in somewhat ad
hominem attacks on the adherents of various theoretical positions.
Mandeville is less interested in pushing a tight logical argument
against a theory than he is in diagnosing the reasons—usually unattractive ones—why someone signed up to that particular theory in
the first place. None of these strategies have much logical force, but
when pushed with the imaginativeness that Mandeville possesses,
their persuasiveness can outstrip their logical validity. Mandeville's way of thinking about a theory is always to ask: cui bono? How
does the person endorsing the theory benefit from their endorsement of it? What is in it for them? The desire for knowledge and
the pursuit of truth are always, of course, possible contenders.
But Mandeville thinks that there are always more likely causes to

consider. When considering why a new theory becomes dominant within any area of inquiry, he thinks it more likely that it suited the material interests of the individuals putting the theory forward:

> The physicians did not begin to reason about physick, and make hypotheses, because they thought that what they wrote was true, and would be of service to their posterity in curing the sick; but to ingratiate themselves with the ages they lived in; and that they did not so much find fault with others to have things mended, as to establish their own reputations upon the ruins of those they overthrew.[30]

The change in dominance of a theory does not happen in a rational fashion but according to rules of demand and self-interested competition in the marketplace of ideas.

Mandeville puts this rhetorical style to use frequently later on in *The Fable of the Bees*. To give a single example, he offers a cheerful debunking of the ethical theory of the Stoics.[31] Stoics claimed that what was truly good in life was happiness. However they held that happiness was not secured by bodily or physical pleasures but instead consisted of a kind of inner contentment to withstand the trials and tribulations of life. But why did they come to this position? For Mandeville, the reason is obvious. In the real world, one can increase the chances of securing great physical happiness through an improvement in one's material conditions, through the gathering of possessions and financial wealth, and so on. However, one's ability to maintain happiness is fragile for the same reason— possessions and wealth can always be lost, and were one to lose those material conditions, one would thereby lose happiness. Stoicism was a philosophy jealously motivated by those without material advantages (or those in fear of losing them):

> They would not allow any thing to be a real good that was liable to be taken from them by others. They wisely considered the instability of fortune, and the favour of princes; the vanity of honour, and popular applause; the precariousness of riches, and all earthly possessions; and therefore placed true happiness in the calm serenity of a contented mind free from guilt and ambition.[32]

In this way, the Stoics tried to turn the tables by making their weakness irrelevant to the question of happiness. In fact those who might *appear* to be in a weak position in material terms—say through poor health, poverty, or lack of social influence—turn out to be in a *strong* position in terms of the true value of life, since it is they who have the opportunity to gain 'serenity of a contented mind' in the face of such hardships. What Mandeville describes is what Nietzsche would later call a 'slave morality'—an entire system of values invented by a group solely to match and justify that group's own idiosyncrasies. Mandeville anticipated Nietzsche by about a century and a half—for Mandeville, philosophical theories about the meaning and value of life were nothing but a way of rationalizing to oneself that one's own disadvantages are in fact advantages.

This rhetorical strategy is on shameless display in the *Treatise* in Mandeville's account of the origin of Galen's medical theories. Galen, according to Mandeville, noted the empiricist methodology of close observation and, more importantly, noted the labour-intensive element of that professional lifestyle. It was for this latter reason that he wrote against the empiricist method and formulated his own theories. Since he himself had no taste for that lifestyle, Galen effectively reimagined medical practice in his own image, arguing what it ought to be by making it accord with his own existing preferences. This kind of rhetorical attack does not disprove Galen's theories any more than Mandeville's account of the motives of the Stoics proves that their theory of happiness is wrong. But in both cases the rhetorical effect is powerful. More importantly, perhaps, in both cases Mandeville draws the reader's attention to the point that theories are always put forward by individuals who do not exist in a vacuum, but rather live and breathe as you and I do, existing under material conditions with particular needs, desires, insecurities, and aspirations. When assessing any theory it is worth at least considering the circumstances under which the theory was formed.

Mandeville keeps his own theory of medical treatment offstage for long portions of the *Treatise*. His preferred account of the workings of the human body follows Locke, and involves an explicit rejection of claims to have found any fundamental answers about the deep causes of things. What can we really say about the human body, he asks? What do we know about how its systems operate at the most minute levels, of how the brain or the intestinal system works, of how internal chemical reactions interact with psychological conditions, of how environment interacts with neurobiology, and so on? At each point at which our knowledge increases, we seem to come to understand the increasing complexity of human biology. In Mandeville's eminently sensible view, everything we come to know militates against the idea that there is an easily graspable system of medical first principles that can postulate a clear cause–effect relationship. The idea that one can say that a symptom can be alleviated by identifying the deep cause of such illness is for Mandeville a fantasy. 'Hypotheses'—by which Mandeville means biological or chemical theories formed in the aid of medical practice—are just empty words that produce satisfaction only for the person who likes to concoct theories. The value to the patient is precisely nil.

When Misomedon asks Philopirio what his hypotheses are, he responds that 'he doesn't make use of any'. He then asks how it is that Philopirio can 'reason about the causes and Seat of the distemper' or 'solve the least of the symptoms'. Misomedon replies, 'I don't pretend to reason about either the one or the other; nor did I ever strive to solve any of its symptoms, otherwise than by removing them.'[33] 'Solving' for Mandeville is something that one might do in the practice of mathematics. What the patient needs is not a theory about their symptoms or a solution to a theoretical puzzle. What the patient needs is just to be alleviated of their ills. A theory about the deep causes of those symptoms is only as good as its usefulness in removing those symptoms from a patient suffering from them. Too often, though, what patients receive is the theory and none of the treatment. They leave the physician's office with a fully worked-out theory of the humours or spirits or particles that affect the human body and a theory about how to manipulate them. But since the identification of the deep causes of the distemper is a fiction, so too is the hope of treating them and reducing the suffering. That we continue with treatments in the face of their recurring failures indicates more about the non-rational forces that govern human behaviour than anything else.

Mandeville does in fact have a view about how the human body works, and Philopirio details it at length in the second dialogue. It is the theory of animal spirits found in Willis and Sydenham. It might seem that in committing to this theory Mandeville is being inconsistent, since he is now claiming himself to have uncovered human beings' true nature. Misomedon in fact challenges Philopirio on just this point, but Mandeville denies he is making the same mistake as other theorists. The difference, as Philopirio points out, is with the way the theory is put forward. Mandeville claims no special insight into the hidden nature of things. The theory of a nervous system that conveys energy around the body is adopted as one possible explanation for what we can observe from human anatomy as well as human behaviour. It is not adopted from a theory devised in the armchair and by a priori reasoning independent of all observation, and based on an abstract concept of the human being. His theory is instead a posteriori and empirical: if observations provide evidence to amend or contradict it, then the theory must be amended or rejected. Anything else would be to fall prey to the rationalistic dogmatism that Mandeville abhors. His opposition, then, is not to theorizing as such, but to theorizing unfettered from close observation of the world around us. The proper empirical methodology is to observe some bodily phenomena, test some responses to those phenomena, form an idea about what has made the difference where there has been a positive result, and stick with that idea as long as it continues generating positive results (and reject it when it stops).

The third dialogue continues the discussion with Misomedon that was taking place in the second, though Misomedon is by now entirely won over to Philopirio's rhetoric. The major change is the introduction of Polytheca, Misomedon's wife, who enters the dialogue to introduce her 'hysterical' symptoms, and to detail the treatment she has adopted, which is to trust apothecaries intimately, and to disdain physicians. Much of the ensuing dialogue consists of bickering between Polytheca and Misomedon on the advantages of physicians over apothecaries. They also discuss the couple's similarly suffering daughter. Philopirio is keen to point out that just as the conditions that affect the hypochondriac have much to do with lifestyle, so too do well-off women's hysterical conditions often stem from their poor diet and their (societally endorsed) inactivity. Mandeville claims that although we can look to emotional triggers for the condition of hypochondria, the more reliable indicator is that the patient enjoys prosperous material conditions such as those that Misomedon and Polytheca have enjoyed for so long: 'Immoderate grief, cares, trouble and disappointments are likely concomitant causes of this disease; but most commonly in such, as either by estate, benefices, or employments have a sufficient revenue to make themselves easy.'[34] The reader does not get to see the improvements that might come about for Polytheca (she leaves the third dialogue still sceptical) or for her daughter, but we are to imagine that Misomedon, who has come to be so enthusiastic about Philopirio himself, will encourage them to adopt the advice. Mandeville's prognosis for Misomedon, however, initially seems bleak. He says that 'an entire cure, so as never to relapse into any of the symptoms . . . is never to be expected' nor will Misomedon's 'vigour ever be restored'; but he continues to say that the symptoms can be managed enough that his 'life again be made easy and comfortable'.[35] Briefly, Philopirio recommends a near total reduction in medicines taken, regular gentle exercise (he especially recommends riding, as Sydenham had done), a simple non-oily fish diet, and the elimination of rich sauces. Moderation, regular and gentle exercise, and a restriction of some of the luxuries of modern life are better treatments that the panoply of drugs that the medical experts recommend.

Interestingly, though, it emerges that the truly crucial aspect of the treatment is the conversation between the two men, one that we readers have just experienced too. Mandeville represents this as the basis of the personal treatment between doctor and patient. The essential development through the dialogues that constitute the *Treatise* is in fact Misomedon's transformation from an angry cynic to a cheerful enthusiast for Philopirio's company. Philopirio uses almost as many classical quotations as Misomedon does, and Mandeville explains apologetically in the preface that Philopirio does this so that he might 'fall in with the humour of his patient'. There is mocking throughout of classical allusions since, while it is no doubt the case that Mandeville also enjoyed showing off how easily he could parody them, the appeal to the ancients is just part of the propaganda of the medical class, and Mandeville's mimicking of it for Misomedon's benefit is simultaneously a satirizing of it for the benefit of the reader.[36] The book, then, is a subtle exercise in both extolling a method—what we would call a 'talking cure'—and giving an example of it.

Crucially, Mandeville has Philopirio practise what he preached by having him engage in time-intensive treatment. On first appearances, Mandeville's focus upon that conversational therapy is peculiar.[37] Given his emphasis on the straightforward empirical method and the prescription of a light diet and gentle exercise as the key elements, why should Mandeville put so much weight upon the methodology of the physician talking to and engaging emotionally with the patient? The answer relates to Mandeville's theory of what kind of *self* the human person really is. Hypochondria and hysteria are crucially relevant illnesses to diagnose, since ailments have physical manifestations as well as psychological ones. Does one treat the human animal as a machine, or does one aim to treat the immortal soul in the machine? Mandeville's approach is predicated on the idea that one needs to treat the consciousness of the patient as much as their body. But he does not take himself to be engaging a detached Cartesian soul—Mandeville's approach is that the connection between mind and body is so intimate that causation can go in both directions, and just as physical improvements can improve mood, improved mood can also quite literally ease our physical ills.

The discussion that Mandeville offers shows his deep familiarity with the theological and philosophical anxieties that permeated the debates between Montaigne, Descartes, Gassendi, and Bayle. When it comes to the question of what the self really is, Mandeville seems inclined to hold that even thinking itself involves nothing more than the movement of the animal spirits in the brain. When challenged by Misomedon that surely it is the immortal soul that performs the operation of thought, Philopirio—agreeable as ever—first of all earnestly agrees. He immediately qualifies this, however, with the claim that the soul is like the craftsman who requires certain tools—namely, the bodily animal spirits in the brain—to perform the craft of thinking. Misomedon then raises an interesting challenge to his own account. He asks how it can be that the soul can both survive after death and yet engage in acts of thinking in the afterlife, if indeed these physical and corporeal elements—the animal spirits themselves—are *also* essential and required for the very act of thinking. Mandeville has Philopirio concede that the point is mysterious, going so far as to say that it is 'incomprehensible that when the body is dead thought should remain'. Nevertheless, Philopirio says that it is 'very immaterial to our business at hand'.[38] One might wonder, though, what business Mandeville had in dropping this philosophical discussion into the middle of a medical text. While he ostensibly argues in favour of the existence of the soul as a Cartesian 'incorporeal being', in the same breath he introduces an argument for the claim that, in fact, incorporeal matter cannot think, and that thought is only ever a function of an embodied mind.

It is in truth hard to appreciate the deeply empirical approach to the human animal that Mandeville adopts without also considering that he is engaged in an interrogation of the very idea of the self. In Mandeville's view, there is no distinct thinking soul, no Cartesian substance to which the word 'self' applies. Rather, the self is something that is in large part formed and constructed in the course of an animal's life, through physical and societal conditions, and through education and enculturation. The thinking self is an idea that the human animal *needs* in order to manage its desires in the complex interactions of social relations. In treating the health of the self under this conception one must first of all consider the impact of those material conditions.

Mandeville is not anti-theory: he himself has a physical theory as to the nature of the human body and its relation to these particular disorders. From our contemporary perspective it is no less fanciful than many of the theories he disparages in the *Treatise*.[39] There are some elements of Mandeville's theory that are not clearly married to his account of animal spirits, however. Adjusting lifestyle—and, more importantly, motivating a patient to want to do it for their doctor—is as effective as any other medical intervention. Moderate exercise and diet are key. These gentle recommendations are premised on the thought that the proper operation of the gut has an intimate connection with our neurological operations and their effect on mood and cognitive function generally.[40]

Mandeville has both Misomedon and the reader gradually come to see that Philopirio's conversation *is* the treatment. Moreover, since Misomedon's obsession was medical theory and practice itself, Philopirio's sympathetic conversation focuses on just that topic, which simultaneously allows Mandeville to present an example of his method in operation and a polemic against opposing schools. In this way, readers of the *Treatise* are invited to observe Misomedon as he describes his symptoms. Since this process of close patient listening is ultimately the method that Mandeville endorses as the proper medical approach, the reader is subtly recruited to endorse Mandeville's own approach, since the reader has been doing the exact same process of observing the patient in the act of reading. It is crucially important, then, that Mandeville wrote the *Treatise* in the form of a dialogue. For what we find here is *both* a discussion of what Mandeville considers the best form of medical practice and an example of it. It is not too hard to believe that what Mandeville wrote was an idealized version of his own actual practice—the first edition of the *Treatise* included means of contacting Mandeville, and so he intended the book to work as advertising for his practice as well as to further his own reputation.[41]

By the end of the *Treatise*, we have a picture of the mature Mandeville as a bold, playful, and thoroughly original thinker, one suspicious not just of rationalizing self-serving theories but of the very idea of identifying any deep rational causes of human behaviour. There are instead patterns of behaviour that can be observed and partly predicted. This is the extent of our knowledge of human beings, however—no insight into the inner workings of things is available to us. Neither is such insight necessary—we can get along well enough interpreting the human animal based on the observable things that it does. More often we do better to observe the more subtle factors that are the true causes of behaviour, those that are not even grasped by the agents themselves. In *The Fable of the Bees* Mandeville would show how these same irrational animal spirits were very much involved in understanding ordinary human behaviour in modern civilized society.

CHAPTER FOUR

Sex in Polite Society

There are few virtuous women who are not weary of their occupation.

—LA ROCHEFOUCAULD, *MAXIMS*, 5:367

THE *TREATISE* WAS clearly an important book for Mandeville, the outcome of reflection on some twenty years of medical practice. It was also a work that expressed many of the views of human nature and society that he held most dear. A couple of years before the first edition of the *Treatise* he had published another work, however, one which, while also a dialogue, was entirely unrelated to his professional and theoretical interests in medicine. This work is remarkable in its own right and shows just how widely Mandeville could cast his anthropological inquiries. *The Virgin Unmask'd* (1709) is a satire upon sexual mores, gender inequality, and the role of popular culture in reinforcing both. The title is alluring, and the average browser of a bookseller's shop might have associated it with other publications of the pornographic variety, whereby an older woman details sexual activity for a naïve younger woman, such as the Abbé du Prat's *Venus in the Cloister* (1683).[1] The opening pages of *The Virgin Unmask'd* are promising in that regard. It is a dialogue between the teenaged Antonia and her aunt Lucinda, and begins with Lucinda chastising Antonia for her low-cut top. A potential reader might have hoped that what would follow would be a detailed account of the risks and temptations (and specifically the varieties) of sexual adventure that a virtuous and excitable young girl must—of course—carefully avoid.

Had any patron, flicking these first pages, subsequently made a purchase they would later have found they had acquired a quite different book. Inside was a roughly presented account of the brutality of modern sexual relations. They would have found in Lucinda a passionate advocate for the prospects of women who managed to steer clear both of marriage and of men altogether. Antonia has lost her parents but has inherited a modest fortune, and Lucinda has raised her as her daughter. Lucinda has never married, because she never had the financial necessity to do so, and has an unremitting distrust of men. She believes that the highest part of her duty in loco parentis is to convince Antonia to be thoroughly fearful of men. Ideally, she would have Antonia remain single all her days.

Readers might have gathered that the work would be an unusual one had they attended to Mandeville's strange writing in the preface to *The Virgin Unmask'd*, which is in fact one of two. In the first preface he engages in some Shandyesque literary game playing *avant la lettre*. Mandeville explains that he originally submitted this work to his publisher without any preface at all, only to be subsequently asked to supply one. Mandeville is initially confused and some farcical dialogue ensues ('. . . the preface! Said I, what do you mean? Mean! Says he, I mean the Preface . . .'). Mandeville baulks: why have prefaces anyway? Why does one not just say what one needs to say in the main body of the book itself? If it does not require saying there, then it does not need saying at all. The publisher persists, the fight escalates, and Mandeville threatens to burn the book altogether rather than submit to the publisher's demands. The publisher tries to soothe Mandeville's ire with a conciliatory drink; they drink perhaps a bit too much, and Mandeville—now in his cups—promises his new best friend not one but *two* prefaces in recompense. Now he has a problem: how will he write two prefaces when he didn't even have an idea for one? Inspiration strikes, and he decides that in the first preface he will tell the story ('as a wheel within a wheel') as to why there are two prefaces.

In the second preface, the tone changes. Mandeville confesses that in fact he has a 'mortal antipathy to prefaces' for the reason that they contain nothing but lies and hypocrisy. The accusation is that no author ever states that their motivations for writing the book are those of financial gain and fame—but these are really the chief incentives. A writer who claims 'that they have no other aim than the reader's good' has told an 'abominable lie'. A recurring theme, seen too in the *Treatise* and that will appear again in *The Fable of the Bees*—that it is impossible for human beings simply to have the well-being of others in their minds—is highlighted from the very beginning. A preface is also where the author adopts a distance from the work and pretends to present themselves separately from the content to follow, for possibly nefarious reasons. Mandeville's aspiration rather is to present the facts as they are, and so he claims to have no need for any such distancing. And yet he does in the end offer not just one but two prefaces, inviting the reader to wonder just how reliable a narrator we can expect him to be, if prefaces are a measure of duplicitous intent. Mandeville does, though, offer the following qualification in the preface. He claims that he is not against marriage per se, but seeks only to expose 'whatever is dreadful' in the institution, and for this reason uses the personage of Lucinda to set out a more complete opposition to it than he holds himself. Whether we are to take Mandeville at his word here is unclear, since it becomes quite obvious that from a woman's perspective, nearly everything about the institution of marriage is indeed dreadful.

The difficulties women incur in managing the emergence of sexual desire prompt the beginning of the dialogue. Lucinda does not shy away from detailing the type of physical behaviour that she has recently observed in the teenage Antonia:

> A hundred pranks you would play with your legs . . . sometimes when you thought you were not observed, how passionately would you throw yourself backward, and clapping your legs alternatively over one another, squeeze your thighs together with all the strength you had, and in a quarter of an hour repeat the same to all the chairs in the room? Many times, Antonia, have I seen you sit in that careless manner, and half shutting your eyes, whilst your head would slowly drop down to one shoulder, bite on your lip with so craving, and so begging a look, that I have pitied you myself. . . . Every action, and every limb, betrayed your desires.[2]

It is around this time that Antonia's spare cash starts to go on 'plays and romances', but it is clear that the awakening of Antonia's romantic sensibility follows from a prior sexual one. Mandeville's account of Antonia's masturbatory aspirations is no doubt meant to titillate, but it is also his aim to draw attention—as he had done with hypochondria in the *Treatise*—to the physical causes of social behaviour. When they pass a good-looking man, Lucinda notes the physical mannerisms that Antonia adopts:

> When he was yet a good way off I saw you raise your body and by alter-
> ing your gait, assume a certain firmness in your steps, that was not
> usual, when he came near, the stretching of your neck had pulled up
> your bubbies, which were then just budding out, he looked upon you
> very hard, you blushed, and your eyes, that looked as if they had been
> newly varnished, were very steadfastly fixed on the ground.[3]

Towards the end of the *Treatise*, Mandeville had made a surprising recommendation for Philopirio's 'hysterical' teenage daughter. Her treatment, it emerges, involves a surprising amount of straightforward physical stimulation. She must receive two vigorous full-body massages a day to get the 'animal spirits' moving. On top of that, Philopirio recommends that they set up a swing for her to use as regularly as Philopirio is to use riding for physical exercise. One can't help but think that part of what Mandeville was recommending was an opportunity for the girl to receive (and to give herself) some innocuous sexual stimulation for the betterment of her physical and mental well-being. In the *Fable*, Mandeville would point out the efforts that we go to in order to deny this carnal side of human nature. If we were found outside of polite society in our natural state and there confronted with our natural sexual urges, he claims, we 'would be at a loss no more than other animals for a present remedy'. In polite society, however, the matter is very different. Here:

> The youth of both sexes are to be armed and fortified against this
> impulse, and from their infancy artfully frightened from the most
> remote approaches of it. The appetite itself, and all the symptoms of it,
> though they are plainly felt and understood, are to be stifled with care
> and severity, and in women flatly disowned, and if there be occasion,
> with obstinacy denied, even when themselves are visibly affected by
> them.[4]

Mandeville mentions here that unsatisfied sexual desire can throw young women 'into distempers' such that 'they must be cured by physick', just as he had detailed in the *Treatise*. The recommendation of a certain kind of self-love is a requirement for young women in any society where female sexual gratification is a perilous pursuit.

In *The Virgin Unmask'd*, it is Antonia's 'bubbies' that afford the pretext for beginning their dialogues. Outside on a hot day, Antonia's cleavage is exposed and her aunt insists that she cover it up. When Antonia claims that it is too hot to cover up, Lucinda replies that it is 'the heat of your blood, your wantonness, and lascivious thoughts, it's they, that are the cause of all your immoderate behaviour'.[5] Antonia is brought to tears by her aunt's eventual comparison of her to a whore. Later Lucinda explains that she lost her cool out of the intense love and fearfulness that she feels for her. She is sure, now that sexual longing is clearly evidenced, that Antonia will not be by her side for long, but that Antonia also will undermine her own happiness in pursuit of romantic love.

Mandeville's bawdy side had already been on display in his first English publication, also his first real attempt at poetry. In *Wishes to a Godson*, he presented 'Leander's Excuse to Cloris', where the higher love of the soul is ridiculed:

> And I, when the Apish act is done,
> Care not how soon the Nymph is gone;
> But to your Charms my constant love is due,
> I can kiss others and still think of you.[6]

If bodily acts constitute the lower, animalistic form of expressing affection, and the admiration of the mind the higher one, then seducing other women while thinking of one's true love must be the purest form of genuine romance. The laddish humour masks a recurrent theme of ridiculing those who would identify a higher and loftier human form of intercourse, one that does not rely upon our bodily animal natures. For Mandeville, the 'apish' nature is far closer to the human one than we care to acknowledge. Moreover, the very idea of separating out a pure ethereal and rational love—a Platonic engagement with the other that transcends our animal being—is marked out for special ridicule in the *Fable*, written two years later. Look into it, Mandeville urges, and you will find that those who advocate this kind of love are the 'pale-faced weakly people of cold and phlegmatic constitutions'. Those of a strong and vital physical constitution, on the other hand, never even entertain the idea of a love 'so spiritual as to exclude all thoughts and wishes that relate to the body'.[7] That other recurring Mandevillean theme—other than that of the denial of our animal natures—is human beings' propensity to rationalize their weaknesses into some special virtue. In this case, those who lack strong sex drives invent the idea of platonic love, he claims, so as to render their incapacity as a higher state of being.

Mandeville is perhaps at his funniest regarding the hypocrisy involved in sexual relations. The most important thing for human beings, as he repeatedly states, is our need to distinguish ourselves from the animals. When non-human animals engage in procreation, they give each other straightforward signals of their intent to do so, so it is therefore of the highest importance to human beings that we never signal our sexual interest directly:

> If a man should tell a woman that he could like no body so well to propagate his species upon as herself, and that he found a violent desire that moment to go about it, and accordingly offered to lay hold of her for that purpose, the consequence would be that he would be called a brute, the woman would run away, and himself never be admitted in any civil company.[8]

What is improper, Mandeville insists, is not the desire but the obvious representation of it to the intended recipient. If, on the other hand, a gentleman were first to approach that young woman's father, gain permission to woo her, flatter her and her family, write love poetry and the like, then engage in a public ceremony, he may at that point realize his desire, as 'the most reserved virgin very tamely suffers him to do what he pleases, and the upshot is, that he obtains what he wanted without having ever asked for it'.[9] As Mandeville points out, everyone in society knows what has just happened, and everyone pretends that they do not. Family come to visit the day after the wedding and act as if their daughter has not been brutishly ravished the night before. In point of fact, a strange transformation has come over the family, who are now desperately keen for reproduction to occur as soon as is physically possible.

Those same brutish inclinations that would have disqualified a suitor from matrimony previously are now viewed as essential for the purposes of a successful marriage:

> The fine gentleman I spoke of need not practice any greater self-denial than the savage. . . . [I]f he is hotter than goats or bulls, as soon as the ceremony is over let him sate and fatigue himself with joy and ecstasies of pleasure, raise and indulge his appetites by turns as extravagantly as his strength and manhood will give him leave.[10]

As Hamlet said, there is nothing either good or bad but thinking makes it so. And in the *Fable* Mandeville insists that the representation of sexual vigour is a vice in one context (before matrimony) but a virtue in another (post matrimony), since in marriage 'the more he wallows in lust and strains every faculty to be abandonedly voluptuous' the more he will gain the approval of the 'prudent, grave and most sober matrons'.[11]

In *The Virgin Unmask'd* the same cynicism had been on display with regard to the romantic ideals of love, but with far less comical intent. Mandeville is brutally frank about how male narratives (many of which still abound today about men's susceptibility to 'bewitching' women, the canniness of the fairer sex, how women are the 'real bosses' in relationships, and so on) are ultimately just so much propaganda functioning to mask women's disempowered status in society. Mandeville has Lucinda describe how the conventions and rituals of romance function to propagate the illusion. When young women excite themselves over the theatricality of courtship they willingly conspire in the undermining of their own power. She is especially irritated by women's girlish gamesmanship—the faux sulks, temper tantrums, the rebukes and teasing invitations for gestures of appeasement from the males over invented slights, which give all the appearance of female control but in reality reflect the opposite:

> What your opinion of wooing may be, I can't tell, but I always thought it very ridiculous. . . . [The woman] is resolved to be very cross, and with abundance of coyness sits in state, insults over the man, and treats him with as much scorn, as if he was not worthy to wipe her shoes; and why does she do all this? For no other reason, but because she

designs to make him her master, and give him all she has in the world. The man, on his side, takes all these indignities in good part, seems to be fond of being ill treated, and with the most profound veneration to his idol, begs on his knees, that a certain modest petition may be granted him; the upshot of which is, that the person, to whom he pays his devotion, would be so kind, as to oblige herself solemnly, before witnesses, upon the penalty of being damned, to be his slave as long as she lives, unless he should happen to die before her.[12]

Lucinda's biting sarcasm is apposite. Why should romance and the rituals accompanying proposals of marriage involve such demonstrations of humility, powerlessness, supplication, and begging on the part of the male? Because he is asking for the most absurd transaction imaginable: for a woman to submit herself to him totally and in exchange for nothing at all, other than the status of being his wife. The man fraudulently declares himself the woman's slave so that she can truly become his. Romantic narratives have an extremely valuable function in the economy of matrimony—they create an ideology that convinces women that this is a good deal. In reality, female achievement is constrained by the societal condition that they marry first.

Mandeville's interest in the status of women in society was by no means limited to *The Virgin Unmask'd*. Richard Steele's *Tatler*, and its central character, Isaac Bickerstaff, had proved an enormous success with English readers. Competitor journals appeared, including the *Female Tatler*, and between 1709 and 1710—the same time as the arrival of *The Virgin Unmask'd*—several issues from 'Lucinda' and 'Artesia' appeared. They were penned by Mandeville. Mandeville had another character, also called Lucinda, report much the same sentiment regarding women's disadvantages: 'Happy are the men, that either with or without wives, may arrive to the top of glory, whilst we poor creatures can deserve but little unless we are first enslaved by them.'[13] In *The Virgin Unmask'd*, Lucinda says that men 'have enslaved our sex: in paradise, man and woman were upon an even foot; see what they have made of us since: is not every woman that is married, a slave to her husband?'[14] Women are enslaved by men for two predominant reasons. Often it is out of financial necessity, and such motives cannot be judged harshly.

But where there is no financial necessity, Lucinda still sees women foolishly entering into voluntary slavery. The reason why they put themselves into the bondage of men, and do so willingly, is predominantly to do with sex. In his later work *A Modest Defence of Publick Stews* (1724), Mandeville writes that inadequate medical attention has been paid to the fact that the clitoris is exclusively an organ of pleasure for women, and that it can possess a wide variety of degrees of sensitivity in different women. The idea that women in general have lesser sex drives is ridiculous, Mandeville claims, and can be belied by a simple social observation: 'there requires no more to convince us of the violence of female desire, when raised to a proper height, but only to consider what terrible risks a woman runs to gratify it'.[15] Women's appetites are strong and natural and difficult to resist, but society demands that women act as if the desires are nearly non-existent. Forced to deny themselves this way, and lacking understanding of their own sexual natures, they channel their energies into romantic fictions that serve to aid their own self-deception and convince themselves that marriage could be a good idea. Only a class of young women undereducated, oversexed, and unsatisfied yet 'taught to hate a whore before they know what the word means' could believe in something such as the value of matrimony.[16]

What does Mandeville make of the women who routinely give up their virtue? In the *Modest Defence*, he provides an analysis of a range of cases of different kinds of women and how they conspire to secure sexual satisfaction while also retaining an honourable image in society. Some manage it more easily than others, but in each case Mandeville implies that the difference between an upstanding and a fallen woman comes down to two factors: firstly, how effectively they have been socially indoctrinated about the shameful nature of their desire and the importance of honour; secondly, how sensitive their capacity for physical pleasure. One woman can have a sense of propriety equal to another's, he claims, but if she has a greater capacity for pleasure then she will be perpetually at greater risk, and will require more effort to avoid vice than her peers. Mandeville concludes that 'the greater part of womenkind hold their virtue very precariously; and that female chastity is, in its own nature, built upon a very *ticklish* foundation'.[17] Behaviour that is usually evaluated as simply a matter of intellectual self-control ought instead to consider the realities of the biology of the human body that drive such behaviour.

For similar reasons, Mandeville has Lucinda claim that the value of marriage should not be judged by the testimony of young wives, who are mere 'giddy-brained things, that knew nothing of the world, before they were married, and have not had leisure yet to reflect on anything, but which way to gratify their appetites, which had first enslaved them'. Instead, the proper judges should be those for whom sexual desire has finally diminished:

> If you would come to a fair trial, then you must take your married women of the same age with the maids, and, if you do so, you will not find one in five hundred, but what has repented a thousand times that ever she submitted to the yoke: whilst all the old maids, as soon as that troublesome itch is over, rejoice at having kept their liberty, and agree unanimously in the comforts of a single life.[18]

Lucinda concedes, though, that it is the peculiar human condition to 'grumble' at whatever one's condition might be, and so instead of taking a straw poll, she tries to convince Antonia of the foulness of men and marriage through some cautionary tales. *The Virgin Unmask'd* tells stories of sexual relations between men and women where women are the clear victims of society's patriarchal standards and of male attitudes towards women generally. As such it inverts much of the comparable literature of the day, which sought to present women as duplicitous, scheming, and dedicated to the taunting of their suitors and the misery of their husbands.[19] One might wonder whether one can take Mandeville at his word when he states in the preface that his intended audience is those naïve young ladies who might think that marriage is always a positive prospect. Given that the title and opening pages of the book are designed to attract *male* attention, it is plausible that Mandeville also sought to influence their social and sexual attitudes.

The Virgin Unmask'd consists in Lucinda recounting to Antonia the stories of two women—Aurelia and Leonora. Aurelia, now a widow living comfortably and happily with her young daughter, is marked by Antonia as an example of a woman whose life does not appear worse off as a result of her marriage. It is an unfortunate example, it emerges, as Lucinda proceeds to detail Aurelia's true marital history. Aurelia has grown up her father's darling, and since he himself has risen up the social ladder, he is both hopeful that his daughter will make a good match and equally wary of unscrupulous suitors. His fears are confirmed when one day, 'coming from Hyde Park, Aurelia fell in love with a gentleman she saw on horseback'.[20] The beginning of the romance is straightforward enough, echoing the reactions to men that Antonia has been recently manifesting. The young man is Dorante, an Irish army officer, and when he approaches Aurelia's father to ask for her hand, he is quickly rebuffed ('the old man, very uneasy at the word . . . "Ireland" . . . gave him a short answer').[21] The father already has a rich, though admittedly physically deformed, suitor in mind for his daughter. When he sees that Aurelia will not be swayed easily, he flies into a rage. He rushes into Aurelia's room and 'beat her most unmercifully'.[22] He locks her in her room and continues his mistreatment for months, even until Aurelia falls ill. Aurelia's mother, who can take no more, arranges for secret meetings between Aurelia and Dorante, and soon they arrange an elopement.

For all his cleverness, sly irony, dissimulation, and detachment, Mandeville's ethical seriousness is unmissable on this occasion. It is all too clearly on display when he describes in frank and simple terms the brutality human beings unleash upon one another. For the role she has played in allowing the elopement to happen, Aurelia's father kicks her mother around the house 'like a football'.[23] When he is done, he puts her out in the street. She dies two weeks later from illness brought on by her injuries. Those who were later to accuse Mandeville of immorality and hatred for human beings had never read *The Virgin Unmask'd*. There is a quality to the recording of the tales that rings true, and just as the *Treatise* had been based on his previous case histories, some of his stories here likely reflect some of his real observations of what life in London in the early eighteenth century was really like, especially those elements that appear less regularly in romantic novels. If Mandeville refuses to flatter the human species, it is because he has seen it in a less than flattering light.

In romantic novels, one never hears of the consequences that arise for a wily mother who puts the couple together despite the disapproval of the father. Neither for the most part does one hear of how things work out for the pair. Orson Welles once noted that a happy ending depends on where one ends one's story, and Aurelia's story really begins only after the romantic union has taken place. As the reader might be now anticipating, it is not a story of domestic bliss and conjugal contentment. If anything, Aurelia's father's suspicions are proven accurate. Dorante, it emerges, is the worst kind of person. They elope to Dublin, where they live contentedly for a while but only because of Dorante's expectation that they will soon receive a generous dowry from Aurelia's father, or at worst a generous inheritance upon his death. It soon becomes clear, however, that Aurelia's father is not one given to forgiveness, and that Aurelia has been entirely written out of his will. At this point, Dorante's true character reveals itself. He is a rogue who lives beyond his means and secures a living when he can from cheating at cards. In general, as Lucinda explains, 'it was not a wife, but money he wanted'.[24] How, Antonia wonders, could Aurelia not have gained even a hint of Dorante's viciousness? She lacked the skills to do so, replies Lucinda. She was one of those young women whose education consisted of being 'taught to sing and dance', whose tutors are bribed to 'wink at their faults', and who learn to spend their time 'cramming themselves with custards and cheesecakes' and giggling in groups as they 'fill one another's heads with so much rubbish of courtship and love', and occasionally whisper a 'bawdy monosyllable, such as boys write upon walls'.[25] How could Aurelia not know better? How could she be so silly? She was raised to be silly. Lucinda wants to tell Antonia these stories now, just at the time of her sexual maturity, when her emerging sexual desires are redirected and transformed into societal norms of trivial and ultimately passive girlish behaviour.

The story of Dorante's married life is one of neglect and then abuse. He takes money from the family purse to pursue his own pleasures and abandons Aurelia whenever he can. When his financial situation is at its worst, he hatches a plan to alleviate their distress. He gets Aurelia's defences down, compliments her, saying that she 'has charms enough to be the mistress of a king' and 'in the same breath' begins to compliment a rich male acquaintance of theirs, who was 'noted for lewdness'.[26] For the next few days, Dorante plots to put them in each other's company, and in the interim preaches to Aurelia on the artificiality of marital fidelity. When this strategy makes only slow progress upon Aurelia's will, he threatens her. She is now still only nineteen, but already has two children, and Dorante orders her to sleep with the gentleman or, he says, 'I can keep you no longer; turn out with your brats'.[27] He sends her to the bedroom, and having finished a final speech, leaves the room, sends the gentleman in, and locks the door behind him. The gentleman attempts to kiss and fondle her but Aurelia puts up stubborn resistance, wrapping herself up in the sheets and avoiding his caresses. The gentleman is unwilling to force himself on Aurelia— not so much out of virtuous self-restraint, Mandeville insists, but rather 'not finding himself in a condition of going through the fatigues of a rape'[28]—and finding her now so resolute to avoid his seduction that she had flung herself onto the floor, he loses interest. Finally grasping her unwillingness, he even gains a little pity for Aurelia, and leaves barely speaking to Dorante.

At this point Antonia wonders again how Aurelia could have been so dim as to not foresee Dorante's plans to prostitute her, but also how she could have been so virtuous as to withhold from her suitor's advances when giving in would have secured financial advantage, and when resisting incurred such violence from her husband. As Lucinda promptly points out—in a way that Mandeville repeats again and again in *The Fable of the Bees*—virtue had nothing to do with it. One can see behaviour whose virtuous appearance belies some less rational motive that explains the same behaviour just as well. Aurelia did not allow herself to have sex with another man, Lucinda reports, simply because she could not conceive of being with anyone other than Dorante. She could not foresee his plot for the same reason—her besottedness made her naïve. Lucinda expresses it with a painful eloquence: 'He was quality, riches, honour, he was everything to her,' and that is why she could not go with another, and not because such actions lacked virtue. Aurelia accepted everything 'what came from him . . . without ever consulting the morality or immorality of what he said or did, if he appeared but gay and good humoured'.[29] The sad truth, Lucinda claims, is that the human heart does not respond to what is morally correct, and women can love their abusers in the very midst of their abuse.

Dorante is unsurprisingly furious at the failure of his attempt to whore Aurelia to his friends. Disappointed to 'find her altogether useless for his purpose' of getting money, he rarely speaks to her when sober, and when drunk, 'she seldom escaped being beaten'.[30] One night he comes in and holds a candle deliberately close to her, and sets her hair on fire. When she speaks back to him 'he gave her an unmerciful blow in the face . . . and made her bloody all over; then dragging her out of the room by one of her arms . . . kicked her downstairs'.[31] Her love for Dorante is now finally gone but she cannot flee from him without any means of caring for her children and is effectively trapped. Eventually he abandons her and their children at his mother's house, where Aurelia is treated as a domestic servant, and her young son, who resembles her more than Dorante, is routinely mistreated.

That Mandeville could write tales like these in 1709 is utterly remarkable. Needless to say, the purchaser of *The Virgin Unmask'd* hoping for erotic distraction would by this point have been thoroughly let down. At various points, Mandeville cleverly uses young Antonia as a substitute for the reader's reactions (much as in the *Treatise*, where Misomedon is both a character, a patient, and a proxy for the interested reader's own medical anxieties). Antonia responds disappointedly to events in the plot, only to be reminded repeatedly by Lucinda that what is being recounted is simply *not* a novel, not one of Antonia's preferred tales of love, disaster, and subsequent romantic triumph. Human beings' feelings are messier and less rational than we would like, and we should not confuse the pathways of real life with the structure of a good story. Antonia asks why Aurelia's feelings did not immediately turn to hate at the first attempt of her being prostituted by Dorante, and wonders why feelings of hate emerged only later after a beating. Lucinda responds:

> Had I been telling you a romance, I would have made use of art; as I know as well as you, niece, what should have been done according to their rules. As soon as Dorante had told her his meaning, and declared himself with that impudence, I should immediately have turned her love into hatred: but in a true story, we must relate things as they happen.[32]

Instead, the facts are that Aurelia—not yet out of her teens—lacked the emotional clarity and strength of mind we expect in heroines.

We expect central characters in stories to overcome their victim-
hood with speed and decisiveness and other virtuous characteristics. In real life, however, victims can possess a diverse range of
character traits, not all of them virtuous or rational. Was not Aurelia a saint, Antonia asks, to suffer so much without complaint for so
long? Not really, responds Lucinda—she was a young foolish girl in
passionate love with an abusive partner. Lucinda is clear that her
'saintly' behaviour had nothing to do with moral virtue at all.[33]

Mandeville has Lucinda save the most difficult part of the story
till now. One night, Dorante comes to Aurelia's bedroom making his
usual insults and threats, and Aurelia's boy, who sleeps in the same
room, rushes to his mother's side to protect her. Dorante grabs his
sword to threaten the young boy, which shocks him enough that he
falls into a series of fits. A fever follows the fits, and the boy dies a
week later. As Lucinda reports it, Aurelia told her this story last of
all and as quickly as possible. Antonia is confused as to why this
incredibly dramatic part of the story was not given more promi-
nence, or recounted in fuller detail; once again it is pointed out
that Aurelia is not trying to tell a story for the entertainment of her
listeners. The most brutal elements of human lives are the hardest
ones to recount.

Aurelia's torment is finally relieved when she learns of the 'joyful
tidings' of Dorante's death after a duel following his having been
caught cheating at cards. More good fortune is forthcoming, as
when Aurelia returns to Dublin to meet some society friends, she
hears that an unknown benefactor is willing to pay for her return
passage to London. The benefactor, it emerges, is a relation of her
dead mother's, who had fallen out with her father and lost touch
with Aurelia. Now this mysterious man wants to make amends
and offers her financial security for life for her and her children. At
the end of the fifth dialogue, as Aurelia's tale is coming to an end,
Lucinda tells how a kind (and handsome) Irish merchant greets
Aurelia on behalf of her benefactor when she arrives in London.
As the tale proceeds, and it emerges that Aurelia chooses to live the
remainder of her life single, Antonia says that she has 'lost a wedding' at the end of the tale. Lucinda points out that the Irish merchant was actually a married man with a family, and admits that the
way she presented this scene in the story 'was a little suspicious, but

I did it to see, how soon you would swallow the hook, if it was covered with that bait'.[34] Antonia and (and we readers alike) *still* have the novelistic romantic framework in mind dictating how the story should end, no matter how frequently the facts speak to a different reality. We are reminded again of the folly that romantic narratives should determine women's lives. Even after we are told a tale of the brutish realities behind tales of romantic love and marriage—domestic abuse, rape, infanticide—we are hardwired for romantic happy endings. It takes a bit more imagination by Antonia—and the reader—to see that Aurelia's widowed single life without a man *is* the happy ending.

Mandeville gives Aurelia's story pride of place in *The Virgin Unmask'd*. The book concludes, though, with the unfinished tale of a second modern heroine, Leonora. Antonia complains to her aunt that she might avoid Aurelia's unhappy fate by making more careful inquiries into her suitor's character. In response Lucinda tells how even a careful girl can be taken advantage of if the man is unscrupulous enough. To illustrate this she tells the tale of how Leonora was targeted by one Alcandor. Alcandor is presented as a kind of genius of duplicity, the 'most skilful dissembler upon Earth'.[35] He is a virulent misogynist, motivated by having been previously jilted by a woman he loved. Since then Alcandor has resolved 'to be revenged on the whole sex' and 'had made it his whole business to deceive and ruin as many as he could'.[36] He dislikes easy conquests and sets out to destroy only those women of great reputation and outstanding virtue. Leonora gains his attention, and since he 'thought attacking her would be a noble enterprise',[37] he sets in motion a plan of unnervingly patient manipulation.

Mandeville details how Alcandor insinuates himself into Leonora's household, playing with her children and taking only a passing interest in the company of Leonora herself. He then slowly and expertly feigns being a man in distress, eager to hide his torment from her. He carefully lets her catch him staring at her, while pretending to be trying to avoid her notice. He makes out that he is falling into a depression, and then an illness, but then won't let Leonora know the cause of it. Finally, as his illness now appears terminal, he at last confesses that his suffering is from the pure love of Leonora's soul and his broken heart in that he cannot be with her. Having made his dying confession, Alcandor fades into exhausted silence.

Here at this high moment of drama, *The Virgin Unmask'd* ends. Lucinda addresses her niece in the final lines: 'Now, Antonia, tell me where you can blame Leonora yet? Consult your pillow upon it and tomorrow you shall know all.'[38] Why does Mandeville choose to end the book in this way? The likely reason is that he hoped to set up a cliffhanger that would stoke public demand for a sequel. In the preface he says that he leaves Leonora's story unfinished so that the reader might expect that Mandeville does 'intend to go on'.[39]

There is also something more subtle going on, perhaps. Leonora, our heroine, is very likely about to abandon her virtue. The aim is clearly to confuse the reader as to what moral is to be drawn from all this, and perhaps to indicate that the idea of drawing any moral from the conjugal and sexual behaviour of human beings is folly. Furthermore, throughout *The Virgin Unmask'd* Mandeville has toyed with the expectations of the reader. The bookshop browser expected pornographic titillation and instead gets an exposé of male dominance in modern society; the romance reader is promised tales of heroines overcoming obstacles, but the tales end without a male coming to the rescue, and so on. The final story ends just as Alcandor is about to realize his half-year-long scheme to get Leonora into bed—might the reader perhaps be experiencing a bit of excitement as well as outrage at the beautiful, virtuous Leonora finally giving in and expressing a bit of physical passion?[40] Mandeville plays with the fact that the lascivious expectations of the reader cannot be eliminated, even after reading two hundred pages on the horrendous plight of women under men's lascivious expectations. Just as in the *Treatise*, he uses the literary device of drawing the reader's attention to their own expectations in order to co-opt them into acknowledging some facts about human nature— even in the intellectual act of reading they are always driven by their animal spirits, their desires and passions. In the *Fable* he goes so far as to say that the human being is nothing but a 'compound of the passions'[41]—we are creatures who lack rational self-control over our desire. The most that we can hope for is some kind of self-understanding—it might not help us reform ourselves and lead us to make better decisions in our lives, but it can at least stop us from forming unrealistic expectations about living lives governed by reason and virtue.

The Virgin Unmask'd is an entirely unique piece of writing. The work has been described as 'a moral dialogue devoted largely to a defense of feminism'.[42] There are certainly enough elements in *The Virgin Unmask'd* to suggest that Mandeville was something of a proto-feminist. He sees the differing positions of women and men in society to be mostly due to circumstance; and he sees women's intellectual disadvantage to be determined entirely by men's educational advantages. More to the point, he explicitly sets out the whole dialogue as a kind of manual for women to protect themselves.

For all the literary techniques employed, there is a sense that Mandeville is writing about behaviour towards women that he has observed personally. Mandeville has a notable sensitivity to the dangers for women that arise from the physical rigours of pregnancy and childbirth, no doubt culled from his first-hand medical experience. Lucinda warns Antonia against the manifold harms of having children, beginning with the sometimes-incapacitating effects of morning sickness followed by the hardships of the physical changes of pregnancy:

> Is it not a thousand pities to see a young brisk woman, well made and fine-limbed, as soon as she is poisoned by man, retch, puke and be sick, ten or twelve times a day, for a month or six weeks, and after that, swell for seven or eight months together, till, like a frog she is nothing else but belly? . . .
>
> . . . But if man was not a venomous creature, how would it be possible, that a hail plump girl of a good complexion should in so little a time, after conversing with him, turn thin-visaged, pale, yellow, and look as if she was bewitched? Not be able to endure the sight of bread, loathe the best of food, and in an instant, get an aversion to twenty things, which she used to admire before.[43]

This, Lucinda points out, is to say nothing of the dangers of childbirth itself. Mandeville even has Lucinda talk about how women are treated with more decency and with greater equality in his homeland of Holland than in England. Here in England, Lucinda

pointedly remarks, it is the respect shown towards delicate women
that holds them back:

> 'Tis that respect and tenderness I hate when it consists only in outward
> show: In Holland women sit in their counting-houses and do business,
> or at least are acquainted with everything their husbands do. But says
> a rascal here, 'no my dear, that is too much trouble' . . . [44]

Lucinda also claims that while men can outpace women in reasoning in almost all instances, she is firm that this is only because men
receive an extensive university education just at the point where
women cease to be educated, and so are left behind.

Mandeville was more explicit about the contingencies of female
inferiority in his contributions to the *Female Tatler*. Isaac Bickerstaff had in the *Tatler* proposed a 'table of fame' of the most eminent human beings to have ever existed: Aristotle, Alexander,
Cicero, and so on—all men. Many of Mandeville's issues concern
how many women from history might have been considered had
one only cared to look. Female leaders, philosophers, and heroines
abound in the history books, though tend not to get mentioned
at all, unless it is for the peculiarly female virtue of chastity. The
reason is straightforward: 'Since men have enslaved us, the greatest part of the world have always debarred our sex from governing, which is the reason that the lives of women have so seldom
been described in history.'[45] More than that, Artesia claims that 'if
women had been at the helm as often as the men, the first would
far outshine the latter'.[46] In one remarkable passage, Artesia rages
against what she sees as a kind of political domination of men
over women, one that is motivated as much by anxiety over female
power as it is by desire for male control:

> Why should we be treated almost as if we were irrational creatures: we
> are industriously kept from the knowledge of Arts and Sciences, if
> we talk politics we are laughed at; to understand Latin is petty treason
> in us; silence is recommended to us a necessary duty, and the greatest
> encomium a man can give his wife is to tell the world that she is obedi-
> ent: the men like wary conquerors, keep us ignorant, because they are
> afraid of us, and that they may the easier maintain their dominion over
> us, they compliment us into idleness, pretending those [pleasantries]

to be the tokens of their affection, when in reality they are the consequences of their tyranny.[47]

Artesia is angriest of all, however, at her fellow women, who accept
this internalized patriarchy and imagine that they are being gifted
with leisure rather than being excluded from the worlds of work,
politics, and creative endeavour.

All of this might suggest a picture of Mandeville as an Enlightenment champion, one who foresaw the basic equality of all human
beings, the contingent societal pressures that place people in
uneven and unjust positions in life, and the importance of gearing
society along moral standards that might afford everyone basic
levels of respect. There are some problems with this picture, however. It might be said that a satire must presuppose some moral
sensibility that the author intends the reader to appreciate, and
in showing that honest maidens are betrayed by duplicitous men,
Mandeville no doubt sets out to satirize the notion that romantic
standards of male chivalry are all that a woman need rely upon.
Mandeville shows how much women are taken advantage of by
such means. However, he does not really put forward any explicit
positive moral lesson—such as that men ought to respect the admirable virtue of women—as a result of the satire. Mandeville's eye for
the double standards between men and women is more motivated
by his alertness to how hypocrisy and self-deception rule in human
behaviour. If he notes that women are taken advantage of despite
their evident virtue, certainly it is to show that the world is a cruel
place that does not respect the virtue of maidens. But it is just as
much to mock the very idea of virtue being some kind of shield for
a young woman in the modern world. The problem with modern
sexual interactions is as much to do with the notion of virtue as
anything else. Virtue is doubly irrelevant: it doesn't really motivate
Aurelia's behaviour, and even when a woman has it—as in Leonora's case—it is of no help to her.

The lesson of the irrelevance of virtue is supposed to draw
our attention to the real forces at work in sexual relations in the
actual world. Lucinda and Antonia continually use commercial
metaphors when sparring with each other. In asking her to cover
up, Lucinda wonders whether Antonia knows that 'when goods

have been much exposed and blown upon' then 'creditable dealers won't meddle with them, unless they can get them for a song'.[48] In response Antonia says that when 'people of skill like the goods, they matter but little what spiteful neighbours speak against them', and a little more pointedly she notes that 'old traders commonly envy young ones'.[49] The stories of *The Virgin Unmask'd* make clear the financial interests that are always at play (the father's and the husband's) and which are ultimately the only way in which a woman can take control of her own life. Romantic love is exposed as nothing but a fiction invented to disguise the realities of the pervasiveness of sexual desire in the species on the one hand, and the commercial transactions of sexual relations on the other.

If romantic relations are in reality nothing but the commerce of desire, then on what grounds does one object to legalized commercial transactions for sex? It is perhaps unsurprising that Mandeville would later argue for the legal regulation of prostitution. The pamphlet *A Modest Defence of Publick Stews*, written at the height of the scandal of *The Fable of the Bees* in 1724, is one of the most influential works of its type ever written. Here Mandeville's ambivalence and ambiguity are on typical display. The subtitle, *An Essay upon Whoring, as It Is Now practiced in These Kingdoms*, seems to indicate again his serious and realist outlook. The emphasis is upon acknowledging the actual practice of prostitution that exists and how to manage that reality, rather than upon the ideal of eliminating the practice by cultivating a better species of human being. On the other hand, Mandeville is continually undermining his own serious tone: the pamphlet is authored by one 'Phil-Porney', meaning 'lover of harlots'. The pseudonym is a challenge in itself, since it directly implies that the whole argument in favour of the legalization of prostitution might be serving an ulterior purpose— namely, that Phil-Porney can indulge his habits more easily. What is more, the original edition of the *Modest Defence* is dedicated to the members of the Societies for the Reformation of Manners. These were the same members who were outraged by *The Fable of the Bees* and would have had its author locked up. In the *Fable*, Mandeville had made many similar arguments in favour of prostitution in remark H. Mandeville's response to the outrage at that remark now is to dedicate a full pamphlet to arguing for the legitimization of prostitution. As such, it is fair to suppose that a degree of provocation is an important goal of the work.

It is incredibly difficult to identify Mandeville's true intentions here. Whenever he states an ethical truth one must be on guard against the temptation to identify this as his primary aim. We contemporary readers would like to say that Mandeville's shocking and mocking literary style is a means to the end of stating some fundamental ethical position. But more often than not, the opposite seems to be the case: Mandeville seems to use the identification of ethical truths as a means to his literary ends. He points out that the lack of regulation of prostitution (brothels had been outlawed by Henry VIII but had routinely been tolerated in most European states before and after that time)[50] has the consequence of encouraging infanticide among prostitutes, and he points out that this is an inhumane consequence.[51] However, it can look like his goal is just to point out the hypocrisy and artificiality of those who claim the moral high ground in insisting upon the criminalization of prostitution. He immediately follows up this accusation of inhumanity with the point that were prostitution legalized and regulated, then the reduction in infanticide would ultimately result in an increase in the availability of cheap labour as more poor children are produced for the workforce. The effect is that of keeping the reader constantly off balance. At one moment we sympathize with Mandeville's sensitivity to the cruel effects of prostitution; at the next moment he is arguing for it to be legalized on cold economic grounds. There is reason to think that Mandeville really believes that these economic grounds are in fact good reasons for the legalization of prostitution. He argues again in *The Fable of the Bees* that available prostitutes would allow an outlet for male passion that would otherwise (inevitably, he thinks) be directed towards the decency of other women in society:

> Where six or seven thousand sailors arrive at once, as it often happens at Amsterdam, that have none but their own sex for many months together, how is it to be supposed that honest women should walk the streets unmolested, if there were no harlots to be had at reasonable prices?[52]

Mandeville says that the women involved are generally 'the scum of the people' and so unbecoming in their appearance and manner than one need not fear the undermining of virtue, since it really could not be the case that 'the better sort of people will be tempted by them'.[53] Here Mandeville's irony is more obviously on display: if the type of woman who becomes a prostitute is so heinous to behold, there can be little risk of moral corruption to discerning and well-bred gentlemen; if someone wants to maintain that there is a genuine risk, then they must acknowledge that the women do not constitute any kind of horrible subclass of human being. Nevertheless, he is worryingly unclear as to his ironic intent when he shockingly states that 'there is a necessity of sacrificing one part of womankind to preserve the other'.[54]

In the *Modest Defence* Mandeville lists a series of ills attached to prostitution: the increase in venereal disease, the break-up of relationships, the ruin of young women, the financial ruin of those addicted to visiting brothels, and the accompanying practice of infanticide. He claims, though, that none of these are the 'necessary effect of whoring' but instead are only the effects of the 'ill management' of prostitution.[55] The establishment of public houses especially for the business of prostitution would have enormous socially beneficial effects. For one thing, it would organize and ameliorate bad behaviour. Those prostitutes who engage in other crimes do so because 'their lewdness cannot supply their wants'—they cannot make a decent living from prostitution alone and so must supplement it with theft, fraud, and so on.[56] If prostitution were organized as a means of making a genuine living, the temptation to further crime would be reduced. For another, organized prostitution can allow for the systematic treatment and prevention of the spread of venereal disease.

The considerations at play here are explicitly mercantile and utilitarian. Mandeville advocates setting up public 'stews' (as brothels were called) for the convenience of the 'man of business' who constitutes the new lifeblood of Great Britain. He has business to be getting on with, and his activity is what keeps the national economy going. He needs sexual release; lacking which, Mandeville claims, he becomes fixated on the sex he is not getting, distracted from his main business, and becomes unproductive. He can try to overcome the needs of the body through pure exercises of reason, though Mandeville thinks it is the lucky fellow who is able to manage it.

Instead, the man of business currently has to waste too much of his valuable time procuring a prostitute. It involves time, physical and legal risk, uncertain price rates, and altogether too much energy. The economic gaiety of the nation demands that its businessmen be able to relieve themselves of their physical burdens in an efficient and hassle-free manner. Mandeville also has an interesting twist on the anti-romantic themes of *The Virgin Unmask'd*. Brothels provide occasions for men to discover the pleasures of sex, he argues. Those chaste men without such experience tend to imagine that sex provides far more satisfaction than it really does. Their minds have been filled with the impossible image of perfect satisfaction within matrimonial bliss, and the truth revealed on the wedding night can be profoundly disillusioning to the point of undermining the marriage. So, for the sake of the preservation of marriage men must be allowed to visit prostitutes.

Mandeville can start to appear as an opportunistic controversialist, as a writer who will endorse any claim just insofar as it might appal the public. Mandeville switches from the humane to the mercenary almost from sentence to sentence. In the dedication to the *Modest Defence*, he questions whether punishments such as flogging have ever been thought to return a harlot to a 'state of innocence'.[57] In the next sentence he compares the prostitute to a piece of meat cut off by the butcher to distract flies from his better cuts, repeating the misogynistic rhetoric of 'sacrificing a small part' so as to secure the 'safety of the rest'.[58] For Mandeville there is surprisingly little sympathy for those who have fallen to the hardships of the sex industry as a result of society's structures. If we attempt to cut through the use of irony and the ambition to provoke, it can still seem that he thinks that it is a plain truth that the social role of prostitute can be an appropriate one, at least for women of a certain kind.

Yet, if he does think this, it is not because he thinks that certain kinds of women are by nature 'lower' in any way. At every point, Mandeville notes that the different standards of behaviour are entirely down to contingent circumstances, and that our animal nature is for the most part the same in every person. This is illustrated by some remarkable passages in the *Fable* detailing the power of shame in our lives.[59] In remark C, Mandeville evocatively describes what it is like to feel shame. It is not a rational state but a physical one, better understood through the medical theory of animal spirits than through sophisticated moral psychology:

> When a man is overwhelmed with shame, he observes a sinking of the spirits; the heart feels cold and condensed, and the blood flies from it to the circumference of the body; the face glows, the neck and part of the breast partake of the fire: he is as heavy as lead; the head is hung down, and the eyes through a mist of confusion are fixed on the ground: no injuries can move him, he is weary of his being, and heartily wishes he could make himself invisible.

And, of course, when we are flattered and full of self-regard, the opposite physical manifestations are no less evident:

> But when, gratifying his vanity, he exults in his pride, he discovers quite contrary symptoms; his spirits swell and fan the arterial blood; a more than ordinary warmth strengthens and dilates the heart; the extremities are cool; he feels light to himself and imagines he could tread on air; his head is held up, his eyes rolled about with sprightliness; he rejoices at his being, is prone to anger, and would be glad that all the world could take notice of him.[60]

For Mandeville we are a species of animal so physically responsive to the commerce of esteem, the to and fro of approval and disapproval, that it can dominate any other aspect of our being. He argues that the impulse to meet the social expectation of others is so strong that when we fail to meet it, the ensuing sense of shame is more powerful than any other drive in the human being's constitution. How else, he asks in remark H of the *Fable*, can we explain the common phenomenon of infanticide? The ordinary motive for why women kill their own children is that they have been conceived out of wedlock. He envisages a scullery maid doing so, and then subsequently conceiving a child after marrying. Is the explanation of why this happened to be that the woman lacked a maternal sensibility and a moral compass in the first instance but regained them in the second? The unpalatable truth—and one must imagine what it would have been like to read sentences such as these in the early eighteenth century, let alone today—is that the power of social approval and our need to secure esteem and avoid shame can be stronger than our love for our own children. He even points out in remark C that prostitutes are less likely to kill their unintended offspring than more respectable and 'virtuous' women, since the former have no loss of status at stake.[61]

This is the kind of insight that goes to the heart of Mandeville's sensibility. He appears a heartless denigrator of the human species when he plainly points out that we would often rather kill a child than lose social standing. He certainly wants to shock the reader with that impression, but this is not the whole intention. Mandeville's further targets are the tendency first of all to ignore the very fact that such events occur, and to ignore that they occur for these very reasons. We can marvel at the human race all the better if we turn our eyes away from such cases, but such cases nevertheless exist. Nothing profound is shown by the fact that human beings often fail to be as morally good as they ought to be. However, Mandeville is not arguing that human beings are inherently bad because they are sometimes bad. His concern is with how we think about cases like these. The conventional response is to explain infanticide in terms of a *moral* failing, to say that what caused the infanticide is an absence of ethical virtue. On the contrary, Mandeville thinks maternal love was equally present in the case of infanticide and in the latter case where the child was kept. What explains the difference in behaviour is nothing more than the presence of social shame in the first case and the presence of social approval in the latter.

The difference is crucial, since it changes how we think about the scullery maid. On the most liberal interpretation of Mandeville's thinking, he is pointing out that the problem is not with the scullery maid but with society. If children born out of wedlock were approved of, then shame would not be at play, and individuals would not be subjected to a psychological pressure few can bear. By attributing the infanticide to a simple failure of moral character, we commit multiple mistakes. Firstly, Mandeville is sceptical as to whether there really is anything like 'moral character'. Secondly he thinks that we simply fail to acknowledge the reality of the scullery maid's social and psychological condition if we attribute her action to a moral failing. We might say, 'well, she just isn't a decent person', ignoring that she would have acted morally had her social situation been different, and ignoring that *we* might have acted similarly had *our* social situation been different. This is not to say that we cannot recognize that infanticide is a horrendous action that ought never to be performed; it is just to acknowledge that moralizing can serve a different function than that of condemning horrendous actions— it also serves the function of distracting ourselves from the contingencies involved in leading an ethically decent life. On this reading, a disposition to moral condemnation can serve as evidence of one's lack of empathy with others, an unwillingness to identify with the frailty of the human condition, and a hard-hearted ambition to hold oneself apart from and higher than others. We condemn others because it makes us feel good about ourselves. By so doing we create and solidify a sense of our own identity, that of the 'decent' ones in society. By so doing, though, we fail to show any humanity at all.

Once again, the temptation is to read Mandeville as the sympathetic champion of those ordinary human beings who fail to live up to the moral standards preached by those in more privileged circumstances. And yet. There is no doubt that Mandeville enjoys lampooning society and exposing hypocrisy. But does he always do so for the further end of promoting progressive values in society? Or does he do so with no further lesson at all, but just for the purpose of exposing societal hypocrisy, enjoyed as an end in itself? Mandeville is ultimately an unlikely champion of the Enlightenment. And as far as his feminism is concerned Mandeville is, as Karen O'Brien puts it, 'only incidentally pro-woman';[62] his discussion of the status of women itself often looks like only a means to his truly preferred end—that of exposing the artificiality both of conventional morality and of society in general.

CHAPTER FIVE

The Grumbling Hive

Vices have a place in the composition of virtues, as poisons have a place in the composition of medicines. Prudence gathers them and tempers them, and puts them to good use against the ills of life.

—LA ROCHEFOUCAULD, *MAXIMS*, 5:182

THE YOUNG PHYSICIAN MANDEVILLE probably arrived in London sometime in the early 1690s. After ten years he had certainly gained enough facility with the language (and no doubt also the financial security as a practising doctor) to allow him to begin writing, his other passion. His first known publications were both in 1703, the first a translation of *Aesop's Fables* from a French edition, the second a satirical poem targeting political pamphleteers. In 1704 he tried his hand at burlesque poetry. In 1705 he wrote some doggerel verse on a political theme. That last attempt was *The Grumbling Hive*, the poem that would later become the basis of *The Fable of the Bees*. We can see in each of these writings the young Mandeville attempting to break into the market by drawing upon his own cultural background, by using satirical writing to political or philosophical ends. There are a range of questions we might ask about Mandeville's literary ambitions. Why did he use verse? Why indeed did he choose satire as his preferred genre? And ultimately, what motivated Mandeville to write in the first place?

Mandeville answered this last question himself in the *Fable*: 'If you ask me, why I have done all this, *cui bono*? And what good these notions will produce? Truly, besides the reader's diversion, I believe none at all.'[1] This is his standard response—Mandeville writes for fun. He says much the same in the preface to *Aesop Dress'd* (1703)— his translation of La Fontaine's variations on *Aesop's Fables*. There he remarks upon the insubstantial nature of the work he is placing before the reader:

> I could wish to have furnished you with something more worthy your precious time: But as you'll find nothing very instructive, so there's little to puzzle your brain. Besides, I desire everybody to read them at the same hours I wrote them; that's when I had nothing else to do.

These explanations function as partial distancing from what is to follow, for if there was no reason for them to be written other than to take up Mandeville's own leisure time, they must be read only for the same reason. There is an implicit ironic relation between the author and the content of his own work—there is no positive message to be accrued from it at all, he insists, no edification or personal improvement to be had from it. Mandeville included a couple of his own invented fables with his translation of Fontaine's, and while dismissing them as clearly inferior to the others, he doesn't indicate which those are, saying he will leave this identification as a game for the reader. Mandeville is no doubt hoping that they will be tricky to pick out and thereby viewed as similar in quality. For all his denials, Mandeville has literary ambition.

Such distancing techniques are part and parcel of the tradition of satirical writing. *The Grumbling Hive* is a crucial work in the history of satire, but, just as with more famous satirical writings before it, it presents an interpretive challenge. Erasmus's *Moriae Encomium* or *The Praise of Folly* (1511) would have been a basic part of Mandeville's education.[2] Erasmus begins similarly by claiming that he is attacking no particular individuals, and that anyway 'any intelligent reader will understand my intention was to divert, not to insult'.[3] Both Erasmus and Mandeville deploy the tactic of claiming their aim is the mere diversion or entertainment of the reader, so as to insulate themselves from rebuke for the attacks that will follow. Erasmus's writing in praise of folly is a classic of the genre of the paradoxical encomium—the extended praise of that which is inherently unpraiseworthy.[4] Erasmus's particular encomium for Folly can run quite close to the bone, however. For it to work as satire, it is important that there is recognition throughout that the praise is false praise, that the character of Folly isn't really due the credit for the achievements attributed to her. And yet Erasmus can often seem to be making a compelling case for Folly's actual achievements. It would be hard to argue with an initial premise claimed by Folly herself early on—namely, that 'it's the nature of human life that no individual can be found who's not subject to great vices and faults'.[5] One style of argument that Folly deploys is to show that achievements that we would normally attribute to the higher side of human nature, such as our rational or benevolent dispositions, are more plausibly explained as made possible by the lower aspects of human nature. If we weren't foolish, we would never be capable of overlooking the evident flaws, inequities, and downright falsehoods that we nevertheless manage to pass over quite consistently within our daily lives. It is this ignorance—wilful or otherwise—that makes all the familiar social relations possible:

> Briefly, no society, no association of people in this world can be happy or last long without my help; no people would put up with their prince, no master endure his servant, no maid stand her mistress, no teacher his pupil, no friend his friend, no wife her husband, no landlord his tenant, no soldier his drinking buddy, no lodger his fellow-lodger—unless they were mistaken, both at the same time or turn and turn about, in each other. Now they flatter one another, now they wisely overlook failings, now they exchange blandishments, foolish but sweeter than honey.[6]

One might wonder which part of this the reader is supposed to recognize as untrue. While other factors may be in play in cementing social relations, it can seem almost obviously true that dissimulation and ignorance play their own role, just as Erasmus describes. If that's the case though, then there is the risk that a reader might lose track of the satirical intent here. A radical thought is opened up, which is that ineradicable *flaws* in human nature nevertheless serve a positive role in human beings' social lives. While on one level we might retain the obvious thought that it is better to be wise than foolish, Erasmus provides an explanation as to why we might not expect or perhaps not even hope for foolishness to be thoroughly eradicated from human nature. Thomas More's *Utopia* (1516) would have been well known to Mandeville (the conclusion of *The Grumbling Hive* was that the aspiration to render the hive honest was 'a vain Eutopia in the brain'),[7] manifesting all the same ambiguity. Is More's Utopia a perfect society merely not yet existing, or somewhere we should be cautious in even dreaming about? Is the contrast of Utopia with this world supposed to reflect poorly on this world or is it a demand for restraint on over-zealous calls for the improvement of society through dreamt-up imaginary worlds that outstrip what human beings are in reality capable of achieving? One of the traditional functions of satire is to teach an implicit lesson of virtue through presenting an ironic explicit endorsement of vice. A typical example might be Swift's *A Modest Proposal* (1729), where the explicit recommendation to the Irish poor to sell their children to be eaten is evidently meant as a clearly vicious way of drawing attention to the necessity of a virtuous response to a starving population.

The Grumbling Hive, however, is not so easily described. Mandeville would claim again and again that his aim in the poem was to ridicule vice. Yet everywhere he was condemned as a champion *for* vice. His satire, like Erasmus's, functions just because it threatens to reveal some uncomfortable truths. Mandeville expressed his admiration for Samuel Butler's *Hudibras* (1684), a mock-heroic satire on the puritanical virtues in England following the Revolution. Butler's justification of his use of these literary forms is itself a form of cynicism regarding human rationality:

> Men take so much delight in lying that truth is sometimes forced to disguise herself in the habit of falsehood to get entertainment as in fables and apologues frequently used by the ancients, and in this she is not at all unjust, for falsehoods do very commonly usurp her person.[8]

The starting premise of Butler's justification of the fable is that human beings are simply not receptive to truths that clash with their self-image. They cannot be told uncomfortable truths head-on. The response to hearing such truths unadorned and flatly stated is a kind of fight-or-flight response whereby the truth is either angrily rejected or haughtily ignored. If one wants one's readers to genuinely consider the uncomfortable truth on offer, then one has to dress it up in some form other than flat-out assertion. One must present the truth indirectly. The paradoxical strategy is that human beings will be more receptive to the truth if it is presented as a myth, fantasy, or fable. When the form is set as an utterly fantastic one, only then can the reader be told the truth.

This paradoxical form of writing is also frequently accompanied with paradoxical content. Often the goal of instructing through fables is that some truth of a moral or otherwise improving kind might be imparted to the reader. But often what is revealed in *Hudibras*—satirically or not—is ambiguity regarding the very distinction between virtue and vice:

> So in the wicked there's no vice,
> Of which saints have not a spice;
> And that thing that's pious in
> The one, in the other is a sin.[9]

At one point Hudibras has to rationalize a way in which he might break an oath that he has made to a woman. His reasoning is a virtuoso piece of self-deception:

> For breaking of an oath, and lying,
> Is but a kind of self-denying,
> A saint-like virtue, and from hence
> Some have broke oaths by providence:
> Some, to the glory of the Lord,
> Perjured themselves and broke their word.[10]

When one breaks a promise, Hudibras reasons, one denies oneself one's own previously made commitment; self-denial is the mark of virtue, since we can be virtuous only by denying our selfish passions; therefore we bring ourselves closer to saintliness and maybe even to God's will when we break promises. Hudibras insists that there is a strict distinction between virtue and vice, but now everything is topsy-turvy, and lies can be made good with a quick bit of sophistry.

There are other reasons, though, why Mandeville would be inclined to use fables in particular. In his *Some Thoughts concerning Education*, John Locke suggested an illustrated edition of *Aesop's Fables* was a crucial tool for the moral instruction of the young.[11] Fables had and continued to have a status as peculiarly edifying reading. For this very reason they would have been tempting to writers like Mandeville as opportunities to subvert the genre through the provision of accounts of human vice and folly. A further, more pragmatic, recommendation for the use of fable was that it had enjoyed a literary vogue during Mandeville's time in London. In the 1690s reworked fables arrived at regular intervals, always placing Aesop at recognizable though not always glamorous locations: in 1698 alone there appeared *Aesop at Amsterdam, Aesop at Epsom, Aesop at Bath, Aesop at Tunbridge,* and *Aesop at Whitehall.*[12] These were often fables written specifically for the purpose of inserting in the standard 'moral' a relevant social or political comment. The anonymous *Aesop at Islington* (1699), for example, begins with 'Of the Countryman and Snake', whereby a charitable and pitying 'yeoman' finds a frozen and starving snake and brings it to his home to care for it. When the snake recovers, it resumes—somewhat predictably—its ordinary snake-like behaviour. Only when the yeoman's family can bear it no more do they respond and 'with many a thwack' drive out the 'saucy interloping snake, to starve abroad again'. The moral of the fable makes the intended message clear:

The Moral

Beware fond Britons how you favourites choose,
No more the scum of other lands maintain;
To softer foreign things forbear;
For all you by the sharpers gain
Will be their old scorned wooden shoes,
And a fool's cap to wear.[13]

This edifying fable is a piece of xenophobic anti-immigration propaganda. The reign of William III had seen what many understood to be a dangerous consequence of the increased trade with the Dutch in luxury goods (those 'softer foreign things') in the form of increased immigration of unwanted Dutch settlers with their 'wooden shoes'. As one such immigrant, Mandeville might have been alert to the warning to decent English people about the dangers of inviting in the 'scum of other lands'.

Mandeville's own 'morals' were often similarly concerned with the political dimension of life also. His own contributions to *Aesop Dress'd* include 'The Carp', a tale of a young carp who visits overseas to learn the ways of other societies (Mandeville himself may have undertaken a grand tour before settling in England) but who falls in with the wrong crowd and ends up dissolute. On the way, the carp encounters a couple of herring who ask him of his own land's political situation:

> Then herring asks, what news of late?
> Which are your ministers of state?
> Indeed, says carp, he could not tell,
> Nor did much care, quoth herring well
> What laws, what form of government?
> Are taxes raised, without consent
> Of parliament? What course of? Pish
> Says the other, I'm a gentle fish
> And we know nothing of those matters.[14]

As Mandeville outlines in the moral at the end, the folly was that of thinking that one might gain common sense through travel if one didn't have it already. Mandeville's own teens involved enough education and experience of the rough and tumble of Rotterdam's political life to ensure that the moral did not apply to him:

The Moral

> Some Fops that visit France and Rome,
> Before they know what's done at home,
> Look like our carp when come again.
> Strange countries may improve a man,
> That knew the world before he went;
> But he, that sets out ignorant,
> Whom only vanity entices,
> Brings nothing from them but their vices.[15]

Mandeville is fast and loose with the translations he provides of Fontaine's own fables, especially when it comes to interpreting the content of the accompanying moral. Translating 'The Frogs Asking for a King', Mandeville sees a lesson that he thinks his new homeland would do well to heed. This fable concerns the discontent that the populace often show for their own form of government without consideration of the consequences of political change:

The frogs, after some ages spent
In democratic government,
Grew weary of it, and agree,
To change it for a monarchy.[16]

This patently unwise course of action is requested in the form of a prayer to Jove, who complies by throwing down a 'king' for them to worship in the form of a log, which splashes into their pond, terrifying them for a while. Eventually they approach and play on it, but aren't satisfied for long:

And soon they're so familiar grown,
That, laying all respect aside,
They jump upon his back, and ride.
The King, says nothing, keeps his peace,
And let's them work him as they please.
But this they hate, they have him move.
A second time they call on Jove.[17]

Predictably irritated, Jove sends a hungry crane:

Who only was for kill, and slay,
And who ate whoever came in his way.
Much louder now the rascals cry;
Deliver us from tyranny![18]

Jove is unmoved and declares that the foolish frogs now have to stick with the strongman form of government they asked for. Mandeville states the moral:

The Moral

Thank God, this fable is not meant,
To Englishmen; they are content,
And hate to change their government.[19]

Mandeville's message to the English is clear enough: their form of constitutional monarchy—neither overrun with the new fad of democratic self-determination nor under the unchecked tyrannical sway of authoritarian monarchs—has in his view the best of both worlds. One had better be careful before changing things.

Mandeville's analysis interestingly suggests that the problem with democracy is just that it leaves things too much up to the demos, the public. They are, after all, only human beings, and are inclined to radical change of their political situation just for the sake of making some change, irrespective of whether it might tend to the better or the worse. If there is no tyrant in place, then the public will inevitably after a matter of time invite one in. If there is already a monarchy in place, even one with radically curtailed powers, then the public at least won't be tempted in that direction.

In 1703 there also appeared *The Pamphleteers: A Satyr*, which was almost certainly penned by Mandeville. It complains of the attacks on the recently deceased William III. The tone is more strident and less playful than in Mandeville's other works, and it may well have been written on commission to remind the public under the new Queen Anne, herself somewhat intolerant of Protestant dissenters, of the memory of William. It reminds the readers of the turmoil and civil strife—not to mention the real threat of what Mandeville perceived as the tyranny and intolerance that would come with a Catholic on the throne of England—that had existed before William's arrival on the scene. It bemoans the ingratitude of the English public towards a monarch always 'striving to appease a grumbling nation that was never at ease'.[20] In Mandeville's mind was what he saw as a peculiarly English tendency towards perpetual discontent with the current state of things. The reading public was mostly unmoved by Mandeville's offerings, however, and so these warnings went for the most part unheard.

At the end of *Aesop Dress'd*, Mandeville says to the reader that if the fables interest them, then he will write more; if not, then not. The next year he reports that the latter was the case—his offering went down like 'chop't hay'; so instead he is going to offer a different dish, 'a little ragout of gods, giants, pins, speeches, starts, meal tubs, and other knickknacks all jumbled together *a la Françoise*'.[21] *Typhon* is a burlesque poem, originally by Scarron, a low retelling of the mythical challenge to Zeus ('Jove') by Typhon. In Mandeville's translation the story involves drinking games, bowling accidents, and a cast of gods resembling louche narcissists and sybaritic aristocrats. The issue of alcohol means Mandeville can have a swipe at the least-favourite aspect of his new English home. This was the advent of the Societies for the Reformation of Manners, groups set up by private individuals to protect society from the sins of modern life (echoing Erasmus's praise of folly, Mandeville in fact dedicates *Typhon* to what he calls the 'Society of F[oo]ls'). The Societies for the Reformation of Manners had sprung up in the 1690s after William had taken the throne.[22] They recommended not just sermonizing against wickedness but actively going into the streets to report immoral behaviour to the magistrates for prosecution, thereby constituting something close to a volunteer morality police. Mandeville is clear as to what he thinks of them:

> For was an age, in which read
> Of hardly one good man in twenty,
> An age, that spoiled by peace and plenty
> Had no reformers, under banners
> Of holy thirst-encountering manners;
> Those champions of society,
> That watch to keep the world adry;
> Whose drummers teach one day in seven
> That the tattoo's the march of heaven.
> I saw it was in that wicked time,
> When quenching thirst was thought no crime.[23]

One of their primary targets was the vice of drinking and associated debaucheries. A frequent refrain in Mandeville's writing is the defence of drinking. The ancient myth of the challenge of Zeus by Typhon is turned into a bowling accident; the gods are presented in various stages of drunken stupor and disgrace when they are hit. Their indignation at the accident—Jove has some glasses broken—is presented as aristocracy outraged at a populace unable to appreciate their betters:

> Can they subsist, ungrateful puppies,
> Without my sunshine, rain, and twenty
> Odd things, of which they have had plenty
> Even when themselves forgot to pray for it?[24]

In *Typhon*, the unruliness of the ruled masses is presented more favourably than it was in 'The Frogs Asking for a King'. When Jove's emissary is sent down to earth to demand submission, Typhon

sends him on his way, complaining that the gods fail even to manage the English weather:

> It is we that should complain; we've reason;
> They have weather in May enough to freeze one.
> And winds, that keep the spring so back,
> Folks think you lost your almanac.[25]

Here, though, the complaint is not that the gods just fail to make
life better for everyone, but that they charge for the pleasure at the
same time and do so without parliamentary consent:

> Though for bare use, despite parliament,
> Your bailiffs gather twelve per cent.
> Tell Jove, I say, that he an ass is,
> For thinking, we should buy him glasses.[26]

One can imagine Mandeville reciting these lines in a tavern; they
are poetic versions of drinking songs. The political themes are clear,
however: the dangers of political regime change are balanced with
an awareness of the intolerable nature of monarchical tyranny. The
gods are drunks and reprobates (and, Mandeville implies, so is he,
and so are his audience, and so are most human beings) and they
preach submission just so that they can continue their debaucheries at the people's expense. At the same time, though, this judgment
is directed less at the gods' drunken behaviour and more at their
hypocrisy, since the whole brouhaha takes place in a land where
everyone, low-born and high, is blessedly free of the moralistic
restriction of the 'champions of sobriety'.

All these themes are present in *The Grumbling Hive*, published the next year in 1705. It appeared in four sheets, taking up
around four hundred short lines of doggerel verse, nowhere near
as long as *Typhon*, though considerably longer than any of Fontaine's fables. It does, however, contain a 'Moral' at the end of it, not
unlike those found in *Aesop Dress'd*. It is printed in the manner of
a political pamphlet. In short, it is a mishmash of various literary
forms from the seventeenth and eighteenth centuries. The full title
is *The Grumbling Hive: or, Knaves Turn'd Honest*. The alternative
title promises a redemptive story as to how a dissolute community
of knaves was brought to the path of honesty. In one sense this is

right: *The Grumbling Hive* is a story of how a corrupt society was cured of its corruption. But it is not a redemptive story. Bees don't show up much in La Fontaine's *Fables*, and one striking feature of Mandeville's use of bees is how little he in fact capitalizes on the metaphorical potential of the beehive in the course of the poem. One reason for this might be that the image of the beehive was such an established trope in literature that the connotations would have been obvious.[27] Mandeville's aim was to subvert those connotations with some of his own. Reference to bees would have been familiar from the context of his own particular education. Willis's medical writings had noted in the *Two Discourses on the Souls of Brutes* that animals frequently do form highly organized systems without having any of the rational capacities of humans: 'We might here also take notice of the most admirable *Repúbliques* of Bees and Ants, in which, without any written Laws . . . the most perfect ways of Government are exercised.'[28] Erasmus had said much the same, having Folly point out that bees are an example of how well we might get on if we left social design to nature rather than to human beings' improving efforts:

> What community is more happy or more remarkable than that of the bees? Though they don't seem even to have all the bodily senses, what has architecture discovered to equal their structures? What philosopher ever devised a better republic than theirs?[29]

Even more strikingly, perhaps, one of Mandeville's most important literary influences, Montaigne, had noted the marvellously efficient way bees operate in 'An Apology for Raymond Sebond': 'Is there any form of body politic more ordered, more varied in its allocation of tasks and duties or maintained with greater constancy than that of the bees?'[30] Montaigne had thought that the capacity of bees to form such complicated, sophisticated, and effective group structures was sufficient grounds to attribute them something like rationality. Mandeville's thinking is similar, but he runs the argument in the opposite direction. He is more inclined to raise the question whether, if bees can form such complex social groups *without* anything like reasoning being at play, it might also be the case that what governs human beings' own societal behaviour is something other than pure abstract rationality.

Montaigne and Willis were only repeating the standard observations regarding bees and ants made by Aristotle in his *Historia animalium*. A sceptical attitude towards the example of bees was part of a famous attack on Aristotle by the notorious Hobbes in the latter's *Leviathan* (1651). While accepting the fact that bees manifested a hugely impressive amount of social organization, Hobbes had ridiculed Aristotle's suggestion that the evidence spoke to a natural tendency in humans to be sociable. Aristotle took this evidence of sociability in the natural kingdom as good reason to suppose that it was no less present in human beings. He maintained that it could thereby explain how and why humans tended to band together to form societies and to rely upon one another in such mutually cooperative ways. According to the Aristotelian analysis bees are naturally industrious team players, always working with an instinctive eye upon the common good of the hive. That is the only plausible explanation as to how and why they would cooperate together to produce such a large and bounteous hive. For Hobbes, who believed that a successful state requires a strong sovereign at its head to enforce the law and hold it together, this comparison is pure fantasy. There are many reasons why the comparison doesn't work, Hobbes says, not least that it ignores the fact that human beings just aren't as nice as bees: humans 'are continually in competition for honour and dignity, which these creatures are not; and consequently amongst men there ariseth on that ground, envy and hatred, and finally war'.[31] This competition for social standing is an exclusively human phenomenon, Hobbes thinks, and the result of this is that what individual humans want as private individuals might differ from what is the good of the whole of society. For bees, however, the situation is simpler, and here private interests and the public good align:

> Amongst these creatures, the common good differs not from the private; and being by nature inclined to their private, they procure thereby the common benefit. But man, whose joy consists in comparing himself with other men, can relish nothing but what is eminent.[32]

Mandeville takes Hobbes's analysis as the starting point of his own.[33] Mandeville's beehive will be one whose inhabitants are— just as Hobbes insists—dominated by their drive towards realizing their own private interests. However, while Hobbes thought that human beings' overarching concern with their own interest precluded them from realizing the common good, Mandeville turns Hobbes's theory on its head. Mandeville's innovation will be a new story about how human beings' selfishness in fact *naturally* tends to the hive's common benefit.

The poem begins with a description of a beehive that was clearly recognizable as England in 1705:

> A spacious hive well stocked with bees,
> That lived in luxury and ease;
> And yet as famed for laws and arms,
> As yielding large and early swarms
> Was counted the great nursery
> Of sciences and industry.[34]

This was a characterization of England from the Dutch outsider, representing to the English all that was good about their own country that they may not themselves have appreciated. At this time England was famed both for its military strength and for its modern legal system, and already Mandeville is drawing attention to the idea that England's strength in these areas is the source ('the great nursery') of what he saw as its advanced culture and prosperity. In fact, it is the shape of the particular political set-up of England that Mandeville emphasizes:

> No bees had better government,
> More fickleness, or less content:
> They were not slaves to tyranny,
> Nor ruled by wild democracy,
> But kings, that could not wrong, because
> Their power was circumscribed by laws.[35]

The mixed monarchy model that followed the Revolution Settlement of 1689 meant that while William and Mary came to the throne they did so under the restriction of parliamentary sovereignty. Mandeville's point from 'The Frogs Asking for a King' was that if the populace were left entirely to themselves to decide their own form of government ('wild democracy') it would risk the consequence of their unwisely ushering in monarchical Catholic tyranny all over again. A parliament and its laws protect the people from a tyrant but also protect the people from themselves.

Mandeville suggests that the beehive thrived because it was populated with 'vast numbers' in which each toiled not for each other's benefit but rather to 'supply each other's lust and vanity'.[36] The hive is a buzzing centre of productivity, but not because everyone has in mind the noble aim of making the hive great; rather it is because each individual bee is straining to get ahead for themselves that the hive itself is so active. This striving is reflected in the fact that the hive is not an egalitarian utopia with each bee granted an equal footing. Rather, it is an inherently hierarchical place, full of the usual inequalities of birth, and opportunities distributed as much by fortune as by industry:

> Some with vast stocks and little pains
> Jumped into business of great gains
> And some were damned to scythes and spaces,
> And all those hard laborious trades;
> Where willing wretches daily sweat
> And wear out strength and limbs to eat.[37]

Another group in the hive were the 'sharpers, parasites, pimps, players, pick-pockets, coiners, quacks, soothsayers'—the criminal class that took advantage of others' labour where they could.[38] At this point Mandeville expresses his first key claim in *The Grumbling Hive*. If the reader thinks that this group—the knaves of society—can be classed as those who earn their living from vice, then they have made a grave mistake. *Everyone* in this society makes their living from vice. Every respectable form of living operates with immoral behaviour tacitly endorsed by some and otherwise ignored by others:

> These were called knaves, but bar the name,
> The grave industrious were the same,
> All trades and places knew some cheat,
> No calling was without deceit.[39]

From here Mandeville mimics a pattern in *The Praise of Folly* and starts to detail in turn the low practices of the various professions and groups that go to make up the bee society. The legal, medical, political, and military classes all come in for characterization as thoroughly knavish. Mandeville wisely begins on the safe ground of criticizing the practices of lawyers, who are characterized as motivated to create legal problems rather than solve them, 'raising feuds' just for the sake of settling them. Their approach to their clients disregarded virtue and instead mimicked the behaviour of the criminals that they prosecute and defend:

> And to defend a wicked cause,
> Examined and surveyed the laws,
> As burglars shops and houses do,
> To find out where they'd best break through.[40]

Mandeville makes sure his own profession is not exempt from his critique. Here he presents in outline the dubious practices that he would later detail in the *Treatise of the Hypochondriack and Hysterick Diseases*:

> Physicians valued fame and wealth
> Above the drooping patient's health,
> Or their own skill: the greatest part
> Studied instead of rules and arts,
> Grave pensive looks and dull behaviour
> To gain the apothecary's favour;
> The praise of midwives, priests, and all,
> That served at birth or funeral.[41]

Just as lawyers create and prolong cases for their own financial gain, so too do doctors create and prolong illnesses for the financial reward that can accrue. Doctors differ, though, in that their more important source of income is not the patients themselves but rather the pharmaceutical providers, and the other ancillary beneficiaries of successful—and unsuccessful—treatment. Both the legal and medical professions are in a strange socio-economic position whereby they must avow to the aims of eliminating something (whether it be illness or illegality) while at the same time they rely upon the existence of that same thing, and sometimes prolong and promote it for that reason. The 'deceit' that Mandeville is claiming is rife throughout society is not just that of a doctor lying to their patient, or a lawyer to their client—they also must, in order for the whole show to work, have thoroughly internalized their own lies and be engaged in as much *self*-deceit as deceit of others. It is not just that every stratum of society must contain knaves, it must be that the knaves are unaware that they are knaves. To this extent, identifying the pickpockets and pimps as vicious criminals serves an important psychological as well as social function—they become the necessary scapegoats when they are exclusively attributed the vice that in fact permeates modern life.

Mandeville is a little gentler on the clergy, but not by much. The beehive contained some priests that were 'learned and eloquent' but thousands that were not:

> Yet all passed muster that could hide
> Their Sloth, Lust, Avarice and Pride.[42]

Qualification for the priesthood is not an ability to overcome temptations of the flesh, but rather the ability to hide the strength of one's desire for them. The priests were 'famed' for these deadly sins, Mandeville claims. He especially points to the same phenomenon he has already mentioned—namely, that within any group there are some industrious, prudent, and altruistic types, and then there are others who capitalize on the self-denying behaviour of their peers. The clergy are just another social group with the same mix of drones and libertines:

> And while these holy drudges starved,
> The lazy ones, for which they served,
> Indulged their ease, with all the graces
> Of health and plenty in their faces.[43]

The military are no better, some seeking glory but losing limbs; some generals routing their foes, while others 'took bribes to let them go'.[44] Government ministers are—perhaps predictably—accused of systematic corruption, bleeding the state dry, hiding their bungs and payoffs under the terminology of legitimacy:

> Calling, whenever they strained their right,
> The slippery trick a perquisite;
> And when folks understood their cant,
> They changed that for emolument;[45]

The judicial system is similarly accused of class-based discrimination and corruption, punishing the lower orders with an establishment populated by their betters, who are well rewarded for their mercilessness. Justice proves not quite blind in the beehive:

> Yet it was thought, the sword she bore
> Checked but the desperate and the poor;
> That, urged by mere necessity,
> Were tied up to the wretched tree
> For crimes which not deserved that fate,
> But to secure the rich and great.[46]

Throughout *The Grumbling Hive* there is what one might take as evidence of a social conscience and an overarching concern for the poor. There can be no doubt that Mandeville is an acute and sensitive observer of the raw deal the working classes received in eighteenth-century London. He sees economic benefits as randomly distributed through society (the labouring poor have been 'damned' to that fate), he sees the tendency to criminality as a consequence of poverty rather than evidence of immorality, and he sees law and government as functioning to preserve wealth in one class and thereby preserve inequality within society as a whole. Yet Mandeville's aim is not to raise up the lower ranks of people to a decent quality of life but rather to drag down the higher orders to a lower moral level. Having established his first point—that every group in society contained immoral behaviour as a matter of course—Mandeville makes his second major claim:

> Thus every part was full of vice,
> Yet the whole mass a paradise.[47]

The overall state of the beehive is one of prosperity: 'flattered in peace, and feared in war',[48] other hives view this beehive with nothing but envy at its wealth, strength, and activity. The reader would struggle to deny either of these claims. Who could deny that early eighteenth-century London was full of the immoral practices Mandeville described? Yet who could deny that eighteenth-century London was undergoing a revolution in economic prosperity? Mandeville's radical claim was to suggest the former *caused* the latter. Somehow the economic activity that is generated by all this low behaviour actually helps rather than hinders the hive:

> Such were the blessings of the state
> Their crimes conspired to make them great.
> And virtue who from politics
> Had learned a thousand cunning tricks,
> Was, by their happy influence,
> Made friends with vice: and ever since
> The worst of all the multitude
> Did something for the common good.[49]

Mandeville does not mean that *every* vicious action brings with it some economic benefit, as his critics seemed to think. He allows that there are some vicious actions that simply don't benefit anyone, other than the perpetrator. Rather, he is saying that every economic benefit involves at least some element of vice. Moreover, Mandeville *is* arguing the converse point, saying that every vicious individual brings some economic benefit about when their vicious actions are thought of in terms of the complex economy of a modern society. The 'crimes' of individuals as they indulged in various vices—actions obviously not undertaken for the sake of the common good—did nevertheless get caught up in the medical and legal machinery of the state and helped to keep it growing. In this way the crimes conspired of their own accord—behind the backs of both those who indulged in them and those who disapproved of them—to generate economic activity in the state.

The radical nature of Mandeville's proposal starts to emerge at this point. When he speaks of virtue 'making friends' with vice, he does not mean that virtue became tolerant of vice. It is not that the virtuous individuals became aware of the economic benefit of vice and came to a rapprochement with vicious individuals for the greater good. Mandeville's point is rather more subtle: the greater economic good is generated by the economic activity of vicious behaviour sometimes being indulged and sometimes being condemned. Economic activity is generated through the endless dynamic between virtue and vice. Keeping this dynamic going is the job of the state. Therefore, while the state shouldn't seek to promote vice, it shouldn't seek to make virtue ubiquitous either; instead, the state should keep both in a perpetual quarrel so that the whole of society can reap the rewards of their endless spat—this is the 'friendship' between virtue and vice that Mandeville sees in successful societies. It is a strange cooperation between parties that takes place despite— or, rather, because of—the best efforts of each to eliminate the other:

> This was the state's craft, that maintained
> The whole of which each part complained:
> This, as in music harmony,
> Made jarrings in the main agree;
> Parties directly opposite,
> Assist each other, as it were for spite.[50]

The self-deception of the virtuous is a crucial part of the dynamic. The virtuous are self-righteous—they condemn vice simply because they think it is bad behaviour. It would not be half as effective if the virtuous were presented with the idea that they ought to condemn vice for the economic benefit that it would bring. Regulations are far more effective when laid down with a categorical fervour—even if they will inevitably be broken. It is a necessary condition of the dynamic being successful, then, that vice is condemned on high-minded moral grounds. It is only if the participants are ignorant of the economic forces driving their activity that the whole system can function well.

Mandeville now makes his third crucial point. An obvious contender for vice is *luxury*. Luxuries are by definition not necessities of life. Anyone possessing a luxury has by definition more than they need. We rail—Mandeville has cleverly invited the reader already to rail—against the blatantly self-interested greed and avarice of lawyers, doctors, and politicians; but anyone who indulges in life's luxuries is no less indulging in some of the seven deadly sins. But instead of restricting ourselves to only what we need, we instead indulge our pride, vanity, greed, and sloth by seeking out more and more material luxuries. Mandeville introduces a theme that would become crucial for eighteenth-century social thought and is still crucial for understanding our modern world—economies function by constantly stimulating these low dispositions. And it is the economic activity generated by this constant stimulation of the less elevated sides of our nature that improves the condition of the poor.

By keeping its people always hungry for the latest superficiality, by rendering us discontented with what we have, society ultimately improves the lot of the poor by virtue of the industries and employment needed to keep up with demand. This has the effect that the poor are far better off than they would have been had the well-off virtuous folk instead opted to help them through a policy of austerity, self-denial, and moral improvement:

> Whilst luxury
> Employed a million of the poor,
> And odious pride a million more:
> Envy itself, and vanity,
> Were ministers of industry.[51]

Not only that, but the worst aspects of vanity become the most valuable. Vanity invented the most outrageous concept it could in order to find new ways to exercise itself—*fashion*:

> Their darling folly, fickleness,
> In diet, furniture and dress,
> That strange ridiculous vice, was made
> The very wheel that turned the trade.
> Their laws and clothes were equally
> Objects of mutability,
> For, what was well done for a time,
> In half a year became a crime;
> Yet while they altered thus their laws,
> Still finding and correcting flaws,
> They mended by inconstancy
> Faults, which no prudence could foresee.[52]

Mandeville is making what might seem to us today an obvious point, that fashion operates to render a commodity valuable and then worthless in turn, so that a new commodity can be sold in its place, and so on indefinitely. Yet Mandeville was the first to push the point and, more importantly, to present it as a good thing. More daring still is Mandeville's conceptual pairing of the planned obsolescence of clothes with that of laws. Changes in the law have the inevitable effect, apart from that of keeping legislators and lawyers well employed, of generating new behaviour from citizens, since that which was allowed yesterday is condemned today, and everyone must now bustle to keep their practices up to code and within the latest regulations. All this regulation generates economic activity—even if the changes are motivated by the inconstancy and vanity of legislators, and if prudence is ineffective against them, then it is clear that vice and not virtue has the whip hand here. It is in this sense that 'vice nursed industry' and 'the very poor lived better than the rich before'.[53] Mandeville is introducing the reading public to an entirely new idea. Something might be valuable because it is useful or well made or durable and long-lasting; but he wants us to see that there is a different kind of value attached to any produced object, which is the value of the economic activity generated in the course of that object being produced. The conditions for the creation of this kind of economic value appear to have their own rules, rules not at all governed by the notions of goodness with which his readers were familiar.

At this point in the poem Mandeville stops his implicit comparison of the beehive with contemporary England, and starts telling the tale of the beehive's downfall. The bees were unhappy. This unhappiness stems from several factors. Firstly, they can't appreciate what they have and instead imagine a more perfect society (one that Mandeville points out was always meant to be realized in the afterlife rather than in this terrestrial one). Secondly, the bees are hypocrites: they look for some imperfection and they find it in the form of the vice of others. They start to ratchet up the rhetoric in order to distract from their own faults: '*Good Gods: had we but honesty!*'[54] Thirdly, they make what Mandeville sees as a fatally flawed inference: from the fact that the current state of society is imperfect, they infer that there is a vice-free society available. As *Typhon* and *The Grumbling Hive* revealed, Mandeville is not claiming that this society is a virtuous one, or one without unfairness, cruelty, and inequality of which any reasonable person might complain—but he does think that it is as good as one might expect in this life.

Unfortunately for the bees, the gods are listening, just as they had been when the frogs had wished for a king. The grumbling of the hive irritates Jove to the extent that he grants them their wish, and he fills their hearts with honesty. Mandeville compares the effect to that of Adam and Eve having eaten from the tree of knowledge: completely owning to oneself and to others all one's foibles and seeing for the first time the nakedness of human folly isn't a pleasant experience. The next effect is that within half an hour there is a price drop from goods' previously overpriced level ('meat fell a penny in the pound').[55] But the more striking consequence is that all the aforementioned professions are decimated:

> The Bar was silent from that day;
> For now the willing debtors pay,
> Even what's by creditors forgot.[56]

Worse still is that every 'vexatious suit' is dropped, and the vast majority of lawyers, previously employed by the luxury of endless court battles, now 'with inkhorns by their side trooped off'. This is a crucial point that Mandeville stresses: it is not just the wicked lawyers who are now stripped of their livelihoods but all of the necessary ancillary professions too. When the justice system is working virtuously, there are simply fewer people in prison, and so no prison industry can be sustained. There is a web of economic activity that had previously thrived and that had raised many out of poverty that is now gone. The same effect occurs in medicine: people still get sick, but only those who have genuinely mastered their profession and are *honestly* confident of bringing about results still practice. This means that there are really very few practising doctors available. Within the clergy, every priest now either dedicates themselves to helping others or withdraws from the clergy. The effect is that a hierarchical and managerially bloated organization is trimmed down into a small charity service. The consequence is perhaps even worse within the political class. Mandeville cleverly suggests that the previous multiplicity of politicians had certainly served the roles of corruptly helping one another out but also in so doing had monitored and thereby regulated the degree of graft that the political class could bear: no single politician ripped off the state too much. But without dishonesty these roles are redundant in any case:

> All places managed first by three,
> Who watched each other's knavery,
> And often for a fellow-feeling,
> Promoted one another's stealing,
> Are happily supplied by one,
> By which some thousands more are gone.[57]

Mandeville mentions that everyone now sells their expensive foreign goods and, freed from the vicissitudes of vanity, wears only one good solid piece of clothing all year round. The importers, traders, and clothiers are all ruined. 'Content', Mandeville points out, is the 'bane of industry'.[58] Simple contentment with one's meagre goods entails a lack of drive to satisfy any other desires; without new desires to be satisfied there is no market for new commodities to satisfy those desires; without a market for new commodities there is no industry, no striving—manufacturing collapses, and even the production of meagre goods becomes difficult. The overall effect is predictable—thousands leave the hive. Equally predictable is that the hive is now correctly viewed as vulnerable by foreign powers. There is a tactical retreat to whatever portion of the hive is defensible by its decreased and militarily unskilled bee population. In the end Mandeville scathingly describes the beehive collapsing, ending its days as a kind of masochistic puritan cult:

> They triumphed not without their cost,
> For many thousand bees were lost.
> Hardened with toil and exercise,
> They counted ease itself a vice;
> Which so improved their temperance;
> That to avoid extravagance,
> They flew into a hollow tree,
> Blessed with content and honesty.[59]

Mandeville concludes his fable with the standard moral:

The Moral

> Then leave complaint: fools only strive
> To make a great and honest hive.
> To enjoy the world's conveniences,
> Be famed in war, yet live in ease,
> Without great vices, is a vain
> *Eutopia* seated in the brain.
> Fraud, luxury and pride must live,
> While we the benefits receive.[60]

Throughout the poem, Mandeville strives to present the badness of these vices as naturally occurring phenomena, and suggests that the benefits to society are as necessarily connected to vice as the pleasure in eating is to the feeling of hunger:

> So vice is beneficial found,
> When it's by justice lopt and bound;
> Nay where the people would be great,
> As necessary to the state,
> As hunger is to make them eat.[61]

He also makes an explicit reference to More's *Utopia* in the moral. It is clear at least that Mandeville thinks that a certain kind of vision of his adopted homeland—that of an England that is perfectly virtuous and perfectly prosperous and perfectly powerful all at the same time—qualifies as utopian in the literal sense. 'Utopias' are literally 'no wheres' and Mandeville's claim is that their only possible location is as figments of someone's brain, motivated, moreover, by the vanity of self-perfection rather than any higher motives. Given his knowledge of his educated readership, Mandeville must have been aware that his recommendation for society would be taken as echoing the one made by Machiavelli for princes:

> Because, carefully taking everything into account, he will discover that something which appears to be a virtue if pursued, will result in his ruin; while some other thing which seems to be a vice, if pursued, will secure his safety and his well-being.[62]

Mandeville isn't, of course, recommending the wholesale pursuit of vice over virtue; then again, neither was Machiavelli. Machiavelli merely suggested that the goal of being a successful prince was a different one from that of being a virtuous person, and that one ought not to conflate political expedience with moral principle. Mandeville is similarly recommending that readers distinguish in their minds the goal of having a flourishing society from the goal of creating a society of morally decent individuals. If the two things are different, then we shouldn't assume a causal connection between the two, that pursuing virtue would automatically realize political or economic success. In fact, Machiavelli and Mandeville are suggesting that there *is* a causal connection, but the opposite of the one supposed: just as a prince's goal of perfecting his virtue would be likely to lead to his downfall, so a state pursuing a goal of perfecting its citizens' virtue would be likely to lead to that society's collapse.

Mandeville couldn't have intended *The Grumbling Hive* as anything other than a provocation. He did not, for instance, write an Erasmian work entitled *In Praise of Vice*. That work would have required an implicit ironic condemnation of vice. Rather, *The Grumbling Hive* is a paradoxical encomium without the paradox. *The Praise of Folly* works as satire because of its irony—*just because* we readers understand that the point is that folly is, after all, just foolishness. That folly is something negative by definition is always kept in the reader's mind. The point of a paradoxical encomium is that it praises that which is by definition unpraiseworthy. As a satire it hopes to reveal some truths along the way—it might be true that many aspects of human behaviour are driven more by folly than by high-minded motives; it might be true that these same foolish motives generate many of the things that we like and of which we approve; but nevertheless, folly is folly. Not so for *The Grumbling Hive*, which merely co-opts the literary form of a paradoxical encomium. Mandeville argues that human behaviour is driven by vicious motives rather than by high-minded moral ones; he also claims that these same vicious motives generate many of the things that *we like* and of which we publicly approve. He doesn't leave us with the straightforward thought that after all vice is vice and we should obviously disapprove of it. Rather, he leaves us with the thought that despite the fact that we should as individuals disapprove of it, *vice can be good*, economically speaking.

Ultimately, it is not quite right to say that Mandeville claimed to write simply for his own diversion and the diversion of the reader. He acknowledges that there are some consequences that one ought to expect from someone reading the thoughts contained in *The Grumbling Hive*:

> That in the first place the people, who continually find fault with others, by reading them, would be taught to look at home, and examining their own consciences, be more ashamed of always railing at what they are more or less guilty of themselves; and that in the next, those who are so fond of the ease and comforts, and reap all the benefits that are the consequences of a great and flourishing nation, would learn more patiently to submit to the inconveniences, which no government upon earth can remedy, when they should see the impossibility of enjoying any great share of the first, without partaking likewise of the latter.[63]

Mandeville's motive is not so much the improvement of society as the discouragement of those who would hope to improve society. It can seem that he is more disturbed by the presence of hypocrisy than by the existence of vice. The core message of *The Grumbling Hive* is that human beings are irreparably imperfect, and beseeching them to be better creatures is all fine and good so long as one doesn't really expect the species actually to change its nature or behaviour as a result. If his theory is correct, then one genuinely paradoxical consequence is that reading *The Grumbling Hive* won't change anything either. It might, however, offer some kind of reality check to those loudest grumblers in the hive.

Aesop Dress'd was a flop, as was *Typhon*. So too was *The Grumbling Hive*. Whatever Mandeville was trying to achieve with the poem, it didn't succeed. He published no more poetry again other than *Wishes to a Godson* (1712), explicitly occasioned as a gift for a friend's son. Instead, he turned his mind to different types of writing (*The Virgin Unmask'd* and the *Treatise* would take the form of dialogues). Mandeville hadn't given up on the message of *The Grumbling Hive*, however: in 1714, he found occasion to publish it again, this time accompanied by an extensive series of lettered remarks expanding on the claims contained in the lines of verse, and a brief essay—'An Enquiry into the Origin of Moral Virtue'. Here he began to lay out what he had learned from his anthropological inquiries into modern society. It would be this examination of the civilized human animal in this new work—*The Fable of the Bees*— that would cement his notoriety. Here he would state, expand, and defend the paradox he had introduced to accompany the work: *Private Vices, Public Benefits*.

CHAPTER SIX

The Contradiction
in the Frame of Man

*Moderation has been turned into a virtue to limit the ambition of
great men, and to comfort average people for their lack of fortune and
lack of merit.*

—LA ROCHEFOUCAULD, *MAXIMS*, 5:308

WHEN MANDEVILLE SOUGHT TO present 1705's *The Grumbling
Hive* to the ungrateful public once again, he chose to publish it
in a very different form. *The Fable of the Bees* arrived in 1714 as a
book beginning with that poem, but this time followed by a series
of lettered endnotes, each referring to a 'Remark'—twenty in all—
expanding on some of the points made in the poem. In between
the poem and the remarks there was also a new essay, 'An Enquiry
into the Origin of Moral Virtue'. In *The Grumbling Hive* Mandeville
described a perfectly honest society as inherently unrealizable, a
'vain Eutopia in the brain'. That message, upsetting though it was,
might have been accepted as a piece of Realpolitik, a consideration
of the limits of human nature when considering the implementa-
tion of social reform. To say that human beings aren't perfectible
isn't to say that they can't be good at all; similarly, to say that a perfectly good society might lack a thriving economic structure might
have been read as nothing more than a (provocative) plea to think
more carefully about how ethical life and economic prosperity are

to be integrated. *The Fable of the Bees* does away with any such moderate interpretations of *The Grumbling Hive*. Throughout the *Fable* Mandeville argues that the very idea of upright behaviour is a fantasy. Perfect human society is impossible not because human beings lack moral perfection—it is because morality itself is a sham.

Mandeville opens the *Fable* with the thought that there is no shortage of writers who will tell us how human beings *ought* to be (a *normative* claim about human nature) but very few who are willing to give a frank *descriptive* account about how human beings really are.[1] On one level, then, Mandeville could avoid the accusation that he is recommending vice by simply pointing out that he isn't recommending anything at all, merely observing the patterns of our behaviour. Few of his readers would have accepted this defence, however, as this would be the expected response from someone seeking to avoid prosecution. Instead, they saw a deeper and more sceptical thesis at work in Mandeville's writing. This thesis is that the descriptive claims set up a radical picture of human nature that debunks the normative ones regarding how human beings should live. Perhaps Mandeville thinks that there's a reason why people so frequently fail to live up to our moral ideals, and that is because they are unreal fictions, imaginings, utopias in the brain. If there is a normative claim discernible in Mandeville's work, it is that we ought not to govern our lives in accordance with utopian fantasies of the superiority of human nature. But why in that case do we have morality at all? What purpose does it play in our lives? What makes us so proud of and married to standards that we all inevitably fail to meet?

The Grumbling Hive had contained two uncomfortable truths, and Mandeville's account of human nature had to be adequate to explain them both. The first was that our world was far more infested with vice than we ordinarily like to admit: not just the criminal professions but *all* professions (and all consumers of their products) were driven by their lower instincts. The second major claim was that being driven by our lower instincts tended to the benefit of society as a whole. His challenge was to explain what kind of creatures we could possibly be such that both these things might be true. When Mandeville presents his own theory of human nature in the *Fable* he does so in terms that his readers would have immediately recognized as Hobbesian in character.[2] Like Hobbes before him, Mandeville claims that human beings are fundamentally self-interested creatures driven by natural desires:

> There is nothing so universally sincere upon earth, as the love which all creatures, that are capable of any, bear to themselves. . . . This is the law of nature, by which no creature is imbued with any appetite or passion but what either directly or indirectly tends to the preservation either of himself or his species. The means by which nature obliges every creature continually to stir in this business of self-preservation are grafted in him, and (in man) called desires.[3]

This is Mandeville's basic level of explanation of the human animal. He finds the exact same biological continuity between us and the beasts—we are physical beings pushed and pulled by forces within our bodies. We are all driven by animal spirits. However, his medical theories lead him to develop this theory in ways unforeseen by Hobbes. Mandeville alludes to this context throughout the text:

> I believe man (besides skin, flesh, bones, etc. that are obvious to the eye) to be a compound of various passions, that all of them, as they are provoked and come uppermost, govern him by turns, whether he will or no.[4]

There are several striking claims here already. Human beings must be governed by their passions, since Mandeville thinks that a human being *just is* a 'compound of various passions'. But then what role *can* rationality have in our behaviour? Mandeville claims that the passions govern our motivations against our own will, implying both that reason is impotent in our actions (anticipating and influencing David Hume's later famous remark that 'reason is and ought to be the slave of the passions')[5] but also that we might lack free will altogether, since on this account our actions are generally pushed by those passions rather than resulting from freedom guided by rational choice.[6]

It does at least *appear* to us that we make rational decisions, however, so Mandeville's theory must be that our apparent ability for rational choice is an illusion. This relates to another implicit claim, which is that Mandeville is presenting an account of how passions operate in ways that are not 'obvious to the eye'. Mandeville had used the same anatomical metaphor in the preface, when suggesting that what drove society was not in fact the externally visible features of society's self-image, but rather involved what lay under the skin, and this was the same with regard to what moves our bodies to action:

> The chief organs and nicest springs more immediately required to con-
> tinue the motion of our machine, are not hard bones, strong muscles
> and nerves, nor the smooth white skin that so beautifully covers them,
> but small trifling films and little pipes that are either overlooked, or else
> seem inconsiderable to vulgar eyes.[7]

Although he presents it as a metaphor, when it comes to human behaviour and society the claim is a literal one.[8] Mandeville's medical theory had it that human beings are literally moved in their behaviour by the ebb and flow of indiscernible animal spirits through the 'little pipes' of the nervous system, running through every part of our bodies, and affecting all of it, not least our brains. The entire range of our behaviour, especially the behaviour in which we take the most pride, can be explained in terms of the move-ment of passions generated by our animal natures. But Mandeville thinks the most adequate and powerful explanation is the one that we are the least willing to accept, and in fact we work hard to keep this side of our nature out of sight. Thus, when Mandeville says that he is 'anatomizing the invisible part of man',[9] it is clear that he sees no discontinuity between his medical and his social investigations. Mandeville's pictures, for all the informality of their presentation, bear a remarkable unity. The movement of the animal spirits means that we are at the behest of our passions, and for any animal who also happens to have developed self-consciousness, this is not nec-essarily a happy existential condition. We are at the mercy of our passions, and we are dimly aware of the fact, but it is such a difficult thought to accept that we construct entire theories so as to rational-ize its denial. Mandeville's account of human nature is a stunningly original account of how human beings evolved socially to cope with this very fact. He takes it that human beings' coping mechanism is one of systematic self-deception about their own true natures. Incredibly, though, he argues that it is this very aspect of our mal-formed nature that has generated such enormous benefits to the species as a whole. Our capacity for species-wide self-delusion is the secret of our success. It has also created a kind of paradoxical second nature: human beings are by nature those animals that deceive themselves as to their true animal natures.

In generating this theory, Mandeville engaged in highly discriminating poaching across a diverse intellectual territory. Perhaps surprisingly, the most accurate description of this intellectual heritage is theological. Mandeville is steeped in Augustinian and Calvinist theology, communicated through his love of French literature and philosophy, especially as it was developed by a range of French thinkers, such as Pierre Nicole, Jacques Abbadie, La Rochefoucauld, and especially Pierre Bayle.[10] Mandeville is not just a conduit for this tradition, however—he twists it, adapts it, and turns it into something new, something different and frequently disturbing. For example, La Rochefoucauld's presence would have been detectable to any reader from the outset of the *Fable*. Although Mandeville claims that he will show how human beings' 'vilest and most hateful qualities'[11] are necessarily the ones that help society flourish, and although he thinks the human being is just an animalistic 'compound of various passions'[12], he insists that none of this will entail any kind of scepticism with regard to his dear readers' grasp of justice or virtue: 'I must desire the reader once for all take notice, that when I say men, I mean neither Jews nor Christians; but mere man, in the state of nature and ignorance of the true deity.'[13] Later, in remark O, he makes a similar crucial qualification:

> Thus I have proved, that the real pleasures of all men in nature are worldly and sensual, if we judge them from their practice; I say all men *in nature*, because devout Christians, who alone are to be excepted here, being regenerated, and preternaturally assisted by divine grace, cannot be said to be in nature.[14]

La Rochefoucauld had deployed the very same distancing technique at the beginning of his *Maxims*, written a half-century earlier:

> The person who wrote [these reflections] considered men only in the deplorable state of nature corrupted by sin; therefore, his way of referring to the innumerable faults to be found in their apparent virtues, does not apply at all to those people whom God preserves from such things by special grace.[15]

They both use the manoeuvre of asserting that what they are talking about is the state of human beings *without* the improving conditions of religion. The analysis that is about to follow might appear misanthropic and immoral, but it will appear so only to the uneducated (or perhaps impious) reader. The intended readership is supposedly those devout types who want to understand more about how low humanity can sink if left without God's assistance. With this disclaimer in place, Mandeville is free to elaborate in cheerful detail the awful ways in which the heathens among us behave towards one another without it reflecting in any way the values of the author. If anyone were to accuse Mandeville of impiety, he could always return to the high ground and to his claim that his work is that of 'the strictest morality'.

The very first remark of the *Fable* had already given the reader a taste of Mandeville's use of humour. In remark A he begins in earnest mode, pointing out that a decent society has a responsibility to provide for the education and the future livelihood of its youth. But what to do if for various reasons young men don't succeed in the profession their parents have set up for them? Some hard-working ones will become journeymen, and studious types will become schoolmasters, but 'what must become of the *lazy* that care for no manner of working, and the *fickle* that hate to be confined to any thing?'[16] Mandeville claims that those who like being entertained end up on the stage; gluttons end up cooking and getting around food in some capacity or other; those without principles but with fast hands become pickpockets, and so on. Last of all, and at the bottom of his dubious hierarchy, Mandeville places his own profession:

> Others again, that have observed the credulity of simple women, and other foolish people, if they have impudence and a little cunning, either set up for doctors or else pretend to tell fortunes; and every one turning the vices and frailties of others to his own advantage endeavours to pick up a living the easiest and shortest way his talent and abilities will let him.[17]

The nub of the style in *The Grumbling Hive* is on show again here. The virtuous question of what to do with the youth is given an answer that everything is best left to vice. There is the self-incriminating thought that even doctors—perhaps especially doctors—are properly understood as individuals possessing less a desire to cure the sick and more a capacity for sleight of hand. It just so happens that sleight of hand can have a home in a civilized profession. There is a claim of equivalence between the high and low ways of life, implying that the pickpocket is just unfortunate that the profession to which their natural abilities—physical sleight of hand— suit them involves a form of taking money from the gullible that has been declared illegal. Those whose abilities are suited to the financial sector are more fortunate, but are not necessarily better people, than pickpockets. Fortune tellers are deemed charlatans, while stock market advisors are deemed serious professionals, but both prognosticate to their own advantage and contrary to evidence, regularly undermining the belief that they know what they are doing. Finally, there is the implied claim of hypocrisy in that those who condemn the immoral pickpocket are those who wilfully ignore that their choice of profession is similarly determined by whatever suits their natural abilities and privilege of birth. This is in essence Mandeville's theory in the *Treatise* about how the modern practice of medicine arose, now applied to civilized professions in general. These kinds of analyses imply that the motives that we cite to ourselves for why we have engaged in our preferred professions—the reasons why we do what we do—are not what we think they are. Most of us take our professional lives to be worthwhile in some broadly ethical sense (or at the very least not to our discredit). Mandeville claims that this is a piece of wilful self-deception.

Throughout the remarks we see that private vices bring public benefits. Every right-minded person deplores avarice and is surely correct in their suspicion that money is at the root of all evil. And yet—would we be better off if we could cure ourselves of materialism and greed? Obviously not: avarice is, Mandeville claims, a 'slave to prodigality'.[18] Most of those greedy for wealth are greedy so that they can spend their wealth, and so it is the opposite of miserliness. Miserliness hides money under the mattress; avarice by its very nature moves money around:

> Avarice, notwithstanding it is the occasion of so many evils, is yet very necessary to the society, to clear and gather what has been dropped and scattered by the contrary vice . . .

... [T]here is a sort of avarice that consists in a greedy desire of riches, in order to spend them, and this often meets with prodigality in the same persons, as is evident in most courtiers and great officers, both civil and military. In their buildings and furniture, equipages and entertainments, their gallantry is displayed with the greatest profusion.[19]

Echoing one of La Rochefoucauld's metaphors, Mandeville says that he views 'avarice and prodigality' as he does 'two contrary poisons in physick, of which it is certain the noxious qualities being by mutual mischief corrected in both, they may assist each other, and often make a good medicine between them'.[20] Conversely, we should be suspicious of frugality, a private virtue that Mandeville is in no doubt turns out to be a public vice. To be frugal in one's life is to manifest 'a mean starving virtue'. It might be wise for the small farm owner in the village to manage their wealth carefully, but that wisdom goes out of the window when we consider the best behaviour for a large booming society:

'Tis an idle dreaming virtue that employs no hands and therefore very useless in a trading country, where there are vast numbers that one way or other must be all set to work. Prodigality has a thousand inventions to keep people from sitting still, that frugality would never think of.[21]

Up is down, night is day, black is white, folly is wise, while wisdom is foolish. What is bad is good, and what is good is bad. While it was shocking to the English reader, Mandeville had drawn upon what was for him a traditional training in how to perform these ethical inversions. La Rochefoucauld famously begins his *Maxims* with the thought that 'our virtues are, most often, only vices in disguise',[22] and many of Mandeville's remarks are directed towards this more radical claim. Human beings are driven by low passions, but we convince ourselves that our behaviour is acceptable and—with a little effort—even virtuous. Both Mandeville and La Rochefoucauld see in every putative occasion of virtue an opportunity to reveal vice. What is generosity? For La Rochefoucauld the answer isn't complicated, as 'what we call generosity is most often merely the vanity of giving, which we like more than the thing we are giving.'[23] The standard reductive technique is to substitute some virtue (generosity) with some vice (vanity) and to imply that the same action (e.g., giving something away to the needy) can be as well explained by appeal to the vice as to the virtue.

There are two readings of La Rochefoucauld's analyses, one far more sceptical than the other. On the less sceptical reading, he is merely claiming that although generosity and so on are undeniably good things, when we examine human psychology it just so happens that reaching these standards is a lot more difficult than we think. On this reading he is merely trying to show that when one thinks one is being generous, it might for all we know just be a case of vanity. For this reason, it behoves all of us to be as scrupulous as possible with regard to our own motives—and perhaps to hope for divine help if we really want to live a good life. However, a stronger sceptical reading is available. On this account La Rochefoucauld is not just attacking our ability to realize these virtues but is attacking the very virtues themselves. The more sceptical reading is that he is claiming that generosity is *nothing but* vanity under a different name. We are deceived when we say to ourselves that there is even any real thing called 'generosity' at all. Despite La Rochefoucauld's professions of Christian sincerity, the stronger sceptical reading becomes hard to resist as we read inversion after inversion of what we might have thought was decent human behaviour. What is humility? Desire for tactical advantage, since 'humility is often merely a pretense of submissiveness, which we use to make other people submit to us.'[24] What is pity? Again, desire for future tactical advantage:

> Pity is often a feeling of our own ills, prompted by the ills of other people. It is a clever way of anticipating the misfortunes that could possibly befall us: we help other people so that they will be obliged to help us when comparable circumstances arise; and the services we render them are, strictly speaking, good deeds that we do for ourselves in advance.[25]

One might think that such cynical analyses of the human heart betrayed a thoroughly immoral or amoral picture of human behaviour. Yet La Rochefoucauld—unlike Mandeville—may well have been sincere in his disclaimer that he was describing only the corruption of minds untouched by God's guidance. La Rochefoucauld might have been merely giving fervent expression to the theological position of Jansenism (named after the Dutch theologian Cornelius Jansen), the French Catholic movement reinvigorating Augustinian thought. Saint Augustine had famously argued for a picture of human beings as fundamentally fallen, thoroughly and forever corrupted by their expulsion from Eden. This tragedy rendered them forever incapable of morally virtuous behaviour, at least through the exercise of their own frail faculties. If genuinely virtuous behaviour ever occurred it was only as a result of *grace*, the addition of divine intervention into the hearts of human beings.

Augustinian thought was revitalized during the Protestant Reformation, in large part owing to the writings of the French theologian John Calvin, with whom the Jansenist sect was frequently associated, despite the latter's Catholic origins.[26] Calvin stressed the corrupted nature of humankind and denigrated the tendency of human beings to extol their power of reason and its ability to guide their moral behaviour. What is it when a heathen has the temerity to suppose that they might be doing good? Nothing but a self-deception, says Calvin, prompted again by vanity:

> Show me, if you can, an individual who, unless he has renounced himself in obedience to the Lord's command, is disposed to do good for its own sake. Those who have not so renounced themselves have followed virtue for the sake of praise. The philosophers who have contended most strongly that virtue is to be desired on her own account, were so inflated with arrogance as to make it apparent that they sought virtue for no other reason than as a ground for indulging in pride.[27]

For Calvin too, moral guidance is possible only through divine grace. Yet God surely does not distribute his grace arbitrarily in the form of a divine lottery. There must be something *in us* that makes the difference when God decides to distribute his good favour upon us. How does one determine that one is worthy of divine grace, then? One central way available to human beings is that of *moderation*. Calvin found in scripture evidence that God's intention for human beings was that they should distinguish themselves from animals by employing their rational capacities for the purpose of restraining their unruly and self-interested desires. Since animals are governed by instinctual desire alone, it is the very capacity to overcome our instinctual drives that distinguishes the human being.[28]

Consider, for example, that classic of Christian instructive writing, Thomas à Kempis's *The Imitation of Christ*, written in the early fifteenth century, and enormously influential for subsequent generations of Christian thinkers such as Luther and Calvin. The crucial path to achieve spiritual wisdom is a negative one, through the denial of the flesh. Our animal natures push us away from holiness but we can get closer to it by moderating our desires through the training of self-denial:

> Happy and wise is he who endeavours to be during his life as he wished to be found at his death. For these things will afford us sure hope of a happy death; perfect contempt of the world; fervent desire to grow in holiness; love of discipline; the practice of penance; ready obedience; self-denial; the bearing of every trial for the love of Christ.[29]

> Our advantage does not consist in winning or increasing possessions; it lies rather in being indifferent to such things, and eradicating the desire for them from our hearts. These harmful desires include not only love of riches, but also ambition for honours and vain praise. Remember that all these things pass away with the world.[30]

Again, while moderation and self-denial are necessary ingredients for a genuinely virtuous life, they are still not sufficient. That extra element, grace, is needed for human beings in order to push them past the finishing line in the race to virtue.

One difficulty with the doctrine of divine grace is that it faces some quite obvious counter-evidence. It just doesn't seem to us to be the case that we require divine assistance in order to engage in everyday moral behaviour. It doesn't appear to us that we need anything other than simply to think for ourselves about what the right thing to do is—and then just to do it. It looks to us as though this is the kind of thing that goes on every day, not just among true Christians but also with those faux Christians among us merely paying lip service to religion, or to practitioners of other faiths, and perhaps even among atheists. Whatever their differences, the Augustinian, Calvinist, and Jansenist traditions all maintained that such appearances must be illusions. The bizarre consequence of this is that from within the most rigorous tradition in Christian theology there sprang a campaign devoted to the kinds of moral scepticism mentioned earlier. The core task of this tradition was to show that what *appears* to be ordinary secular moral behaviour is in fact nothing of the kind. The path to elite holiness requires first of all demonstrating that the apparent evidence of ordinary human beings' goodness is in fact something not at all to the credit of the species.

One of the most prominent French Jansenists, Pierre Nicole, argued for the importance of grace by denigrating the most obvious evidence of simple moral behaviour. This required elaborating the basic Hobbesian idea of human beings as fundamentally driven by their self-interested desires (ironically enough, since Hobbes's thought was widely perceived to be atheistic). On this elaborated account, humans quickly learn that in social settings the display of one's desires as clearly self-interested tends to undermine their effectiveness. Where we require the cooperation of others to realize our goals, the display of our naked self-interest frustrates those aims, as it can incur the resentment and opposition of others. Nicole is at one here with what Erasmus had claimed in *The Praise of Folly*—what is required for successful social interaction among flawed creatures such as ourselves is an abundance of dissimulation and deceit. For Nicole, this is because we must hide the fact of our self-interest in order to realize our aims. We have here the type of paradoxical account of human nature in which Mandeville would revel. If we are genuinely driven by self-love, it claims, then the naturally arising phenomenon we would expect would be our strenuous efforts at disguising that self-love.

For example: what, according to Nicole, is charity? A desire to hide that our motivations are in fact selfish:

> It is this which inclines those who are sensible of the hatred of men, and who love not to expose themselves thereunto to endeavour to withdraw . . . their self-love from the sight of others, to disguise and counterfeit it, never to show it under its natural shape, to imitate the behaviour of those who would entirely exempt from it; that is to say, persons animated with the spirit of charity.[31]

Nicole attests that this disposition towards 'counterfeit charity' is so ingrained into human psychology that it is 'almost impossible to know . . . what distinguishes it from charity'.[32] This is not least because of the fact that counterfeit charity produces the same results as the real thing. Nicole doesn't say, of course, what a reader might now wonder, which is whether it is necessary to this story that real charity ever existed at all. It is certainly consistent with Nicole's account that all the beneficial consequences of human charity could have come about in a society where no real charity had ever emerged. The benefits could just as well come about in a society where each member was attempting to hide their self-interest from the other—all that is required is that they are under the same delusion, that they think the other person is manifesting real charity. A society where each member was determined not merely to imitate charity but also to hide that fact from other members might amount to a society with just as many good deeds in it as a society filled with genuinely charitable souls.

It is with such theological sources in mind that Mandeville constructed his paradoxical thought experiments. Perhaps a society manifesting *fake* virtue would produce just as many benefits as one manifesting real virtue? Perhaps a society with fake virtue would even produce *more* benefits than one with real virtue would have done? Mandeville wouldn't even have had to look too far for this latter thought, either. As Jacob Viner has pointed out, Pierre Nicole himself had expressed something like this very thought in his defence of true virtue and religion.[33] In his multivolume (and hugely influential) *Essais de morale*, Nicole had acknowledged that since so much of the social interaction of human beings in fact depends on the fake virtue displayed by the corrupted common folk, it would be somewhat disastrous for society, especially in terms of its trade and commerce, were the uneducated masses to acquire the real virtue that he and others of a similar religious bent possessed. This appears to be a problem: the maintenance of a healthy economy is a necessary background condition in order to create the material comforts and the leisure time for those few blessed with grace to meditate on God's perfection. The complete conversion of the entire population to true religious virtue would create a society of pious but not very industrious meditators. Then there would be no one left to set up and maintain the social structures that meditation requires—here, true morality would be paradoxically 'detrimental to the reestablishment of true morality'.[34] Nicole doesn't blink at this consequence however. Universal salvation was never part of his Jansenist outlook anyway. It was an unfortunate fact that vast swathes of humanity weren't to be saved because they simply didn't achieve real virtue, and perhaps this was God's plan too, because it at least allowed for society to produce material conditions that allowed some (such as Nicole) to attain true virtue in comfort. Nicole had therefore already argued for there being a positive role for widespread fake virtue, in that it produces more benefits than a society of genuinely virtuous souls would ever do.

This is exactly the scandalous claim of *The Grumbling Hive*. Mandeville has all these religious manoeuvres in mind when he presents modern society's underlying workings in *The Fable of the Bees*. Mandevillean analyses are ones that claim that most actions are what he—following Nicole—calls *counterfeited* virtue, actions that do not consist in a rational victory over the temptation of some desire, but instead are properly understood in terms of 'a conquest which one passion obtains over another'.[35] In particular, whenever 'virtue' is observed, it is to be interpreted as an occasion of pride or shame overcoming some other desire. Whenever 'virtue' is observed it is not our pure rational capacities motivating us to do the right thing for its own sake. It is for this reason that Mandeville says that 'the seeds of most virtues are contained' in pride and shame.[36] Mandeville doesn't offer here any explanation as to *why* pride and shame specifically are quite so powerful within our moral psychology. He does, though, hint that the standard practices of childrearing tend to make us creatures possessed of a 'greediness . . . after the esteem of others'.[37] Parents instruct their children through expressions of approval and disapproval regarding certain actions long before the children have enough intellectual capacity to understand just what it is that makes these things right or wrong. We are first formed as persons through intense conditioning in the economy of esteem. Parents lack the time, the will, and often the ability to explain to children why they ought to do the things that society demands—it is more important that the child simply does them. The most effective way of instructing the young therefore is through rewarding children with praise when they perform good actions and shaming them when they go wrong.

With this child development thesis in play, Mandeville can begin to motivate the thought that there is just one of our interests that has the power to curb all the others. Human beings are the creatures who take pleasure in moderating their pleasures. Whenever we curb our passions we gain the approval of others, and when the approval of others is more pleasurable than the original passion we have denied ourselves, then the deal done with oneself is a good one. Similarly, whenever we curb our passions, we thereby avoid the shaming looks of others. Shame—the sense of being *seen as* being in the wrong—is so unpleasant to us that we will forgo whatever desire we want to satisfy if we grasp that doing so might incur this feeling. By the time we are small children, this anticipation of the shaming looks of others is thoroughly internalized (as we have seen, girls are 'taught to hate a whore before they know what the word means').[38] By that stage, we don't even require the actual presence of any observer shaming us to forgo the desire; we will forgo it by ourselves through imagining the shameful look that *would* have arisen were we to have been observed.

When Mandeville offers his own analyses of virtues, they are debunking performances very similar to those of La Rochefoucauld or Nicole. Mandeville clearly has fun with the genre. What is modesty? According to Mandeville, it is the drive we have to secure the approval of others by showing that we can control our desires. When someone picks the 'worst out of the dish', Mandeville points out, it is highly implausible to attribute them the regular desire for the smaller portion of food.[39] Rather, they have a stronger desire to be perceived as not being greedy. The realization of this perception is far more pleasurable to us than the small amount of extra food would have been. A small bit of loss in physical pleasure generates a profit in the economy of esteem. The same basic economic dynamic plays itself through all our manners, Mandeville claims, and it is the most prevalent where the desires are strongest. It is for this reason that the approval of others has such an important role in sexual manners—seeming lustful is, for example, viewed as animalistic and shameful, and so we work hard to avoid any appearance that our interactions with others might be motivated by sexual desire. What is honour? A contrived notion indicating a special ability to keep to one's commitments that is possessed only by a very few—honour 'in great families . . . is like the gout, generally counted hereditary, and all lords' children are born with it'.[40] Throughout Mandeville points out how anything might be done in the name of honour if it can be stoked up, even to the point of taking one's own life. But in this, as with all other virtues, the real motivation for the actions is the sense of pride we get from being perceived as honourable. For this reward 'there is no pitch of self-denial that a man of pride and constitution cannot reach, nor any passion so violent but he'll sacrifice it to another which is superior to it'.[41]

Like Montaigne, Calvin, Nicole, and La Rochefoucauld before him, Mandeville's denigration of ordinary virtues such as modesty, patience, chastity, frugality, and the like reveals all to be occasions of our overweening *pride*. That human beings are fundamentally governed by pride—recall that it is what Montaigne called our *maladie originelle*—is central to Mandeville's studies of the controversy of animal minds as well as to his medical studies of the animal spirits that govern our behaviour. Yet Mandeville differs from his predecessors in certain key respects. For one, he is utterly sceptical about the role of self-denial. Unlike Calvin, for whom at least self-denial was the path to godliness, Mandeville has a more radical take on human foibles: the self-denial of our desires is always an occasion of pride, of showing others just how self-controlled we can be. Moreover, Mandeville's entire attack on frugality implies an antagonism to the Calvinist recommendation of moderation. Here he seems to bring in La Rochefoucauld *against* Calvin. While Calvin recommends moderation as the cure for pride and corruption, moderation itself is a 'virtue' that came to La Rochefoucauld's suspicious attention. Moderation, he claimed, had been *turned* into a virtue, and what's more, for low reasons: it is an expression of our envy of those who succeed through the realization of their powerful desires.[42] We cope with our jealousy by creating a new value—moderation through rational self-control—so we can scold the powerful for their immodesty and thereby feel superior to those to whom we are in reality inferior by comparison.

It is unlikely that the educated reader in early eighteenth-century England would have failed to notice that the *Fable*'s sceptical attitudes towards the value of self-denial and moderation (what

David Hume would later refer to as 'monkish virtues') were anti-religious in tone.[43] Mandeville's mock-Calvinism would not have been mistaken for the real thing, no matter how thick the ironic piety in which he wrapped his message. Just to be sure, though, Mandeville added a short essay after *The Grumbling Hive* entitled 'Enquiry into the Origin of Moral Virtue'. He had already argued that some of the ordinary virtues like modesty, frugality, chastity, charity, and so on were really just pride in disguise. Even if one accepted these sceptical analyses, it might be claimed that Mandeville hadn't touched upon the final and most important virtue that governs human beings' lives. This is the idea of *moral* virtue, or the capacity we humans have to choose to do something just because it seems to us to be 'the right thing to do'.[44] In the 'Enquiry' Mandeville extends the exact same sceptical analysis even to the basic idea of moral virtue, to the very idea of doing an action just because it is good in itself. It was the answer that he presents in this essay that would be seized upon by critics when the scandal of the *Fable* finally broke. The 'Enquiry' does exactly what it says, which is to propose a theory of how the very idea of moral virtue came about. The answer would surely be that God gave us the capacity to distinguish right from wrong and that's that; however, Mandeville has already specified that he is interested in the origin of that concept of morality that has been deployed in non-Christian societies. Given that such societies lacked the exclusive divine guidance that Christian culture received, how did *they* come to the notion?

The 'Enquiry' begins by reminding the reader that human beings are animals. The first line states that 'all untaught animals are only solicitous of pleasing themselves'; several pages later, after the theory has been presented, Mandeville claims that 'this . . . was the manner after which savage man was broke'—the story being told is one about how the human animal was changed from being wild to being domesticated. This is in essence Mandeville's account of the origin of morality. It is not that human beings were civilized in order that they might more fully realize their natural moral capacity, it is that morality just emerged as a by-product of the process of civilizing human beings into a manageable kind of social order. In his later sequel to *The Fable of the Bees* in 1732, Mandeville offers the following characterization of vice:

Vice proceeds from the same origin in men, as it does in horses; the desire of uncontrolled liberty, and impatience of restraint, are not more visible in the one, than they are in the other; and a man is then called vicious, when, breaking the curb of precepts and prohibitions, he wildly follows the unbridled appetites of his untaught or ill-managed nature.[45]

The notion of virtue is tied to the actions of staying within set rules and norms (whatever they might be); the notion of vice is tied to those actions where we are *unruly*, where our instincts, desires, and interests push us in ways that happen to go against those norms. In both cases, the notions of right and wrong are generated by the fact that human beings have been trained in various ways, some of which match their animal desires, and some of which do not.

Mandeville's account of how we came to be this peculiar variety of house-broken animal starts from a Hobbesian premise. In our pre-societal state we simply followed our own desires without care or concern for others. In the state of nature, we pursued our own ends in an exclusively self-interested manner. For Hobbes, the question was why human beings left the state of nature in order to form modern society; Mandeville sets up the 'Enquiry' by asking what he takes to be the more important question of how it is that such societies, even if formed at first for mutual advantage, somehow managed to hold themselves together for any length of time. Perhaps some animals can withhold from pursuing all their desires for a little while in order to keep the peace, but for humans the challenge is particularly acute. They have the double affliction of possessing a wider range of desires compared with other animals as well as having a highly developed rational capacity for figuring out different ways to gratify those desires. The result, Mandeville notes, is that 'no species of animal is, without the curb of government, less capable of agreeing long together in multitudes than that of man'.[46]

An obvious expedient for the management of wild human beings would be force, and a system of punishments. However, he claims that the natural desires of human beings are too strong to be controlled in this manner. Moreover, a system of governance is not a particularly cost-effective strategy for those in charge of the regulation of behaviour. A better—one might say, inspired—idea would be for the members of society to *regulate themselves*:

The chief thing, therefore, which lawgivers and other wise men, that have laboured for the establishment of society, have endeavoured, has been to make the people they were to govern believe that it was more beneficial for everybody to conquer than indulge his appetites, and much better to mind the public than what seemed his private interest.[47]

But why would anyone do that? Given that the self-interested motivational structure is a fundamental natural fact about human beings, one can't really be transformed so as to ignore or forget this fact. The task of the lawmakers looks straightforwardly contradictory: there is nothing in it *for me* to deny my own desires, just as there is nothing in it for me to act in support of other people's interests. In order to pull the trick off, one would have to give the individual a reason to go against their own nature. It would have to be a powerful motive that is immensely satisfying when gratified, since the whole idea is that we forego all our other natural pleasures just to receive this one single benefit. But what would compensate for the loss? What would be an adequate 'reward for the violence which by so doing they of necessity must commit upon themselves'? It is obvious that there is in fact no actual pleasure so intense that it could compensate for all the self-denial this orderly behaviour would entail. Since there was no real reward to be handed out, the lawgivers 'were forced to contrive an imaginary one'.[48] It had to be something on the one hand so attractive that it might offset all the denied passions and yet on the other hand obviously had to be entirely fictitious, so as not to cost the lawgivers anything in reality.

What was required was some special natural feature of the human animal that could be turned towards the project of domestication. The politicians noticed, Mandeville claims, that among the range of human desires, one of the most powerful, and one used most routinely by parents in bringing unruly children to some level of orderly behaviour, was that of positive and negative reinforcement through the mechanisms of praise and shame. We take huge positive motivation from actions that incur flattery from others when we do them, and are adversely motivated from anything that brings blame, mockery, or scorn from those around us. Whether or not the actual action is pleasurable, we take care for how others will react if we are to do it. What was required, then, was a theory that suggested that the very activity of denying one's desires was *itself* somehow a praiseworthy thing to do, and that following one's natural desires was somehow unnatural.

The theory that the political elite invented was that human beings are special. It maintained that human beings are different from all other animals and that they occupy a higher and more exalted status than them in the hierarchy of nature. The theory extolled the 'excellency of our nature above other animals' and particularly with regard to our capacity for rational deliberation and reflection in deciding whether or not to pursue this or that desire. The politicians put it about:

> how unbecoming it was the dignity of such sublime creatures to be solicitous about gratifying those appetites, which they had in common with brutes, and at the same time unmindful of those higher qualities that gave them the preeminence over all visible beings. They indeed confessed that those impulses of nature were very pressing, that it was troublesome to resist, and very difficult wholly to subdue them. But this they only used as an argument to demonstrate how glorious the conquest of them was on the one hand, and how scandalous on the other not to attempt it.[49]

The incredibly radical notion that Mandeville introduces is that at some point in history we were presented with a new and entirely false picture of what our nature actually is, a picture entirely contrary to what our nature really is. Our first natural instinct is to strive to realize our own desires; but we were then presented with a new, second social nature, which claimed the exact opposite: it insisted that the more we *resisted* desires the more we would realize our essentially human character. The only reason why members of the human species would happily indulge in behaviour that is so patently disadvantageous to their individual interests is because of the immense influence of our pride and its gratification in terms of social esteem. Having insisted he is not at all directing his analysis at Christians, Mandeville then goes on to do just that, and to present an account of how the Calvinist model of virtue through moderation and rational self-control was invented in the first place.

As Mandeville notes, the theory works particularly well because our motivation is not just to distinguish ourselves from other animals, but primarily to distinguish ourselves from our fellow human beings. We are all animals, and we all inevitably fail to live up to this new standard of human nature, which is after all an attempt to do the impossible, to eliminate any trace of animality from ourselves. But from the fact of this inevitable failure comes the consequence that human beings will invariably fail to different degrees on different occasions. The lawgivers and politicians took advantage of these facts and 'divided the whole species into two classes'. On the one hand there are the high-minded rational agents who could always control their passions; on the other there are the 'abject, low-minded people, that always hunting after immediate enjoyment, were wholly incapable of self-denial'.[50] Whatever the pleasure there is to be had in sensuality, it pales in comparison to the pleasure of being recognized as a higher kind of person, the possessor of a beautiful soul that might qualify us for an afterlife; whatever the pain involved in denying oneself the basic pleasures that our bodies insist upon, it still is nothing compared to the pain of being thought of by others as being of some kind of lowly sort.

A neat feature of this theory is that it proceeded in a way that recognized and took advantage of something that Mandeville thinks *is* in fact a distinguishing feature of human beings. We are unusually different from other animals, he thinks, in having an entirely overdeveloped need for esteem. Unlike other creatures, we really will live or die to achieve and protect our good names. But this feature gets turned upon itself in our modern world to incredible effect. For in this world the most naturally thrusting of us now want to win reputation according to the rules of this new story about the best human behaviour, with the result that it is *especially* 'the fiercest, most resolute, and best among them' who are motivated to 'endure a thousand inconveniences, and undergo as many hardships, that they may have the pleasure of counting themselves men of the [higher] class, and consequently appropriating to themselves all the excellences they have heard of it'.[51] In this way, the more self-denial that is displayed, the more pay-off in social approval that is garnered. The paradoxical result is that the most self-interested in society are always the ones demonstrating their ability to go without, to deny their own interests.

This was the origin of the very idea of moral behaviour, Mandeville claims. Helping others in need is the paradigmatic example of forgoing the activity of chasing after your own needs. Restraint from violence, giving away one's property, and sexual continence all became the marks of what makes a *good* person, a person who simply does the *right* thing. Any desires that were pursued unchecked, and which were pursued without consideration of how it might affect others, were given a new name: vice. On the other hand, those that were directed at stultifying those desires, and of acting 'contrary to the impulse of nature' itself were given another new name: virtue. Human beings were given a new purpose in life: 'the conquest of [their] own passions out of a rational ambition of being good'.[52] The 'moral virtues are the political offspring which flattery begot upon pride'.[53] Of course, Mandeville can't help but note that a further benefit of this theory was not just that the politicians managed to hold society together. They were not motivated by their own sense of civic duty and responsibility to others. They were keen to produce a marvellously passive populace, a herd of human beings who somehow managed to render themselves bovine. This has many beneficial consequences for those who manage the herd:

> It is evident that the first rudiments of morality, broached by skilful politicians, to render men useful to each other as well as tractable, were chiefly contrived that the ambitious might reap the more benefit from, and govern vast numbers of them with the greater ease and security.[54]

Morality is not just an arbitrary convention but a deliberately installed conspiracy to convince the average human being that they ought not to strive to dominate so that a select few might benefit from the timidity of the rest.

What, then, is moral virtue? Nothing but the pride we take at denying our true animal natures. Why do we take such pride? An entirely contingent historical event whereby a few conspired to control the many for their own benefit. It is worth pausing on this wild claim. All of Mandeville's comments and remarks in the *Fable* could be viewed as aimed towards the lesser sceptical claim that, grand though virtue is, we human beings are routinely unable to realize it. That would have confirmed Mandeville's statement that the *Fable* is a work of the 'strictest morality'. His aim is firstly just to set the bar high in terms of what the definition of morality really is and then to draw the unfortunate conclusion that genuine moral behaviour is a rare phenomenon. In this regard Mandeville could more easily claim his own sincerity and his continuity with the religious tradition.

In the 'Enquiry', though, Mandeville does something very different. Here, his attack is not on our ability to realize the idea of moral virtue, it is an attack on that very idea itself. It is one thing to say that human beings cannot regularly realize a standard, another thing entirely to say that the standard in question is not even real. This scepticism is far more radical. What's more, it presents the reader with a clearly ironic reading of the *Fable*'s agenda. Recall that Mandeville had sought to insulate himself from the accusation of scepticism by claiming that everything that he will write in the *Fable* concerns only human beings insofar as they lack the moral virtue given exclusively by true religion. Yet within those very pages Mandeville then offers a story about how the very idea of moral virtue is a myth. The perspicacious reader is supposed to note immediately that this debunks Mandeville's initial caveat that he is not questioning the virtue of the true Christian. In fact, far from insulating Christian virtue from critique, it is Christian morality that Mandeville has specifically within his sights.[55]

Mandeville clearly has not just politics and morality but religion too as one of his targets. The echoes of the commitments of Hobbes—long thought an atheist in all right-minded circles—would have been unmistakable to his readers. More to the point, everything Mandeville said about the origin of morality fitted with an attack on the origin of Christian morality. The aspiration to become higher beings of angelic purity, the mortification of the flesh, and so on are all the rudiments of that religious system. In his later *Free Thoughts on Religion, The Church and National Happiness* (1720) Mandeville would characterize the role of religion just as the conniving politician had hoped: 'The chief duty then of real religion among Christians consists in a sacrifice of the heart, and is a task of self-denial, with the utmost severity against nature to be performed on ourselves.'[56] Mandeville in fact frequently baits his reader with hints of atheism.[57] For example, in the *Fable* he offers a decisively insincere defence of himself from the accusation of impiety. He cannot be blamed for all these theories, he claims. After all, they just serve to keep the honest individual even more honest, by making them aware of the power of self-deception and the 'secret stratagems of self-love'.[58] Human beings love to hear a theory that presents them well, and they hate to hear one that runs the species down—which, of course, is exactly in keeping with his theory that we are governed by our pride. As an aside he remarks that some theories are so unlikely that they probably wouldn't have been taken up at all if it weren't for the benefits that might accrue to us if they just so happened to turn out to be true. As a good example, he can't help but note that a good example might be the idea of an immortal soul that is preserved into an afterlife.[59]

In his *Various Thoughts on the Occasion of a Comet* (1682), Pierre Bayle had pointed out that astonishing events shouldn't be interpreted as divine signs sent to protect humanity from atheism. There were in fact many ways in which societies could protect themselves from atheism:

> ... [The] magistrates concerned with civil affairs and with those of religion took great care to keep men in a state of dependence by means of the brake that is the fear of gods. It has been recognized in all times that religion was one of the bonds of society and that the subjects were never kept in a state of obedience better than when one could have the minister of the gods intervene. . . . This is why politics wished to have managed carefully all that would be suited to foment the zeal for religion in men's minds.[60]

The message is clear enough: religion can and has been used as an essential form of social control. Politicians require subjects in a 'state of obedience', and that is handily what religion provides.

Key to Mandeville's debunking of morality and religion, then, is a return to Montaigne's central claim about human beings—that of the role played by *pride* and the drive for social esteem. What is pride?

> Pride is that natural faculty by which every mortal that has understanding over-values, and imagines better things of himself than any impartial judge, thoroughly acquainted with all his qualities and circumstances, could allow him. We are possessed of no other quality so beneficial to society, and so necessary to render it wealthy and flourishing as this, yet it is that which is most generally detested.[61]

Mandeville would have been familiar with the Earl of Rochester's infamous poem, 'A Satire against Reason and Mankind' (1679), where Rochester argued that not only are human beings distinguished from other animals by virtue of their pride, but that the particular form of pride is that human beings love to think of themselves as *rational*:

> Were I (who to my cost already am
> One of those strange, prodigious creatures, man)
> A spirit free to choose, for my own share
> What case of flesh and blood I pleased to wear,
> I'd be a dog, a monkey, or a bear,
> Or anything but that vain animal,
> Who is so proud of being rational.[62]

Mandeville's account of pride is essentially Erasmian—it presents it as a form of ignorance and folly. By defining pride as a capacity for *over*valuing, he claims that its basic function is to represent ourselves other than as we really are. It is our prideful natures, then, that make us so singularly interested in the opinion of others, since the good opinion of others confirms the inflated value we have of ourselves. Pride therefore inaugurates the economy of esteem, where we all become traders in praise, flattery, and shame. La Rochefoucauld had seen the centrality of pride to behaviour, as had the French theologian and moralist Jacques Abbadie. Abbadie went further and anticipated Mandeville's situating of pride at the centre of all valuable human achievements:

> It is this desire to obtain an esteem in the world, that renders us affable
> and complaisant, obliging and civil; that makes us love decency and
> sweetness of conversation. . . . [T]he finest arts, the most lofty sci-
> ences, the wisest governments, the most just establishments, in gen-
> eral, most that is admirable in reasonable society, proceeds from this
> natural desire of glory. . . . Let us not fancy, that our own corruption
> and concupiscence brought this excellent benefit to mankind; doubt-
> less the wise instructions of the author of nature had the chiefest hand
> in this matter.[63]

Abbadie sees immediately the controversial implications of his view and suggests that the only answer is that there must be a divine providence at play behind the scenes in allowing human beings' frailties to have such a positive role in the organization of life. Mandeville repeats Abbadie's appeal to providence at the end of the 'Enquiry': thank heavens, Mandeville says, that it appears that the Lord has made it such that through all our wickedness and vice we might actually end up better off—could there be any better proof of the existence of our divine benefactor? Anyone who had perceived the atheist implications of the essay could be in no doubt as to the profoundly ironic tone of Mandeville's rhetoric here. Mandeville sees religion and politics conspiring together upon human beings' natural weakness so as to co-opt them into a masochistic cult that worships self-denial. The name of the peculiar institution they set up for the purposes of social control is called morality.

No astute reader could have been mistaken as to Mandeville's true intentions or taken in by his protestations of piety. William Law shows some acuity of mind when he ridicules Mandeville's claim at the beginning of the 'Enquiry' that he is talking only of the nature of human beings without religion:

> The absurdity of this apology will appear from hence; Let us suppose that you had been making an *Enquiry into the Origin of the World*, and should declare that it arose from a *causal concourse of atoms*, and then tell your scrupulous reader, by way of excuse, that you did not mean the world, which *Jews* and *Christians* dwell upon, but that which is inhabited *by man in his state of nature and ignorance of the true deity*. Could any thing be more weak or senseless than such an Apology? Yet it is exactly the same as that which you have here made.[64]

Law sees through Mandeville's pretence immediately (which, it should be said, was exactly Mandeville's hope). He compares Mandeville to a hypothetical writer describing Lucretius's notoriously atheistical account of how the universe came into being—that is, randomly, through a chance 'concourse of atoms'. Law asks: could we really think that this radical theory, once stated, can be taken back with the qualification that is true for heathens but false for Christians? The universe was made by God or it was not; it emerged randomly or it did not. When Mandeville speaks of the origin of moral virtue, Law claims, he does not *really* mean 'virtue as it is practiced by heathens', or 'counterfeit virtue'. Mandeville just means to debunk virtue itself, and *all* our talk of 'virtue'.

The 'Enquiry' is ultimately a wicked inversion of Calvinist theology. Calvin had warned of the dangers of pride and false virtue; instead, he recommended self-denial and moderation as the path to true virtue and obedience to God's laws. In the 'Enquiry' Mandeville represents Calvin's cure as the politician's con. Self-denial and moderation are not the cure to pride; pride is the passion that inclines us to believe in self-denial and moderation in the first place. Believing ourselves to be paragons of self-denial and champions of moderation is the way in which we think of ourselves as a higher species of animal. It is when we are following Calvin's cure for our prideful corruption that we then are at our most prideful. Within the Calvinist system there is a tight connection between social order and order of one's own passions. Religion's recommendation of moderation is the means to both. Mandeville slyly endorses both these claims. Christian religion *is* the means to self-governance, and self-governance *is* the means to social order—that is why politicians invented and promoted Christian religion in the first place. This is not exactly what Calvin had in mind.

In *The Praise of Folly*, Erasmus had said that reason 'shouts out her prohibitions until she is hoarse' before we instead follow whatever our desires demand.[65] In *Various Thoughts on the Occasion of a Comet*, Bayle had commented that we might 'let a man be as reasonable a creature as you like; it is no less true that he almost never acts in accordance with his principles'.[66] Mandeville echoes these thoughts with his claim that it is part of our nature that we are just not the kind of animals who are able to let rational principles govern our actual behaviour: 'This contradiction in the frame of man is the reason that the theory of virtue is so well understood, and the practice of it so rarely to be met with.'[67] The contradiction in the frame of man, as we have seen, is very deeply instilled. It is a contradiction between what human beings *are* and what human beings like to think they are. No wonder virtue is so rarely met with, since the very idea of moral virtue was introduced as an impossible ambition, one to keep human beings endlessly striving in their self-denial and thereby made immeasurably easier to handle. Human beings, it turns out, will meekly defer the gratification of their real needs and desires forever if offered imaginary rewards. Yet more paradoxical still is that this masochistic self-deception turns *to our benefit* in the long run, in allowing us to get along and prosper in society. He says that this contradiction in the frame of man is not in fact 'injurious' but rather a 'compliment to human nature'.[68] Mandeville then has one final paradox to offer. It is that natural facts about what human beings are like—what role pride plays in the natural economy of their passions—have ultimately led us to invent fictions with which to constrain one another's behaviour. Moral talk is perhaps more than a useful fiction, it is in a sense a *natural* fiction, a peculiarly distinct manifestation of the human animal's tendency to self-deception. Perhaps in human beings the myth of morality just is the exercise of the human being's capacity for self-deception par excellence. We can no more do without it than we can cease to be human. But for all that, morality *is* a fiction, and Mandeville wants us to know it.

CHAPTER SEVEN

Politics and the Ideology of Virtue

Hypocrisy is a kind of homage that vice pays to virtue.

—LA ROCHEFOUCAULD, *MAXIMS*, 5:218

FROM WHAT HAS BEEN SEEN so far, one might think that Mandeville's motives for writing were first and foremost intellectual. His works were intended to be appreciated in the cool hours of leisure by an educated audience and were designed to amuse by challenging set notions of human nature and ethical life. One could take the view that *The Fable of the Bees* was primarily a work of philosophical anthropology and one could see Mandeville as a detached observer exposing the follies of mankind. The *Fable* is a humorous tale about human beings and the nature of moral behaviour in commercial society. If there are any further motives to be suspected, it might be those of literary ambition and perhaps a love of mischief. Yet there is an entirely different prism through which Mandeville's writings can be read. Most of his writings were made as direct interventions in the political situation in Great Britain in the first three decades of the eighteenth century. There is a case to be made that such direct political engagement was frequently Mandeville's primary motive for writing.[1] Mandeville's style was social satire, and his intellectual passion was philosophical anthropology, but his motives were political. The events that occasioned the writing of *The Grumbling*

Hive in 1705, the first edition of *The Fable of the Bees* in 1714, and its reissue in 1723 were all local political events taking place in London. What's more, when the scandal regarding the *Fable* broke in 1723 it was because it was caught up in events in which Mandeville had no hand, and his subsequent notoriety was not directly a result of his theories at all.[2]

In the simplest terms, Mandeville was a Whig propagandist. While the distinction between the Tory and Whig factions of Parliament is crucial to understanding late seventeenth- and early eighteenth-century British culture, the terms nevertheless lack any succinct definition, as we shall see. It is perhaps more straightforward to explain the difference in terms of their attitudes towards the Glorious Revolution of 1688. William III was invited to the throne of England, which is an extraordinary enough event, one adequately explained only by the desperate demand for stability in England following the preceding forty years of religious and social uncertainty. The Civil War and the Protectorate under Oliver Cromwell had, among other things, made the ruling property-owning class aware of the precarity of their social and economic position. The Restoration of Charles II in 1660 had brought back a series of ideological commitments that this class hoped would solidify the political hierarchy in England and their own futures with it. They argued for the divine right of kings, the crucial importance of respecting hereditary succession, and the vital recognition that political stability requires the authority of the monarch. The stability of England depended on the idea that the authority of the Crown could never be justifiably violated again by violent uprising, and that citizens thereby owed the monarch the doctrine of so-called 'passive obedience'. These commitments served the interests of both the landed class and the Anglican Church alike.

The issue of religious tolerance had been fatal to this new ideology, however. Charles's successor, James II, had sought repeatedly to introduce new elements of religious toleration into English society. These moves towards toleration were perceived as motivated by a covert agenda, and it was thought that James's manoeuvres were aimed towards re-establishing royal absolutism. They were also perceived as a means to the end of detaching the throne from the Protestant Church of England, thereby making space for the reintroduction of the Catholic Church into the fabric of society. In the eyes of James's opponents these manoeuvres offered the double threat of royal tyranny and the return of a collapse of Church and state. Whether this was James's intention is debatable, yet it is undeniable that his high-handed methods for securing his aims were such that conflict was unavoidable. When he produced what many presumed would be a likely Catholic heir, tensions rose inexorably and a return to civil war seemed imminent. It was in this context that representatives of the ruling political class took the extraordinary step of inviting the Dutch monarch, William of Orange, to take up the throne of England. What transpired was a mostly peaceful transition of power, when James fled to France and William acceded to the throne, under the banner of securing freedom from religious tyranny. The Glorious Revolution in 1688 was a precarious attempt at securing that liberty in perpetuity.

Mandeville arrived in England probably in the early 1690s, his prospects in Rotterdam having been ruined as a result of his participation in the Costerman affair. He no doubt saw straight away that his interests aligned with those of the Whig faction in Parliament. Whigs were the political party more inclined to be concerned with individual liberty, freedom of expression, toleration, and the resistance of tyranny in general. Yet this would be to oversimplify matters. Mandeville was an opportunistic writer who naturally found himself aligned with Whig interests, yet it remains a matter of speculation as to whether he really was a Whig or—perhaps more pertinently—whether any Whigs would have wished to count him as one of their own. He has sometimes been identified as an 'independent Whig', and this has some truth to it, though it would not be wrong if one instead described him as merely occasionally Whiggish. There were few Whigs who would be willing to own to any of Mandeville's views on morality, human nature, religion, and society.[3]

As I have been urging, Mandeville has a unified picture of human nature and how it plays out in various spheres of life, and so he couldn't express one Whiggish political view without accompanying it with some scandalous opinion, and so could never occupy a central place in the Whig political cadres. It is also unlikely that he held any such ambition. A better interpretive assumption might be that Mandeville was motivated more than anything by the need to promote religious tolerance. His intellectual temperament, however, forbade him from expressing it in anything like these straightforward terms. He could only ever be an ally to toleration by presenting himself as a radical outlier from received norms. And yet the strategy clearly risked triggering a reactionary response, since the case against political absolutism would be made by an immoral rogue. It cannot be that Mandeville didn't perceive this risk. He often mentions the paradox that, if his theories regarding human beings' self-deceiving and hypocritical natures are correct, then the predicted response is that his theories should be universally rejected. His theory maintained that human beings are unable to see themselves as they are, and that they engage in endless moralistic rationalizing in an effort to perpetuate their self-deception. It is difficult, then, to see Mandeville as in the business of changing hearts and minds. So long as he introduced a reading public to the very idea that human nature is quite different from how it was assumed to be by the dominant public discourse, his aims would be realized well enough.

The England that Mandeville discovered was to his liking. It was a place where he could make a living. For one thing, William's rise to the British throne encouraged an influx of Dutch immigrants, including many physicians. The first mention we have of Mandeville is in the 1693 records of the College of Physicians, who note him as one of several medics practising in London without their approval.[4] He would therefore also have found that England was not a straightforwardly tolerant place in which to live. However, this does indicate that by this time his practice was established and successful enough to come to the attention of the authorities, and he wasn't subsequently denied a licence to practise and deported, as others were. He married Ruth Elizabeth Laurence in 1698, his wife giving birth to a child later that year.[5] The medical establishment was not the only part of society suspicious of new practices imported from abroad. He would be aware, however, of the attention that was being paid to outsiders and the concern regarding their presence. Mandeville may well have noticed the anti-Dutch pamphlet *Aesop at Islington* (1699), discussed previously, or similar publications. The message in them was clear enough: the recent influx of the Dutch and their luxury products would inevitably lead to a movement of wealth out of Britain, and the British would find themselves the dupes left wearing Dutch clogs out of economic necessity rather than fashion. Some might have noted though it was in fact Britain's reputation for religious tolerance that was a factor in attracting the skilled migrant labour that was helping it to thrive.[6]

Mandeville's fortunes were to some degree tied to the English perception of the Dutch in general and of William III in particular. The irony couldn't have been lost on him. The cause of Mandeville's banishment from Rotterdam was his involvement in the Costerman affair, and Mandeville's downfall had been decided by the influence of William in support of his favourite over that of Mandeville. As a consequence, Mandeville emigrated to a country that turned out to be ruled by that very same man. Mandeville perhaps thought that William III ruling in England wasn't quite the same proposition as his ruling in the Dutch Republic. England's interest in William was that he might be a source of security for the Church of England, the independence of Parliament, and the liberty of its people; William's interest in England was that it might provide a source of revenue for his Continental wars against France. Mandeville must have had mixed feelings in this regard—he had seen first-hand the effects of Louis XIV's revocation of the Edict of Nantes, and the expulsion of Protestants (like his teacher Pierre Bayle) to Rotterdam. Whatever he thought of William's own motives, Mandeville saw in William the best supporter of the kind of society that would be tolerant of 'freethinking', not least his own.

Mandeville's motives for aligning with the Whigs are, then, straightforward enough, even if the division between 'Whig' and 'Tory' is not. Factions developed within each party, sometimes moving one group of the Whigs closer to the Tories in their views. Some general attitudes can be discerned as associated with one group rather than another. The Tories in general were anxious about the economic and social changes reshaping England and were concerned to advocate in favour of a return to civic virtue, and a conception of the unity of the nation that this would bring with it. In general, Tory 'sympathies lay with the men of the land—the peers and gentry living upon Britain's rolling acres, natural leaders of a stratified, deferential, and unitary society'.[7] The events of the previous three decades had led to an inevitable split within the Tory Party between Jacobites, who remained loyal to the ousted James and who viewed the Stuart line as the rightful monarchs, and those who were willing to accept William for the sake of order and stability. While the former camp was seen as sympathetic to the reintroduction of Catholicism, the latter camp had made its peace with the Glorious Revolution and valued the stability brought under William (and later Queen Anne). The Glorious Revolution was seen by some Tories as an opportunity to bring about new ideals in English politics and social life in general. There were, of course, many Tories who *professed* to be members of the latter camp while secretly being members of the former. Mandeville writes as if he is of the view that a Tory should be assumed to be a crypto-Jacobite until proven otherwise.

The Whigs, on the other hand, were those more straightforwardly enthusiastic about the Glorious Revolution and the innovations in English society that followed. Yet they too were not without their internal divisions and complications. One of the key issues was with regard to how the Glorious Revolution had happened. For some Whigs it had simply been an unavoidable reaction ever since James had threatened to overstep his domain and force a change in the constitution in a tyrannical manner. His 'abdication' further supported the claim that it had been a matter of practical necessity. There was a philosophical argument explaining why it had to happen, one which derived from the work of the philosopher John Locke. Locke's writing implied that the actions of James had constituted an attack on the natural rights of England's citizens, and that as a result the contract between subjects and their king had been broken. While for some Whigs this was now an opportunity for republicanism to gain a permanent foothold in English politics, other Whigs thought that this argument was a step too far. It implied a decisive shift in political authority away from the Crown and towards those who were supposed to be its subjects. On such Lockean grounds any wild populist reordering of the political structure of society might be justified. Internal Whig divisions also emerged therefore, often along lines sympathetic to Tory concerns, such as that of retaining the established place of the landed gentry within the social, economic, and political hierarchy.

Tories ultimately accepted William's ascent to the throne on the grounds of the impossibility of defending James's absconding from it. The civil war that had been averted was too powerful a fact to ignore. Yet certain mental gymnastics were required in order to maintain that the divine right of kings, so long a Tory commitment, had been respected throughout this transition of power. They could make a case for it by virtue of the fact that William's wife, Mary, was James's daughter—one just had to ignore the existence of James's son. Later the Act of Settlement (1701)—still in place today—would declare that no Catholic could ever hold the Crown, but even then the very idea of the divine right of kings had begun to take on a strange position in Tory consciousness. Those unwilling to excite themselves into supporting Jacobite uprisings would have to ignore the political realities of the new world after the Glorious Revolution. Those still harking after the divine right of kings had to ignore the fact that things had changed, and—insofar as the avoidance of social breakdown was concerned—changed utterly. For Mandeville there is a special kind of pernicious hypocrisy inherent in this outlook, what Isaac Kramnick has referred to as the 'politics of nostalgia'.[8] Rhetoric arguing for a return to past values was combined with a desire to maintain the status quo within a contemporary society that had, as a matter of fact, developed very different values. Mandeville's attitude to what we would now think of as conservatism is not at all uncritical—a core part of his attack on the political scene will be its impossible fondness for myths of the past. His critique is focused upon two camps, however. On the one hand, he is opposed to those who think that the return to some previous form of government is on the table, when in fact the material conditions of modern life have changed so radically as to render that impossible; on the other hand, he is no less opposed to those who are fully aware of this contradiction but who disingenuously use the politics of nostalgia for strategic aims. Mandeville would target ignorant and knowing hypocrites alike.

Within this highly complex political arena, a key strategic battle emerged with regard to the question as to who could own the language of *virtue*. A widely read anonymous pamphlet *Reflexions upon the Moral State of the Nation* (1701) argued that there was corruption throughout the highest strata of society, corruption that would inevitably undermine the entire nation:

> For such an *ill complexion of affairs* in a State, resembles that dyscracy [bodily disorder], or universal distemper of humours in a natural body; whereof every one is physician enough to foresee the event: and the abounding of vice in any nation, doth not only as a meritorious cause sooner or later pull down the *divine vengeance* upon it, but in its natural course directly tends to make people as *wretched* and *miserable*, as they have been *base* and *vile*, in all the instances of wickedness and folly.[9]

The author of this pamphlet insisted on the need for broad educational reforms for the purposes of improving the moral character of the nation—the 'reformation of manners'—from the bottom up. Mandeville would no doubt have been struck by the medical metaphor, not to mention the blasé confidence with which it is predicted that indulging licentious pleasures will naturally make us unhappy. If the analysis for rectifying the immoral effects were to be undertaken from the bottom up, the diagnosis of the cause of those effects was just the opposite. The author of the *Reflexions* had quoted *Oceana* (1656) by the political theorist James Harrington. Harrington had been keen to point out how the determination of a nation's political and moral character ran from its highest echelons down to its lowest, since 'the vices of the people are from their governors, those of the governors from their laws and orders, and those of the laws and orders from their legislators'.[10] *Oceana* was an image of a state opposed to the one put forward in Hobbes's *Leviathan* (1651), and opposed in particular to Hobbes's picture of political authority residing absolutely in the sovereign. Instead, Harrington's vision was one whereby order was maintained by way of power residing with the landed gentry and aristocracy. The proper functioning of the state was guaranteed by the fact that the legislators themselves had the national interest as *their* interest, and were guided by that first and foremost. Since James had demonstrated how aspirations to religious tyranny can be manifested by a sovereign, it was clearly up to someone else to uphold virtue and thereby maintain the good of the nation.

In the same year of the *Reflexions*, the writer Charles Davenant wrote his popular 'Essay on the Balance of Power' (1701) and claimed—despite his own Whig sympathies—that the problem of corruption was one that had already set in thoroughly within English society. Once again, the metaphor of an illness in the body is deployed:

> There is no truer mark that a government is near its utter destruction, than when the people are observed to be careless and unconcerned at a time when they are pressed and encompassed with dangers of the highest nature. This State lethargy is such an apoplectic symptom as is commonly the forerunner of death to the body politic.[11]

However, for Davenant the complacency was not towards the threat of Louis and French tyranny overtaking their native soil—it was rather a threat from within. A new condition had arisen England, one which was causing the highest born in the land to have their concerns directed from the good of the nation to their own personal gain:

> Many of the first rank, for birth, parts, title, and fortune, instead of bending their thoughts how to serve their country, are either meanly contriving how a change may be made whereby they may better themselves, or, which is as bad, they imagine all will be well if a few of their friends are at the helm, as if any good to the public could be expected from a little shifting of hands.[12]

Davenant maintained that the 'little public spirit that remained among us is in a manner quite extinguished', and that instead 'self-interest runs through all our actions, and mixes in all our councils and if truly examined is the very rise and spring of all our present mischiefs'.[13] Davenant captured—or perhaps even created—the spirit of the times, which was that things were changing too quickly and for the worse. The main effect of this acceleration anxiety was that greed and self-interest were undermining the fabric of social solidarity and national strength. What was required was the creation of a virtuous citizen. Here the notion of 'virtue' involved was that of civic virtue, the participation of an individual in the form of governing when motivated by a prioritization of the public good over whatever private interests one might have. In 1696 Davenant had written 'An Essay on Public Virtue', where he argued that a neo-Harringtonian concern for civic duty and the common good was not just morally correct but also necessary for the establishment of a strong and prosperous state:

> Where ever this public spirit reigns: and where this zeal for the common good lives in the minds of men; that state will flourish in riches and power, and where ever it declines or is set at nought: weakness, disorder and poverty must be expected.[14]

Especially noteworthy is Davenant's evocation of the success and failures of ancient societies. Sparta, Athens, and Rome, it was claimed, had thrived primarily as an effect of the love of 'native soil' and prioritization of the public interest by its citizenry. Rome lost its way, he claimed, and nearly fell to Catiline's plotting just because its citizens had become enamoured of the possibility of accruing great personal wealth rather than establishing a powerful state. The position in eighteenth-century England was now little different, and 'the busy men of the town . . . who talk and appear most about, have a different interest than that of their country'.[15] They are interested in whether *their* fortunes might be affected by the fortunes of England, and that is the full extent of their patriotism. If and when the pursuit of private interest fails to align with the good of the country, then the country is lost. The moral weakening of the population is a sure preamble to national weakness, since 'where there is a general neglect of national interest [Englishmen] grow luxurious, proud, false, and effeminate: and a people so depraved is commonly the prey of some neighbour, seasoned with more wise and better principles'.[16]

While Davenant insisted upon harking to the past for guidance, the question of just which ancient city-state a modern one should emulate would become an increasingly tense theme. François Fénelon's *Telemachus* (1699) became an enormously influential work, second only to the Bible in terms of its publication rate in the eighteenth century. It told the tale of Odysseus's son Telemachus, and the education he receives from his teacher, Mentor, as he learns to become a prince. The work is supposed to offer a kind of virtuous riposte to Machiavelli's political advice in *The Prince*. Mentor is adamant that the path to righteousness is the Spartan one, whereby virtue is cultivated through the elimination of vice. Vice is eliminated by national self-discipline and the self-denial of luxuries. Mentor and Telemachus arrive at a land called Salente, and Mentor is afforded the opportunity to instruct its ruler how to govern. Mentor wastes no time in identifying the sources of vice: foreign luxury. He prohibits the importation of luxury goods that adorn people's persons and homes. He insists upon the regulation of dress and diet across the land; he instructs the people to train themselves to moderate their desires and do without fancy sauces for their dishes. Mentor 'endeavoured to retrench that pomp and luxury by which the morals of a people are corrupted: he aimed at reducing everything to a noble simplicity and frugality'.[17] Davenant similarly saw that the corruption that had overtaken Rome and Salente was starting to take a hold in England, and he thought that the disciplined and self-denying virtue that the Spartans had exemplified was desperately needed.

What factors led to this dangerous situation whereby England was now so willingly enfeebling itself in a morass of moral depravity? The reality was that William's reign in England had changed the nature of national governance forever, and any defender of William had to come to terms with those changes.[18] The Glorious Revolution had instigated a financial revolution that in turn radically altered the political scene in England. William's invasion had been, of course, motivated by a desire to protect England for Protestantism and from a potential invasion from the French Catholic king. But William arguably lacked any particular interest in England beyond his own broader geopolitical concerns. He saw in England a source of further tax revenues that could sustain his fight against Louis in Continental Europe and thereby considered the arrangement to be of mutual benefit. It was to this end that a land tax was introduced, much to the annoyance of the landed gentry, who had in any case been seeing diminishing rental returns in recent decades. The cost of the subsequent wars was enormous, however—nearly £5 million a year, 75 per cent of government expenditure. By the end of 1713, government debt was £30 million.[19]

In the 1690s financial instruments were created to generate newly required revenue. The private individual, whether of great or meagre means, was invited to invest in the government for a return that was both generous and guaranteed. Soon, investment in William's war effort poured in from every quarter, with the predictable result that the financially buoyed William increased the scope and ambition of his campaigns. Before too long, the government owed enormous sums to a tiny section of the public. Soon it involved figures that the government would be simply unable to repay if investors looked to recall their investment. Not only that, but the investments were identified as financial products, things that themselves could become the object of trade, just like any other property. Government behaviour was now tied to the financial markets in a way that it never had been before, and there was a real transfer of power away from the traditional branches of government. Moreover, since the prospect of their continuing to provide a return to investors was tied to the prospects of William successfully continuing his campaign against Louis, a certain demographic of society had an interest in perpetuating the war, a motive that was neither the interest of patriotism nor opposition to monarchical tyranny nor freedom of religious expression. The success or failure of William's campaign, and the lives of the soldiers fighting in it, could be a source of enormous personal wealth for private individuals if they predicted the course of the war correctly.

A further aspect to the financial revolution was that it soon became government policy that the proper way to manage the debt to investors was not to generate sufficient income so as to pay it all back—the figure had grown just too large. Instead, the aim was merely to generate the means to pay back the interest on the investment, with the capital sum left untouched. It was in this manner that the British national debt was born, soon to become a permanent reality. An institution for the management of this debt was required, and the Bank of England came into being in 1694—another permanent reality. The Bank of England was only the most notable bank to come into existence during this period—there were twenty-four private banks in London alone in 1725, twenty-nine in 1754, forty-two in 1770, and sixty-two in 1792.[20] In 1711 the South Sea Company was formed and granted sole access to South American markets in exchange for taking on £9 million of the government debt. The shares in the company drew enormous interest from a range of members of society, as the highest nobleman and

the middling merchant alike saw the same financial opportunities. They can reasonably be said to have been equally neglectful
of the risks.

Apart from the questionable probity of a nation willing itself into
permanent debt, there was yet another unanticipated consequence.
A previous form of parliamentary opposition from factions opposed
to government domination had been simply to refuse to endorse
the collection of taxes. Now, however, refusal to gather taxes didn't
merely threaten to impede the government's ambitions, it would
undermine its ability to pay back the interest on the loans to investors. The threat had worked previously only because it was of the
non-nuclear variety—were it to be wielded now, however, it could
bring about a financial crisis that would have hurt all parties' interests catastrophically. In the eyes of many, the national debt functioned to de-tooth opposition to the ruling party and undermined
the checks and balances of successful politics; at the very least it
could be said that the threat of the debt meant that opposition parties were newly and permanently disadvantaged in their strategic
options. William had financialized English politics in a way that
had previously been unimaginable. The monarch, Parliament, the
gentry, and the merchant class were now all merchants of power,
trading with one another in increasingly complex ways.

A difficulty for those troubled by this new destabilization of the
political order was that things had undeniably improved. That economic prosperity had been generated for England (now Great
Britain, after the Act of Union in 1707) was undeniable. That Act
of Union had, among other things, opened up a free trade zone
for British manufacturing. England had already been a relatively
unregulated market compared with European competitors, with
comparatively fewer customs and taxes for goods making their way
across the country. In the late seventeenth century, England had
become for the first time a grain exporter: rising from only two
thousand quarters per annum in the 1660s, English grain exports
reached over three hundred thousand quarters per annum between
1675 and 1677, and that figure continued to rise until about the
middle of the eighteenth century.[21] Agricultural improvements
meant that England became one of the main cereal producers for
Europe. This, however, brought considerable problems of its own:

wages for workers were increasing as competition with manufacturing grew; a huge surplus of grain meant that prices continued to fall; grain that wasn't exported was directed into the new distilling business. The gin craze of the early eighteenth century and its attached alcohol-related social problems were caused more by a rural surplus of grain than by an urban deficit in propriety. Land taxes were introduced from the 1690s onwards, though rents themselves were sluggish.[22] The consequence was that farmers were financially vulnerable, and the rents paid by those farmers to the landowners suffered as well.[23] Wool production was one of the largest industries, but even exports of non-cloth goods doubled between 1660 and 1700.[24] Financial pressure thus fell on the countryside, while the cities boomed. The war effort also afforded enormous opportunities to individuals and their employees. For a single example, the ironmonger Ambrose Crowley employed a workforce of nearly a thousand, housing them and providing for their medical care himself, financially secure by virtue of the demand set by the navy.

Things were in general looking distinctly brighter for a new professional class that seemed to rise up from nowhere. This new demographic of merchants and lawyers, medics and civil servants, found themselves at the centre of bustling economic activity. Moreover, they began to recognize themselves as a distinct social group, neither aristocrats nor those isolated few who earned their wealth from the land. Nor were they part of the great majority who provided manual labour on that land. They had their own financial interests that were to a large degree independent of their country's economic history. They had their own trade, their own styles and desirable commodities, their own culture and language of commerce. In this new economic climate, they were the group that increasingly appeared to be at the centre of power. It would be naïve to say that prior to William's reign, economic concerns hadn't determined political ideology, but what changed was the *kind* of economic factors at stake, and the immediate political consequences of that change were profound. This generated an entirely new anxiety in British political life, one regarding the rising relevance of what we now call the financial sector and its impact on society more broadly. Later, in his *Free Thoughts on Religion, the Church, and National Happiness* (1720) Mandeville stated

Harrington's old maxim that 'dominion follows property', and claimed that so it had been for all recorded history.[25] But Mandeville was being disingenuous here—he knew that the meaning of the maxim had changed utterly. By 'property' Harrington had of course meant land; Mandeville knew that 'property' now meant simply capital, and that this was something new, something that had been wrenched free from the British soil.

Jonathan Swift, too, noted what was happening, and wrote that these new military men who were populating William's forces were not quite the heroes of old; they were rather 'a species of men quite different from any that were ever known before the Revolution' in that these new men's 'fortunes lie in funds and stocks; so that power, which according to the old maxim was used to follow land, is now gone over to money'.[26] The anxiety felt in early eighteenth-century England, then, was perhaps one with which we are not unfamiliar today. Mandeville's opponents argued that the creation of public debt meant that financial practices (and their increasingly international character) would govern national political institutions. Whereas the constraint of international finance upon national self-determination was offensive enough, they would also claim that global financial practices would ultimately destabilize political institutions. Whether one considers the South Sea Bubble of 1720, the stock market crash of 1927, or the financial crisis of 2008, one might concede that they had a point. Yet it was difficult to ignore the fact the new commercial society was, for all its short-term financial catastrophes, on a clear trajectory towards prosperity. Early eighteenth-century Great Britain was the original case study for both the promise of and the problems with capitalism's relationship with politics.

It is within this heated economic and political scene that an eleven-page pamphlet appeared anonymously, entitled *The Pamphleteers: A Satire* (1703). Its author was Bernard Mandeville. The occasion for this, his first real publication for the mass market, was the death of King William III the previous year. Its title page features a quote from Juvenal: 'semper ego auditor tantum?' (am I always to be a listener?). Mandeville had been in the country for a decade or so, and had to date not written much. What he had written had been most likely for the benefit of a small few of his acquaintances. Here, though, the epigram is a declaration of intent: he is stating his impatience. He has been a Dutch immigrant working to fit in and build a place in British society, but now he is announcing his desire to speak about his new home. What is remarkable is that *The Pamphleteers* is a defence of the memory of William, the very man who had instigated Mandeville's flight from Rotterdam after the Costerman affair. Mandeville had different feelings about William as a British monarch, or at least he saw good enough reason to put any negative feelings he bore towards him aside for the purpose of current political concerns. This goes some way to explaining Mandeville's enthusiasm for William III in his early political pamphlets. It was not so much enthusiasm for William per se as it was for any head of state in the British political system. The mixed monarchy system in Britain entailed a curtailment of the powers a monarch such as William had wielded in the Dutch Republic. If we take him at his word in this pamphlet, Mandeville's concern is that opposition to the reign of the new monarch, Queen Anne, might gradually lead to conditions of religious intolerance, specifically of the Catholic variety. Anne, who was thirty-seven when she took the throne, had no surviving children, and though a devout Protestant, the question of her suitability to produce an heir and continue the Protestant line within British royalty was pressing.

In *The Pamphleteers* Mandeville engages in some quite obvious and, it must be said, not particularly impressive versifying extolling William's greatness, and condemning those who would pour scorn on his memory. He reminds his new countrymen that William was all that stood between England and French Catholic tyranny. William prevailed militarily, while the domestic politicians did nothing:

> Whilst on the attempt vain politicians gazed,
> The work was done, and Europe stood amazed.
> He reaped the glory, we the benefit,
> But oh! How soon can English men forget?[27]

The problem, Mandeville points out—as perhaps he thought only a foreigner could—is that Britain was 'a grumbling nation, never at ease'.[28] This will be his main sociological observation of the British. Davenant had written in the 1690s that the nation was sick, corrupted, weak, and unwell. Mandeville wonders: what exactly could he be talking about? When *he* looks around he sees a prospering society vigorously contesting international wars and, what's more, triumphing in them. Why this constant refrain that things are going so very badly? Why so much anxiety regarding the health of the body politic? Mandeville has spent enough time in the country to grasp that the theme of the decline of virtue had become the dominant form of political rhetoric, aimed at generating a kind of moral panic regarding the shifting flow of power.

Mandeville attempts to turn that rhetoric on its head whenever he can. In his rendering of the fable 'The Frogs Asking for a King' he had presented the British as ignorantly asking for any king—even James II—to oppress them, complaining that their own condition was too bad to bear. In *The Pamphleteers* he asks his readers to see just what is going on when some complain of William's distribution of gifts—accusations of corruption are in fact motivated by crypto-Jacobitism:

> Under pretence of railing at his grants,
> They vent their spleen against all Protestants.[29]

In the later *Free Thoughts* Mandeville concedes that Great Britain is in fact unwell, but not from what its detractors claim. It is suffering from the very medical condition in which Mandeville himself happens to specialize. Great Britain is suffering from hypochondria—a general negative disturbance of mood without any discernible physical conditions underlying it: 'Should any state physician behold our goodly countenance, and have felt our low dispirited pulse, examine into the real cause of all our grievances, he must infallibly pronounce the nation hypp'd.'[30] It is a constant refrain in Mandeville's writings that the popular consciousness of the British nation is genuinely unhappy, but that the source of this unhappiness is not anything to do with reality and is instead a kind of national neurosis. The country's material condition has never been better, in Mandeville's view, but there is a relentless narrative put forward that things have never been worse. More importantly, though, Mandeville wants to point out that any nostalgic narrative is in reality a cover for the protection of the interests of a certain class of society, rather than a principled argument for how a modern society ought to be run. He has no time for moral arguments for a return to what we would now call a rent-seeking economy run by the 1 per cent. The reality, he thinks, is that power and money were being diverted from their traditional beneficiaries to new ones—the resulting moral rhetoric, calls for austerity, and demands for the restoration of national greatness were merely the panicked propaganda of a ruling class on the way out.[31]

This puts an entirely different context on the publication of *The Grumbling Hive* in 1705. Of course, that poem's purpose was just what it appeared to be—a comic diatribe against those bees who would grumble their way to virtue, and render the nation impoverished along the way. Yet 1705 was also the year of a general election in England, and so it becomes clear that it is first and foremost a *political* pamphlet in the spirit of *The Pamphleteers*. It was to counteract the increasingly audible attacks on John Churchill, the Duke of Marlborough, and his wife, Sarah Churchill, the latter who exerted a notoriously powerful influence upon Queen Anne. The Battle of Blenheim in 1704 had been feted as a historic win in the War of the Spanish Succession, as it established a military status abroad that England hadn't known in centuries. Tories, however, were reasonably suspicious that Sarah was now even more emboldened in promoting Whig policies to Anne. They spread the (quite reasonable) suspicion that the Churchills, having gained so much reward for past successes, were now dragging on the war for their own financial gain. Whether or not this was the case, it seems that Mandeville thought it was probably true. He doesn't take the line that Marlborough was a true patriot and thereby above reproach. Instead, he points out that England is great, and its greatness is due to men like Marlborough. Perhaps he is venal, perhaps Blenheim Palace is a bit much—but who cares? Marlborough is a winner, and when he wins, England wins. It is due to him that those in the British hive are 'famed in war, yet live in ease'.[32] The publication of *The Grumbling Hive*, then, had a very specific purpose. It was an attempt to rebuff those critics of Marlborough and the Whigs who supported the War of the Spanish Succession. These critics, Mandeville insisted, just didn't know what was involved in making a hive truly great. What is the plan for national greatness from the opposition, exactly? It is to somehow retain greatness for Great Britain while depopulating it of great individuals. It is a policy of filling the land with small, mean, penny-pinching types, piously moral individuals of the smallest stature. Or so Mandeville would have his readers believe.

Mandeville's first introduction of the beehive had little effect on the reading public. If anything, the moral rhetoric he was opposing intensified in the following years. In Addison and Steele's *Tatler* in 1710, he would read that 'public spirit . . . ought to be the first and principal motive of all . . . actions' and that the decay in public spirit could be attributed to the greed of the new class overtaking society, the 'men of business':

> It were to be wished, that love of their country were the first princi-
> ple of action in men of business, even for their own sakes; for, when
> the world begins to examine into their conduct, the generality . . . will
> judge of them by no other method, than that of how profitable their
> administration has been to the whole.[33]

Mandeville's writing output was in this period focused upon the *Female Tatler*, that competitor publication to Addison and Steele's, vying for attention and distinguishing itself with the inclusion of central female characters.[34] In the same year, Mandeville wrote there that, on the contrary, 'if the most public-spirited man in the universe will be pleased strictly to examine himself, he will find that he has never committed any action deliberately but for his own sake'.[35] What emerges is a sense of Mandeville always writing in various forms, always with the same agenda in mind: defending the new self-interested bourgeois mercantile class as the basis of a new society, one promising to replace religious ideology with commerce and international trade.

Matters changed dramatically when Sarah Churchill overplayed her domineering hand with the queen and subsequently fell from grace. This allowed for a Tory ascendency, under Henry St. John, Lord Bolingbroke, and Robert Harley. They finally forced the Treaty of Utrecht (1713), ending that costly commitment to European conflict (Swift's *The Conduct of the Allies* (1711) had been hugely successful in generating opposition to the war and aiding Harley's case—it was also an outright attack on the Dutch Republic's role in geopolitical matters). Mandeville's mind now returned to the threat of Jacobitism.

He can hardly be accused of paranoia in this regard—there would be failed Jacobite invasions in 1715 and 1719. The Act of Settlement would have been a tenuous piece of legislation upon which to hang one's hopes if Bolingbroke and Harley were to have their way. The Tories in ascendency spelled the rise of Jacobitism from within.

The rhetoric of virtue which Mandeville had tried to mute in 1705 was now instead reaching a higher and higher pitch. Although it was more frequently supported by Tories, zealots within both the Tory and Whig factions populated the Societies for the Reformation of Manners. The ideology of virtue was becoming the lingua franca of British politics.[36] There were no notable opposing voices to their rhetoric. Mandeville's interests obviously aligned with the Whigs, but to his mind they were in general agreement with the Tories with regard to the politics of virtue as the path to national greatness. Whereas the Tories thought it required a return to the virtues of obedience to the divine right of kings, the Whigs thought it required a proper inauguration of moral norms from top to bottom in civic life. It is important to recall that when Mandeville opposes the Societies, it is not just on abstract points of principle. Their members are not just prigs: they actively pursue the punishment of others, reporting drinking, gambling, and so on wherever they see it. Since they have no legal powers, their industry is that of informing on the private lives of others. Not only that, but they often pay others a fee to do the dirty work of informing for them. Neighbour observes neighbour, ready to report them for whatever is spied through twitching curtains. The moral policing of one another is turned into a cottage industry. Despite an apparent concern with the morally corrupting influence of commerce, the societies had themselves turned morality into a commercial activity. Even Jonathan Swift, a defender of the Tory interest and the ideals of the societies, noted that they 'had grown a trade to enrich little knavish informers of the meanest rank'.[37] In Mandeville's view, the ideology of virtue had real-world effects on individuals' liberty to pursue their own preferred vices, an exact foreshadowing of the tyranny to be found in a state run by religious orthodoxy.

Mandeville wrote *The Fable of the Bees* in 1714 in this dramatic atmosphere, where rhetoric to rebut the Tories and that to correct the Whigs were now needed in equal measure. The language of virtue and public spiritedness had by now become ubiquitous in public discourse. In 1713, *The Groans of Great Britain* was composed, probably by the writer Charles Gildon.[38] As the title insists, the population of Great Britain is in great pain, and their groans can be heard if only the politicians will listen. Gildon was a committed Whig, but he had entirely internalized the political ideology of virtue. Gildon's aim is 'to establish the good of my country and government'.[39] His rhetoric recalls how all great societies were run in accordance with just laws, and that Great Britain should be no different. How is national goodness—'a common wealth'—to be established? Through virtue, Gildon claims: it is through the 'growth of a wise, polite, honest and frugal people, a people where *a public spirit* . . . was evident in all their heads and leaders, and . . . as eminent in the common people themselves'.[40] Gildon co-opts Fénelon's theme from *Telemachus*, and claims that the British lack the wisdom to govern themselves in the manner of the ancient Greek city-states, and that they are therefore 'wholly incapable of being a commonwealth'.[41] But the lack of wisdom is not the central problem:

> Besides this wisdom, there is necessary a *Public Spirit*, which we call virtue; for without this virtue liberty can never subsist. There must be a love of your country, or of the public good, above all other considerations whatsoever; and entire deference to its laws and manners.[42]

According to Gildon, history teaches that there is only one true path to virtue and public spirit, and that is frugality and self-restraint:

> Poverty, or at least an unavaricious frugality is the inseparable companion of liberty and public virtue; avarice and luxury are always the attendants of riches, and these have always been the corrupters of mankind. While the Spartans observed those laws of Lycurgus which banished gold, avarice, and luxury, their state and their liberties flourished and made them formidable. Before the conquest of Asia Rome had virtue, Rome had liberty; but with the spoils of that country, wealth, luxury, and avarice entered, and vanquished the vanquishers of the known world, and soon ate up their public virtue, and with that the Roman liberty.[43]

Gildon is even exceptionally clear that the corruption that happens at the individual, 'private' level inevitably leads to the undermining of the state at the 'public' level. Avarice, he claims, 'diverts a man from a public to a private spirit [and] must contribute to the common destruction'.[44]

There are few works that anticipate Mandeville's juxtaposition of private and public interests more than *The Groans of Great Britain*.[45] When Mandeville reprints *The Grumbling Hive* just the following year, he entitles it *The Fable of the Bees or, Private Vices, Public Benefits*—explicitly framing his point in terms of the relationship between Gildon's contrast of private and public interests. He now takes all of Gildon's claims and reverses them. Following private interest *is* in the public good; luxury and avarice are in fact what make for a bustling and thriving society; individuals need have no concern for 'public spirit' in order to contribute healthily to that bustling hive; frugality is actually what marks a nation in decline; most importantly of all, the perfect pursuit of *virtue*, not of vice, is what inevitably leads to 'common destruction'. Mandeville's addition of the notorious 'Enquiry Concerning the Origin of Moral Virtue' in 1714, with its conspiracy theory story of the origin of morality, served to counter the idea that Gildon's 'heads and leaders' of society might be ones who most manifest virtue and public spirit. On the contrary, Mandeville's 'wise politicians' were the very ones who invented the ideas of virtue and public spirit in the first place, and did so just for the purpose that the common people would live lives of onerous obedience while the elite pursued their own desires unchecked. The 'cunning politicians' to whom Mandeville refers throughout the *Fable* are not just fictional characters from society's ancient past—they are specifically Harley, Bolingbroke, and all those who evoke and reanimate ideas of strict morality for their own political advantage. They are also their pious mouthpieces, like Addison, Steele, and Gildon, whose self-important solemnity allows them to serve as useful idiots for Tory interests. Mandeville's conclusion to that essay can even be seen as mockery of Gildon's religious defence of his theory. Gildon claims that God made human beings sociable and rational for a specific reason—so that they could use their sociability and rationality to their benefit. It followed, therefore, that avarice and vice are opposed to both society and God:

> God made man a rational and sociable creature; nay He has put him under so great a necessity of society, that he cannot subsist without

the Benefits of it. Those, therefore, who promote doctrines destructive of that society must necessarily be odious to its wise author, Eternal Providence, as those on the contrary must be most agreeable to that who advance maxims most conducive to the public good.[46]

Mandeville concludes *his* essay by agreeing with Gildon's premise that whatever promotes sociability and benefit must be part of a divine design for human beings. However, since it turns out that vice and the manipulation of politicians are what promote the common good, then this deception, he wickedly suggests, must be part of God's mysterious plan:

> Nothing can render the unsearchable depth of the Divine Wisdom more conspicuous, than that man, whom providence had designed for society, should . . . by his own frailties and imperfections be led into the road to temporal happiness.[47]

Throughout the *Fable,* Mandeville's tales of duplicitous merchants, preening social climbers, pickpockets and prostitutes, chemists, lawyers, medics, and writers are all designed to direct the reader's attention away from Alexander the Great, Lycurgus, Socrates, Cicero, great monarchs of old, or even monarchs of the recent past. His aim is to draw the reader's attention to how life is being lived in London in 1714, and how very different it is from anything else that has come before. The new society is run by the economic activity of a range of people, some whose professions fall within the law, some without, but all of whom contribute to the prosperity of the whole. If the question is 'what would make Great Britain great again?' then the answer is 'the things that are making it great now'. There is no need for a return to the order established by the divine right of kings, nor the order that might be brought about by the establishment of a republic of citizens possessing 'natural rights'. The hive is thriving without harking back to absolute monarchies of the past nor yearning for the progressive reforms of a utopian future.

The question of who would succeed Anne had becoming pressing, as she had been severely ill for some time. Her death in 1714, and the identification of the Hanoverian George I as the next proper Protestant in line for the throne, was an opportunity for even more political turmoil—and more pamphleteering. In the same year as

The Fable of the Bees, Mandeville published *The Mischiefs That Ought Justly to Be Apprehended from a Whig Government*, arguing unsurprisingly that they were in fact far and few between. The *Mischiefs* pamphlet was published anonymously, and this is also unsurprising, since if it was intended to be really effective, it would surely do better if not associated with the author of the work who claimed that vice was good and morality an invention. Given its radical claims, it is unclear in fact just what Mandeville was thinking the likely beneficial political effect of the argument of the *Fable* was going to be. It can't be viewed as directed primarily towards defending the Whigs, since most Whigs would prefer not to be associated with Mandeville's debunking of morality.[48]

It is striking that Mandeville was at this time, in fact, very close to the centre of power by virtue of the close friendship he had developed with Thomas Parker, Lord Chief Justice from 1710 to 1718 (and then Lord Chancellor 1718–24), who also earned the title of Earl of Macclesfield. Mandeville was a regular dinner guest and a valued wit and confidante. Mandeville never sought out any kind of public office, so far as we know, but with his connection to Macclesfield we can see how well-informed he must have been with regard to the political scene. When George I came to the throne in 1714 it was, in fact, Macclesfield who as Lord Chief Justice acted as regent and spoke for him in Parliament. By all accounts, Macclesfield especially valued Mandeville's commentary not as a fellow political player but as a controversialist who might appal the more pompous attendees at his table (it was at Macclesfield's dinner table that Mandeville met Addison and later declared him a 'parson in a tye wig').[49] Although there is no reason to doubt the genuineness of their relationship, it clearly did not extend to any kind of public political activity in partnership. Both Mandeville and Macclesfield were perhaps cognizant that this was not in keeping with Mandeville's temperament as it expressed itself in *The Fable of the Bees*.

It is quite plausible, however, that Mandeville's anonymous pamphleteering might have taken place with Macclesfield's encouragement. In the *Mischiefs* he is chiefly concerned with allaying public fear about the installation of a German king on the British throne, so soon after having to endure a Dutch one. The point— once again—is that a foreign king sympathetic to Whig interests is less a mischief for Great Britain than the Tory alternative of the Old Pretender. The Whigs stand for monarchy (and not the 'wild democracy' of republicanism), but a monarchy checked by the rule of law:

> For a *Whig* is one who stands up for Liberty and Property and the welfare of the nation; that is obedient and submissive to his sovereign, as long as he rules by law and endeavours to promote the good of his subjects, but thinks it lawful whenever the King or his favourites invade the constitution and break upon the privileges of the people to resist both him and his ministers.[50]

Mandeville claims that resisting a tyrant is always justifiable, and that a just king would have no need of a 'Doctrine of Non-Resistance'. Here he addresses in a more gentle fashion a theme he would return to in a later edition of the *Fable*—the doctrine of passive obedience. Defending himself against the charge that he prefers a nation bedevilled with vice, Mandeville vigorously denies it, and claims that he thinks the population of a nation where vice had been extinguished would be clearly superior:

> It is impossible, that such a change of circumstances should not influence the manners of a nation, and render them temperate, honest, and sincere, and from the next generation we might reasonably expect a more healthy and robust offspring than the present; an harmless innocent and well-meaning people, that would never dispute the doctrine of passive obedience: nor any other orthodox principles, but be submissive to superiors, and unanimous in religious worship.[51]

The ironic intent would be obvious to any reader—the ideology of virtue is there to produce passive political subjects, and the production of passive political subjects is there to enable tyranny. The same theme can be seen clearly in Mandeville's *Free Thoughts on Religion, the Church, and National Happiness* (1720), which is a work devoted mostly to theological debates. It borrows freely from Pierre Bayle, and was another critical flop for Mandeville at the time of its publication. Here, too, after some three hundred pages of reflection on predestination and divine mysteries, Mandeville turns to what was quite possibly his ulterior motive in writing the book, which is to reiterate that there is no divine right of kings such as would require obedience directly from subjects to their king, unless that king's rule was ratified by law.[52] It represents an ongoing Mandevillean theme that the intersection of religion and politics in cultural life primarily functions to sow discontent. In the *Mischiefs* pamphlet, he criticizes 'high-flying priests' who agitate that everything is unwell in the nation. The 'more the Kingdom flourishes', Mandeville complains, 'the more they grumble, like physicians, who are never less satisfied than when everybody else is well'.[53] Here he swipes at his own profession so as to make his point once again: when all is well with a nation, there will still be forces whose interest it is to say that everything is dire, and the louder those cries are, the more we should suspect what real agenda those complaints serve.

In 1705 Mandeville had argued that vices were both ineliminable within the human constitution and that they tended to the good of society as a whole, but his writing did not incur much attention, let alone criticism. In 1714, he had argued that moral virtue itself was a con, an invention of politicians to keep the herd of society adequately docile. Again, no hue and cry emerged, undoubtedly to his great disappointment. In 1723, Mandeville reissued the *Fable of the Bees* with some additions. This time the reaction was different. The *Fable* was presented to the Middlesex Court. Countless writers lined up to condemn his work, from outraged sermonizers to sophisticated moral theorists. Mandeville spent the rest of his life delightedly engaged in as much further writing as he could manage, producing both strenuous denials of his immoralism on the one hand and just as many new immoral provocations on the other. It raises the question of just what had changed between 1704 and 1723 in London such that a work first ignored was later quickly propelled to a notoriety comparable to Hobbes's *Leviathan* or Machiavelli's *The Prince*.

The short answer is that the political circumstances had changed. This implies that it was nothing to do with the message of the *Fable* itself but rather that the spirit of the times had changed such as to warrant its condemnation in 1723. It also implies that Mandeville was an innocent victim of political polemic. Neither is the case, however. The political tensions addressed by the *Fable* had continued to simmer in the preceding two decades, and Mandeville had tried to insert himself in the discussion at every opportunity. Mandeville had been provoking the British reading public and political class since he began writing, albeit to little effect. In 1723, however, his provocations finally got a response. What had changed in the interim was an even greater anxiety regarding the implications for society of the new economic and political realities, and an increased feeling that they had been accompanied with a serious decline in civic standards. Three events are particularly relevant: firstly, the catastrophe of the South Sea Bubble in 1720; secondly, the publication of *Cato's Letters*, composed by John Trenchard and Thomas Gordon and published to special notice between 1720 and 1723; thirdly, the so-called Atterbury Plot of 1723. Each of these events played a role in what was in the end a somewhat arbitrary catapulting of Mandeville to notoriety.

The South Sea Bubble story is well known.[54] The South Sea Company was created in 1711 and had been granted monopoly rights for the slave trade. However, the function of the company was that of relieving the aforementioned government debt, as investors in William's (and then Anne's) foreign wars could find themselves with a solid investment but not with capital that was easily tradeable or made liquid. To allow for this to take place the South Sea Company underwrote the government debt. It wasn't until 1719 that the company attempted an ambitious conversion of £1 million of government debt into company shares. The swap was successful for all involved, and the following April the government approved another debt conversion—this time for £30 million. Word leaked out of the secure return that the shares underwriting the government debt would bring, and speculation ran rife through different strata of society. The original flotation share price had been around £100; by the summer of 1720 it reached £1000. Then in September the price fell dramatically back towards its original level. Overstretched individuals were ruined, as were a range of companies connected to the South Sea Company. There was a parliamentary investigation, and insider trading was discovered. The world had seen its first major financial scandal. It had been driven by greed and the pursuit of profit, motivated by the government's self-serving interests, themselves fuelled by individual hubris and national desire for military domination. Mandeville's remedy for the hive's problems had been to allow self-interest to run unchecked. Had anyone bothered to read *The Fable of the Bees* in 1714, they might have blamed it for the South Sea Bubble. Anyone reading it after 1720 could see it only as an offensive and outrageous defence of the worst parts of society. The trade of stocks had been opposed previously only by those resistant to change and the new realities of commercial society, but now it was felt first-hand what havoc those new financial realities might bring to ordinary life.

The mood of civic virtue in opposition to individual self-interest had been in any case rising in British culture. Joseph Addison's play *Cato, a Tragedy* was first performed in 1713, and was enormously successful in subsequent years; it set the new tone, detailing Cato's principled taking of his own life rather than submitting to the tyranny of Caesar's impending dictatorship. Just as Fénelon had harked back to Sparta to summon up an image of public engagement through self-denial, Addison presented the public with an individual leader who lived and died in accordance with the ideals of the Roman republic. Cato was in this regard everything that John Churchill was not; a political leader quite different to those who sought recognition in military glory and one who eschewed personal ambition and its trappings in the face of a culture of massive wealth among its political leaders, and incredible corruption alongside it.

'Cato' was also the nom de plume of Trenchard and Gordon. Most of the very first letters they published were on the South Sea scandal, calling for punishment and railing against the corruption that had set in throughout government and that had clearly set the conditions for the catastrophe to occur. Though Whiggish in their sympathies, they reiterated the moral priorities Addison had promoted—great individuals were those who pursued the public interest, and not their own:

> It was otherwise at Athens and Rome; where, though particular men, and even great men, were often treated with much freedom and severity, when they deserved it; yet the people, the body of the people, were spoken of with the utmost regard and reverence.[55]

The South Sea Bubble fever that had torn through society had changed the ordinary person—the 'raging passion for immoderate gain had made men universally and intensely hard-hearted: They were every where devouring one another'.[56] From the Tory perspective, it appeared as if Trenchard and Gordon were wrenching the rhetoric of virtue away from them, and securing the moral high ground. The Tories should have monopolized that rhetoric after the fiasco of the South Sea Bubble, which after all had happened under Whig stewardship. That they were unable to do so owed in part to the so-called Atterbury Plot. The bishop of Rochester, Francis Atterbury, had been discovered to have been in regular contact with the family of the Old Pretender, and was conniving with other nobles for yet another Jacobite uprising (the last one having been in 1715). The plot was discovered in 1721, and Atterbury was arrested and imprisoned. Whereas George's ascension to the throne had been accompanied by public riots (coordinated by Tories) in opposition to a German monarch only a few years previously, now the Tories were decidedly on the back foot, and their commitment to the Protestant succession was a source of severe scepticism in all quarters.

It was in this feverish context that Mandeville reissued the *Fable* in 1723. He had added two new essays to this edition. One was 'A Search into the Nature of Society'. The 'Search' defends Mandeville's conception of virtue as self-denial, taking special aim at the philosopher Shaftesbury's fanciful theory that we each possess a moral sense that always allows our personal interests to tend to the good of the universe as a whole. Mandeville also takes the opportunity in this essay to give his views on Cato. There is no mistaking his ironic tone: 'How strict and severe was the morality of Cato, how steady and unaffected the virtue of that grand asserter of Roman liberty!'[57] On the other hand, he continues, there is a tendency, when evoking great figures of the past, to pass over some salient facts, such as that Cato was also a politician, and a proud elitist one, for whom defeat was worse than death. He was also in constant rivalry with Caesar, and desperately wanted to achieve what Caesar now seemed on the verge of achieving—a kind of immortality. In the end, what exactly should we say motivated Cato's suicide? To Mandeville it is simply obvious that, for all the plays and letters to newspapers extolling Cato's commitment to civic duty and the public spirit, it was the 'implacable hatred and superlative envy he bore to the glory, the real greatness and personal merit of Caesar,

[that] had for a long time swayed all his actions under the most noble pretences'.[58] Although Mandeville sided with Trenchard and Gordon against a common enemy of Tory Jacobitism, he had no time for their pious invocation of the moral paragons of yore. Just as Marlborough was no political devil, Cato was no political saint.

Mandeville added one more essay that he hoped would provoke in a way that his previous writings had failed to do. This was 'An Essay on Charity, and Charity Schools'. In this essay he attacked the institution of charity schools: voluntary organizations, usually set up in parishes to provide a basic education for the poorest members of society. Mandeville's attack on the charity schools demonstrates just how intense his hatred of the motives behind the Societies for the Reformation of Manners really was. Mandeville acknowledges that anyone criticizing the schools—which, after all, remove starving children from the street and provide them with shelter, clothing, safety, and an education—'is in danger of being stoned by the rabble'.[59] Any such opponent must be 'an uncharitable, hard-hearted and inhuman, if not a wicked, profane, and atheistical wretch'.[60] Mandeville's line, though, is that he must nevertheless point out some grounds of opposition to charity schools. And it is the issue of charity schools that in effect caused the scandal of *The Fable of the Bees* and is the reason Mandeville is remembered at all today.

As outrageous as it might at first appear, Mandeville was not alone in criticizing charity schools. In that same summer of 1723, they had been subjected to a fierce attack from another writer—'Cato'. In this case it was one of Trenchard's essays—similarly entitled 'Of Charity, and Charity-Schools'—that had raised again what had in fact been a long-standing concern with the schools. The accusation was that they were in fact a cover for a very specific form of religious indoctrination. Whereas there had been in the time of William a healthy 'detestation of popery' in the land, now the Jacobites in the schools had 'corrupted all the youth whose education has been trusted to them, and who could be corrupted; so that at the end of near forty years, the Revolution is worse established than when it began'.[61] Trenchard argued that the real purpose of the charity schools was indoctrination in anti-Whiggism and support for the return of the Old Pretender. There was some evidence for this: as Mandeville mentions in his essay, there were a curious number of charity school children involved in the Tory-organized public riots against George's coronation.

The scandal of *The Fable of the Bees* was created when it was 'presented' to the Middlesex County Court (which covered the London area) alongside Cato's essay. The reasons these texts were presented to the grand jury are not straightforward. As W. A. Speck has shown, the particular context of the submission involved complex local politics concerning the Whig and Tory candidates for the election of a sheriff, an election that had been mired in controversy.[62] The Tory candidates had prevailed, but in the course of the campaign they had gained support from various quarters that had renowned Jacobite sympathies. Thus, in order to secure their position and draw attention away from themselves, they went on the offensive, and attacked what they saw as one of the most prominent Whig propagandists on the grounds of heresy and sedition. Their attack was on 'Cato' first and foremost, since it was 'Cato' who was the most effective rhetorician connecting Toryism with Jacobitism. They accused 'Cato' of denying the Trinity and claimed that by opposing the work of charity schools, the 'instruction of youth in the principles of the Christian religion [is] exploded with the greatest malice and falsity'. This is perhaps a thin basis upon which to indict a letter to a newspaper before a grand jury. What they required was a further target that they could link to 'Cato'. Mandeville's essay against charity schools had also just arrived, and was handily nestled among writings of such moral turpitude (Prostitution defended! Morality a fraud!) that the charges that *both* these authors were aiming to 'run down religion and virtue as prejudicial to society' might just stick.[63] It was for this reason that *The Fable of the Bees* was brought to court and this is how Mandeville's writings were finally brought to full public attention.

Mandeville's essay is directed, of course, to the very same end as Trenchard's, though it is not in his temperament to express his purpose as directly as 'Cato' did. Instead, he attacks charity schools on a range of outrageous grounds, and allows the reader to infer his real intent. There is a sincerely held core argument in the essay, though Mandeville takes some time to get to it. He employs a scattershot approach, whereby a range of interesting arguments sit side by side with some not quite as valid provocations so as to generate an overall rhetorical affect. There is certainly to be found within his prose a line of argument that would become a classic trope in conservative thinking.[64] This is not a knee-jerk opposition to progressive initiatives but the idea that it is neither possible nor desirable to assign the responsibility for the cultivation of human values to large institutions. This task is properly assigned to smaller social groups, such as the family, or one's immediate circle of acquaintances. Insofar as human beings are improvable—and Mandeville doubts that they are very much—'it is the precept and the example of parents, and those they eat, drink and converse with, that have an influence upon the minds of children'.[65] If anyone can set a child on the path of being a law-abiding and productive member of society, it is a parent, who does so through their good example. If a loving parent through all their efforts cannot reform the child, a state institution won't do any better. It would be entirely anachronistic to see Mandeville as anticipating 'family values' rhetoric, however. His claims here are of a piece with his overall social anthropology and his repeated emphasis that the norms of society are only ever inaugurated, enforced, and preserved through human beings' incessant negotiation for status and esteem. It is the securing of praise and the avoidance of criticism and blame that drive all our standards of behaviour, and our interest in these norms is disproportionately influenced by the enforcement of standards from those with whom we have the most intimate social contact.

A second conservative trope is to deny that the cause of ills in society is the lack of an education for its population, rather than material conditions such as a lack of work. Education would be a good solution if the problem were ignorance, Mandeville claims; but it is not. The cause of criminal mischief in society is the absence of something more worthwhile for the criminals to do—specifically, work. As it happens, Mandeville claims, charity schools just *don't* prepare the poor for work. They instead contribute to the problem rather than solving it by creating a class of overeducated ne'er do wells. The graduates of charity schools will possess reading and writing skills but lack vocational skills and moreover a sense of industry, and will be even less familiar with the value of hard work than they were when they first entered. Mandeville attacks the idea that lack of education creates crime with a further series of deliberately provocative counterclaims: criminals don't lack intelligence, since a successful criminal has a kind of genius about them, and so lack of education can't be the cause of crime; it's rather the leniency and the absence of a strictly enforced death penalty that encourages crime; finally, the majority of crime is caused by victims not showing enough common sense in protecting themselves and their property.

The attack has some of the characteristic features of Mandeville's subtle negotiation with satire. Can he possibly have sincerely meant all these things? He clearly enjoys the expected outrage from his praising of the criminal mind, yet there is surely nothing controversial in whether more or less intelligence has been manifested in this or that crime. The aim is rather to get the reader to start thinking about intellectual quality and moral virtue as different kinds of thing. He can't possibly think though that improving the material conditions of those in poverty won't disincline *some* of them to crime. The aim is rather that of piercing the idealized rhetoric regarding lifting the poor up to virtue. He does this by way of some hard-nosed observations regarding what human beings are actually like. The causes of crime are manifold; one could argue that tighter punishments, or more vigilance in ordinary behaviour, or any number of other things could produce a reduction. A lack of education among the criminal class is not the decisive factor in the matter. If it is not the decisive factor in the matter though then perhaps the rhetoric of charity schools is intended to distract from some other covert function at which they really aim.

However, when Mandeville does get to his central argument, it emerges as one difficult to dismiss as the mere piercing of moralistic bombast. Charity schools must be resisted, he claims, because they aim to remove everyone out of a poor underclass; but society *requires* a poor underclass if it is to prosper:

> It is impossible that a society can long subsist, and suffer many of its members to live in idleness, and enjoy all the ease and pleasure they can invent, without having at the same time great multitudes of people that to make good this defect will condescend to be quite the reverse, and by use and patience inure their bodies to work for others and themselves besides. . . .

... If such a people there must be, as no great nation can be happy without vast numbers of them, would not a wise legislature cultivate the breed of them with all imaginable care, and provide against their scarcity as he would prevent the scarcity of provision itself?[66]

It is obvious that the educational aspirations of the charity school movement run entirely counter to this being achieved, since an educated underclass would inevitably become too demanding and unruly: 'It is requisite that great numbers should be ignorant as well as poor. Knowledge both enlarges and multiplies our desires, and the fewer things a man wishes for, the more easily his necessities may be supplied.'[67] Thirty years later, Jean-Jacques Rousseau would take Mandeville's point and run it in an entirely opposite direction. Seeing nothing but corruption in the incipient consumer culture of Paris, he noted that it was modern 'knowledge' that increased our desires to a point where they could never really be satisfied.[68] The only recourse was a return to a simplicity that perhaps the uneducated peasant knew better than the city-dweller languishing in luxury. But for Mandeville such rhetoric is only ever made by those who are already the happy beneficiaries of privilege. Usually what such passionate advocates of the wholesomeness of agrarian simplicity end up doing is buying a summer home in the country. The message of the 'Charity' essay is rather that if you think that the comforts of modern life are a good thing, then you had better be committed to keeping the means of its production in place, and the means to the production of modern luxuries is a large workforce who can't afford them themselves.

One has to ask whether Mandeville could have been sincere in this view. It is in one sense a perfectly clear application of the argument from *The Grumbling Hive*—were virtue to rule a society (in this case, the virtue of charity), that society would undermine the economic prosperity which brings overall benefit to the whole. Yet Mandeville couldn't possibly have thought that any good Christian reader would endorse *as a good idea* the notion that a responsible government adopt a deliberate policy of keeping the poor in poverty and of keeping the uneducated stupid. Perhaps he did think this, and our outrage is just the result of a further three hundred years of moral education and progress, the Victorian projects

against poverty, the rise of egalitarianism in modern liberal societies, and some sensitivity to Marx's thought that class oppression is
central to capitalism's proper functioning. Nonetheless, one need
not have this education just to find the view appalling. It would
have been found reprehensible at the time by anyone sympathetic
to Christian thought. Christian teaching identified the poor as
blessed, and the rightful inheritors of the Kingdom of Heaven; it
does not follow that we thereby do them a good turn by keeping
them in poverty.

There are in fact some reasons to doubt that Mandeville thought
that the best course of action for a government really was to
ensure the perpetuation of an economic and social underclass. For
example, Mandeville notes at one point that 'in a free nation where
slaves are not allowed of, the surest wealth consists in a multitude of
laborious poor'.[69] He surely cannot have been blind to the thought
that any reader would have had, which is that a perpetual multitude of laborious poor *is* in effect a slave class, a way of sanctioning
one within a society that otherwise likes to think of itself as a free
nation. Perhaps Mandeville was inviting the reader to think this
very thought. Could he then perhaps have been entirely ironic here?
Perhaps Mandeville personally had no opposition to the reduction
of poverty and hardship but was instead attacking merely the inef-
ficacious means to that end that charity schools represented. Perhaps he did think that such institutions serve the function of virtue
signalling for their well-heeled benefactors. He was perhaps sincere
in the thought that they fail to bring about a sustainable higher
quality of life for the worst off in society, just because they fail to
take into account the realities of the need for a labour force in a
prosperous society. The better way to improve their lot would be
to improve their working conditions, not to pluck them from those
conditions altogether, plant them into a genteel educational setting,
and then transpose them back out into the street again once our
consciences have been sufficiently caressed.

It is later on that Mandeville gets to his real point, which isn't
about the importance of maintaining a working poor, or anxieties about social revolt. His real point is the same one made more
explicitly by 'Cato', which is that the charity school has become a
place of religious instruction:

> Whatever is necessary to salvation and requisite for poor labouring
> people to know concerning religion, that children learn at school, may
> fully as well either by preaching or catechizing be taught at Church,
> from which or some other place of worship I would not have the mean-
> est of a Parish that is able to walk to it be absent on Sundays.[70]

Mandeville disingenuously stresses that his concern is that the
charity schools might inappropriately compete with the Church
and he claims that it is for the preservation of the dignity of the
Sabbath day that he opposes the schools. The manoeuvre is a cunning one, as it stresses that the real agenda of those schools is religious indoctrination, not education. As with all satire, there is an
ethical undertone needed in order for the whole thing to work.
And there is such an undertone just occasionally detectable in the
'Charity' essay. He raises and dismisses two arguments for charity
schools from opposed ideological viewpoints. To those supporters
who think that they improve religious commitment, Mandeville
responds that they might do, but at too great an expense for what
can be got at church for free anyway. To those who support charity
schools on the diametrically opposed grounds—that education in
fact liberates, and people who 'can judge for themselves' will soon
learn how to be 'priest-rid'—Mandeville argues that the success of
setting up a culture comprising those 'who will but think for themselves and refuse to have their reason imposed upon by the priests'
will be better achieved among the higher classes and within fee-
paying institutions.[71] Mandeville pretends to endorse neither camp,
though he is more eloquent with regard to the latter one. Instead he
asserts—almost in passing—his real grounds for abolishing charity
schools, which are that the education comes at a cost, and that cost
is indoctrination:

> I know it will be every urged against me that it is barbarous the children
> of the poor should have no opportunity of exerting themselves, as long
> as God has not debarred them from natural parts and genius more than
> the rich. But I cannot think this is harder, than it is that they should
> not have the same money as long as they have the same inclinations to
> spend as others.[72]

The education people receive at the charity schools is one that they
are to exercise in pursuit of the same interests and 'inclinations'

POLITICS AND THE IDEOLOGY OF VIRTUE   [189]

that their educators possess. Mandeville thinks it is no worse for him to say the poor should have no money than that they should have money on condition that they live their lives in a way others dictate. A free education is worthless if it does not enable freedom of thought. Public education is no way of making society priest-rid if it is the priests providing the education.

It is also possible that Mandeville sincerely thinks that a certain kind of value—that of the moral improvement of human beings—is being tied to the possibility of education here in a way that is pernicious. It is pernicious because it downgrades something he stresses later in the same essay—the variability of what 'happiness' might amount to for different people. The moralizing education of the poor comes with an implied restriction of a higher value, that of creating a society where everyone may pursue happiness in their own fashion. It is possible that Mandeville truly believed that such institutional improving of individuals is infantilizing—it is a form of dominating them, and forcing consciousness into the same ideology of virtue that he had always argued against. Mandeville's pre-eminent concern might not be with cultivating the capacity for everyone to realize the freedom to think for themselves, which is a somewhat intellectualized ideal for someone like Mandeville to endorse above all others. Rather, it might be that he thinks society ought to make possible the freedom to *live* in one's own way, a capacity which does not mandate spiritual or even intellectual improvement. Nevertheless, one can't help but think that Mandeville's prose in fact reveals a shared sympathy with the ensuing Enlightenment's claim that the conditions for realizing freedom of thinking *and* freedom of living are necessarily secular.

When considering Mandeville's politics, it is worth recalling the formative details of his early life in Rotterdam once again and the centrality of the Costerman affair to his intellectual trajectory. As a teenager, Mandeville had attacked the corrupt bailiff Van Zuijlen in print; William had come to Van Zuijlen's aid, which in turn had led to Mandeville and his beloved father being banished from the city. William helped Van Zuijlen because the latter was an elder in the Calvinist Church, and William required support from that Church in order to maintain his rule. Dutch Calvinist doctrine was marked by both religious intolerance and passive obedience. Much of Mandeville's debunking of morality is marked by his first adopting strict Calvinist standards of self-denial and purity of spirit, only then to lament that those standards are rarely met, but his real opposition is to those standards themselves—it was the Calvinist influence in the state that contributed to his own emigration to England in the first place. When Mandeville rails against crypto-Catholic agendas in politics, it should be viewed within this broader framework. His life was shaped by religious intolerance and the influence of the Church upon the state—in Rotterdam that threat was Calvinist; in London the looming threat was Catholic.

In the end, most of Mandeville's writings were political. His politics were shaped by the revocation of the Edict of Nantes, by the forced emigration of his teacher Pierre Bayle, that high priest of religious toleration. They were shaped by his father's and his own persecution in the Costerman affair, and his own flight to England as a result. His politics in one sense begins and ends with the thought that the pursuit of happiness could occur only in the absence of oppression. In *Free Thoughts*, Mandeville writes in the first-person plural in the chapter 'Of National Happiness'. He writes as one of the British and against the land of his birth. He argues that whereas 'in Holland the magistrates of every city are arbitrary in many things and men are capitally punished without public trial',[73] the central political character of Great Britain is recognizably the theme of freedom from oppression:

> But what we, and only we may boast of, is, that throughout the globe there is not a country, great or small, where the men of the highest rank can do less injury to their inferiors, and even the lowest with impunity than in England. This privilege, without which all the joys and comforts of life are precarious, is the grand characteristic of English liberty, and a felicity which is not in the power of wit or eloquence to over-rate.[74]

What Mandeville wants to make his readers aware of is the opportunity at the beginning of the eighteenth century to forgo the social aim of moral virtue and instead pursue the goal of freedom from oppression. At the very least, he wants his readers to see that 'virtue' as used in public discourse is not in fact a moral term at all; first and foremost, it is a political one. As such, the politics of virtue is an ideological tool, and it can be used for good or ill. He thereby opened up a way of thinking about human society that wouldn't be more fully explored until the nineteenth and twentieth centuries. Mandeville's uncovering of the function of ideology in political language is the very beginning of political critique.

In 1713, not long before the first edition of the *Fable*, Queen Anne had been presented with a natural history text by one Joseph Warder, a work that would have a surprising popularity and be reprinted many times, entitled *The True Amazons: or, The Monarchy of Bees*.[75] In the cloyingly sycophantic dedication, Warder outlined the reason for his dedication of the work—a study of bees—to Anne:

> I have . . . conversed with these innocent creatures the bees, and have not failed . . . to inform myself, by the most curious observations of their nature and economy, wherein I find so many things that resemble your Majesty's happy state and government, that all the while I was writing of this book, I could not forbear wishing I might dedicate it to your Majesty. . . . But oh, what harmony, what lovely order is there in the government of the bees![76]

Warder's fantasy was that British society naturally mimicked the innocent workings of the beehive. Mandeville exposed that fantasy for what it was and showed the British that they inhabited a different kind of hive, one possessing its own lovely order, one governed by a strange new rationality, one that emerged from within the new commercial activity of society. The aim of politics should in the end be only to understand and manage the forces that really govern the bees.

CHAPTER EIGHT

Merchants of Morality

There are people who have the approval of society, though their only merits are the vices useful for the transactions of daily life.

—LA ROCHEFOUCAULD, *MAXIMS*, 5:273

THERE IS ONE FIELD IN which Mandeville's name is regularly cited today, and where his views are acknowledged as insightful, if not prophetic. Historians of economic thought see him as a pioneering figure.[1] In 1966, F. A. Hayek gave a lecture to the British Academy identifying Mandeville as one of the 'Master Minds' of economics. Hayek, however, acknowledged that his choice was a controversial one, not least because in his own view 'what Mandeville has to say on technical economics seems to me to be rather mediocre, or at least unoriginal'.[2] As Hayek noted, his eminent adversary J. M. Keynes had also praised Mandeville in his *General Theory of Employment, Interest, and Money* (1936).[3] Yet what we find in the *General Theory* are a few pages praising Mandeville's anticipation of the so-called 'paradox of thrift'—the claim that individual saving and frugality, while sensible for the individual in most cases, might be detrimental to society's economy as a whole, since there would be in such cases less discretionary spending and as a result less economic activity. This is an important insight, yet it falls short of an economic theory, and in a sense neither Keynes nor Hayek really praises Mandeville as an economist at all. Hayek's comments are justified, and so the question becomes why Keynes, Hayek, and generations of economists after them nevertheless came to recognize Mandeville as one of their own.

Hayek and Keynes are surely correct to see him as absolutely crucial for the development of modern economic thought. Mandeville's
groundbreaking contribution, itself made possible by his controversialist disposition, is explained as a far simpler insight. It is that
he asks us to *see as an economist*. *The Fable of the Bees* abounds in
examples of everyday social phenomena, of human interactions
generally, explained and discussed as examples of economic activity.
It is not that Mandeville invented the idea of economic activity—it
is that he took it that there is no area of human life that couldn't be
anthropologically analysed in terms of economic activity. He looked
upon social conventions, social interactions, and social mores as
not just interacting with but as governed by economic factors. In so
doing, he brought a conceptual apparatus to domains where it had
never been applied before. Mandeville stressed a basic injunction—
to see like an economist—and showed how an economist simply
produces different answers to familiar questions. The counterintuitive character of the answers was meant to highlight the possibility
that one could look at human society from utterly different stand-
points. Mandeville's writings on economic matters involve no real
economic theory or, as Hayek pointed out, any technical applica-
tions at all. What makes Mandeville a seminal economic thinker is
that his views cannot be understood without appeal to 'the paradox
of thrift', 'the household fallacy', 'the law of unanticipated consequences', 'the invisible hand', 'spontaneous order', and 'laissez-faire',
the concepts of self-regulating systems and competitive individual
behaviour, all key phrases and notions for anyone approaching any
subject matter from an economic point of view.

An essential part of his approach is to view the human animal as
a system of interconnected circuits, conduits through which non-
rational 'animal spirits' move from part to part generating heat,
energy, and activity, excesses here and depletions there. Mandeville
thought that the individual human animal's physiology worked
this way in a quite literal sense, but that it also properly characterized the workings of the species considered in terms of its group
dynamics. Societies of human beings are similarly run by the flow
of animal spirits, and movements and interactions that might look
unbalanced, irregular, or even malfunctioning at the individual
level can be seen as just part of the back and forth of a properly

working system when viewed at the group level. The way to see this shift—that what is good at the micro level might be different from what works at the macro level—shows up in the distinction between personal ethical rules and economic benefits for society as a whole. Economic thinking, therefore, is Mandeville's way of identifying this difference and of expressing his general theory regarding the nature of the human animal and its behaviour.

Mandeville brings his economic point of view to bear on three different types of relation: firstly, how states ought to interact with other states; secondly, how states ought to interact with the individuals that make them up; thirdly, how individuals ought to interact with one another. In each case, thinking in economic terms brings a way of understanding how benefit can be brought to a society, ways that are obscured, distorted, or flatly contradicted when we take the individual point of view on the same issues.

The primary case of how states interact with one another was of course international trade; the more specific and pressing issue was the exportation and importation of luxury goods. It is important to appreciate just how fast and exciting the emergence of luxury goods must have seemed in the early eighteenth century. The increase in luxury goods was a feature of the increase in consumption in general. In 1700, London used up eight hundred thousand tonnes of coal. By the middle of the century that figure had nearly doubled; by the end it had nearly tripled.[4] Consumption increased both in quantity and diversity, as commodities such as sugar and tobacco were produced and imported from colonial territories.[5] The question was whether or not this was all a good thing. As we have seen, the issue of whether or not England was to be a warlike and dominating Sparta was one that was deployed for various political purposes. Sparta was warlike and dominating by virtue of the austere self-disciplining of its own culture; Rome had been similarly triumphant before luxurious decadence had brought it to its knees. The emerging materialist culture was seen as the warning sign for the decline of Great Britain. The philosopher the Earl of Shaftesbury, one of Mandeville's favourite targets, gave a simple expression to the idea of the corruption of urban sophisticates and the contrasting virtue of the simple rural folk unsullied by prosperity:

We see the enormous growth of luxury in capital cities, such as have been long the seat of empire. We see what improvements are made in vice of every kind where numbers of men are maintained in lazy opulence and wanton plenty. It is otherwise with those who are taken up in honest and due employment and have been well inured to it from their youth. This we may observe in the hardy remote provincials, the inhabitants of smaller towns and the industrious sort of common people, where it is rare to meet with any instances of those irregularities which are known in courts and palaces and in the rich foundations of easy and pampered priests.[6]

Here the effect is moral illness but the cause is economic. If only Great Britain could reduce its dependency on the importation of foreign goods, and instead cultivate national self-sufficiency by regulating its desires to what it produces, then the moral fabric of society could be protected.

Mandeville is, of course, deeply opposed to the claim that luxury is inherently corrupting. Apart from anything else, 'luxury' is incredibly poorly defined. We might start by thinking of it negatively, as anything that is not a necessity. Yet that doesn't mark out anything in particular, and is in any case a moveable line, since what is regarded as a luxury by one generation is viewed as a necessity by the next. If we consider Abraham Maslow's 'hierarchy of needs', we find food, water, warmth, shelter, and sleep at the bottom. Were we to consider everything higher up that hierarchy to be a luxury, then we would find that almost everything in the modern world is a luxury, and would have to conclude—as Rousseau would in fact later do—that the modern world is inherently corrupting.[7] More offensive to Mandeville than the idea of urban environments as corrupting is the idea of rural ones as edifying. Shaftesbury's prose aims at the valorization of agrarian simplicity. Mandeville is suspicious as to whether Shaftesbury has much personal experience of the moral character of the simple folk; one suspects he hadn't. Shaftesbury's claim presumes that the effect of being a member of the group of 'hardy remote provincials' is that one is simply too busy getting food on the table to even have a chance to be corrupted by luxury goods. In fact, Shaftesbury's rhetoric is rather closer to the Protestant work ethic, and the idea that some kind of moral

goodness attains to a person just by virtue of their being industrious. As Mandeville is aware, advocates of these views rarely give
up their worldly goods themselves and take up honest work in the
fields. Someone might even think it straightforwardly unlikely that
one's moral character improves the poorer one becomes.

As James Harris has convincingly argued, Mandeville's rhetoric
in *The Virgin Unmask'd* and the *Fable* can be understood in the
political context of the anticipated demise of Anne and the introduction of Dutch values once George took the throne.[8] It became a
live issue then as to what exactly those Dutch values were. The British reading public had long had an image of those values in the
work of Sir William Temple, whose *Observations upon the United
Provinces of the Netherlands* had been regularly reprinted since its
first appearance in 1673. There, Temple had speculated that the
cause of Dutch success had to do with the national characteristics
of the people, since their resources and geographical advantages
were in fact few. There were two national characteristics, Temple
argued, that accounted for a great deal of Dutch prosperity, and
they were industry and frugality. These features were originally
determined by the simple facts of scarcity of resources and a large
population making industry and parsimony a necessity. But they
had so long been adopted by the population, Temple wrote, that
the Dutch now lived in accordance with the virtues for their own
sake. Crucially, this manifested itself in terms of the relationship
between exports and imports and in their attitudes towards the status of luxury goods. The chief aim of the Dutch was to encourage
manufacture, trade, and the exportation of luxury goods as much
as possible—this was the virtue of industry—and to resist indulging in those goods themselves as much as possible—this was the
virtue of frugality. This showed, Temple thought, that certain fashionable 'maxims', such as that the 'encouragement of excess and
luxury . . . is of advantage to trade', are, as he puts it, 'not so certain'.
On the contrary, conspicuous consumption of luxury goods sets an
example for idleness, which undermines industry, and then renders
a nation poorer still. Moreover, by being so covetous of imported
goods, the British 'by buying more than we sell . . . shall come to
be poor'.[9] These were the universal truths where economics and
morality aligned: the laws of trade are that those who work harder

and export more will be better off overall than those nations that consume more and are reliant upon imports to do so.

Mandeville's own views were quite different.[10] He had, as we have seen, his own political motives for being opposed to the rhetoric of virtue in determining a nation's direction. But as a Dutchman he also thought these claims were simply false, not least with regard to the economic benefits of the domestic consumption of luxury goods.[11] He takes issue with Temple's image of the Dutch whenever he can (in *The Virgin Unmask'd* his interlocutors somewhat implausibly break off their discussion of sex and marriage for reflection upon Dutch trade). He criticized the idea that the Dutch's lack of consumption of luxury goods was motivated by abstemiousness or parsimoniousness as a national character trait. Temple had written that the Dutch 'furnish infinite luxury, which they never practice; and traffic in pleasures, which they never taste'.[12] But the Dutch resisted luxuries not out of some sense of the value of self-denial, but because of the particular contingent features of their condition. Their abstemiousness was caused, Mandeville claims, simply by the fact that these goods were far more highly taxed for the ordinary Dutch individual than Temple had been aware. Not only was the image of Dutch industry false, it was also false that frugal behaviour was a source of prosperity. Temple had clearly thought it impressive that in the Dutch Provinces 'among the whole body of civil magistrates, the merchants, the rich traders, and citizens in general, the fashions continue the same' and that 'men leave off their clothes, only because they are worn out and not because they are out of fashion'.[13] But this is no spur to an energetic economy, Mandeville argues in the *Fable*; on the contrary, the constant changes in fashion in how to adorn our homes and our persons generate enormous economic activity. The moral is that the British will not become great like the Dutch by emulating the Dutch in their particular behaviours and social norms.

Mandeville's thinking is in large part directed towards resisting moral interpretations of what are for him just obviously economic and non-moral aspects of life. In remark Q of the *Fable* Mandeville distinguishes between two senses of 'frugal': in the one case there is the frugality that is demonstrated when a person moderates their spending to their income; in the other case there is the frugality of going without luxuries or anything superfluous to one's needs. The first type of frugality is one of which Mandeville thoroughly approves, since it is simply a piece of common sense not to spend more than one has (or than one can comfortably borrow). This, he thinks, is nothing more than the general recommendation to be practically minded. The second sense, though, is one of which he thoroughly disapproves, since it is the *ethical* notion of frugality, the idea of being frugal as something intrinsically good or as an end in itself. In keeping with the general tenor of his thinking, Mandeville thinks this latter 'virtue' is a fiction. Here, though, we can see how ethics and economics intertwine in important ways. Mandeville can see how one might come to think of frugality as a purely ethical virtue, rather than a piece of prudential rationality, because it is in fact so ubiquitous in our lives. It is very frequently the case that being frugal in the non-ethical, prudential meaning of the term is a good—in fact, vital—rational recommendation for an individual or a household. From this one could come to believe that it is some kind of stand-alone truth, transcending individual circumstances and context. However, frugality is always just a means to an end, he insists, the end of preserving one's happiness (in this case, by avoiding ruin). The case of frugality is a helpful one for Mandeville, since it not only highlights the importance of thinking like an economist when analysing social behaviour but also dovetails with his sceptical thinking regarding the fallacies that humans make in confounding mere means to an end with ends in themselves.

Mandeville thinks there is another fallacy at play in the rhetoric of private virtue, one that is, again, properly exposed by consideration of economic factors. The paradox of thrift might be thought to be a particular case of the so-called 'household fallacy', which is the claim that economic policy that constitutes a good plan for a household might by extension hold for the nation. It is this shift in a way of thinking that is, I would argue, the most important aspect of Mandeville's contribution to economic thought. There was a rich theological tradition that Mandeville drew upon, one that claimed that God's ways are mysterious and that human planning has to work within the constraint of these inexplicable rules. But this implies that there might be some larger forces at play in human society and history, ones that go beyond what we can readily understand at the human level. Mandeville claims that there *are* larger laws at play in human society, which have emerged in its evolving history, but they are not the mysteries of a transcendent cosmic order. They are rather the *natural* rules that govern human life at the macro level. It was Mandeville who first articulated the thought that thêse rules are not providence but nature; they can be seen as the rules of how nature—in this case, in the form of large groups of highly social animals—regulates individuals' behaviour to the benefit of the group.[14] The rules that regulate the system are not identical to the rules that regulate the individual players within the system. This is why errors like the household fallacy emerge. They fail to acknowledge that there might be rules for how a good system ought to behave that are entirely distinct from familiar rules about how a good individual ought to behave.

The second dimension of Mandeville's economic way of thinking, of how the state should relate to the individual, can be illustrated with regard to three pressing issues of his day: the practice of theftbote, the problem of prostitution, and the proper approach to the alleviation of poverty. The issue of theftbote, the practice of paying thieves or their intermediaries for the return of stolen goods, is discussed in his 1725 pamphlet *An Enquiry into the Causes of the Frequent Executions at Tyburn*, which was a collection of shorter pieces he had published in the *British Journal* previously. It is striking that these pieces appeared in the years immediately after his notoriety had been assured. There were two topics covered in the pamphlet, the first being that of the practice of theftbote, the second that relating to the efficacy of public executions for maintain social order. Perhaps surprisingly, the first issue was arguably the one of greater social concern at the time. By the early 1720s, Jonathan Wild had set up a criminal business never before seen in London. His public persona was that of a 'thief-taker', one who would recover stolen goods and capture thieves, who would then be destined for the gallows.[15] His private persona was that he was the head of organized burglary and theft in London. He thereby worked businesses on both sides of the law. More importantly, the business of theft had evolved into something else: the business of theft and return. Wild would engineer the theft of some item, and if it wasn't more valuable as melted-down bullion, he would immediately place an advertisement offering himself as a go-between for its return to its rightful owner.

One might have thought that this is a case ripe for a Mandevillean defence. There is some obviously immoral behaviour taking place, yet there is also an economic activity that requires analysis separate from its moral condemnation. It would have been a typical move for Mandeville to come now to theftbote's defence, to argue for the general welfare of the public that is generated by the return of stolen goods, and how an economic activity ineffectively managed by the law courts might be better regulated by market behaviour. This is not what Mandeville argues, however. His case is that theftbote is properly a felony and one punishable to a degree comparable to the initial crime of theft itself. His argument is simply that the practice of buying back one's stolen goods increases the demand for stolen goods, which encourages more theft. Mandeville does not regard the theft of one's possessions as a good thing. He exhorts his readers to look at theftbote not as a way of redeeming one's own goods (he acknowledges it is helpful in this regard) but to consider how 'the whole suffers by the redemption'.[16] The act of securing one's stolen goods is not to be considered as merely an individual transaction but as a single data point in the generation of a system of supply and demand within a typical economic system. To engage in theftbote is 'as sure a way to keep up the breed of rogues, and promote the interest of them, as either our fishery or the coal trade are constant nurseries of sailors'.[17]

It is worth considering the case of theftbote with regard to the image of the wicked and immoral Mandeville. Here we have a case where he clearly advocates for an increase in the regulation and punishment of immoral behaviour for the greater good of society. His call here is in fact for legal reform, on the grounds that something that has been allowed to become a commercial activity regulated only by the self-interest of its practitioners should instead be curtailed by the law. While it might seem surprising then that Mandeville opposes theftbote, it is in fact very much in keeping with fundamental aspects of his thinking. It should be kept in mind that in promoting his view he is firstly attacking some established practice, which is always his preference. What's more, he sees in the case of theftbote an example of the fallacy of composition, the general fallacy of which the household fallacy is a special case, and which is at the heart of the message of *The Grumbling Hive*. There he had argued that what is bad for individuals is not thereby bad for society as a whole, despite the fact that society's composition is nothing but the totality of individuals. Even though vice is bad for every individual, some vice is good for society as a whole. In this case, Mandeville sees the fallacy at work again, though now with the values inverted. Since no one can see the harm in an individual transaction between an honest person who has lost their goods and the person who took them, they presume that the practice in general is acceptable. Now, however, he makes the point that what is good for the individual can be bad for society as a whole. Thinking from the perspective of the good of the system is Mandeville's fundamental concern.

One might still argue that even from the perspective of the system there are grounds for defending theftbote. It could be claimed that the harm of theft, even if encouraged by theftbote, is more than counterbalanced by the additional economic activity that is generated. The organization of the practice, the hiring of go-betweens, the printing of advertisements, the bureaucracy of the entire practice—all this surely generates economic benefit. Mandeville's opposition here reveals a deeper concern. His worry is that it undermines the very concept of property. The concept of property is that one has goods that one has rights over by virtue of one's labour, and that it is one's own discretion to dispose of them as one sees fit. It is simply part of the idea of property that one can still have rights over it even if someone else has taken possession of it. To allow theftbote, Mandeville thinks, implies that one might still have to buy back that to which one already has a right, and thereby blurs the boundaries of the notion of property itself. The worry is not just an abstract point of philosophical principle, though, since Mandeville thinks that this feature of property is what ordinary people rely upon as part of their investment in commercial activity as a way of life. 'There is no greater encouragement for men,' Mandeville claims, 'to follow any labour or handicraft than that they are paid as soon as they are done their work, without any further trouble'.[18] Laws against theft are there to ensure that lack of 'further trouble', and theftbote is merely a genteel way of undermining the idea that one has rights to the fruit of one's labours. Mandeville's opposition to theftbote is not a moralizing position and not an expression of horror at the normalization of theft. He thinks that it undermines the rights to property upon which trade and the general public good depend, and so his attack is still thoroughly economic in approach.

Mandeville had made a more notorious economic argument the year before he wrote *An Enquiry into the Causes of the Frequent Executions at Tyburn*. In 1724, he published *A Modest Defence of Publick Stews*, in which he argued for the legalization of prostitution. In the case of theftbote he argued for the economic benefits of the criminalization of an activity many ordinary people viewed as morally acceptable; in the case of prostitution he argued for the legalization of an activity many ordinary people viewed as morally unacceptable. He had already argued for the legalization of prostitution (in remark H of the *Fable*) and no doubt sought to capitalize on his newfound notoriety by publishing an extended version of one of its most scandalous parts. Several things jump out as one reads the *Modest Defence*, not least the practical approach Mandeville is recommending, and the consideration of the ways in which what is essentially a commercial activity can be recognized as such. Putting aside the vast amount of baiting of his conservative opponents and the inside jokes presented for his preferred reader, there nevertheless still remain proposals for the management of prostitution in society that Mandeville thinks eminently sensible. The practicality of the proposals is if anything more striking in the light of what Mandeville knows would be their inevitable rejection by the society of his day.

Central to his rhetoric is that the procurement of sex cannot be abolished so long as human nature exists, and that although it is undoubtedly a 'crime' against decency, we can 'divert it with policy, and prevent the mischief though we can't prevent the crime'.[19] The pragmatic and realist rhetoric is that if human nature can't be changed so as to eliminate altogether a certain kind of undesired activity, it is in fact the duty of the state to ensure that such activity takes place with the minimum of harm to society as a whole. To do this, Mandeville claims, a radical change in society is needed:

> When I talked of encouraging public whoring, I would be understood
> to mean, not only the erecting [of] public stews, as I first hinted, but

also the endowing [of] them with such privileges and immunities, and at the same time giving such discouragement to private whoring, as may be most effectual to turn the general stream of lewdness into this common channel.[20]

Mandeville proposes 'a hundred or more' public houses equipped with managing 'matrons', liquor licences, and rules for conduct. There would be an infirmary and house physicians. There would be different rates to appeal to customers of different incomes, and to match workers based upon their looks 'or other Qualifications'. Each sex worker would be taxed at a reasonable rate, and this tax would go towards an official inspector's fees, medical costs, pensions for 'superannuated courtesans', and a fund for 'the maintenance of bastard orphans'.[21] Mandeville's proposal and even his language are thoroughly economic, even when his tongue is in his cheek. He raises the worry that importation of prostitutes might have to take place if 'supplies should not prove sufficient to answer the greatness of the demand'.[22] Part of his argument is that the establishment of public stews would reduce the amount of prostitution that currently takes place. He argues that more women are drawn into prostitution than is necessary or should occur. Women who have suffered some disgrace as a result of their sexual behaviour find themselves excluded from polite society, and frequently find themselves cast into the role of a 'harlot', and only then take on that role out of economic necessity. Yet, Mandeville claims, if men's sexual energies were directed towards public stews, fewer women would be seduced by callous and enterprising men, and their virtue would be saved. There is also an implied appeal to the idea that market forces will tend to find the proper equilibrium between supply and demand, and he forecasts that soon after the establishment of the stews 'we shall not have one woman employed in the public service more than is absolutely necessary, nor one less than is fully sufficient'.[23]

As Laura Rosenthal and Emily Nacol have each importantly pointed out, Mandeville is clearly implying that there is an element of trade at play in sexual relations in all strata of society.[24] The reason why there is money to be made from the satisfaction of sexual desire in the first place is because virtue creates that demand.

By declaring themselves too decent to engage in sex for sex's sake, virtuous women create a seller's market for sex, where supply lags far behind demand. Prostitutes provide two essential societal functions, then: on the one hand they provide supply for the sexual demand, but by trading sex for money, they also reaffirm virtuous women's higher social status. They confirm that those women are the ones who partake in virtue for virtue's sake. This is vital for the economy of esteem into which women are raised for the purposes of securing profitable marriages. With a vital flow of sexual energy directed away from them and towards prostitutes, the risk of their being debauched is substantially reduced, and the chances of their making wholesome marriage matches are thereby increased. Therefore, each economy—the economy of sex and the economy of esteem—is promoted by dint of being distinguished from the other. Despite the deliberately shocking claim—made half-seriously, half-jokingly—that the legalization of prostitution would inevitably reduce the amount of sin and lewdness in society, Mandeville clearly has genuine concerns that he thinks justify the legalization on ethical grounds. Part of his analysis is that the hyper-moralized status of sexual vice makes the risk of women being 'debauched' too high. His casually cruel line from remark H that we need prostitutes lest returning sailors ravish our more precious virtuous daughters belies the thoughts, more directly expressed in *The Virgin Unmask'd*: that men are both sexually relentless and in positions of power over women; that women are highly sexed creatures just like men; and that the combination of the two, along with the norms of sexual morality, puts women more at risk than men.

One cannot help but wonder how many of the ill effects of this combination of factors were ones that Mandeville dealt with himself in his medical practice. One reason why prostitution must be organized, he claims, is that the 'French pox'—syphilis—is ruinous of lives and cannot be treated effectively if its main form of transmission is via an activity that is itself unregulated. It is wilful moralism to say that it affects only wrongdoers, since 'men give it to their wives, women to their husbands, or perhaps their children; they to their nurses, and the nurses again to other children'.[25] The costs of subterfuge, constant medical treatment, and so on tend to have a destabilizing effect on men's lives in general, but Mandeville is keen to point out 'the injury it does to particular persons and families . . . by alienating the affections of wives from their husbands, which often proves prejudicial to both, and sometimes fatal to whole families'.[26] Mandeville wants us to look squarely at the reality of sexual behaviour and to acknowledge the enormous social and emotional costs that human beings bear as a result of it. Finally, there is the phenomenon of infanticide due to unwanted pregnancies, one to which Mandeville returns again and again in a variety of his writings. He cannot see that the legalization and regulation of prostitution would do anything but reduce the number of infant deaths. These thoughts—far from amoral cynical humour—are ones that he thinks are available to us once we stop thinking in terms of reforming society by rigidifying moral norms of individual conduct. Instead, we must start thinking about achieving real reductions in human suffering by acknowledging patterns of human behaviour, including the regular deviance from sexual norms within a society, and the consequences. When we look on human society as a system of patterns of behaviour, new solutions recommend themselves for its management.

While ethical arguments appear to be on offer in the cases of theftbote and prostitution, it is on the topic of poverty that we perhaps see Mandeville at his worst. As we have already seen, the context of 'An Essay on Charity, and Charity Schools' was Mandeville's opposition to the charity school movement and his perception of their covert religious and political agendas. Nevertheless, many would have seen the argument for the perpetuation of an uneducated working class as in keeping with the overall amoral economic reasoning of *The Grumbling Hive*. The central claim is that attempts to eradicate either vice or poverty are equally hypocritical ventures, since the projects are embarked upon only by those already in a position of prosperity, and that very prosperity depends on the perpetual maintenance of a poverty-stricken underclass servicing privilege. It might seem at first as if Mandeville has no conception that being born into privilege affords opportunities to those who would not otherwise show the aptitude to realize them. More importantly, perhaps, Mandeville shows no concern with the idea that a lack of privilege debars individuals from opportunities for which they have sufficient aptitude. He appears entirely unaware of the very idea of a class system perpetuating exploitation by way of the prevention of social mobility. Yet this cannot be the case, since Mandeville's whole rhetoric is based upon the charge of hypocrisy, and the hypocrisy in question is exactly the charge that those advocates of charity schools preach social mobility while benefitting from the absence of it. The entire thrust of his argument is that the system of modern commercial society functions by virtue of its perpetuating inequalities and exploiting the working class. The problem with Mandeville is not that he lacks an understanding of this truth but that he endorses it.[27]

Mandeville's endorsement of capitalist exploitation does come with some notable qualifications. His language is harsh, yet it should be noted that he is not so much arguing for the perpetuation of poverty as requesting that advocates of charity schools acknowledge that the suppression of wage levels is an essential element of what they take to be a properly functioning economy. He claims that 'the greatest grievance of farmers, gardeners and others, where hard labour is required, and dirty work to be done is that they can't get servants for the same wages they use to have them at'.[28] Wage inflation is a natural phenomenon anyway, Mandeville implies, and so it behoves us employers to operate counterbalancing forces to keep wage expectations down. The motivation for this is not private benefit but the wealth of the public in general:

> It is in our power to have a much greater plenty than we enjoy, if agriculture and fishery were taken care of as they might be; but we are so little capable of increasing our labour, that we have hardly Poor enough to do what is necessary to make us subsist. The proportion of the society is spoiled and the bulk of the nation, which should everywhere consist of labouring poor, that are unacquainted with everything but their work, is too little for the other parts. In all business where downright labour is shunned or overpaid, there is plenty of people. To one merchant you have ten book-keepers . . . and everywhere in the country the farmer wants hands.[29]

Again Mandeville is requesting that the reader consider the issue in terms of the supply and demand of labour, and the manipulation of wage levels that is required in order to manage supply. Mandeville's innovation here is his insistence that a putatively social and moral issue—the education of the unskilled labourer—has to be considered within an image of society considered as a nexus of social, political, and economic factors. At some point the reforming spirit of progressive politics will have to ask itself who will dig the ditches and bake the bread, and it should ask itself that question before and not after shortages arrive.[30] A generous interpretation of Mandeville's interjection here is that he is willing to adopt the persona of an advocate for keeping the poor starving just so he can make a plea for the relevance of economic considerations with regard to the management of society.

Once one considers all the rhetorical ends to which Mandeville is conspiring, however, it is difficult to attribute strong claims to him with any confidence. The attack on religiosity in society is clearly his primary target. He does not look down on the poor and judge them harshly, he claims. What Mandeville claims to despise is the 'petty reverence for poor that runs through most multitudes'.[31] He thinks that this comes from the thought that the poor are especially blessed, and for that reason owed special care in providing them with a good life. But Mandeville doesn't think any human beings are blessed, and he thinks there is no single form of the good life.[32] Happiness is a motley concept, a placeholder for whatever set of desires a particular person, or culture, or historical era, projects onto it. What is on offer in the charity schools is one particular conception of the good life, a kind of intellectual cultivation that leads to Christian piety. Mandeville thinks that indoctrination into Christian devotion is an explicit requirement for anyone requiring charitable aid.

There are even some grounds for doubting the sincerity of any of Mandeville's claims in the 'Essay on Charity'. At one point, he points out that educating the people is a dangerous business, since once educated they are inclined to get ideas of their own. There is an ironic reading of the 'Essay on Charity', which points out that the improvement of the working class will lead to the undermining of the ruling class, so that the ruling class had better watch which institutions they promote and how far they intend to improve the lower orders. Mandeville claims to be appalled when he recounts hearing of collective bargaining by porters for their services. He notes that the workers might unionize and expect rights along with the provision of their labour. He might just be having fun with the Societies for the Reformation of Manners, pointing out the actual repressive social agenda behind the apparent emancipatory one. It is possible, though, that Mandeville might have been drawing attention to the unionizing activity of the footmen with private approval, and that his aim is to appal those upper-class endorsers of charity schools, whom he knew would oppose it. If this ironic reading is possible, then Mandeville's actual own views regarding the necessity of maintaining a poor labouring class can be cast into some doubt.

Flashes of this more radical Mandeville emerge here and there. In *The Virgin Unmask'd* in 1708, Mandeville has Antonia note that a major aspect of social inequality, the 'subordinations of the degrees of people', is that it perpetuates itself.[33] In Holland, he asserts, the lowest person is so proud of their liberty that the ordinary person is routinely 'saucy'—they often show outrageous disregard to the highest magistrate (as, one is reminded, the young Mandeville did during the Costerman affair); in France, the difference between the nobility and the ordinary person is vast. The effect of this is that in France the ordinary people live in great poverty but are relatively unperturbed by it, at least compared with their equivalents in other countries:

> Where the poor set such a small value upon themselves and esteem the better sort far above their own rank, it must follow that they will work much cheaper, and be contented to live much meaner, than where they are so haughty.[34]

In fact—and this is rather surprising for the politically conservative image of Mandeville—he says that differences in poverty in different states are determined by their model of government more than anything else. In a commonwealth, the pride a human being takes in their liberty precludes them from accepting low rates of pay:

> Where nations are equal in riches and plenty, the lowest rank of people will not be so poor in a commonwealth, as in a kingdom; and that they must still be more superlatively mean in an absolute, than in a limited monarchy.[35]

Writing as a Dutchman in Great Britain, there is an obvious and controversial inference to be drawn. In Great Britain, the poverty of the French people and the tyranny of its form of government are deplored. Yet the poverty is explained by the low self-regard the ordinary person has for themselves in an absolute monarchy. Great Britain is then compared unfavourably to Holland. The former is still a monarchy, albeit one limited by Parliament, and this explains why it is populated by working classes that have only occasional flashes of their own self-worth. The workforce's self-esteem is frequently undermined by the structure of Great Britain's social strata, by the preservation of an aristocratic class. Mandeville obviously holds that economic structures determine political ones, but he also thinks the opposite can be the case, and that economic behaviour can be influenced by the political self-image of economic agents. William Temple, too, had noted that the examples from history of successful trading states had always been commonwealths. But he makes it plain that he doesn't think that a commonwealth is the only form of government that encourages trade, and that a society 'may thrive under good princes and legal monarchies, as well as under free states'.[36] What is inimical to trade, Temple says, is 'arbitrary and tyrannical power', when ordinary subjects have no sense of their security or have no trust in their neighbours.[37] Mandeville, though, makes a far more radical claim: he argues that tyrannical power in an absolute monarchy has its own economic benefits, since by keeping the self-esteem of its subjects low it keeps labour costs down. Given Mandeville's lifelong opposition to religious tyranny and absolute monarchy, the ironic implication is that he thinks more secularized and less authoritarian political structures tend to reduce wage inequality and increase the living standards of the worst off in society.

It is clear that Mandeville also takes issue with the idea that there are certain national characteristics associated with the Dutch or the French, such as those of industry and prodigality respectively. There are no national moral characteristics, Mandeville claims, no 'Country Vices', just ordinary human desires that are common to all. There are also prudent and less prudent ways to realize them. It is these latter things that vary from country to country. If a state is prosperous and if there are many employment opportunities, then a worker might be able to afford to take it easy in one job, since they know they can get another. If the country is prosperous and the cost of living low, a poor person can nevertheless manage to be comfortable doing less work than they would need to elsewhere. The very same person in a different state—like Holland, Mandeville comments—where land is scarce and resources precious, will need to develop a different attitude in order to get by. There is no national character, only contingent circumstances to which the human being must adapt.

This chimes with Mandeville's wonderful example of the porter from remark V of the *Fable*, which relates to the third dimension of economic thinking, on how individuals relate to one another. He tells of a gentleman who tries to procure a porter to take a message for him for a penny. The porter says he will do the work for two pence, and when the gentleman refuses the higher rate the porter declines the work, saying that he would rather 'play for nothing than work for nothing'.[38] The gentleman is offended at the porter's haughty idleness, and his preference for inactivity over honest work. Later that evening, the gentleman finds himself in desperate need of a messenger to pick up a bill of exchange late at night. The night is cold and windy, and the gentleman has to offer a crown to an agent to procure any porter willing to do the work and be back by midnight. Just before the stroke of midnight, an exhausted and sodden porter returns. While congratulating the porter for his industry and speed, the gentleman notices that the man he is praising is the same porter from that morning. Mandeville's point is that the porter is neither lazy nor industrious—he simply had an intuitive grasp of the value of his own labour in the context of the situation. In the morning the porter declines to supply his labour to the gentleman—the reason he does this is that he has other opportunities to sell his labour at a higher rate. It is not, as the gentleman supposes, that he lacks a sense of industry. It is economically rational behaviour to refuse to work rather than drive down one's own rates for the sake of immediate reward. Later, when the gentleman needs work done urgently, the demand is high, but the time-sensitive nature of the task means that supply is limited—he has to offer more money to entice someone to do the hard task at that late time of night. When he finds someone to do the task, he praises the person's industry, and is surprised to learn that it is the same individual from that morning. But he shouldn't have been surprised, Mandeville implies, since the porter was motivated by the same thing in the evening as he was in the morning: an evaluation of whether the reward was adequate to the labour he was to expend. He was not a paragon of industry in the evening any more than he was shiftless in the morning.

The example connects Mandeville's economic thinking to this claim regarding political structures. In an absolute monarchy, where there is a range of conventional prohibitions upon social interaction between the upper and lower classes, the impossibility of the advancement of the lower orders is regularly reinforced. It is not just the vast inequality but the cultural attitudes towards upward mobility that, in Mandeville's view, determine labour costs. Where no one imagines a real opportunity to improve their position in society, one comes to think of one's value in society as fixed, and as having an upper threshold whereby that value is expressed monetarily. This, Mandeville says, means that the individual in an absolute monarchy is less intuitively aware of the value of their own labour, and so is less inclined to behave as the porter in England does and less disposed to bargain well, and so is more disposed to accept lower rates for their labour. Although the outcome of this analysis is an effect on labour costs, Mandeville is not at all an economic determinist, claiming that the course of history and political institutions is determined by the laws of economics pushing and pulling us where they will. On the contrary, the laws of supply and demand are themselves affected by political power structures and by what we might now call class ideology.

The majority of Mandeville's most important ideas are ones made famous by his successors. The most notable example of this is the notion of the division of labour, which though introduced by Mandeville is more commonly associated with Adam Smith's development of it in *An Inquiry into the Nature and Causes of the Wealth of Nations* (1776). Mandeville introduces the idea in his remarkable 'crimson cloth' passage:

> What a bustle is there to be made in several parts of the world, before a fine scarlet or crimson cloth can be produced, what multiplicity of

trades and artificers must be employed! Not only such as are obvious, as wool-combers, spinners, the weaver, the cloth-worker, the scourer, the dyer, the setter, the drawer and the acker; but others that are more remote and might seem foreign to it; as the mill-wright, the pewterer and the chemist, which yet are all necessary as well as a great number of other handicrafts to have the tools, utensils, and other implements belonging to the trades already named: but all these things are done at home and may be performed without extraordinary fatigue or danger; the most frightful prospect is left behind, when we reflect on the toil and hazard that are to be undergone abroad, the vast seas we are to go over, the different climates we are to endure, and the several nations we must be obliged to for their assistance.[39]

The day of the artisan, one who brought a product from conception to actuality simply with the fruit of their own individual labour, is over. Taking just a single product as an example, Mandeville traces the range of labourers and types of labour that must all be in play just for that single product to exist, and this is not to mention the manufacturing required for all the tools particular to their related supporting industries. The point is reminiscent of the central scandalous thesis of *The Grumbling Hive* and the idea that one kind of product, the treatment of gout say, must involve an enormous range of doctors, medicine makers, sellers of books on treatments, delivery agents, and so on. One might think that the best benefit to society would be the elimination of gout, but this is to ignore the way economies in societies actually operate.

The division of labour theme goes to the heart of Mandeville's economic way of thinking, but it is striking that he again presents the case in terms of contrasting political regimes. He imagines that the production of that single piece of crimson cloth, if idly desired by a supremely powerful monarch, would be the very epitome of tyranny. It would require sending one's obedient servants across the seas on incredibly perilous missions for the correct dyes and manufacturing materials, and then ordering a range of individuals to work on whatever tasks the monarch decided were required for that single item. The difference with how the modern world has actually evolved could not be more striking. In the era that Britain was leaving, industry depended on hierarchically

controlled monopolies distributed by royal favour at court. Breaking into those industries was a tightly regulated practice. In the
modern era, industries emerge spontaneously, and anyone is free to
pursue them if they have enough will and initiative. No one today,
Mandeville notes, has their wills coerced in the production of that
crimson cloth. There is consumer desire, and those who are willing
to sail abroad to retrieve the materials so as to satisfy those desires
do so; if they don't wish to do so, they do something else, and some
other sailor inevitably takes on the job because *they* desire the
profit on offer. No one complains of the work, but rather thinks
that the ability to earn a livelihood is a blessing compared with
the opportunities offered to their parents before them. Everywhere
one looks, Mandeville says, families are improving their material
conditions without a sovereign telling them how they ought to live.
Key to this is that there is no constraint on what drives trade. What
is truly remarkable is that the supply lines, companies, insurance
agents, maritime merchants, and a range of other professions are
all brought into being in securing the crimson cloth in a way that
requires that they *still exist* after the cloth is produced. There is
an enormous difference in the economic productivity introduced
into a society when it is allowed to operate organically through
the enterprise of individuals. In the case of the absolute monarch,
the whim is achieved after great individual labour, but nothing
structural has changed in society once the poor servants have done
their work. When the crimson cloth is demanded by consumer
desire, however, then that desire is satisfied through the establishment of a commercial structure in society that perpetuates society's
overall economic benefit.

It does not matter what particular thing consumers demand as
long as there is consumer demand. Mandeville says:

> What a vast traffic is drove . . . what a variety of labour is performed in
> the world to the maintenance of thousands of families that altogether
> depend on two silly if not odious customs; the taking of snuff and the
> smoking of tobacco; both of which it is certain do infinitely more hurt
> than good to those that are addicted to them!'[40]

He also considers the benefits not of vices but of misfortune and the
imperfection of things in general. In a long passage he imagines

the possibility of a perfectly long-lasting ship that always manages
to set sail in fair seas and with good winds. The amount of economic activity that would be lost, without the need for repairs and
the replacement of various parts of the ship, would be considerable. Similarly, the opportunities that would be forgone by those
looking to replace the business lost in storms or other disasters
would have a deleterious effect on trade in general, driving down
commerce rather than improving it. Mandeville has a keen sense
of the advantages of the obsolescence of material products, though
the point goes significantly deeper than that. He is always trying to draw our attention to the ways in which a thriving system
works, and to how a genuinely buzzing beehive is achieved through
constant demolitions and rebuildings, repairs and removals, calam-
ities and constructions. What looks like a bad outcome might be so
only relatively, to the individuals in close proximity to the event (to
the sailors on the ship that is lost at sea, one might think). There
are different perspectives which one could take on the same event,
and if one is thinking in economic terms, then the perspective one
should take is a very broad one. When one does this one starts to
see imperfections, whether in humans or their environments, as
part of the necessary stimuli for a dynamic system to do its work:

> But the necessities, the vices and imperfections of man, together
> with the various inclemencies of the air and other elements, contain
> in them the seeds of all arts, industry and labour: it is the extremities of
> heat and cold, the inconstancy and badness of seasons, the violence and
> uncertainty of winds, the vast power and treachery of water, the rage and
> untractableness of fire, and the stubbornness and sterility of the earth,
> that rack our invention how we shall either avoid the mischiefs they may
> produce, or correct the malignity of them and turn their several forces to
> our own advantage a thousand different ways; while we are employed in
> supplying the infinite variety of our wants, which will ever be multiplied
> as our knowledge is enlarged, and our desires increase.[41]

Here he returns to what he sees as the ludicrous opposition to luxury, given that the increase in our desires is a natural by-product of
the increase in our knowledge of how the risks of nature might be
managed, and the management of the risks of nature is simply the
human condition.

Mandeville's economic way of thinking also helps us to understand his concerns about morality as traditionally conceived—that is, as a set of things that are 'intrinsically good', 'right on principle', or 'good in themselves'. Following these passages on the division of labour, he writes:

> It is in morality as it is in nature, there is nothing so perfectly good in creatures that it cannot be hurtful to any one of the society, nor any thing so entirely evil, but it may prove beneficial to some part or other of the creation: so that things are only good and evil in reference to something else, and according to the light and position they are regarded in.[42]

His view here is less radically relativist than it might at first seem. He wants us to acknowledge that what we mean by 'good' is up for grabs, theoretically speaking, and that the judgment of whether or not something is good or evil will require first a consideration of it from different perspectives, and secondly an acknowledgement that something can be good from one of those perspectives and evil from another. After all that, it might be that we decide that one of those perspectives is the important one. First, though, we must acknowledge this general truth about values considered as a natural phenomenon within the dynamic system that is human society. There is still the radical point that these different orders of value, the moral and the economic, can be at odds with each other in very obvious cases. In remark B of the *Fable* Mandeville gives us a story of the duplicitous and manoeuvring activities of two stock traders, on the face of it close friends. What the friends understand is that the withholding of information in a duplicitous manner is exactly the kind of behaviour that is appropriate for securing a market advantage. It is what the other friend would do in the same circumstances. When one friend learns that the other has deceived him, he will be angry no doubt, but not morally resentful, for the very reason that he would do the same in similar circumstances. Yet there is no doubt that all this behaviour does not sit well with a commandment that thou shalt not lie. The 'golden rule' from the Bible, that one ought not to do anything that one would not have done to oneself, is conspicuously non-applicable here. Mandeville says that 'this is called fair dealing; but I am sure neither of them would have desired to be done by, as they did to each other'.[43] What is a sin in one context is fair dealing in another. A range of business behaviours—for example, driving down prices to put a competitor under pressure, or buying them out when they are financially vulnerable—are all rough treatment that is nevertheless understood by their practitioners to be part of the basic elements of business.

In general, Mandeville urges his readers not to moralize non-moral things. He frequently states that human beings in general find leisure preferable to work. They would prefer inactivity rather than activity. There are no doubt thrusting industrious types among us, but most of them have a desire for wealth or ambition for some status as the motive for their industry. Mandeville can't see that inactivity could ever really be a vice in itself. The only mistake is not to work when work is what is required for one's needs and wants. What is it, then, to be 'lazy' or 'hard-working'? For Mandeville, these are nothing but moralized constructs used to add an extra layer of value onto behaviour that is really about differences of opinion regarding the value of labour. What we tend to project onto a person—or sometimes even a nationality—in terms of virtues or vices of character reflect a failure to recognize that the behaviour we are observing is simply normal human economic behaviour.

There are also interesting connections to consider with regard to the theory of the division of labour and moralized conceptions of work. There are ideals of self-determination, autonomy, freedom, and artistic self-expression that are occasionally idealized in the image of the artisan, who moves from a pure conception of something with the individual power of their mind and then brings it into being with the power of their hands. This powerful individual might then exchange their unique product for other equally unique products, in a community of individual artist-kings. Mandeville anticipates pious homilies about the simple artisan as economic saint, one whose products are laden with the value of their very being, and whose labour is imbued with a kind of sacrosanct dignity. Labour, for Mandeville, is what people do to keep themselves in enough comfort to allow them to realize their pleasures. His very first remark in the *Fable* makes the same point—people have different levels of energy and different pleasures, and society has evolved marvellously to accommodate this fact. Of course, now we call these social roles 'professions' and tell ourselves that our pursuit of them can sometimes be 'vocations', or at the very least labours of love. For Mandeville, this is just entirely post hoc rationalization of the fact that as human beings with material needs, we have to do something to satisfy them, and what profession we choose is best explained as our doing whatever it is that will allow us to secure a living while not bending our natural dispositions too much out of shape. In short, we labour to the degree to which it suits us and no more.

It is perhaps no surprise that Mandeville has been seen as one of the originators of the concept of 'laissez-faire', that of letting the market achieve its results through its own inner workings and without intervention or regulation.[44] Mandeville has no explicit concept of laissez-faire, of course. His main agenda is to reveal the prevalence of economic considerations governing human behaviour, for which talk of social or moral virtues serves often as a cover. His audience is one who is unfamiliar with the very idea of rendering economic considerations first in the order of explanations, so his concern is to show just how much can be explained by economic factors. Mandeville's conception of what we today call economic behaviour is one where there is a dynamic interplay between commercial interests and social and legal regulation. There is no economic activity in the justice system if there is no set of laws for it to implement, and it is when vice is 'lopt and bound' by justice that the greatest economic activity consistent with 'aggrandizing the nation' is achieved. Just as William Temple had stressed the importance of political stability for economic prosperity, so too did Mandeville stress that the strict curbs of the rule of law play just as much a role in the development of a prosperous nation as do the wild enthusiasms of a self-interested consumer market. In remark L he comments that:

> Trade is the principal but not the only requisite to aggrandize a nation: there are other things to be taken care of besides. The *meum* and *tuum* must be secured, crimes punished, and all other laws concerning the administration of justice, wisely contrived, and strictly executed.[45]

The rule of law and the protection of what's mine and what's yours (the '*meum* and *tuum*') are necessary ingredients in promoting the greatness of a state—there is a clear denial here that a reduction in regulation will entail an increase in prosperity. The same 'dextrous' politicians who manipulate the morals of the population also have a responsibility to manage trade, and this can involve 'laying heavy impositions on some goods, or totally prohibiting them, and lowering the duties on others'.[46] It seems obvious that if great amounts of governmental regulation could be satisfactorily borne by a society of self-interested people then Mandeville would be for it. The question is only whether it will produce that strange dynamic mixture of opposing forces—the result of people sometimes meeting and sometimes *failing* to meet the standards required by societal regulations—that generates economic benefits for society as a whole. If Mandeville thought it would increase national prosperity as a whole he would by force of his own logic be in favour of increasing the amount of government regulation.

Mandeville's commitment to laissez-faire economics, such as it is, ought to be put in the historical context of the jumble of early eighteenth-century British writings on society. Economic activity was exploding, and people simply didn't know what to make of it.[47] What Mandeville contributed to was a new way of looking at ordinary activities, and this new way of looking became far more common after *The Fable of the Bees*. We can see this by considering two pieces by Mandeville's contemporary Jonathan Swift. In 1728 Swift published the pamphlet *An Answer to a Paper, Called 'A Memorial of the Poor Inhabitants, Tradesmen and Labourers of the Kingdom of Ireland'*, responding to a previous one which had proposed large tax increases on luxury goods. Swift responds that the idea that one can tax one's way out of economic difficulties is a fiction, and that he will tell his correspondent 'a secret, which I learned many years ago from the Commissioners of the Customs in *London*'.[48] What Swift discovered there was an instance of what was to be known as the Laffer curve, that increases in taxation do not always simply result in increases in revenue for the government. Although it is a well-known law of arithmetic that an increased tax will generate an increased revenue, this neglects a different law of economics, which is that at a certain point an increase in taxation will simply deter people from trade in that commodity. If the increase is too much, the government will retard business so much that it will end up generating less taxable income than it would have done had it kept the tax rate lower:

> They said, when any commodity appeared to be taxed above a moderate rate, the consequence was to lessen that branch of the revenue by one half, and one of those gentleman pleasantly told me, that the mistake of parliaments on such occasions was owing to an error computing two and two to make four. Whereas in the business of laying heaving impositions, two and two never made more than one, which happened by lessening the import, and the strong temptation of running [smuggling] such goods as paid high duties.[49]

To see like an economist is not to see like a mathematician, where the answers will always be straightforward. Rather, to see like an economist is to think about the arithmetic of rates of taxation in the context of their likely and predictable effects on human beings' group behaviour. Raising the taxes on an activity will always generate more tax revenue, *unless* the raising disincentivizes that activity—and it always does. Tax the legal trade too much and one encourages the black-market trade. For Swift, there is no point in expressing disapproval at this fact, let alone shock or outrage. That black-market trading is illegal or immoral is a fine point for leisurely discussion, but not for determining the best course of action for the prosperity of a people. Swift's point regarding the side effects of excessive taxation would be taken up in the economic writings of David Hume, Adam Smith, Alexander Hamilton, and others.[50] By the end of the eighteenth century, it was widely known just as a piece of ordinary common sense.

In the following year, Swift anonymously published a second pamphlet, one that has become rather better known. In *A Modest Proposal for Preventing the Children of Poor People from Being a Burden to Their Parents, or Country, and for Making Them Beneficial to the Public*, Swift targeted and combined two of Mandeville's most controversial issues: how to manage poverty effectively and how to keep a clear eye on whatever is to the public benefit, irrespective of how it might be regarded in terms of private virtue or vice. The problem was the 'prodigious number of children' in Ireland keeping their parents in poverty because of the cost of maintaining them. The side effects of this state of affairs were manifold: women were removed from the workplace while doing childcare, there was increased begging and thievery, emigration, and ultimately the perpetuation of national poverty. As Swift acknowledges, there have been many well-intentioned schemes for the alleviation of Irish poverty, ones that had all had little effect. Swift's proposal is that the children of Ireland have an obvious use that could be expediently exploited to the public good:

> I have been assured by a very knowing *American* of my acquaintance in *London*, that a young healthy child well nursed is at a year old a most delicious, nourishing, and wholesome food, whether *stewed, roasted, baked,* or *boiled,* and I make no doubt that it will equally serve in a *fricassee* or *ragout.*[51]

Swift runs through some calculations of the number of childbearing women ('Breeders') available in the country, their likely output, the number of meals that could be generated per child, and so on. He perceives immense benefits, not least that the Irish tenants will have an extra asset that they can exchange in lieu of rent to their English landlords. It would even 'be a great inducement to marriage' and 'increase the care and tenderness of mothers towards their children', when at present abortion and infanticide were prevalent practices. With a new system for how childbearing might be esteemed, 'we should soon see an honest emulation among the married women, *which of them could bring the fattest child to the market*', and 'men would become as fond of their wives, during the time of pregnancy, as they are now of their *mares* in foal . . . nor [would they] offer to beat or kick them (as is too frequent a practice) for fear of miscarriage'.[52] For Swift, then, the consideration of the public benefits of the modest proposal over any private moral scruples leads straightforwardly to better outcomes:

> I profess in the sincerity of my heart that I have not the least personal interest in endeavouring to promote this necessary work, since having no other motive than the *public good of my country*, by *advancing our trade, providing for infants, relieving the poor and giving some pleasure to the rich.*[53]

The prose, with its contrast of private interest and concern with the public good, the promotion of trade, the relief of the poor through tough but pragmatic policies, is thoroughly Mandevillean. It is of course also entirely *anti*-Mandevillean. Swift's satire focuses on the complete detachability of economic and consequentialist thinking from the concerns of morality. His satire functions because the economic proposals *make sense* economically. When we see like an economist, when we understand the costs and benefits to the group, we abstract from considerations that govern behaviour from the first-personal point of view, and then we often abstract from consideration of what really matters.[54] Swift and Mandeville are both convinced of the necessity of grasping that economic consequences are simply distinct from issues of individual morality. Mandeville never claimed that individual morality should be abandoned whenever a more promising economic fix offered itself. Yet Swift is ready to press the point that if Mandeville is right on the distinctness of the economic and moral orders of value then what might be prohibited by the moral order could be necessitated by the economic order. Swift's satire was occasioned by the perversity, complacency, and arrogance of British attitudes towards Irish suffering, but it can be viewed also as a powerful expression of a new general anxiety, that once the possibility of looking at the world like an economist has been recognized, it can never again be ignored.[55]

What, then, are we to make of Mandeville as an economist? His economic analyses always turn on the thoughts that unanticipated consequences can arise in an economic system, and that some kind of systemic benefits can emerge unplanned through the conflict of forces internal to that system. Hayek, then, was quite justified in his complaint that Mandeville's legacy should really be 'the definite breakthrough in modern thought [of] the twin ideas of evolution and of the spontaneous formation of an order', and that the reason his legacy was neglected was that he chose to express his ideas by way of the contrast between private and public interests.[56] One can make the distinction between individual benefits and benefits to the system overall, and suggest that the latter can nevertheless spring naturally from the former. These claims, however, are not particularly controversial in themselves, and perhaps can be cashed out in a variety of ways that might be palatable to the educated inquirer. This was not Mandeville's strategy, however. As Hayek puts it:

By making his starting-point the particular moral contrast between the selfishness of the motives and the benefits which the resulting actions conferred on others, Mandeville saddled himself with an incubus of which neither he nor his successors to the present day could ever quite free themselves.[57]

One might sympathize with those who feel that their advocacy of free-market solutions to social problems inevitably leads them to be characterized as apologists for rampant selfishness. The deeper point of Mandeville's 'breakthrough' was not at all tied to the idea that greed is good. It is not that immoral attitudes at the individual level always produce benefits for society as a whole. It is rather simply that the order of the system as a whole is morally *neutral*: whatever benefits accrue as a result of evolutionary developments and emerging order within the system are different in kind from individual-level moral considerations.[58] One might decide to regulate the market for moral reasons, but even in doing that one must surely acknowledge that the rational rules that govern the markets are different in kind from the rational rules that govern individual behaviour. Whatever approach one takes, one must see the situation clearly, and that means seeing it on Mandeville's terms.

Mandeville's thought, then, is not best understood as claiming that economic considerations should always trump moral ones. His aim is to show how economics permeates life at every scale of consideration. Moral considerations are just one further currency within this economy of esteem, he thinks, and if we examine how we work and trade in moral status then we will have learned all there is to know about morality. We do not need a philosophical examination of the nature of moral virtue; an analysis in terms of what we would now call the behavioural economics of virtue-*signalling* will tell us all there ever was to say about virtue. This is not as cynical as it sounds; Mandeville is in one sense sincere when he states himself in favour of the moral norms of the day. He is not denying that we are moral agents, but he is inviting us to reconsider just what this means. To be a moral agent for Mandeville is to be (in Irving Goffman's phrase) a 'merchant of morality'.[59] Morality is the currency with which human social trade takes place, and as such is no less real than the currency with which we purchase material goods.

In the end there is little to suggest that Mandeville endorsed a claim that what makes an action legitimate or illegitimate is to be decided by what economic benefit it brings. It is one thing to mock those who are so righteous as to refuse to consider the economic effects of their moralizing rhetoric; it is another to say that one should evaluate every policy solely in terms of its economic effects. Yet because Mandeville was clearly doing the former, it is sometimes presumed that he was also claiming the latter. It is worth repeating that his claim in *The Fable of the Bees* is not that unchecked desires tend to the economic benefit of society as a whole. His explicit claim is that the public benefits that accrue to society as a whole are as a result of human beings' ineliminable passions being regulated, curtailed, and punished within an organized social system. His claim is that economic benefit is different from moral behaviour, and to think that the former might be generated by the latter alone is fanciful self-deception. It is more accurate to say, perhaps, that he firstly accuses his opponents of positing a positive causal connection between private virtue and public benefit. Once on notice that morality and economics come apart, and that they can even be opposed, he points out the emptiness and hypocrisy of those who would advocate morality in every domain of social life, since these advocates are almost all without fail preaching from a position of already-secured economic benefit. They can quite literally afford to virtue-signal to their hearts' content.

The Grumbling Hive is a thought experiment regarding what would happen if human beings were capable of organizing their social and economic life in accordance with strictly adhered to moral rules. Mandeville firmly believes that human beings simply are not creatures who are capable of living in accordance with moral rules in this fashion. His purpose in making the unintended consequences of a moralized society clear is to expose that it is a 'vain utopia of the brain', one that is not a mere progressive ideal but a misshapen fantasy premised on a mischaracterization of human nature. His second claim regarding unanticipated consequences is that our imperfect natures demand that when we attempt to live in accordance with morality we set ourselves up to fail. However, *failing* to live up to the societal rules that we set ourselves can sometimes itself generate economic activity that benefits society as a whole. That the parts of the individual human being that we deplore nevertheless tend to the benefit of the species as a whole is a remarkable claim. Mandeville realized that underlying his account of human beings as merchants of morality was a theory of human nature that returned him to his first medical studies on the nature of animals. What he now needed to account for was just what exactly was going on when success came out of failure, when nature seemed to work behind our backs and yet to our benefit, when order emerged spontaneously out of disorder.

CHAPTER NINE

Spontaneous Order

In the depths of our minds, it seems, nature has hidden away talents and
forms of cleverness unknown to us; only the passions have the power of
bringing them to light, something giving us surer and more complete
insights than art could possibly do.

—LA ROCHEFOUCAULD, *MAXIMS*, 5:404)

MANDEVILLE RECEIVED WHAT MUST have been a very gratifying, if delayed, amount of moral outrage regarding the pernicious ideas in *The Fable of the Bees*. When one looks to Mandeville's publishing ambitions immediately after the scandal broke in 1723 one sees that he quickly set about writing a two-pronged response: on the one hand he wrote hurt denials of the charge that he was a libertine whose intent was to 'debauch the nation'. His constant refrain thereafter—from the 'Vindication of the Book' he published in 1724 to *A Letter to Dion* in 1732 (Mandeville's last published work and a response to the philosopher George Berkeley's objections to his licentious system)—is that he is terribly confused as to how anyone could have mistaken his writings for ones that promote immorality. On the other hand, he also set about writing as many shocking things as possible: he also sat down to write *A Modest Defence of Publick Stews* in 1724. Engaging in literary activities such as these is how Mandeville enjoyed himself in the last decade of his life.

Yet among the outraged responses to *The Fable of the Bees* there were some astutely reasoned critiques also. Some writers took Mandeville's views seriously enough to try to refute them, and many thinkers raised serious theoretical objections to the portrait of humanity that Mandeville had painted. Towards the end of his life there is a discernible shift in his writing output, marked by the publication of *The Fable of the Bees Part II* (1729) and the *Enquiry into the Origin of Honour and the Usefulness of Christianity in War* (1732), of which the latter could well be considered *The Fable of the Bees Part III*, so continuous is it with the preceding text.[1] There is no more Whig pamphleteering, ('I have nothing to do with Whigs or Tories'),[2] no more goading of the Societies for the Reformation of Manners. These texts are not directly concerned with the politics of the day in the same way that so much of what he had written previously had been. Nor are these works even particularly concerned with the paradox of private vices and public benefits. Mandeville seems less concerned to support his previous claim regarding the economic benefits of immoral behaviour. He has a more serious agenda now, which is to set out his theory of human nature and society in a developed way, one that is continuous with his previous writing but that sets it on a sounder footing against the objections he had received. These final works did not attract the acrimony of the public at the time, nor have they gained much sustained scholarly attention since.[3]

What we do not find, however, is Mandeville setting out his serious agenda by writing in a serious way. These works are not set out as analytical accounts of human moral psychology and social anthropology, ones that address each of his interlocutors explicitly in turn, evaluate the merits of the objections, and note the adjustments to his theory that those objections require in a fair and even-handed manner. To write in such a way now would be to abdicate Mandeville's own deepest-held philosophical and aesthetic commitments. In any case, Mandeville had not written in an academic style since he was a student at Leiden, and then it was only because he had to. The *Fable II* and the *Enquiry* are still thoroughly Mandevillean in style, in that they deploy irony, dissimulation, distraction, humour, and rhetoric to make their case. Nevertheless, it is clear that Mandeville is trying to use the opportunity of his notoriety to express what he takes to be his more significant thoughts about what it is to be a human being, a project that is in some ways more continuous with his medical theory in the *Treatise of the*

Hypochondriack and Hysterick Passions —which he had republished in 1730—than it is with *The Fable of the Bees*.

One very notable feature of these works is that in them Mandeville returns to the literary form that he had last adopted in the *Treatise*, that of dialogue. What he acknowledges, and spends some time discussing in *Fable II*'s preface, is that this mode of expression is one that is particularly prone to abuse. He claims that we find, even in the dialogues of Plato or those of Cicero later, a tendency to present straw men, opponents who offer opposition so weak as to strain credulity. Some figure resists a point of view on one page but only a few pages later can be seen to be acquiescing or even enthusiastically agreeing with every proposal that the writer's protagonist now makes. Ultimately, Mandeville confesses that he has no defence against these concerns—in fact, he happily and brazenly engages in these very excesses. As the dialogues progress we indeed find that the disputants, Horatio and Cleomenes, aren't at loggerheads for very long. Cleomenes is Mandeville's spokesperson, and is supposed to be a friend of the author of *The Fable of the Bees*; Horatio is a young gentleman who has not read it but knows of its reputation, and is deeply upset by Cleomenes's enthusiasm for it. *Fable II* starts off with this social awkwardness between them, and Cleomenes hopes to reconcile with Horatio by promising that he has abandoned all his allegiance to Mandeville's thought. He hasn't, of course, but this hooks Horatio in, and by the third dialogue Horatio himself is mostly a convert. His function in the conversations is merely to request more detail and clarification, and he rarely offers any resistance.

In the preface Mandeville says that, despite its drawbacks, he will proceed with the dialogue form anyway, on the grounds that a reputable philosopher such as Pierre Gassendi has used it and 'not only explained and illustrated his system, but likewise refuted his adversaries'.[4] We are put on notice from the beginning with regard to the aims and methods of Mandeville's forthcoming inquiry. He has told us that inquiries such as these can appear biased and self-serving and lack the appropriate standards of impartial argumentative evaluation; he has told us he is going to use the dialogue form anyway, since it suits his aims best. The reference to Gassendi serves a precise function. The clued-in reader is supposed to infer that the text to follow will be less concerned with strict proof and deduction from a priori principles as could be found, for example, in Descartes's *Meditations*. It is worth noting that Gassendi did *not* in fact usually write dialogues; however, as a devotee of the philosophy of Epicurus, Gassendi *did* insist upon the empirical examination of nature, the priority of experience in understanding the physical world, and the eschewing of abstract theorizing in the absence of corroborating evidence.[5] Mandeville is signalling in his usual indirect manner that the forthcoming work is for those who are perhaps already of an empiricist disposition.

Such readers aren't in any case the kind of people who believe that claims about human nature and morality are established through logical proof or mathematical demonstration. Mandeville thinks that Gassendi 'refuted his adversaries' well enough without such arguments. We find that in *Fable II* Mandeville straightforwardly asserts that 'knowing *a priori* belongs to God only, and divine wisdom acts with an original certainty of which what we call demonstration is but an imperfect borrowed copy'.[6] In the *Treatise*, Mandeville's patient had asked for a medical theory and was refused one—instead, Mandeville's protagonist simply insists on listening and talking about common interests until a rapport is built that is strong enough for the patient to listen to his modest advice. Here, Horatio's conversion to Cleomenes's way of thinking happens relatively abruptly. Cleomenes discusses the example of duelling as a morally problematic case of honourable action, knowing that Horatio's conscience is troubled by a duel that he fought in his youth. Just as in the *Treatise*, Mandeville is attempting to match literary form to the philosophical content. His philosophical view is that human beings are not the kind of beings upon whom abstract deductive reasoning has any effect, and in his dialogues individuals are convinced through rhetorical and persuasive strategies that sometimes accompany argument and sometimes replace it altogether.[7]

Whatever one may think about his methodology, it is certainly the case that the theory that Mandeville presents in *Fable II* and the *Enquiry* is one he thinks is true. These works attempt to justify and elaborate the broad picture of human nature he presented in the *Treatise* and *The Fable of the Bees*, while also maintaining the elusive ironic stance that permeates so much of his preceding writing.

He is responding to his opponents in his own fashion. Moreover, it is with these later works that we see that Mandeville is not only a genius synthesizer of the thoughts of others but just how much he is an original thinker in his own right. The later works have three entirely novel elements that together form the essence of his mature theory. The first element is the introduction of the passion of *self-liking*, which is the natural drive a creature has to display its own value in an exaggerated fashion.[8] The second element is the idea that gradual and arbitrary historical development is adequate to explain things that now appear as something designed and purposeful. While the idea isn't original with Mandeville, he was the first to claim that this idea could be applied to the human mind itself. The ways in which we think and reason—the phenomenon of human consciousness itself—might have developed as a defining part of our biological constitution not because they serve any designated purpose but rather because they are the product of gradual historical processes. Mandeville proposes what is clearly a proto-evolutionary theory of the mind.

The third element is the notion that with the combination of the previous two elements we can explain an enormous range of phenomena whereby patterns have been introduced into human social relations considered as a system. Social relations are the product of immensely long natural-historical processes. Through enormous procedures of trial and error, patterns of human behaviour emerged that constitute effective ways for large groups to handle and regulate the phenomenon that individuals have a natural tendency towards overvaluing aspects of their own being. The result is the gradual emergence of a self-regulating system that produces beneficial functions for the species overall. Nature produces order spontaneously without the elements within the system—in this case, those elements are *us*—having any conscious or rational idea of how or why the system works.[9] What matters to the system is that they follow their own natural roles, which are determined by their natural drives and instinct. The picture Mandeville presents is, then, ultimately one that explains how private benefits generate public benefits, yet this political point pales into insignificance in comparison to the import of the theory itself, which is nothing less than a theory of the evolution of human society.[10]

One finds that Mandeville rarely identifies the opponents he takes seriously. He does not set out their positions scrupulously with an aspiration to evaluate the correct viewpoint on the level ground of philosophical argument. Mandeville begins and ends *Fable II* by mentioning the falsity of Shaftesbury's views.[11] He singles out Shaftesbury, just as he did in *The Fable of the Bees*, for several reasons. Shaftesbury was a prominent and renowned philosopher who maintained two claims entirely antithetical to Mandeville's position and so was a natural target for attack and ridicule. In his *Inquiry Concerning Virtue or Merit* (1711) Shaftesbury maintained, firstly, that human beings are imbued with a natural 'moral sense' and, secondly, that individuals realize the public good when they follow what that individual moral sense recommends. Since our moral sense is pleasing to us, he claims, as well as being beneficial for the whole, then 'virtue and interest may be found at last to agree'.[12] An essential part of Shaftesbury's thought was how what was right for the individual would inevitably be right for the whole of society. This is a truth about the structure of the natural world, he claimed, that of there being a 'a system of all animals: an animal order or economy according to which the animal affairs are regulated and disposed'.[13]

One of the particular reasons why Shaftesbury is a target for Mandeville is that he suggests that morality is a naturally occurring and real phenomenon. Mandeville never loses his conviction that moral virtue is explained similarly to the social development of a religious framework. He is eager to debunk the idea that we proceed from some natural and simple grasp of right and wrong that is detachable from a supernatural framework. Shaftesbury's means of claiming that every individual has a private interest in maintaining the public good is so hopeful and ecstatic, however, as to nearly compete with supernatural explanations. He claims that each human being perceives the beauty of systematic order and the unpleasantness of disorder and that this is enough to regulate our behaviour in a virtuous fashion:

> In the meanest subjects of the world, the appearance of order gains upon the mind and draws the affection towards it. But if the order of the world itself appears just and beautiful, the admiration and esteem

of order must run higher and the elegant passion or love of beauty, which is so advantageous to virtue, must be the more improved by its exercise in so ample and magnificent a subject.[14]

Mandeville mocked Shaftesbury in *The Fable of the Bees*—and continues to mock him in *Fable II*—as a Pollyanna-like figure, one who always sees the very best in every aspect of human nature. Yet what perhaps really accounts for Mandeville's ongoing interest in contrasting his position with Shaftesbury's is that, ironically, many of the themes of his account are present in Mandeville's own mature theory: an attempt to take a naturalistic perspective, an eagerness to draw comparisons and analogies between how humans and other animals behave, and a focus on how micro-level behaviour is to be understood at the macro level of systems. Mandeville's project can be thought of as trying to show that when these elements are truly understood then conclusions diametrically opposed to Shaftesbury's can be drawn.

If one wants to understand the final response to Shaftesbury in *Fable II*, however, one must examine what Mandeville is most obviously doing in the later works that differs from what came before. When one does this one can make a plausible case that he was in large part responding to problems raised regarding *The Fable of the Bees* by the Church of England priest and theologian William Law.[15] Law wrote his *Remarks upon a Late Book, Entitled the 'Fable of the Bees'* in 1724, immediately after the scandal broke. At over a hundred pages, it was in effect the first extended published engagement with Mandeville's thought. It was the outraged reaction Mandeville had been waiting for since at least 1705. It was also a work that was cited as particularly powerful by other critics of Mandeville, such as Richard Fiddes and Alexander Innes. It contains objections that anticipate ones made by more famous philosophers, such as Joseph Butler and David Hume, in subsequent years.[16] Moreover, Law's attack would have been a very engaging read for Mandeville—the *Remarks* is a fascinating mixture of po-faced religious polemic, satirical swipes, and astute philosophical analysis. Law sees exactly what Mandeville is up to. He grasps that humour and mockery might be needed just as much as argument in order to combat Mandeville's immoral and irreligious agenda. He also grasps that

Mandeville's fundamental claims are that we are animals and that specifically human moral notions were invented as part of the process of bringing humans out of a 'savage' animalistic state and into civil society. Therefore, morals are invented and artificial. Law cleverly ignores the outrageous material on charity schools and prostitution, and instead attacks these larger claims, the ones with implications for human nature, religion, and morality.

Law's own rhetoric is no doubt powerful. He notes that Mandeville presumes that the change of humans from savages into moral agents is best explained as occurring by their being deceived into an invented institution of morality. This, Law says, makes as much sense as saying that the curing of the mentally unwell is an account of their being deceived into the invention of rationality—why not rather say that in both cases they were *helped* and *educated* into grasping something real?[17] Law outlines the conspiracy theory of clever politicians and theorists inventing morality presented in Mandeville's 'Enquiry into the Origin of Moral Virtue' and then engages in some snarky mockery:

> What a graphic description is here! One would think that you had been an eye witness to all that passed and that you held the candle to those first philosophers when they were so carefully peeping into human nature. You don't love to dwell on these little matters, or else you could have told us the philosopher's name, who first discovered this *flattery*; how long he looked before he found it; how he proved it to be agreeable to pride; what disputes happened upon the occasion; and how many ages of the world had passed before this consultation of the philosophers.[18]

Law remarks that a few easy reflections on the supposed event that Mandeville claims inaugurated the very practice of morality reveals a noteworthy point—it never happened. Law similarly engages in superb mockery of Mandeville's general reasoning regarding the function of pride, showing that it could be wielded to give an absurd conspiracy theory origin for any distinguishing feature of the human species. Law wonders whether Mandeville has come across the work '*Origin of the erect posture of mankind*', in which clever politicians 'extolled the excellency of his shape above other animals and told him what a grovelling thing it was to creep on all four like the meanest animals'.[19] This precedes an even more substantial criticism, which is that Mandeville has introduced an unnatural explanation of morality that ignores the plain evidence of experience:

> Had there ever been a time when there was nothing of [moral virtue] in the world, it could no more have been introduced than the faculties of *seeing* and *hearing* could have been contrived by men who were *blind* and *deaf*. Were not the first principles and reasons of morality connatural to us, and essential to our minds, there would have been nothing for the moral philosophers to have improved upon. Nor indeed can any arts or sciences be formed but in such matters as where nature has taken the first steps herself, and shown certain principles to proceed upon. *Perspective* supposes an agreement in the different appearance of objects. *Music* supposes a . . . perception of various sounds, and *moral philosophy* supposes an acknowledged difference of good and evil. Were we not all naturally *mathematicians* and *logicians*, there would be no such sciences; for science is only an improvement of those first principles or ways of thinking which nature has given us.[20]

At first, Law's objection here might seem to miss the point of Mandeville's theory. Law claims that we would have needed some prior grasp of morality if politicians were ever to flatter us successfully and manipulate us into obeying it. But Mandeville had explicitly denied this exact point—what we already had was not an interest in morality but an interest in being a creature of a higher status than other animals. We were creatures who grasped the idea of esteem and had a prior interest in ascribing value to ourselves; Mandeville claimed that it was *this* prior prideful disposition that allowed politicians to manipulate us into thinking that what being a higher animal really meant was being a moral animal—they then stipulated that this entailed living a life of self-denial in the service of others. There is no need according to Mandeville's original account to take it that human beings already had an interest in specifically moral concepts.

In another sense, however, Law's critique of the conspiracy theory account is very much on point. The conspiracy theory is something that Mandeville has just presented with no details, no supporting historical evidence, and there is no good reason to think it ever occurred, other than that it would suit Mandeville's apparent legitimation of private vice. More than this, though, Law very perceptively points out that we wouldn't say that the development of musical theory—experts telling us what musical beauty consists in—*created* our very capacity to hear harmony in the first place. Nor would we say that the development of abstract mathematical theory *created* our abilities to add and subtract apples and oranges. So why would we think that the development of moral theory itself *created* our capacity to perceive the difference between right and wrong? Surely the common-sense approach would suggest that the cause and the effect are the other way around—we came up with moral theory to describe something that human beings were already registering in their minds. Law cleverly suggests that, for all Mandeville's rhetoric about bringing the scientific and medical approach to the human animal, it is more respectful to our experience of human nature to think that we have moral theories because there really is an objective moral order. We have musical and mathematical theory today because human beings have always had a natural grasp of harmony and number; we have moral theory because human beings have always had a *natural* grasp of morality.

Law is pressing on a particularly sensitive spot, since Mandeville's theory is one that proudly proclaims the ultimately natural and animalistic character of human activity. The fact that Mandeville offers a *non*-naturalistic conspiracy theory as his explanation of where moral activity came from reveals a deep tension in his story. A real flaw in Mandeville's early theory is the sheer implausibility of maintaining that there was some social event, of there being a secret cabal of politicians who out of nothing came up with the idea of morality itself. Much later Samuel Taylor Coleridge would dismiss the theory, and even questioned Mandeville's own sincerity in propagating it, along similar lines:

> If I could ever believe that Mandeville really meant anything more by his Fable of the Bees than a *bonne bouche* of solemn raillery, I should like to ask those man-shaped apes who have taken up his suggestions in earnest, and seriously maintained them as bases for a rational account of man and the world—how they explain the very existence of those dexterous cheats, those superior charlatans, the legislators and

philosophers, who have known how to play so well upon the peacock-like vanity and follies of their fellow mortals.[21]

This relates to another worry, which is whether Mandeville's theory of human psychology in *The Fable of the Bees* is really up to task of explaining the whole origin of moral behaviour. Mandeville deliberately echoes Hobbes's talk of a wild state of nature where subjects are violently competing for resources. Mandeville suggests that our violent and varied passions make us particularly tricky to manage in an ordered and law-governed society. The 'natural' feature of human beings that politicians focused upon, he claims, is their capacity for pride, and it is by manipulating this element of their psychology that politicians invented morality and thereby turned us into docile and submissive political subjects. There are at least two concerns with this. Firstly, one might think that pride, which is connected with our sense of esteem and concern with how we appear to others, is arguably a relatively rarefied late-stage development of human psychology, one that surely came into play only *after* we had come together in social groups, and after we had already found good reasons for the minimal cooperation that society requires. We would then already have had natural reasons to interact helpfully with others before we became socially preoccupied with our status and self-image. Secondly, it is essential to Mandeville's account that not only is pride a fundamentally natural passion but that it is the pre-eminent passion within the physiology of the human animal. It is unclear why this should be so. Mandeville's debt to Hobbes is one that stresses that the natural state of the human being is one whereby the individual's self-preservation is the pre-eminent concern. Hunger, aggression, fear, and sexual desire are all understood as basic passions that characterize the human being's needs as a savage in the state of nature. It seems prima facie implausible that pride would be even present itself as one of the basic passions out in the wild. Yet Mandeville's theory states that pride is not only present in the wild human animal but is a naturally *stronger* drive than any other, stronger even than all the others combined.

Yet another concern is that Mandeville hasn't really given us an account as to why pride should even be as egotistical as he claims it is. It is perfectly normal for individuals to take pride in works simply for the reason that they are objectively well done, and the fact that one takes pride in doing something doesn't mean that one's motive was fundamentally self-interested. One's motive might have simply been *to do the right thing*, and the pride one takes in doing it might just be a side-effect. Mandeville's claim is that all our moral actions can be explained as ultimately self-regarding in their motivations, yet it isn't obvious that saying they all are accompanied by pride shows that our actions are ultimately self-regarding.[22] A final worry, one pushed particularly by Francis Hutcheson in his *Inquiry into the Original of Our Ideas of Beauty and Virtue* (1725), is that Mandeville is obviously ignoring the possibility that kindness and benevolence to others might in fact themselves be thoroughly natural phenomena. There is obvious evidence of care and affection from parents to children that is observable across a range of species of animal—why would we think that the love of a mother for a child is not simply a natural instinct? It is true no doubt that there might be some pleasure for the parent in giving parental love, but it seems highly unlikely that parents show that love solely for the purpose of their own pleasure.[23] If one concedes this, however, then has one not conceded that we naturally have some passions that are inherently directed towards the benefit of someone other than ourselves? It can begin to seem that Mandeville's insistence on reducing every apparent human phenomenon to self-love is proof only that for someone with a hammer everything looks like a nail. His dogmatic commitment to his theory blinds him to the plain facts regarding nature.

A large part of Mandeville's methodology might be thought of as anti-theoretical and empiricist in character. Mandeville insists he engages in no a priori abstract deductive reasoning from self-evident first principles. He has no theory concocted from the armchair, ready-made to explain the world. His method, he claims, is that of observation, of seeking the simplest and most illuminating explanations based upon the data presented from experience. He resists offering grand theories of the universe or fundamental axioms that govern reality. He simply offers what makes the most sense of what we see around us. Yet, as Law claims, it does not seem that Mandeville's theory is in fact the simplest and most sensible account of what we see around us. Confronted with the evidence of apparently naturally benevolent behaviour in ourselves and other animals, Mandeville insists that the simplest explanation is not that they have benevolent passions but that they are fundamentally self-interested animals. Yet this strains credulity—as Francis Hutcheson complains, Mandeville explains everything in terms of self-love, and ends up 'transforming self-love into a thousand different faces'. This approach was similarly ridiculed by Joseph Butler, who, in his *Sermons Preached at the Rolls Chapel* in 1726, imagines Hobbes (though it is quite likely that Mandeville was being targeted as Hobbes's contemporary disciple) engaging in an inquiry into the nature of charity only to discover that the true motive behind it is our love of the demonstration of our own power over others. This is absurd, Butler states, and asks which is more likely: that the proper explanation of why we help people is that we want to dominate them, or that Hobbes and Mandeville have just become confused over what they are talking about.[24] David Hume, in his *An Enquiry concerning the Principles of Morals* (1751), would later express the general worry about Mandeville's method as being contrary to common sense and reasonable scientific methods of explanation:

> The most obvious objection to the selfish hypothesis, is, that, as it is contrary to common feeling and our most unprejudiced notions, there is required the highest stretch of philosophy to establish so extraordinary a paradox. To the most careless observer, there appear to be such dispositions as benevolence and generosity; such affections as love, friendship, compassion, gratitude. These sentiments have their causes, effects, objects, and operations, marked by common language and observation, and plainly distinguished from those of the selfish passions. And as this is the obvious appearance of things, it must be admitted; till some hypothesis be discovered, which, by penetrating deeper into human nature, may prove the former affections to be nothing but modifications of the latter. All attempts of this kind have hitherto proved fruitless, and seem to have proceeded entirely, from that love of *simplicity*, which has been the source of much false reasoning in philosophy.[25]

There can be no denying that these critics have a point. Mandeville's modest, empiricist, and anti-theoretical approach in fact covers over a (particularly ironic) kind of false humility. As becomes clear throughout *Fable II*, Mandeville is presenting things from an Epicurean perspective, specifically as it is expressed in Lucretius's

Epicurean poem *De rerum natura* (*On the Nature of Things*), written in the first century BCE. What we find in *De rerum natura* is
very much a theory—it is a didactic poem, intended to help those
benighted by religion enlighten themselves through science and
philosophy. Moreover, by subscribing to it, Mandeville is assum-
ing quite a deal more knowledge than he is letting on. There is a
sense in which he really does see himself as 'penetrating deeper into
human nature', as Hume accuses. According to Lucretius, the universe is composed of atoms and the space between them, nothing
else; the origin of the universe was a random and contingent business, lacking any design or plan; animals are just material things
responding to the mechanics of that atomistic reality; human
beings are just animals of the same kind, our thoughts and beliefs
and conscious life a manifestation of nothing but the movement of
our material constitution; the fundamental drives of the human
being involve the pursuit of its own pleasures and interests; religion is the product of superstition and human fear. All of Mandeville's writings—his medical theorization, his account of humans
as governed by 'animal spirits' that influence their consciousness,
his opposition to narratives that put the human being in a special
place in the cosmic hierarchy, his insistence on the social functions
of organized religion—are in step with a fundamentally Epicurean
viewpoint. The most important point of all, perhaps, is that the
Epicurean viewpoint was seen in the seventeenth and eighteenth
centuries as the scientific model adopted by the atheist.

When Law attacks Mandeville from a theological perspective
he assumes that the statements of devoutness in *The Fable of the
Bees* are thoroughly disingenuous. *Fable II* abounds in discussion of
theological topics, and Mandeville—as in all his works—professes
his sincere faith throughout. Yet as the text proceeds it becomes
obvious that what Mandeville is putting forward is decidedly
anti-theological. To take a single example of Mandeville's satirical
intent—and evidence of the importance of Law's critique—consider
the case of Noah. Law complained that Mandeville's atheistical
intentions in *The Fable of the Bees* were obvious, and his claims of
piety an imposture. Mandeville had insisted that he was not talking about the origins of morality for his good Christian readers,
which were a matter of religious teaching and revelation, but only

for those heathen tribes not related to us. As mentioned previously, Law responds that this makes as much sense as saying that one's theory of physics is true for heathens only, and has no implications as to how atoms interact for Christians.[26] Similarly, the idea that morality was invented for heathen races makes no sense for a genuine Christian, Law claims, since a genuine Christian would be committed to the claim that *all* races are descended from Noah after the Flood, and all races must thereby have at least some historical connection with true religious teaching.[27] In the fifth dialogue of the *Fable II*, Mandeville's characters engage in a curious discussion—à propos of not very much, it must be said—as to how the human species is entirely descended from Noah, as scripture demands. Law is receiving a response. Mandeville's representative, Cleomenes, insists upon the truth of scripture and the consistency of *The Fable of the Bees* with it, despite his noting point after point against the plausibility of our being descended from Noah. In the sixth dialogue his interlocutor Horatio notes that Cleomenes 'contentedly swallows everything that is said of Noah and his Ark' but disregards as ridiculous superstition anything from other traditions. Horatio continues the interrogation in exasperation:

HOR: Yes, yes. Do you believe Hesiod?

CLEO: No.

HOR: Ovid's *Metamorphosis*?

CLEO: No.

HOR: But you believe the Story of Adam and Eve, and Paradise.

CLEO: Yes.

HOR: That they were produced at once, I mean at their full growth; he from a Lump of Earth, and she from one of his ribs?

CLEO: Yes.

HOR: And that as soon as they were made, they could speak, reason, and were imbued with Knowledge?

CLEO: Yes.

HOR: In short, you believe the Innocence, the Delight, and all the Wonders of Paradise, that are related by one Man; at the same time that you will not believe what has been told us by many, of the Uprightness, the Concord, and the Happiness of a Golden Age.

CLEO: That's very true.[28]

Whenever confronted with some ridiculous consequence of his continued espousal of Christianity, Cleomenes has a tendency towards brief dogmatic answers in defence. By contrast, Mandeville has Cleomenes insist just two pages later that there are other theories that, unlike the story of Adam and Eve, are truly ridiculous:

> CLEO: . . . Do you believe there ever was a man who made himself?
>
> HOR: No: that's a plain contradiction.
>
> CLEO: Then it is manifest the first man must have been made by something; and what I say of man, I may say of all matter and motion in general. The doctrine of *Epicurus*, that everything is derived from the concourse and fortuitous jumble of atoms, is monstrous and extravagant beyond all other follies.[29]

For the reader who knows *The Fable of the Bees*, who grasped the significance of the reference to the fellow Epicurean Gassendi in the preface of *Fable II*, and who perhaps even recognized the uncited quotation of Lucretius's *De rerum natura* itself that Mandeville made a little earlier,[30] there can be no mistaking Mandeville's irony here. Religion is absurd, and the theory that the universe came about randomly, for no particular design or reason, is if anything the more sensible theory, one that requires a smaller challenge to our understanding than does an appeal to a supernatural first cause. Here is an example, too, of how Mandeville delights in irritating opponents such as Law. When confronted with a clear instance of inconsistency with regard to his self-proclaimed religiosity, Mandeville simply revels in being caught out and just commits the same crime again. He reiterates that he is a sincere Christian, and expresses this by having his representative stubbornly maintain his belief in scripture in the face of overwhelmingly sensible objections. As a taunting flourish, he has his representative denounce the very position Law knows to be the one Mandeville really holds.[31]

Fable II is primarily aimed, however, at doing what Law claimed *The Fable of the Bees* failed to do—giving a *naturalistic* and Epicurean account of the origins of ordered human society complete with its norms and conventions. How is it that human beings have come to form such a society? What are the minimal attributes of human beings that we must imagine them possessing in order for them to have progressed from a state of disordered savagery to the civilized and ordered condition in which we mostly find ourselves today? Why did this transformation happen with the human animal and not with other species? The account in *The Fable of the Bees* of the trickery of clever politicians now emerges primarily as a piece of polemic, designed to outrage the reading public and the Tory factions who were piously advocating the divine nature of human virtue for their own political purposes. In *Fable II* Mandeville puts forward what he thinks is in fact the true story of the origin of society and morals. The conspiracy theory of *The Fable of the Bees* had society and morals formed by way of a one-off event: a specific nefarious design of a political elite. What Mandeville lacked previously was anything like a compelling theory as to *why* this all should be the case, an account of why we are *naturally* inclined to create social norms that ultimately only limit the pursuit of our other natural desires. What is needed is the underlying natural explanation for why the world is this way, why the interaction of self-interested desires with social constructs generates overall positive benefits for society.[32]

The key insight that Mandeville wants to convey is that the coherence of society, the sociability we show and maintain towards one another, the peace and order that our institutions provide, all emerged *gradually* over enormous lengths of human history, without any planning or design, and without anything like a particular politician's ambition to set things up in a particular form—such as through the institution of a Christian ethic. It arose, Mandeville claims, without any human beings ever having such a specific Christian ambition on a particular occasion, but instead gradually through some general drive to dominate and control others, which is adapted by successive leaders, and which leads through incremental change to the institution of the moral norms with which we are now familiar. As he suggests again and again, human beings are so dictated by pride, vanity, and self-regard that we find it extremely difficult to bring ourselves to think that this could be true. Mandeville was repeatedly accused of seeking 'low' or base explanations for the extraordinary aspects of human beings. His response is that he has not been seeking low or base explanations at all, just those ones that are suggested by observation of the world around us. His explanations appear low only because we have an inherent bias towards looking higher when explaining human nature:

> We are so full of our own species and the excellency of it that we have no leisure seriously to consider the system of this Earth; I mean the plan on which the economy of it is built, in relation to the living creatures that are in and upon it.[33]

Mandeville's theory includes an account of why we might be naturally disinclined to accept it. It is a cunning rhetorical move against those who say that his theory is forced or unscientific. If Mandeville's theory is correct, we have reason to be suspicious of our own rational objections to it, since he will have produced a radically new and potentially disturbing notion of what human rationality really is.

It is in *Fable II* that we see the tremendous—and often unacknowledged—originality of Mandeville's thought. This is evident with regard to his first innovation, which is to distinguish *self-love* from a new passion, which he calls *self-liking*. Self-love is best thought of simply as the motivation of self-interest, or the pursuit of anything insofar as it brings a reward to oneself. Self-liking is a passion or disposition that is particularly about esteem and the practice of displaying and recognizing value. We are all capable of valuing different things, but, Mandeville claims, human beings are always disposed to *value themselves* far more heavily than anything else. The difference might be put like this: self-love makes me seek my own pleasure above anyone else's; self-liking makes me think that my own pleasures are *more important* than anyone else's. It can seem, then, that self-liking is a disposition that is inherently self-conscious, since it involves thinking about own one's pleasure (rather than just seeking it). However, Mandeville claims that many other non-human animals possess self-liking also. So what exactly *is* self-liking? Cleomenes describes it first as a natural phenomenon:

> I fancy that to increase the care in creatures to preserve themselves, nature has given them an instinct, by which every individual values itself above its real worth. . . . [T]he more mettle and liveliness creatures have, the more visible this liking is; and . . . in those of the same kind, the greater spirits they are of, and the more they excel in the

perfections of their species, the fonder they are of showing it: in most birds it is evident, especially in those that have extraordinary finery to display: in a horse it is more conspicuous than in any other irrational creature: it is more apparent in the swiftest, the strongest, the most healthy and vigorous.[34]

Mandeville's hypothesis here is extraordinary: he suggests what might sound to us today as a proto-evolutionary account of the origin of value.[35] Firstly, he claims that it is uncontroversial that all animals seek their own self-preservation, and that they have a natural drive or interest in protecting their own life. He suggests, though, that it is far more advantageous—one is tempted to say it aids natural selection—if one creature's drive to self-preservation is stronger than that of others. Yet there is no objective reason why one creature's self-preservation should be more important than any other's. To overcome this unfortunate fact about reality, some creatures have developed the capacity to represent themselves as better than they are, in the hope of attracting a mate or intimidating a rival. Bright feathers, an imperious gait, and so on are all ways in which animals naturally represent their inherent value as greater than it is. Self-liking, therefore, is Mandeville's blanket term for whenever physical or behavioural traits perform the function of signalling one's superiority to others.

Generating signals that one is superior and worthier of self-preservation can become a self-fulfilling prophecy. If resources are scarce, and there is objectively speaking no reason why I should fill my belly rather than you filling yours, then neither of us ought to have a stronger motive than the other as far as the motive of self-interest is concerned. One of us might develop a stronger motive to fight for the food if that person had the attitude that satisfying one's own hunger was somehow *more important* than the other person satisfying theirs. The false belief that one's interests are more important might in fact make us more tenacious in the scramble for resources, and thereby more successful in getting them. Mandeville remarkably connects how a physical disposition in birds simply to grow bright plumage, the behavioural disposition in horses towards strutting and head nodding, and the intellectual disposition in human beings to think of themselves as important as manifestations of the same drive that serves to reinforce and boost our self-interested instincts. One might think that the rudiments sketched here could be put to use for a kind of social Darwinism, whereby a naturally superior group is singled out for preferential status in society. Some of the things Mandeville says seem to mark out the human being with a strong disposition to self-liking as one of the thrusting and bustling examples of humanity that ought to be admired, as a kind of natural *Übermensch*, one who must not now be tied down by society's mores but allowed to pursue their private vices as they feel like it. The story Mandeville actually develops from this proto-evolutionary story is a good deal more complicated than this Nietzschean caricature, however. Mandeville suggests that the drive to self-liking manifests in human beings in conjunction with their developing rational capacities. Crucially, we are also beings possessing the capacity for self-consciousness. Unlike the bird or horse, the human being's self-attributed importance is something of which it is immediately *aware*—unlike with other animals, humans manifest their disposition of self-liking by consciously thinking of themselves as each more important than the other.

The particularly human variant, which we might call *self-conscious self-liking*, is crucial to Mandeville's story. It is this particular manifestation of the natural drive that creates the immensely varied and complex phenomena that constitute humans' social relations. This is because self-liking is a natural and irresistible drive to represent something that is in fact *false*. It is a tendency to display our value in a fashion that doesn't actually correspond to reality. Self-liking in human beings, Mandeville says,

> seems to be accompanied with a diffidence, arising from a consciousness, or at least an apprehension, that we do over-value ourselves: it is this that makes us so fond of the approbation, liking and assent of others: because they strengthen and confirm us in the good opinion we have of ourselves.[36]

Mandeville's evolutionary psychology, though brief and sketchy, can be reconstructed as follows. It is a fundamental part of self-liking, Mandeville claims, that it does not represent reality accurately. It is of course not true that my desires are more important than yours in any cosmic sense. Being a self-conscious being in the world, I run up against this fact whenever I try to realize my desires and find that others are doing the same. Despite this, I still can't help but value the satisfaction of my interests more highly than I value the satisfaction of yours, since it is still a natural disposition for a creature to value itself 'above its real worth', a disposition we have to 'over-value ourselves'. To ask us to think otherwise is akin to asking a peacock not to display its plumage to attract a mate. Given that the drive is fundamental to a human being's self-preservation, it creates a perpetual illusion about ourselves which we can't dispel, no matter how frequently we encounter disconfirming evidence. The result is that human beings are desperately inclined towards accepting *confirming* evidence that we really are as valuable as we think we are. In essence, Mandeville suggests that human consciousness is fundamentally characterized by an ineliminable form of confirmation bias. What it is to be conscious is to be a creature possessing a theory about itself—that it is important relative to all other creatures—and to be always on the lookout for evidence that would confirm that theory and ignoring or misinterpreting evidence that might contradict it. We are naturally self-deceiving creatures at the deepest level.

Being accepted, praised, or flattered by others is the fundamental currency of self-conscious self-liking. Our self-consciousness immediately creates a condition of painful cognitive dissonance in the human being, between that false self-image we maintain and what reality seems to claim in opposition. When we are praised or admired it confirms the image of ourselves that we possess, and the cognitive dissonance is briefly alleviated. What this means is that, since self-liking is an essential accompaniment of the very drive to self-preservation itself, we value the esteem of others just as highly—and, Mandeville claims, *even more highly*—than any other desired thing. It is the confirmation of the 'good opinion of ourselves' that becomes pre-eminent, since this is what soothes the difficulty of being conscious. This, Mandeville claims, is really the only possible explanation of the clear empirical evidence of suicides from pride, shame, or points of principle. No other creatures value things more than they value their own lives. Humans, by contrast, live and die not for the preservation of their lives but for the preservation of their good name.

Self-liking is a helpful way of disambiguating different ways in which we think of how some individuals' behaviour can be ego-centric. One might be straightforwardly selfish and take the larger share of resources on offer, and this would be the motivation of self-love in action. Yet frequently we see behaviour that is consciously intended to benefit others and yet engaged upon for less than noble reasons. There are those who clearly engage in acts of generosity and charity, yet who seem to be unable to separate the goodness of those acts from the self-regarding aspects of the performative gestures. This isn't quite selfish behaviour—one might give away all that one possesses—yet it is nevertheless a performative act, and the subject is primarily interested in how well their sacrifice must appear to observers. In Mandeville's view, it is this aspect of self-liking that produces all the behaviour that we have come to recognize as the remarkably social nature of human beings. He claims that if a human 'savage' were ruled only by self-love, then they would have always remained relatively solitary and content so long as their needs for food, shelter, and sex were met. It is self-liking that makes them strive for more:

> Self-love would first make it scrape together everything it wanted for sustenance, provide against the injuries of the air, and do everything to make itself and young ones secure. Self-liking would make it seek for opportunities by gestures, looks, and sounds, to display the value it has for itself, superior to what it has for others. . . . He would be highly delighted with, and love everybody whom he thought to have a good opinion of him, especially those, that by words or gestures should own it to his face.[37]

The gratification of self-liking is so connected to the original drive for self-preservation that, he thinks, it constitutes a 'cordial that contributes to his health'.[38] It literally puffs us up, makes us stand up straight, gives us energy and focus and drive for the tasks of the day. Mandeville's conjectures regarding early human development are ingenious, since they allow him to explain a fundamental natural phenomenon that had preoccupied philosophers—the fact of the stunningly common phenomenon of human sociability—without attributing any specifically social instinct to humanity. Human beings do not, on this account, possess any special disposition different from other animals, no species-exclusive drive to come together and interact positively with others out of altruism or solidarity or mutual recognition, and certainly have no rational or moral interest in taking others' concerns on board. What we *do* have is a fundamentally natural drive, and this *does* lead us to interact positively with other humans, but this drive has its source in something in fact shared with other animals—a disposition towards displaying oneself as superior.

Horatio presents a straightforward and sensible challenge against all these claims.[39] Cleomenes states that human beings are fundamentally self-regarding and self-deceiving, and that their true motives are always hidden from themselves. But how can Mandeville *himself* know these things? How can Mandeville know both that we cannot know human motives and that human motives are always self-regarding ones? It seems as if Mandeville's theory contradicts itself, since on the one hand it ascribes us a kind of knowledge of human nature, and on the other hand denies that we ever have any such knowledge. In response, Mandeville simply offers more observations on human frailties that, he claims, demonstrate how pride more than anything else determines our conduct. The response is consonant with the one given in the *Treatise of the Hypochondriack and Hysterick Passions* when Mandeville's representative was asked for his theory of the fundamental operations of the human body. There he claims to have no theory whatsoever, only a few hypotheses based upon amassing as large a number and range of empirical observations as possible. In *Fable II* we find the following exchange:

> HOR: Do you argue or pretend to prove anything from those
> conjectures?
> CLEO: No; I never reason but from the plain observations which
> everybody may make on man, the *phenomena* that appear in the
> lesser world.[40]

Mandeville does not care to prove his position against those who might be opposed to it; he seeks only to illustrate his system to those who might already be sympathetic to it, to those who are already inclined to take empirical explanations as far as possible.

It is in this spirit that we can say that Mandeville does have an answer to Law's complaint regarding the time and place of the crafty politicians' manipulation of humanity. Mandeville has outlined the basic biological mechanism in accordance with which human beings are most susceptive to pride. But how exactly did that susceptibility get manipulated by politicians for the purposes of governing and social control? Horatio raises Law's objection as it relates first to rules of etiquette, which Mandeville thinks are the most typical norms whereby we demonstrate our superiority in a socially acceptable way, by manifesting how we can constrain our desires:

> HOR: ... [P]ray, can you inform me, when or which way, what we call good manners or politeness came into the world? What moralist or politician was it, that could teach men to be proud of hiding their pride?
>
> CLEO: The restless industry of man to supply his wants, and his constant endeavours to meliorate his condition upon earth, have produced and brought to perfection many useful arts and sciences, of which the beginning are of uncertain eras, and to which we can assign no other causes, than human sagacity in general and the joint labour of many ages, in which men have always employed themselves in studying and contriving ways and means to soothe their various appetites, and make the best of their infirmities.[41]

The spirit of the reasoning here is thoroughly Epicurean. Lucretius concludes book 5 of *De rerum natura* with an appeal to how everything in modern civilization, no matter how complex, can be seen to be the product of a long process of natural human activity, rather than as any kind of sudden gift from the gods:

> Navigation, agriculture, city walls, laws, arms, roads, clothing, and all other practical inventions, as well as every one of life's rewards and refinements, poems, pictures, and polished statues of exquisite workmanship, all without exception were gradually taught by experience and the inventiveness of the energetic mind, as mankind progressed step by step. Then by slow degrees time evolves every discovery, and reason raises it up into the regions of light. Men saw one thing after another become clear in their minds, until each art reached the peak of perfection.[42]

The standard Epicurean stance is to explain the origin of complex phenomena not in terms of a single act of invention but as a series of small simple changes over large—sometimes very large—spans of time, whereby complexity is achieved incrementally. If something emerges that looks purposeful, planned, and ordered, the intuitive thought is that it is the result of someone's or something's premeditated design, plan, or purpose. Lucretius begs us to see that this is a fallacy:

> Once you obtain a firm grasp of these facts, you see that nature is her own mistress and is exempt from the oppression of arrogant despots, accomplishing everything by herself, spontaneously and independently, free from the jurisdiction of the gods.[43]

Mandeville's task is to make sense of how it could be that the explicit norms of politeness and morality which humans live by today could have come about in the same incremental way. Mandeville's way of meeting this challenge is to take a premise of another of Law's own objections and use it against him. Law had complained that we see no problem in saying that there was an appreciation of music and mathematics before there was anything like musical or mathematical theory. Mandeville fully agrees, and argues that it is obvious that the fundamental practical goal of the self-liking subject—that is, to hide its pride from others—was profoundly understood by human beings even without their being consciously aware of it.

He thinks he can justify this counterintuitive claim by appeal to two far more straightforward notions, those of *know-how* and the *division of labour*. Mandeville explicates the former with the example of children taking a running jump. It is clear, he says, that children know how taking a run before leaping will improve their velocity, and so on. It is equally clear that they have no concept of velocity, and no matter how well calculated are the angles of their leaps, children have no grasp of geometry. They know *how* to take advantage of physics and geometry, but they are not in the least aware *that* they have this understanding. Horatio rightly objects that 'bodily motion is one thing and the exercise of the understanding is another.'[44] One might say that knowing how to move our bodies requires no conscious awareness of the principles involved. Cleomenes wants us to believe that the observance of social norms, which is an inherently self-conscious activity, is similarly mastered as a kind of know-how without any kind of awareness of the principles that are driving that behaviour. This is one of Mandeville's most imaginative moves—to suggest that we might be grasping some rule that is crucial to our conscious life but are doing so subconsciously. If we can say—just as Law did—that we show a grasp of mathematics or physics in our behaviour without understanding it consciously, then Mandeville thinks we can say that we might grasp the mechanisms of self-liking without ever grasping them consciously.

To complete the account, Mandeville appeals to the division of labour. He famously returns to the analogy of shipbuilding, used to such effect with regard to the division of labour in 'A Search into the Nature of Society' in the first part of the *Fable*. In observing a modern man-of-war, says Cleomenes, we can't help but marvel at the complexity and ingenuity of the design. However, it is obvious that whoever was involved with the design of the ship did not imagine the fundamentals of navigation and seaworthiness for the first time. Every feature of the ship is an expression of a shared and inherited knowledge passed down over generations of seafarers. What's more, Cleomenes points out that, although there are treatises today that employ abstract mathematics to describe the angle of a rudder, and so on, no one shipbuilder in history has ever had all those kinds of abstract reasonings before their mind. They instead worked by way of experiment, by trial and error over centuries, and eventually hit upon the things that seemed to them to work best. At no point, however, was abstract reasoning or general principles of correct shipbuilding operational in their actions. The point of the analogy is that intelligent design can emerge without there ever having been intelligent designers, even when we are talking about the conscious activity of human thought:

> CLEO: . . . [W]e often ascribe to the excellency of man's genius and the
> depth of his penetration what is in reality owing to length of time
> and the experience of many generations, all of them very little dif-
> fering from one another in natural parts and sagacity.[45]

Mandeville moves swiftly from the case of shipbuilding to the evolution of social norms, and suggests that it is not hard to imagine how other-regarding attitudes developed once we take into account the combination of self-liking's need to conceal itself and the labour divided between generations in developing those norms:

> CLEO: . . . When once the generality begin to conceal the high value they have for themselves, men must become more tolerable to one another. Now new improvements must be made every day, till some of them grow impudent enough, not only to deny the high value they have for themselves, but likewise to pretend that they have greater value for others than they have for themselves.[46]

Manners and morals are the means by which we have over the centuries rationalized to ourselves our ineliminable egotism. When we see today that we have a norm to help those in need, which seems to us to be an obvious intellectual achievement of grasping a principle of morally right action, it is in fact a consequence of generations' labour in social conditioning about the need to mask our natural narcissism.[47]

These, then, are the rudiments of Mandeville's naturalistic response to his critics. He does not have to 'bend self-love into a thousand different faces', he would respond—self-liking is sufficient and can do the work in explaining our apparently selfless concern for others. When we are applauded for extolling the virtues of fairness, impartiality, equality, and self-sacrifice, we achieve the intended result of securing the admiration of others while covering up our true motives, even to ourselves. In this entirely paradoxical way, the more human beings are motivated on the surface of their consciousness to extol morality, the more evident it is that they are motivated below the surface by the love of praise. The result is the emergence of social norms without any explicit reasoning or design in favour of them:

> CLEO: . . . [This is] certainly the philosophical reason of the alterations that are made in the behaviour of men by their being civilized: but all this is done without reflection, and men by degrees, and great length of time, fall as it were into these things spontaneously.[48]

Here is one of the key moves in Mandeville's view of human nature—the reason *why* human beings fall into such behaviour is just nothing more than that it is nature's tendency to self-organize itself into ordered patterns. The patterns emerge 'spontaneously' from nature itself, without any divine action, just as Lucretius had maintained. How and why nature does this is a mystery, but no more so than the mysteries of creation to be found in scripture. In this way, the appeal to the shared generational labour returns again to explain the basic phenomenon of sociability. A plain Aristotelian explanation of our eagerness to engage and be sociable with others is that we are naturally sociable creatures, in the sense that among all our other drives for food, sex, and so on we have a distinct drive to interact with others for our mutual benefit. Mandeville's claim is that there is no *distinct* drive to benevolent sociability in the human animal. Human beings *are* naturally sociable, but this sociability is in fact the effect of a different cause—namely, the combination of the self-regarding nature of human individuals interacting over centuries.[49] All the institutions of society have evolved to accommodate this need for sociability, and thus we are a species that has self-organized into complex social orders without ever consciously countenancing any such plan.

Mandeville's philosophy is hugely important for its reconceptualization and revaluation of the idea of self-interest. Prior to Mandeville's writings, 'self-love' could simply be aligned with 'selfishness', but after his works no such simple alignment was possible. Mandeville's earlier theory showed that self-love was at the heart of all human action, and that it produced positive consequences for society, and so couldn't be unequivocally denigrated as the negative aspect of human motivation. His later works, and the development of self-liking in particular, strengthened that thesis even more. Self-interest became inextricably connected with the desire for the esteem of others. When cast in this light, the 'selfish hypothesis', as it is sometimes called, becomes indistinguishable from the claim that in all our actions our concern for the recognition and acknowledgement of others is always at play. This starts to recast self-interest in a far more positive light, and opened up the door for subsequent philosophers such as Adam Smith, Kant, Hegel, and others to investigate how basic ideas of esteem, respect, and social recognition are a central part of our moral concerns. Mandeville's accounts of self-love and self-liking were put forward to undermine the idea of moral action as a product of rationality. What he put in its place, however, has the rudiments of a powerful moral psychology all of its own. That 'being good' was always a complex matter of thinking about what the right thing to do is, thinking how others might see me when I do it, thinking how I might regard myself if I don't, and so on, no longer seemed like a radically sceptical theory, and instead came to appear more like a positive theory of real human ethical behaviour.

Mandeville's presentation of complex and beneficial social behaviour emerging as a spontaneous order has similarly been massively influential.[50] As we have seen, it is the undeniable predecessor of Adam Smith's account of the 'invisible hand' that aids commercial life by generating benefits for the group that are not intended by its individuals.[51] Adam Ferguson in his *Essay on the History of Civil Society* (1767) famously described spontaneous order as 'the result of human action, but not the execution of human design'.[52] Generations of thinkers have subscribed to Mandeville's innovations while attempting to distance themselves from his perceived immorality and irreligiosity. The central motivation for the notion of spontaneous order for Mandeville, however, was as a means of explaining phenomena not as the work of divine providence but a simple, if no less mysterious, fact of human nature. It is not as great an exaggeration as it might seem to say that Mandeville's insight inaugurated a way of thinking about and analysing human social life never previously countenanced. Mandeville introduced the idea of thinking from the perspective of a system and not from the perspective of the elements within that system (even though that is what we are). There are surely aspects of life where an individual's thinking about what is best for everyone is the correct way to proceed; but there may be domains where what works best is precisely a result of us *not* doing this. It might be that there are areas of human behaviour that function well *just because* everyone acts out of self-interest and not out of concern for others.

Imagine, for example, any busy railway station at rush hour. Over the space of an hour thousands of people crisscross the central concourse at a variety of angles, changing directions rapidly to get to their platform, the exit, the coffee stand, the bathroom; people turn back, change their mind, constantly adjusting to avoid bumping into one another. Just *how do* people manage to avoid one another quite so successfully, given the chaotic nature of the enterprise? Why isn't the average rush hour a constant succession of bumps, clashes, and conflicts? One hypothesis is that human beings are generally concerned with the welfare of others, and coordinate all their actions—including concourse-crossing plans—in accordance with a rational rule about accommodating the well-being of the group. One of the problems with this otherwise attractive hypothesis is just its obvious falsity: no one in the history of mankind has crossed a railway platform with the intention of bringing about the best result for humanity. Instead, another hypothesis suggests itself. When people weave and zigzag their way along, what they each have in their minds is just the thought: *how can I get over there now in the quickest way possible?* Just barging in a straight line doesn't work—the time it takes to barge past the bodies and negotiate the ensuing conflicts is longer than the time it takes to weave past them. In fact, when things do go wrong it is more often than not owing to our being overly considerate of others, as when people conscientiously hesitate and second-guess what others might do ('After you'; 'No—after you'). Were this to be the norm everyone adopted, no one would get anywhere. Politeness has a proper place in this domain, of course, but it is not the thing that is primarily governing our behaviour and allowing us to be effectively cooperative with one another. There is a kind of rational order that emerges, but it doesn't emerge because people are *trying* to realize that rational order. There is a benefit that accrues for the group as a whole, but it doesn't accrue because the players are acting for the benefit of the group as a whole. The rational order and benefit for the whole emerges only because the individuals follow their own self-interest and place that at the top of the list in their motivations. The rationality of societal behaviour emerges from behind the backs of its own participants.

Back in *The Fable of the Bees*, Mandeville had remarked on the need for a shift of perspective to see how nature really works to our benefit:

> The short-sighted vulgar in the chain of causes seldom can see further than one link; but those who can enlarge their view, and will give

themselves the leisure of gazing on the prospect of concatenated events, may, in a hundred places, see *good* spring up and pullulate from *evil*, as naturally as chickens do from eggs.[53]

When in *Fable II* Horatio asks how early humans ever managed to succeed against the wild beasts of nature, Cleomenes replies bluntly: 'Providence'. The ironic message is on display again. Appeals to divine providence are appeals to the universe being set up for the purpose of humanity's succeeding in various ways, or of humanity itself being designed with some higher purpose in mind. Mandeville twists the appeal to providential reasoning in the opposite direction. One can appeal to 'providence' as the basis of how things emerge within nature without any rational predesigned plan. Appealing to this naturalistic notion of providence allows one to avoid the fallacy of saying that because we can play the violin with our fingers and opposable thumbs, the human hand was therefore designed with violins in mind. Lucretius had warned against this kind of reasoning centuries before:

> I am extremely anxious that you should carefully avoid the mistake of supposing the lustrous eyes were created to enable us to see. . . . All such explanations are propounded preposterously with topsy-turvy reasoning. In fact, no part of our body was created to the end that we might use it, but what has been created gives rise to its own function. Sight did not exist before the birth of the eyes. . . . In short, I maintain that all the organs were in being before there was any function for them to fulfill. They cannot, then, have grown for the purpose of being used.[54]

While, of course, eyes perform the function of seeing, it is a fallacy to infer from this that they were designed for some predetermined aim of granting humans sight. Lucretius is saying that since it is possible that our organs gradually developed and we realized biological functions after a certain amount of physical development, we can say that our organs found their purpose along the way.

Mandeville exhibits this exact attitude with regard to the evolution of human sociability, and uses natural analogies to stress the point. The human being is naturally social, but it does not follow that the human being has been *designed for* sociability. We can slip into thinking of the human being as having a special purpose or design, but this is the same kind of fallacy, he says, as thinking that grapes are designed to make wine.[55] Grapes have properties that allow for them to be worked upon, developed, and changed into wine, but these other factors are obviously just as essential to the production of wine as the properties of grapes themselves. There is also a kind of contingency involved with these other elements. Just the fact that grapes allow for wine to be made from them doesn't mean that it was somehow cosmically ordained that wine would be made—many of the features of the world can be as easily or better explained as happy accidents. When Mandeville, therefore, says that the human being is naturally designed for society in the same way that grapes are naturally designed to make wine, he is offering the reader a different way of thinking about the development of our species. There are certainly unique and crucial identifying features that make us the kind of animal we are, but we cannot infer from that anything more than that we are a species that has happened to develop in certain specific ways. There is a clear anticipation of the ways in which evolutionary theory can expose the fallacy of teleological characterizations of the human species. Mandeville did not anticipate Darwinian evolution—he has no sense of one species developing from another, of natural selection, and so on—but he did see a kind of fallacy that could be exposed by taking a point of view that stresses the historical and dynamic forces at play in nature.

Mandeville's central paradox in *Fable II* is not that private immorality produces economic benefits, though he of course still maintains that claim. That paradox now emerges as a special case of a more general one concerning human nature. This is that self-liking, which 'in its nature seems to be destructive to sociableness and society, and never fails, in untaught men, to render them insufferable to one another', is nevertheless the very origin of politeness and manners, of social norms in general, and thereby the cause of 'innumerable benefits, as well for the ease and comfort as the welfare and safety of congregate bodies'.[56] Self-liking, which is nothing but the inherent disposition we all have to put self-regard at the centre of everything, is the fount of sociability, of solidarity, and even of altruism. Mandeville in fact goes further than this, and claims that not only are the negative dispositions perfectly adequate to explain the origin of all the features of human society that we value, but that the positive dispositions of human nature are *not* adequate to the job. If there were such a thing as natural human benevolence, he claims, human society would not have developed as it has done:

> There are many other things from which it is plain that such a real love of man from his species would have been altogether inconsistent with the present scheme; the world must have been desitute of all that industry that is owing to envy and emulation; no society could have been easy with being a flourishing people at the expense of their neigh-bours, or enduring to be counted a formidable nation. All men would have been levellers, government would have been unnecessary, and there could have been no great bustle in the world.[57]

Fable II is full of the kind of paradoxical analyses familiar from his French intellectual inheritance, but now explained in terms of Mandeville's naturalistic thinking. He still maintains the funda-mental thesis of *The Fable of the Bees*, which is that private vices bring public benefits, but this truth is now seen in the context of a view of human nature of enormous breadth.

With this in mind, it also complicates the image of Mandeville as a straightforward debunker of morality. If anything, his posi-tion is even more radical than that. To see this, one has to recall first of all that part of the theory in *The Fable of the Bees* was that our desires being checked and regulated by social constraints—including the norms of moral virtue—produces all the prosper-ity and activity of modern commercial society and ultimately increases the common good. *Both* of these elements are crucial for the functioning of any social system. On the one hand, Mandev-ille argues that there cannot be anything like *real* virtue as it is promoted in the pulpit and by zealous politicians; there are only the artificial constructions of virtue that we have made for our-selves. On the other hand, he appreciates the benefit, and in some admittedly paradoxical sense, the *naturalness* of artificial virtue. Moral virtue is a human artifice, but it is very much in our nature to create artifices of just this kind for the purpose of regulating our social interaction. And it is very much a fact about *nature* that the perpetual tussle between desire and self-regulation results in benefits for the species.

What message are readers supposed to take away regarding Mandeville's analysis of moral theory, however? Are we to accept all the dictates of morality just as they are, since ultimately they too contribute to the overall benefit of society? It is possible that Mandeville recommends a kind of conservatism, advocates living in accordance with morals and spirits of one's time and society. On the other hand, one cannot help but see that what Mandeville is anticipating is that something like 'morality' is being torn away from any religious context—not least in its being co-opted by the politicians of his day—and has come to be viewed as an independent reality in its own right, separate from any of its theological origins. What he has no time for is that educated people nevertheless believe in some abstract reality called 'morality' that is supposed to guide our behaviour through the rational appreciation of eternal principles. The reason he is even more violently opposed to Shaftesbury, Hutcheson, and the like is that they aspire to explain the reality of morality independently of religion. Mandeville sees where the modern world is headed, breaking away from religion but not from what he thinks is a masochistic and life-sapping ideology of self-denial.

Mandeville's radical point of departure was the thought that what was good at the level of individual behaviour might prove bad when evaluated at the level of society as a whole. It is natural to think that if a piece of behaviour is good for me, and if society is made up of individuals just like me, then that piece of behaviour will still be good if pursued by everyone in society. But this, it turns out, is exactly *not* the case. It suggests a challenge to the philosopher Immanuel Kant's moral philosophy before it was ever formulated. Kant would hold that in order to determine whether something is the right thing to do, one must imagine whether it's rational that *everyone* should do it. The rational action, he says, is the one that can be universalized. In this way, Kant's primary thought is that rationality is the kind of thing that makes sense at the individual *and* the group level. But Mandeville already anticipated this thought and denied it. What is rational for the individual is one thing; what is rational for the group, another. When thinking about what is rational and good for society as a whole it just won't do to project the standard of individual morality onto the group. It is perhaps for this reason that Mandeville picked out Shaftesbury for particular contempt. One of the fundamental claims of Shaftesbury's system is that what is what is good for the individual by their own lights tends towards the goodness of society, indeed the universe—as a whole. The pre-eminent responsibility, therefore, lands upon every individual to tend to their own subjective appraisal of what the morally virtuous thing to do is, lest they let down the universe as a whole.

Mandeville's denial of this ultimately involves a remarkably unsettling theory of human action. Mandeville takes Lucretius's starting points and weaves them together with the social and psychological theories of Hobbes, Montaigne, La Rochefoucauld, and Nicole. The result is a picture of human rationality very different to the one we hold today. The consciousness of human beings, their cited beliefs regarding value, reasons for acting, principled commitments, and so forth, is no longer the locus of inquiry if one is interested in the *rationality* of human behaviour. These contents of consciousness are themselves the products of an evolutionarily determined disposition to self-deception and self-aggrandizement. The real function of these aspects of our conscious lives is just to regulate the passions, drives, and instincts that work through us, behind the curtain of what we think we are doing. Yet this deceptive function of consciousness at the same time reveals the truth, since the tussle between our passions and our regulatory confabulations is ultimately to our benefit. There is a rationality at work, but it is nature's rationality. Human behaviour, it turns out, *is* rational, if only we take a broad enough perspective and understand that 'being rational' is not a matter of conscious thinking—the activity of Descartes's or Kant's pure self—it is instead a matter of allowing nature's own rationality to do its work within human behaviour. Similarly, there is a sense in which there *is* a wise providence at work for Mandeville. Nature tends to work to our advantage, though never in any predesigned way that we can plan for or anticipate. We can see the real sense in which nature truly works *for* us, but only if we first understand how nature works *through* us.

CHAPTER TEN

Concealment
and Disclosure

We are sometimes as different from ourselves as we are from other people.

—LA ROCHEFOUCAULD, *MAXIMS*, 5:135

IN 1712, AN anonymous contributor to the *Spectator*—possibly Alexander Pope—wrote of the nearly transcendent pleasures associated with retreating from the bustle and heat of the city so as to appreciate the calm tranquillity of nature that can be found in an evening in a well-tended garden:

> The moon shone bright, and seemed then most agreeably to supply the place of the sun, obliging me with as much light as was necessary to discover a thousand pleasing objects, and at the same time divested of all power of heat. The reflection of it in the water, the fanning of the wind rustling on the leaves, the singing of the thrush and nightingale, and the coolness of the walks, all conspired to make me lay aside all displeasing thoughts, and brought me into such a tranquillity of mind, as is I believe the next happiness to that of hereafter.[1]

Around the time of the vast expansion of commercial activity in urban areas, a need to distinguish oneself by extolling the simple virtues of the countryside emerged. When the lesser sort of person flocked to the city, the better sort of person aspired to leave it. They did not actually leave it, of course, since that was where the power and opportunity still lay, after all, but rather cultivated a disdainful pose towards the urban. What the well-bred man required was a rural retreat, wherein the real value of life could be occasionally appreciated, away from the artifice and filth of the city.

Twenty years later, in his 'Epistle to Bathurst', Pope would write of how it had come about that an entire nation had '*sunk in lucre's sordid charms*'

> At length corruption, like a general flood
> (So long by watchful ministers withstood)
> Shall deluge all; and avarice, creeping on,
> Spread like a low-born mist and block the sun;
> Statesmen and patriot ply alike the stocks,
> Peeress and Butler share alike the box,
> And judges job, and bishops bite the town,
> And mighty dukes pack cards for half a crown.[2]

Had Mandeville read these lines he might have noted in passing that Pope himself had lost everything in the South Sea Bubble and had survived only through the support of his well-heeled social connections. Pope's pious condemnation of the greed of the city is really the bitterness of the investor burned by his own avarice. When Pope reflects from his garden bench upon the follies of human avarice in the city, the hypocrisy on display is immense.

Mandeville would have had no interest in country retreats anyway. He lived for city life. He lived all his life in cities because he was a student of human nature, and in his view the tremendous bustle of the city was where he saw nature in its brightest display. In a remarkably prescient observation, Mandeville saw that the new commercial forces were enervating the upper class's ability to distinguish themselves as superior within society. If goods and property could be owned by all, something else was needed to distinguish one's own superiority. The new means of distinguishing oneself was the pursuit of a new special state of mind—contentment, satisfied reflection on one's condition. The idea was so new that its proponents stated outright how its purpose was that of class distinction. Richard Steele's persona in the *Tatler*, Isaac Bickerstaff, argued that the 'calm and elegant satisfaction which the vulgar call melancholy is the true end and proper delight of men of

knowledge'. It is striking that Steele wants to commend to his readers what they might be experiencing as negative: the melancholic
inactivity of the well-bred is in fact a positive condition. They
shouldn't be disturbed by but rather be proud of their reflective
self-absorption, since 'the pleasures of ordinary people are in their
passions'.[3] What is perhaps crucial for considering Mandeville's
own world view is how Steele framed the enjoyment of our passions as nothing less than the abandonment of the search for self-
knowledge, since 'what we take for diversion, which is a kind of
forgetting our selves, is but a mean way of entertainment, in comparison of that which is considering, knowing, and enjoying our
selves'.[4] The pleasures of knowing one's own self are the highest,
and they so distinguish a person that the 'vulgar' wouldn't even
recognize the activity as pleasurable, since it is so different from
the coarse and beastly pleasures of the body.

Mandeville, of course, was having none of this. The next year, in
the *Female Tatler*, he has his spokesperson, Artesia, suggest that it
is not the vulgar who are operating under an illusion of what happiness is, but rather the 'philosophers' who are trying to convince
others—and ultimately themselves—that there exists some higher
good to be secured than those 'vulgar' passions. There is instead,
they claim, the 'contentment' of the ancient Stoics, whereby someone secures 'a happiness out of a continual delight in his present
condition, from which nothing from without can either bribe
or frighten him'.[5] This new thing—true happiness, unlimited
contentment—is a fantasy that has been absurdly fetishized for no
good reason other than marking oneself out from the rest of the
crowd. It is in the bustle of the crowd—in the cities—where happiness is really found:

> [A] great many people, that end their days in the pursuit of wealth,
> and have in reality no other delight than . . . the toil of life, receive more
> inward satisfaction, and enjoy greater happiness in the midst of noise
> and hurry, than others, that retiring themselves from the world, boast
> of their content with so much arrogance.[6]

Mandeville would stay in London until his death, 'in the midst of
noise and hurry', in pursuit of the happiness appropriate to members of his species. He would not retire to the country in search of

a happiness that never existed, realizing an authentic 'self' that he never believed in anyway.

During his earliest studies at Leiden, Mandeville became convinced that we are far more akin to other animals than we are prepared to accept. There is a different attitude towards human beings taken up by those who have literally seen under our skins, who have marvelled at the complex 'little pipes' that run the human machine, of which we are aware only when they break down. Yet those little pipes run the human animal constantly, he thought, and to understand humanity we need to understand what is going on under the skin. Mandeville had all the tools at his service to set out a radical new picture of the human being. He had a scientific basis in his medical theories for the organization of the human being's biology and of the mind–body interface; he had an account of the rudiments of social organization and how it was built on those biological mechanisms; he had a complex psychological theory based upon the giving and taking of markers of esteem as the glue that held human society together; he had innovative ideas regarding how material conditions affected social values, and the connection between economic behaviour and social cohesion. All of these elements hang together in a remarkably connected way. Mandeville could have written a grand opus entitled *A Theory of Human Nature*, setting it all out. Why didn't he?

My aim has been to provide a kind of outline of the figure of Mandeville's thought that emerges when it is presumed that there is and was intended to be some intellectual continuity throughout all his writings. Mandeville's thought is in my view a unified, if not exactly systematic, world view. He does not deduce a system from first principles or have a worked-out account of every aspect of human nature. On the contrary, I have tried to argue that it would be antithetical to his world view to provide any such system. He is fundamentally shaped by his theory of human beings' animal nature, and everything flows from there. Human beings are not rational creatures in the sense hoped for by Descartes; instead, we are simply animals governed by passions and animal spirits. Yet this simplicity is complicated massively by the fact of our self-consciousness. While Descartes, Kant, and others see an intimate connection between self-consciousness and the capacity for scientific knowledge, principled a priori reasoning, and the like, Mandeville sees in self-consciousness only the evolution of a passion—the desire to win esteem. The sinews of self-consciousness itself are developed reflexively by this desire. Rudimentary self-consciousness manifests in our desire to seek recognition from others. In the course of time we become more aware of ourselves *as* selves as a result of our instinctual drive to trade with others in the economy of esteem.

In his lectures published as *Freud and Philosophy*, the French philosopher Paul Ricoeur spoke of the 'masters of the school of suspicion'.[7] These were the thinkers who introduced the thought that our ordinary consciousness might in fact be inherently deceptive. Far from trusting one's own conscience and consciousness, one ought to be suspicious of it, since our very consciousness has been formed by factors of which we are unaware and which have a very different agenda of their own. Ricoeur thought that there were three 'masters' of the school of suspicion: Nietzsche, Marx, and Freud. I have tried to argue here that Bernard Mandeville was the first master of suspicion. We are only starting to come to terms with Mandeville's thought that we are animals. But we have yet to come to terms with his thought about what distinguishes the human animal from other species. I have tried to show how the qualification one must make here makes all the difference. We are animals, but animals quite unlike any other. We are animals whose animal nature drives us in a very specific way: *we are the animals who deny that they are animals*. There is a specific human nature that Mandeville saw, and paradox was at the heart of it. He would have applauded the science fiction writer Robert A. Heinlein's claim: 'Man is not a rational animal; he is a rationalizing animal.'[8] Mandeville's evolutionary theory explains our hiddenness from ourselves as a structural feature of human consciousness. The theory of gradual historical development was brought to bear on the phenomenon of human thinking itself. That which is the most intimate aspect of how we think, what we understand, or the beliefs to which we are committed, is explained as slowly developed for social reasons now resting in the human mind as if it comprised just simple truths grasped by our reason.

Another paradoxical element of his account of human nature is that it is our social nature that is partly the cause of the difficulty. 'It is incredible,' he says, 'how prone we are to imitation, and how strangely, unknown to ourselves, we are shaped and fashioned after the models and examples that are often set before us'.[9] Mandeville thinks of us as an imitatory species, and it is perhaps because we are creatures who think and behave in instinctive imitation of those around us that we are unknown to ourselves. Our first ideas of who we are emerge from imitating others, and so we construct our ideas, even our conceptions of our own selves, second-hand. What kind of authenticity is ever available to an animal like this? There is no moment of pure, conscious self-realization, such as Descartes's 'I think, therefore I am.' Whatever else we doubt, Descartes claimed, we are at least sure that 'this is me now thinking'. All your thoughts, Mandeville wants to say in response, are yours of course, but what you are thinking about yourself is only there because it is purloined from others.

This is the core intellectual content of Mandeville's thought, a content he matches with the literary form of his works. Mandeville grabs references and passages from various sources, internalizes them, reshapes them, and represents them to the reader. It isn't that he is an unoriginal pilferer—he is an original pilferer. And in his writing, he recreates at the level of form that which he espouses at the level of content—human beings are copiers, their true selves are hidden, and they reveal more truth about humanity when they conceal, dissimulate, and deflect than when they attempt to speak sincerely. Mandeville regularly noted that if his theory of human nature in civilized society were true, then the proper confirming evidence would be that it would be denied everywhere—another paradox. He is only the messenger, he would lament, but as such would have to be vilified as immoral, when all he was doing was explaining the prevalence of immorality in society. In his last work, *A Letter to Dion*, he writes that:

> [He who] dares to expose vice, and the luxury of the time he lives in, pulls off the disguises of artful Men, and [examines] in the false pretences which are made to virtue . . . an author, I say, who dares to do this in a great and opulent and flourishing nation, can never fail of drawing upon him a great number of enemies. Few men can bear with patience to see those things detected which it is their interest, and they take pains to conceal.[10]

These are the reasons why Mandeville never wrote *A Theory of Human Nature*. Satire is, at the very least, the earnest statement of that which is not. Satire had to be the literary form to which Mandeville was committed, since with satire form would match content. Mandeville's subject is in a sense always human nature, and human nature is in his view a paradoxical thing. Mandeville was also writing a theory of the nature of the modern human animal, one that was emerging in the new economic culture that was also just coming into being and that has exploded in the three hundred years since. The theory was one that the public of the time were unable to confront head-on. As J.G.A. Pocock put it, with Mandeville's writings 'the specter of false consciousness had arisen, and was proving more frightening than that of Machiavellian realpolitik'.[11] In 1982 the German philosopher Jürgen Habermas would refer to Mandeville (alongside Hobbes and Machiavelli) as one of the '*dark* writers of the bourgeoisie', and the phrase is quite apposite.[12] Mandeville saw a new class of human society emerging, and had an account of what its nature was that was darker than it liked to think. A literal and sincere statement of that modern emerging nature would be impossible. Mandeville was a prophet of modernity. If false consciousness is the spirit of modernity, irony became the necessary medium of its prophet.[13]

One might reasonably object that there are less intellectualized reasons for Mandeville's form of expression. If one is writing under conditions of censorship and criminal persecution for the propagation of destabilizing thoughts, then that is a reason to deny the message one expresses. If the age isn't ready to hear the thoughts, that is a good reason to wrap the message in irony for one's own well-being. Irony and humour are also pleasurable both to write and to read. David Hume famously confessed that his fundamental motivation for his earliest writings on metaphysics, the theory of knowledge, and morality was in fact literary fame. In London in the early part of the eighteenth century, the goal of many young men writing on these themes was not to become a Plato or Aristotle, Saint Thomas Aquinas or Descartes. It was to become Addison or Steele. It was to become part of that select group who wrote in the *Spectator* and other new literary magazines. It was to become someone who wrote wittily, perceptively, scandalously, or humanely on the nature of modern society. It was to be one who could comment on the fine detail of current political intrigues, who grasped the burgeoning relevance of international commerce, who revelled in the distinctly urban character of eighteenth-century London. It was to be someone who could observe and mock the social mores of the time, though also having the ability to adopt a tone of moral seriousness when required. It was, in short, the aspiration to join the republic of letters. This was Hume's original motivation, and I would argue that it was Mandeville's also. His provocations, his scandal-mongering, his calculated crudeness, and swift sophistication were all directed to impress and amuse a class of readers and writers that had only relatively recently come into existence.

These are no doubt adequate explanations for why Mandeville wrote as he did. There is a more fundamental and complex reason for his concealment of his true opinion, however. Mandeville is educated in the paradoxical tradition. He understands that if his theory is true, then no one knows themselves, and we are constantly oscillating between the public presentation of self—a constructed fantasy—and a private image of one's true, deep, self—a greater fantasy still. What could it possibly be to reveal one's true motives on such a model of the human self? Frank, literal, and sincere disclosure is both philosophically and aesthetically anathema to Mandeville's mode of thought. The implication is that being concealed from ourselves is what we ought to expect—it is a natural fact of human beings that we are the creatures who misrepresent their own nature to themselves. But human beings have the capacity to glance obliquely at *this* fact—the very fact regarding our doubled self-deception (deception *by* the self about *what* the self is). It is a fact of human nature that frames the way we see the world, but sometimes the frame itself can seem almost to appear within our peripheral vision. It behoves the species to attend to these subtle glances whenever they are afforded to us, Mandeville thinks. What is inexcusable is for those who proclaim an interest of any sort in human nature to ignore the very same disposition to doubled self-deception. Those who do so really do abdicate the burden of inquiry while paying lip service to it; then they actively strive to make us 'altogether unknown' to ourselves while solemnly claiming to investigate the nature of the human being.

What is less appreciated by readers of Mandeville's works is that he takes none of his theory to have any kind of pessimistic implications regarding human existence. On the contrary, it is clear that he thought the new, emerging economic order offered something like happiness for human beings, despite his not believing in there being any single form of it that one could define. What comes across more than the aim of the pursuit of happiness, perhaps, is the pursuit of the minimization of suffering and oppression. Mandeville the man was, by all accounts, a cheerful type. And he was trying to offer reasons to be cheerful, reasons that could be grasped only once certain illusions about the human being had been thoroughly dispelled. He needed to point out that the pursuit of rarefied notions of happiness was self-defeating. Since the rarefied notion was a figment of the imagination, the pursuit of it could produce at best delayed gratification. The rarefied notion of happiness is a construction invented by philosophers, he thinks, and promulgated by poets, both equally deluded. They search for happiness as if it is a single state, a super condition that once achieved will change the nature of the constantly desiring human being:

> No sort of people brag more of being contented than your poets, because they over-value themselves, and are lazy, which generally makes them poor; but nothing is more ridiculous in them, than that in the midst of their boasting of what they are, they so often make wishes to be what they are not; always pretending to be sure, that if once they enjoyed that, they would never desire more, when they might more reasonably think that their wish being obtained, the very addition they received to what they had before, would put them upon wishing for something else.[14]

Having a side of ourselves that is hidden from view and that might be the side that motivates most of our actions is familiar enough to our post-Freudian minds. Freud was making a descriptive claim that we will most likely struggle to know ourselves. Mandeville thinks that the fact that we are unknown to ourselves is just a natural fact about human beings, not one to be remedied by wishful thinking or by dreams of self-actualization. Anyone consulting the oracle at Delphi could read the inscription there—the imperative to 'Know Thyself'. But Mandeville asks: why know thyself? It's not possible to do so; in fact, it is against our very nature.

And anyway, we get along so interestingly being the dissimulating animals that we are. It is true, as Pocock commented, that according to Mandeville's theories, 'social morality was becoming divorced from personal morality, and from the ego's confidence in its own integrity and reality'.[15] For Pocock, Mandeville makes us 'unreal'. It is bad enough to be told that human beings are driven by their desires, it is another thing to be told that even one's desires are not what they seem to be. Mandeville's story presents the most intimate forms of human consciousness, our commitments and our awareness of our own beliefs, as fundamentally illusory and shaped all the way down by an internalized ideology.

Yet for all this, one must work hard to see him really as a 'Mandevil', as a vicious and cruel sceptical misanthrope. I have instead tried to present him as motivated by the idea that human beings are most cruel towards one another when motivated by the ideology of moral virtue and by an exalted self-image of their own species. Unserious satire and laughter are needed just because the subject matter is so serious:

> By flattering our pride and still increasing the good opinion we have of ourselves on the one hand, and inspiring us on the other with a superlative dread and mortal aversion against shame, the artful moralists have taught us cheerfully to encounter our selves, and if not subdue, at least so to conceal and disguise our darling passion lust, that we scarce know it when we meet with it in our own breasts; oh! The mighty prize we have in view for all our self-denial! Can any man be so serious as to abstain from laughter, when he considers that for so much deceit and insincerity practiced upon our selves as well as others, we have no other recompense than the vain satisfaction of making our species appear more exalted and remote from that of other animals, than it really is; and we in our consciences know it to be?[16]

The least one can do in favour of humanity, if one really cares about actual flesh and blood human beings, is to puncture the inflated constructions of ourselves that do so much damage, and cause so much suffering. When Mandeville attacks the practice of flogging prostitutes, so enthusiastically endorsed by the Societies for the Reformation of Manners, it is not on the basis that it is an affront to the fundamental dignity of human beings. That is the type of reasoning that would become commonplace by the end of the eighteenth century. At the beginning of the eighteenth century, Mandeville's attack is not even on the basis that it is intolerably cruel, though I think it is obviously the case that he thought it *was* intolerably cruel. Instead, Mandeville just remarks that it is rather difficult to flog virtue into a person. His condemnation of intolerable cruelty is merely sardonic.

Mandeville emerges as far less misanthropic than a contemporary to whom I have regularly compared him, Jonathan Swift. In a famous letter to Pope in 1725, Swift qualified the sense in which he himself might be accused of misanthropy. The human beings he was to present as the wild, vicious Yahoos in *Gulliver's Travels* and the viciousness of the satire in the 'Modest Proposal' would all tend to turn the stomach of their readers. Whereas Swift always had a moral point, it seemed to come from a dark place regarding his estimation of his fellow human beings. He acknowledged as much in the letter:

> I have ever hated all nations, professions, and communities, and all my love is toward individuals: for instance, I hate the tribe of lawyers, but I love Counsellor Such-a-one, and Judge Such-a-one: so with physicians—I will not speak of my own trade—soldiers, English, Scotch, French, and the rest. But principally I hate and detest that animal called man, although I heartily love John, Peter, Thomas, and so forth.[17]

I would claim that Mandeville, like Swift, has concern for individual human beings in mind despite his insistence on bringing the species down from its exalted level. And yet, I think we find more consideration for human beings in Mandeville's writings than we do in Swift's. In *The Tale of the Tub*, Swift wrote one of his most infamous satirical lines, possibly also recounting the public flogging of a prostitute: 'Last week I saw a woman flay'd, and you will hardly believe, how much it altered her person for the worse.'[18] There is really nothing in Mandeville's writings that is quite as brutal as this little line of Swift's. Mandeville wants to draw our attention to the perversity of those who would flog women in the name of virtue. Cover Swift's line in as many layers of irony as one likes, there is a fundamental coldness towards human creatures, a profound disappointment in the fact that we are animals with unattractive insides, a self-disgust that we never find with Mandeville.

Mandeville's opposition to moral brigades is that they try to improve the species. The material conditions of human beings *are* improvable, though, since when their material conditions are better then the species has fewer occasions to tear at itself. Mandeville wants the lot of human beings to be better than it is, but the way to achieve it is negative, by treating its diseased disposition—its *maladie originelle*—on the first occasion of symptoms being manifested. Just like his representative in the *Treatise*, he never attempts the positive goal of curing humanity of its own nature. Setting up moral codes and standards, writing paeans to the irreducible dignity of human beings, and making statements of inalienable fundamental truths about the value of our species are just more attempts to cure human beings of the condition of being human.[19] They end up— inevitably—as just more symptoms of the disease, offering more opportunities for happy narratives under the cover of which we can perpetuate our self-satisfied hypocrisy.

This has been an attempt to understand the mind of Bernard Mandeville through his published works, though we read so little of the historical person that one might almost think that he strove to keep himself concealed. We get glimpses here and there, some from his own writings, some from other sources. Mandeville exemplifies Terence's slogan of finding nothing human alien. All human features, whether we call them virtues or vices, whether we attribute them positive or negative values, are nevertheless *human* features, and he is interested in them for that reason. What he opposes are conceptions of the human being that pretend to present certain features of ourselves as merely 'alien' aspects, and furthermore pretend to identify the 'good' part of the human animal. Mandeville cannot bring himself to believe that the pleasures involved in living, in all their diversity and peculiarity, are evils. The immense intellectual pleasure one takes in discovering and understanding the warp and woof of human nature cannot be anything other than a celebration of that very nature. In this way, some of Mandeville's description of Cleomenes in the *Fable II* sounds very much like autobiography:

> The very relish of life, he said, was accompanied by an elevation of mind that seemed to be inseparable from his being. Whatever principle was the cause of this, he was convinced within himself that the sacrifice of the heart which the Gospel requires consisted in the utter

extirpation of that principle; confessing at the same time that his satisfaction he found in himself, this elevation of mind caused his chief pleasure; and that in all comforts of life, it made the greatest part of his enjoyment.[20]

He had a strong aversion to rigorists of all sorts; and when he saw men quarrelling about forms of creeds, and the interpretation of obscure places, and requiring of others the strictest compliance to their own opinions in disputable matters, it raised his indignation to see the generality of them want charity, and many of them scandalously remiss, in the plainest and most necessary duties.[21]

In the *Treatise*, Mandeville's character Philopirio explains why he has never set up a larger medical practice and propounded his theories that way. The account is one we could plausibly attribute to Mandeville himself:

I could never go through a multiplicity of business. Everybody ought to consult his own temper and abilities in all undertakings. I hate a crowd, and I hate to be in a hurry. Besides, I am naturally slow, and could no more attend a dozen patients in a day, and think of them as I should do, than I could fly. I must own to you likewise, that I am a little selfish, and can't help minding my own enjoyments, and my own diversion, and in short, my own good, as well as the good of others. I can, and do heartily admire at those public-spirited people that can slave at an employment from early in the morning, 'till late at night, and sacrifice every inch of themselves to their callings; but I could never have had the power to imitate them: Not that I love to be idle; but I want to be employed to my own liking; and if a man gives away to others two thirds of the time he is awake, I think he deserves to have the rest for himself.[22]

Perhaps this is why Mandeville doesn't seem to have sought political advancement of any kind. It was simply not suited to his temperament, and he was too interested in securing financial comfort through his medical practice and fame through his writings. It is worth noting that when in the *Free Thoughts* he explains why anyone becomes a courtier, he gives the reasons why one *wouldn't*:

A person who is contented with what he has, that hates noise and insincerity, and having no revenge to execute, or other irregular passion to gratify, is one who knows how to value his own liberty, and desires nothing slavish of others; such a person, I say, what should he do at court?[23]

Perhaps we can infer that Mandeville is not at court or seeking office because he does not think of himself as one of those types, but is instead a man 'who has a polite learning, and a good fortune [who] understands the worth of things, and has a true taste of life' and so he is one who 'may better divert himself almost anywhere else'.[24]

In the end, though, we don't know much of Mandeville's character at all, since most of the records are reports condemning him. We can find snippets here and there. As F. B. Kaye notes, the accusation that Mandeville's writings were funded by the gin trade have no discernible basis in fact, and were promulgated by a notoriously unreliable source, the writer Sir John Hawkins. While denouncing him, Hawkins mentions that he 'once heard a London physician . . . mention him as a good sort of man'.[25] The Earl of Macclesfield loved his conversation; Benjamin Franklin found him 'a most facetious, entertaining companion'.[26] Those who denounced him were generally not of his acquaintance; those who knew him personally spoke well of him. When Mandeville speaks of the socially conditioned nature of human attitudes, the images of children are used again and again. Mandeville had a fine eye for the domestic, and one wonders what his relations were like with his own children, Michael (to whom he left the majority of his estate in his will) and Penelope (to whom he left twenty shillings to purchase a wedding ring).

We can determine something from one of the few letters we have that is written in Mandeville's own hand. Composed in 1726, it is to Lord Macclesfield, to report that Michael is seriously unwell. Here we can finally hear Mandeville's own voice, the one he worked so hard to conceal from the public:

> My Lord,
>
> My son is extremely ill. Last Tuesday he was seized with a terrible cold fit that lasted about three hours and was succeeded by a hot, which continued with great insistence till Friday morning, when he had an intermission of about three hours: then another cold

fit came upon him; three hours after it heat returned
which he labours under still. I never heard or read of
any agues with fair intermissions, where a first fit was
of that continuance. . . . The pain in his head and back
are so raging that they overcome his great patience,
a sight of which is very afflicting to me. Next Monday
I shall take a liberty of writing again. I hope your
lord and all his family are well. Pray, my humble duty
to Lady Macclesfield and . . . to Lady Betty, I am my
Lord,

> Your Lordship's most
> faithful and obedient
> servant,
> B. Mandeville[27]

Mandeville's writing is sparse and factual, yet all the more affecting for that. He is writing to a social superior, Lord Macclesfield,
some years after the latter's fall from power. Yet there is a directness
within the formality. He gives more information of the details than
is really needed. He is not explaining why he must cancel an engagement, not asking for anything or expecting anything in response. He
writes to Lady Macclesfield and the Macclesfields' daughter ('Lady
Betty') as much as he does to Macclesfield himself. The anxiety and
pain and frustration that he, the physician, does not understand
how to treat the fever that might soon kill his son are plain. Michael
survived the illness and then survived his father. Bernard Mandeville died on a Sunday, on the 21 January 1733, in Hackney. Perhaps
the newspaper record of his death would have pleased him, since he
knew how it would infuriate those who thought of him as a devil.
Perhaps he would have been amused himself at how it ironed out
the contradictory aspects of his personality. Or perhaps it simply
recorded the man as others knew him:

> On Sunday morning last died at Hackney, in the 63rd year of his age,
> Bernard Mandeville M.D. Author of the Fable of the Bees, of a Treatise
> of the Hypochondriac and Hysteric Passions and several other curious
> pieces, some of which have been published in foreign languages. He
> had an extensive genius, uncommon wit, and strong judgment. He was

thoroughly versed in the learning of the ancients, well skilled in many parts of philosophy, and a curious searcher into human nature; which accomplishments rendered him a valuable and entertaining companion, and justly procured him the esteem of men of sense and literature. In his profession he was of known benevolence and humanity; in his private character, a sincere friend; and in the whole conduct of life, a gentleman of great probity and integrity.[28]

ACKNOWLEDGEMENTS

IN COMPOSING THIS BOOK, I was very lucky early on to have attended several conferences on Mandeville in Coimbra, Rotterdam, and Helsinki. The latter conference, organized by Mikko Tolonen in 2014, was where I began seriously on my Mandeville studies. It turns out that researchers with an interest in Mandeville form the best of scholarly communities. I benefitted enormously from conversations at that and the other conferences, conversations which continued later with Hal Cook, Remy Debes, Aaron Garrett, the late Stephen Gaukroger, James Harris, Sir Malcolm Jack, Eric Schliesser, Tim Stuart-Buttle, Spiros Tegos, and of course Mikko Tolonen himself. I also have greatly benefitted from David Wootton's conversation and scholarship, as well as his careful and helpful reading of the full draft, one that caught many mistakes and infelicities. I am very grateful to the two anonymous readers for Princeton University Press, who provided me with many helpful comments and corrected a good few errors. Robin Douglass kindly read a full draft of the manuscript and provided me with many useful comments, and I have also benefitted greatly from his recent book on Mandeville's political philosophy. Clare Carlisle read an early chapter and gave me very valuable feedback, as well as much-needed encouragement over the years since.

Much of this work was done on research leave from King's College London, where the Department of Philosophy, and my many friends in it, have been particularly supportive of this project. I am especially grateful to Ben Tate at Princeton University Press, whose enthusiasm for the project never faltered, even when the project stuttered owing to the interruptions of parenthood, pandemics, and illness. His encouragement has been invaluable. I am also incredibly grateful for the editorial work of Jenny Wolkowicki and especially for the close eye of Maia Vaswani.

I owe the most of all to Rebecca Vincent, who read substantial parts of this thesis and made them readable. The parts that remain unreadable are my own responsibility. Her never-ending support, as well as her critical interrogation of what I was trying to say and why, brought the project into a focus that it severely lacked beforehand. Her stylistic advice reinvigorated the writing process for me enormously. There are several senses in which but for her the book would never have been finished, and this work is dedicated to her in love and gratitude.

NOTES

Notes to the Introduction

1. For some accounts of this influence: Douglass, 'Morality and Sociability'; Jack, 'One State of Nature'; Hurtado Prieto, 'Bernard Mandeville's Heir'; Sagar, 'Smith and Rousseau'.

2. For helpful sketches on his life: Kaye's introduction to Mandeville, *Fable of the Bees*; Hundert, *Enlightenment's Fable*, ch. 1; Goldsmith's introduction to Mandeville, *By a Society of Ladies*; R. Cook, *Bernard Mandeville*, ch. 1. On the paucity of biographical details: Primer, *Mandeville Studies*, ix. For works on Mandeville's thought, Hundert's *Enlightenment's Fable* is still the superlative source, and my indebtedness to that work is evident throughout this one; other important works to which I am indebted are R. Cook's *Bernard Mandeville*, Douglass's *Mandeville's Fable*, Goldsmith's *Private Vices, Public Benefits*, Hilton's *Bitter Honey*, Horne's *Social Thought*, Monro's *Ambivalence of Bernard Mandeville*, Schneider's *Paradox and Society*, and Tolonen's *Mandeville and Hume*.

Chapter 1

1. *Presentment to the Middlesex County Court*, quoted in Mandeville, *Fable of the Bees*, 1:385. All references to *The Fable of the Bees* will be to F. B. Kaye's incomparable 1924 edition of both volumes. Kaye uses the 1732 edition of the *Fable* for his text, and I will follow suit. The reference system will indicate the volume of the *Fable* followed by the page number in the 1988 reprint of Kaye's edition.

2. Milton, *Paradise Lost*, bk. 4, 110.

3. I have modified and modernized spelling and punctuation from the originals for all quotations in this work.

4. Mandeville, *Fable of the Bees*, 1:28.

5. Mandeville, 1:28–29.

6. Mandeville, 1:32–33.

7. Mandeville, 1:34.

8. Mandeville, 1:34.

9. This process was arguably begun in the previous century and did not reach its zenith until the next, yet the early eighteenth century is the moment when anxiety over the shifting of power entered political and intellectual consciousness.

10. Of course, the notions of capitalism and class, and analyses of their attendant anxieties, were not in play in Mandeville's time, yet they are useful concepts for understanding Mandeville's keen appreciation of economic forces in society, the role of social mobility, the regulation of trade, and the power of markets.

11. Burrow, *Civil Society and Government*, 10. Many of the following sources of early responses to Mandeville have been gathered in Stafford's *Private Vices, Public Benefits?*

12. Law, *Remarks upon a Late Book*, 3.

13. Mandeville, *Fable of the Bees*, 1: 72, remark C.

14. Fiddes, *General Treatise of Morality*, xi.

15. Fiddes, xxix.

16. Fiddes, lxviii.

17. Fiddes, cxxxix.

18. Dennis, *Vice and Luxury*, xii.

19. Dennis, xvi.

20. Bluett, *Enquiry*, iii.
21. Mandeville, *Fable of the Bees*, 1:ix.
22. Fiddes, *General Treatise of Morality*, lxxx.
23. Walker, *Necessity and Advantages*, 8.
24. Hendley, *Defence*, 41.
25. Mandeville, *Fable of the Bees* 1:391, 'Vindication of the Book'.
26. The rumour seems to have been first put into print by Johnson's biographer Hawkins: Hawkins, *Life of Samuel Johnson*, 263. For Mandeville on gin, see Anderson's 'Bernard Mandeville on Gin'.
27. *London Evening Post*, no. 39 (March 7–9, 1728).
28. Campbell and Innes, *Arete-Logica*, iv–v.
29. Campbell and Innes, xxii.
30. *Craftsman*, no. 312 (1731): 54.
31. Anonymous, *Character of the Times*, 5.
32. Anonymous, 10.
33. Swift, *Miscellanies*, 160.
34. This kind of prank was a familiar form of literary entertainment at the time, the most notable occurrence being Swift's own harassment (under the pseudonym of Isaac Bickerstaff) of the astrologer John Partridge. Bickerstaff mocked Partridge's profession by predicting Partridge's own death. Bickerstaff later confirmed that Partridge had died, despite Partridge's insistent and indignant assertions to the contrary.
35. Warburton, *Divine Legation of Moses*, bk. 1, sec. 6, 129.
36. Pope, *Dunciad*, bk. 2, line 414, 117.
37. Fielding, *Miscellaneous Works*, 104.
38. Hundert argues for the significance of Mandeville for Fielding's work in his *Enlightenment's Fable*, 153–68.
39. For the French reception of the *Fable*, see Muceni's 'Mandeville and France'.
40. Wesley, *Journal*, 383, entry for April 14, 1756.
41. Wesley, 383, entry for April 14, 1756.
42. Mandeville, *Fable of the Bees*, 1:229, remark T.
43. Mandeville, *Fable of the Bees*, 1:401, 'Vindication of the Book'.
44. Johnson, in Pope, *Works of the English Poets*, 167n.
45. Pilkington, *An Infallible Scheme to Pay the Publick Debt of Ireland in Six Months* (1732), quoted in Swift, *Miscellanies*, 105.
46. Robinson and Sadler, *Diary, Reminiscences*, 252.
47. Johnson, in Boswell's *Life*, edited by Hill (1887), 3: vi. Johnson is frequently quoted as saying that the *Fable* was a book that every young man had on his bookshelf, though only in the belief that it was a wicked work. I haven't been able to confirm the source of this quotation, however, and it may be apocryphal.
48. For *Le Mondain* and Du Châtelet: Voltaire, *Works*, 84–88; Du Châtelet, *Philosophical and Scientific Writings*. For the early French reception of the *Fable of the Bees*: Muceni, 'Mandeville and France'.
49. For the topic of human nature in the eighteenth century, see in particular Garrett's 'Anthropology' and 'Human Nature'; for Hume's science of man, see Biro's 'Hume's New Science' and Demeter's 'Science'; for a discussion of Mandeville's relationship to the science of human nature, see Castiglione's 'Considering Things Minutely'.
50. For the influence of Mandeville upon Smith: Çeşmeli, 'Is Adam Smith Heir'; Hurtado Prieto, 'Bernard Mandeville's Heir'; Kerkhof, 'A Fatal Attraction?'; Oliveira, 'Mandeville and Smith'; Pongiglione, 'Bernard Mandeville's Influence'.
51. See Hume, *Treatise of Human Nature*; Kant, *Critique of Practical Reason*; J.-J. Rousseau, *Discourses*; Smith, *Theory of Moral Sentiments* and *Wealth of Nations*.
52. Marx, 'Theories of Surplus-Value', in *Karl Marx: A Reader*, 321.

53. For a discussion of the relevance of Mandeville for Darwin, see Alter's 'Mandeville's Ship'. For the relevance of Mandeville to Keynes, Hayek, and laissez-faire in general, see Keynes's *General Theory of Employment*, Hayek's *Trend of Economic Thinking*, and Rosenberg's 'Mandeville and Laissez-Faire'.

54. Dumont, *From Mandeville to Marx*, ch. 5.

55. Schneider, *Paradox and Society*.

56. For some examples: Backhouse, *Penguin History of Economics*; Spiegel, *Growth of Economic Thought*; Viner, *Intellectual History of Economics*.

57. Mandeville, *Fable of the Bees*, 1: 39.

58. Hume, *Treatise of Human Nature*, 4, introduction. Hume was writing at a time when the outrage against Mandeville was perhaps at its highest pitch, and the very inclusion of the Man-Devil on his list of greats was no doubt an attempt on Hume's part to be deliberately provocative. My view of Mandeville's significance for subsequent eighteenth-century European thought agrees with that of Hundert, who in his vital work claimed that what Mandeville offered was a 'highly articulated, conceptually challenging, science of man' (Hundert, *Enlightenment's Fable*, 13). The reading of Mandeville that I argue for here stresses that exactly what was conceptually challenging about Mandeville's anthropology was not in fact his prioritization of economic concerns nor even his apparent moral scepticism. Rather, it was firstly that it that it stressed the explanation of putatively distinctive human rational capacities as continuous with non-human animal passions, and secondly that it put forward a conception of human psychology where self-deception was an essential cognitive mechanism for the human mind's proper functioning.

59. For a helpful brief overview of Mandeville's reception, see the epilogue to Hundert's *Enlightenment's Fable*.

Chapter 2

1. As mentioned, little is in fact known about Mandeville's life. Standard biographical information can be found in Kaye's introduction to *The Fable of the Bees* and also H. Cook's 'Bernard Mandeville' and Hundert's *Enlightenment's Fable*. For discussions of the medical context of Mandeville's thought: Collins, 'Private Vices, Public Benefits'; H. Cook, *Matters of Exchange*, ch. 10, and 'Bernard Mandeville'; R. Cook, *Bernard Mandeville*, ch. 4; Goldsmith, *Private Vices, Public Benefits*, 139–45; Hilton, *Bitter Honey*; Horne, *Social Thought*, 41; Hundert, *Enlightenment's Fable*, 35–49; Kleiman-Lafon, 'Healing Power of Words'; Kleiman-Lafon's introduction to Mandeville, *Hypochondriack and Hysterick Diseases*; Monro, *Ambivalence of Bernard Mandeville*, ch. 3; Romão, 'Mandeville'; G. Rousseau, 'Mandeville and Europe'.

2. Dekker, 'Private Vices, Public Virtues'.

3. I have excluded the *Free Thoughts* from my analysis in this work, not from lack of interest but because the complex religious and political context of its writing is too intricate to summarize efficiently. It is also my view that Mandeville's quasi-plagiaristic writing here reveals more his opportunistic attitude towards polemic than any sincere will to engage in theological dispute, rendering the work something of an outlier in my view. However, the *Free Thoughts* is an undeniably rich work that not only shows familiarity with those theological disputes but also is an important document with regard to the religious controversies of early eighteenth-century Britain.

4. For an important discussion of Bayle's position on morality, see Wootton's 'Pierre Bayle, Libertine?'

5. For helpful translations of Mandeville's Latin works, I am indebted to the excellent dissertation by McKee: 'An Anatomy of Power: The Early Works of Bernard Mandeville'.

6. We owe the detailed account of this event and its relevance to Mandeville's development to the detective work in Dekker's 'Private Vices, Public Virtues'. The presentation that follows derives from his account.

7. From here on, I will refer to human animals as 'humans' and non-human animals as 'animals'.

8. Montaigne, *Essays*, 505.

9. Montaigne, 505.

10. Montaigne, 505.

11. Montaigne, 514.

12. Montaigne, 515.

13. Montaigne, 514.

14. Montaigne, 513.

15. Descartes, 'Discourse on Method, Part VI', in *Philosophical Writings*, 1:141.

16. More, *Utopia*, bk. 2, 95.

17. Descartes, *Philosophical Essays and Correspondence*, 276. For discussion: Clarke, *Descartes's Theory of Mind*; Cottingham, '"A Brute to the Brutes?"'; McKee, 'Anatomy of Power'; Melehy, 'Silencing the Animals'.

18. Descartes, *Philosophical Writings*, 3:302.

19. Descartes, 3:304.

20. Descartes, 1:188.

21. Descartes, 1:269.

22. Descartes, 1:270–71.

23. For an in-depth account of seventeenth- and eighteenth-century thought that pays proper attention to the notion of animal suffering in God's creation, see Van der Lugt's *Dark Matters*.

24. Willis, *Two Discourses*, 24.

25. Willis, 27.

26. Locke, *Essay concerning Human Understanding*, bk. 4, ch. 3, sec. 23.

27. Locke, bk. 4, ch. 3, sec. 4.

28. Sydenham, *Epistolary Dissertation*, in *Works*, 90.

29. Sydenham, *Works*, 106.

30. Sydenham, 85.

31. Baglivi, *Practice of Physick*, x. There are no significant differences between the 1704 and 1723 editions.

32. Baglivi, 17.

33. Baglivi, 17.

34. Baglivi, 29.

35. Baglivi, 51.

36. Baglivi, 40.

37. Mandeville, *Hypochondriack and Hysterick Diseases*, 28.

Chapter 3

1. This edition was the third edition, there having been a second edition in 1728. However, the second edition was basically a reprint of the first, while the third edition is a substantial revision: the title was changed, around one hundred pages of extra text were added, and footnotes providing English translations of the numerous Latin quotations were also added.

2. Mandeville, *Hypochondriack and Hysterick Diseases*, 27.

3. Mandeville, 25.

4. Mandeville, 25.

5. Mandeville, 26. For the topic of pride in this period, see Lovejoy's '"Pride"'. A classic account of Mandeville's theory of pride can be found in Heath's 'Mandeville's Bewitching Engine'. For more recent explorations of Mandeville's account of pride: Douglass, 'Dark Side of Recognition'; Verburg, 'Bernard Mandeville's Vision'.

6. Mandeville, *Hypochondriack and Hysterick Diseases*, 79–80.

7. Mandeville, 53.

8. Mandeville, 27.

9. Mandeville, 41.

10. Mandeville, 43.

11. Mandeville, 44.

12. Mandeville, 46.

13. Mandeville, 47.

14. Mandeville, 51.

15. Mandeville, 51.

16. Mandeville, 49.

17. Hilton, *Bitter Honey*, 99.

18. Mandeville, *Hypochondriack and Hysterick Diseases*, 23.

19. Mandeville, 23.

20. Mandeville, 52–53; see also Monro, *Ambivalence of Bernard Mandeville*.

21. Mandeville, *Hypochondriack and Hysterick Diseases*, 54.

22. Mandeville, 54.

23. Mandeville, 53–54.

24. Mandeville, 63.

25. Mandeville, 64.

26. Mandeville, 63. The example of the Van Dyck painting might bring to mind the well-known anecdote in Gladwell's *Blink* where an art expert is correctly convinced of the inauthenticity of an artwork despite being unable to articulate the exact grounds for their judgment.

27. H. Cook, *Matters of Exchange*, 405–6.

28. Mandeville, *Hypochondriack and Hysterick Diseases*, 26.

29. Mandeville, 63.

30. Mandeville, 63.

31. Mandeville, *Fable of the Bees*, 1:150–51, remark O.

32. Mandeville, *Fable of the Bees*, 1:140, remark O.

33. Quoted in Monro, *Ambivalence of Bernard Mandeville*, 53.

34. Mandeville, *Hypochondriack and Hysterick Diseases*, 125.

35. Mandeville, 125.

36. Hilton, *Bitter Honey*, 13.

37. For a discussion: Hilton, *Bitter Honey*; Kleiman-Lafon, 'Healing Power of Words'; Simonazzi, 'Bernard Mandeville on Hypochondria'.

38. Mandeville, *Hypochondriack and Hysterick Diseases*, 102, perhaps punning dreadfully on 'immaterial'.

39. As pointed out by R. Cook in *Bernard Mandeville*, 74.

40. This is a thesis that is receiving some scientific support these days, and has been popularly conveyed in Enders's *Gut: The Inside Story of Our Body's Most Underrated Organ*.

41. Hilton, *Bitter Honey*, 94.

Chapter 4

1. Vichert, 'Mandeville's *The Virgin Unmask'd*', 1. For discussion of *The Virgin Unmask'd* see chapter 3 of R. Cook's *Bernard Mandeville*. The best treatments of the status of women in Mandeville's thought are to be found in Garrett's 'Women' and O'Brien's *Women and Enlightenment*, 19–27 and ch. 1.

2. Mandeville, *Virgin Unmask'd*, 21. See also Mandeville, *Fable of the Bees*, 1:143, remark N.

3. Mandeville, *Virgin Unmask'd*, 19.

4. Mandeville, *Fable of the Bees*, 1:143, remark N.

5. Mandeville, *Virgin Unmask'd*, 2.

6. Mandeville, *Wishes to a Godson*, 14.

7. Mandeville, *Fable of the Bees*, 1:144, remark N.

8. Mandeville, 1:72, remark C.

9. Mandeville, 1:73, remark C.

10. Mandeville, 1:73, remark C.

11. Mandeville, 1:74, remark C.

12. Mandeville, *Virgin Unmask'd*, 30.

13. Mandeville, *By a Society of Ladies*, 119.

14. Mandeville, *Virgin Unmask'd*, 129.

15. Mandeville, *Modest Defence*, 76.

16. Mandeville, 76.

17. Mandeville, 79.

18. Mandeville, *Virgin Unmask'd*, 32.

19. For discussion, see Vichert's 'Mandeville's *The Virgin Unmask'd*'.

20. Mandeville, *Virgin Unmask'd*, 38.

21. Mandeville, 39.

22. Mandeville, 40.

23. Mandeville, 41.

24. Mandeville, 52.

25. Mandeville, 49.

26. Mandeville, 52.

27. Mandeville, 62.

28. Mandeville, 68.

29. Mandeville, 74.

30. Mandeville, 69.

31. Mandeville, 83.

32. Mandeville, 87.

33. Mandeville, 67. For more detail on this point, see Vichert's 'Mandeville's *The Virgin Unmask'd*'.

34. Mandeville, *Virgin Unmask'd*, 108.

35. Mandeville, 204.

36. Mandeville, 205.

37. Mandeville, 205.

38. Mandeville, 214.

39. As Cook notes, there is a pattern in Mandeville's writing of leaving works open-ended, sometimes in explicit acknowledgement that he will continue only if there is public demand for more (R. Cook, *Bernard Mandeville*, 45).

40. Vichert, 'Mandeville's *The Virgin Unmask'd*', 8.

41. Mandeville, *Fable of the Bees*, 1:39, introduction.

42. Vichert, 'Mandeville's *The Virgin Unmask'd*', 1.

43. Mandeville, *Virgin Unmask'd*, 119–20.

44. Mandeville, 128.

45. Mandeville, *By a Society of Ladies*, 171, no. 88.

46. Mandeville, 172, no. 88.

47. Mandeville, 174.

48. Mandeville, *Virgin Unmask'd*, 12.

49. Mandeville, 13.

50. For discussion: Karras, 'Regulation of Brothels'.

51. Though Cook notes that Mandeville seems appalled mostly at the waste of potential labour force that results (R. Cook, *Bernard Mandeville*, 102).

52. Mandeville, *Fable of the Bees*, 1:95, 96, remark H.

53. Mandeville, 1:96–97, remark H.

54. Mandeville, 1:99, 100, remark H.

55. Mandeville, *Modest Defence*, 57.

56. Mandeville, 63.

57. Mandeville, 49.

58. Mandeville, 50.

59. For a discussion of the development of the concept of shame, see Dawson's 'Shame'.

60. Mandeville, *Fable of the Bees*, 1:57, 67–68, remark C.

61. I'm grateful to Robin Douglass for drawing my attention to this parallel claim.

62. O'Brien, *Women and Enlightenment*, 21.

Chapter 5

1. Mandeville, *Fable of the Bees*, 1:8. For discussion of Mandeville's literary style: R. Cook, *Bernard Mandeville*, ch. 2; Hundert, *Enlightenment's Fable*, 116–26; Monro, *Ambivalence of Bernard Mandeville*, ch. 2; Noel, *Theories of the Fable*, ch. 3.

2. For discussion of the influence of Erasmus on Mandeville, see Primer's 'Erasmus and Bernard Mandeville'.

3. Erasmus, *Praise of Folly*, 5.

4. For discussion of the paradoxical encomium, see Colie's *Paradoxia Epidemica* and Miller's 'Paradoxical Encomium'.

5. Erasmus, *Praise of Folly*, 21.

6. Erasmus, 22.

7. Mandeville, *Fable of the Bees*, 1:36.

8. S. Butler, 'Miscellaneous Observations and Reflections on Various Subjects', in *Characters and Passages*, 401, quoted in Leyburn, 'Hudibras'.

9. Butler, *Hudibras*, 169, pt 2, canto 2, 243–46.

10. Butler, 166, pt 2, canto 2, 133–38.

11. Locke, *Some Thoughts concerning Education* 122, sec. 167.

12. For discussion of the role of fable at the time: Daniel, 'Political and Philosophical Uses'; Loveridge, *History of Augustan Fable*. For a discussion of how the use of fable informs Mandeville's theory in particular: Gaston, 'Fables of Pity'.

13. Anonymous, *Aesop at Islington*, 3.

14. Mandeville, *Aesop Dress'd*, 25.

15. Mandeville, 26.

16. Mandeville, 76.

17. Mandeville, 77.

18. Mandeville, 77.

19. Mandeville, 78.

20. Mandeville, *Pamphleteers: A Satyr*, 6.

21. Mandeville, *Typhon*, preface.

22. See Jack, *Corruption and Progress*, ch. 2.

23. Mandeville, *Typhon*, 5–6.

24. Mandeville, 25.

25. Mandeville, 45.

26. Mandeville, 45.

27. For discussion see Farrell, 'Mandeville's Bee Analogy'.

28. Willis, *Two Discourses*, 35.

29. Erasmus, *Praise of Folly*, 34.

30. Montaigne, *Essays*, 508.

31. Hobbes, *Leviathan*, 119, ch. 17.

32. Hobbes, 119, ch. 17,

33. A recent study connecting Hobbes to Mandeville with regard to sociability can be found in chapter 1 of Sagar's *Opinion of Mankind*.

34. Mandeville, *Fable of the Bees*, 1:17.

35. Mandeville, 1:17.

36. Mandeville, 1:18.
37. Mandeville, 1:18–19.
38. Mandeville, 1:19.
39. Mandeville, 1:19–20.
40. Mandeville, 1:20.
41. Mandeville, 1:20.
42. Mandeville, 1:21.
43. Mandeville, 1:21.
44. Mandeville, 1:22.
45. Mandeville, 1:22.
46. Mandeville, 1:23–24.
47. Mandeville, 1:24.
48. Mandeville, 1:24.
49. Mandeville, 1:24.
50. Mandeville, 1:24–25.
51. Mandeville, 1:25.
52. Mandeville, 1:25.
53. Mandeville, 1:26.
54. Mandeville, 1:27.
55. Mandeville, 1:28.
56. Mandeville, 1:28.
57. Mandeville, 1:31.
58. Mandeville, 1:34.
59. Mandeville, 1:35.
60. Mandeville, 1:36.
61. Mandeville, 1:37.
62. Machiavelli, *Prince*, 54, sec. 15.
63. Mandeville, *Fable of the Bees*, 1:8, preface.

Chapter 6

1. Mandeville, *Fable of the Bees*, 1:39, introduction.
2. For Hobbes's influence on Mandeville: Runciman, *Political Hypocrisy*, ch. 2; Sagar, *Opinion of Mankind*; Young, 'Mandeville'.
3. Mandeville, *Fable of the Bees*, 1:200, remark R.
4. Mandeville, 1:39, introduction; see also Mandeville, *Origin of Honour*, 31.
5. Hume, *Treatise of Human Nature*, 2.3.3.
6. This theme is explored in interesting detail in Daniel's 'Myth and Rationality' and in a different way by Allen in 'Burning the *Fable*'.
7. Mandeville, *Fable of the Bees*, 1:4, preface.
8. For the importance of Mandeville's medical thought to his political and philosophical theories: H. Cook, 'Mandeville and the Therapy' and 'Treating of Bodies Medical'; Romão, 'Mandeville'.
9. Mandeville, *Fable of the Bees*, 1:145, remark O.
10. For discussion of Mandeville's debt to the French *moralistes*: Horne, *Social Thought*, ch. 2; Hundert, *Enlightenment's Fable*, 96–105; Schneider, *Paradox and Society*, 68–76. For a compelling case of just how relevant Bayle's writings were to the details of Mandeville's, see Robertson's *Case for the Enlightenment*, 261–80
11. Mandeville, *Fable of the Bees*, 1:4, preface.
12. Mandeville, 1:39, introduction.
13. Mandeville, 1:40, introduction.
14. Mandeville, 1:166, remark O.

15. La Rochefoucauld, *Maxims*, 3, 'The Publisher to the Reader'. The point is noted by Hundert in *Enlightenment's Fable*, 32–33.

16. Mandeville, *Fable of the Bees*, 1:60, remark A.

17. Mandeville, 1:60, remark A.

18. Mandeville, 1:25, 1:101, remark I.

19. Mandeville, 1:101–2, remark I.

20. Mandeville, 1:106, remark K. See the epigram to this chapter.

21. Mandeville, 1:101, remark I.

22. La Rochefoucauld, *Maxims*, 3.

23. La Rochefoucauld, 75, V:263.

24. La Rochefoucauld, 7, V:254.

25. La Rochefoucauld, 75, V:264.

26. For some excellent recent work on the relations between Augustinian theology and French philosophy see Moriarty, *Fallen Nature* and *Disguised Vices*.

27. Calvin, *Institutes*, vol. 2, bk. 3, ch. 7, p. 8.

28. See, for example, Calvin's Commentary on Jude 10, cited in Bouwsma's *John Calvin*, 76. For discussion of Calvin on moderation in ethics, see Haas's 'Calvin's Ethics'.

29. À Kempis, *Imitation of Christ*, ch. 23, 'A Meditation on Death', 58.

30. À Kempis, ch. 27, 'How Self-Love Hinders Our Search for God', 130.

31. Nicole, *Moral Essayes*, vol. 3, second treatise, 'Of Charity, and Self-Love', 136.

32. Nicole, 135.

33. I'm deeply indebted here to Viner's formative work here (*Intellectual History of Economics*, 186–88; see also Viner, *Role of Providence*).

34. Nicole, *Essais de morale*, ch. 6, sec. 20, 125—my translation.

35. Mandeville, *Fable of the Bees*, 1:230, remark T.

36. Mandeville, 1:67, remark C.

37. Mandeville, 1:68, remark C.

38. Mandeville, *Modest Defence*, 76.

39. Mandeville, *Fable of the Bees*, 1:78, remark C.

40. Mandeville, 1:199, remark R.

41. Mandeville, 1:214, remark R. For fuller discussions of Mandeville's account of honour: Branchi, *Pride, Manners, and Morals*; Douglass, *Mandeville's Fable*, ch. 5; Olsthoorn, 'Bernard Mandeville on Honor'.

42. La Rochefoucauld, *Maxims*, 5:308. See the epigram to this chapter.

43. This is not to say that interpreting Mandeville's moral theory is straightforward. Kaye, for example, thinks that Mandeville developed two sincerely held moral theories, Christian asceticism and utilitarianism, and that the *Fable* is an exercise in revelling in their paradoxical incompatibility (Kaye, introduction to Mandeville, *Fable of the Bees*, 1:lv). While many saw him as a debunker of traditional Christian morality, some interpret him as remaining true to those ideals, and as advocating only the weaker kind of scepticism (i.e., that these are genuine standards of real virtue that we are merely unable to consistently realize)—see, for example, Lamprecht's '*Fable of the Bees*' and chapter 7 of Monro's *Ambivalence of Bernard Mandeville*. More recently, Roger Crisp has argued that Mandeville 'wishes to promote a view of his own which rests on what he saw as a firm Christian foundation' (Crisp, 'Mandeville', 61), and that he sincerely 'recommends a life of humility, piety, and frugality' (72.) One needs to ask what role is attributed to satire in Mandeville's writings on these readings, a point made originally by Harth in 'Satiric Purpose'. Kyle Scott believes that there is satire in Mandeville's writings but that it is directed towards the immorality of commercial society (Scott, 'Mandeville's Paradox as Satire'). As should already be clear, the story presented here is of a somewhat different Mandeville. The Mandeville Crisp and Scott accurately perceive is one who is no doubt promoting a work of the 'strictest morality' in terms his readers would have recognized as Calvinist; the reading I offer here though presumes that Mandeville's intended satire extends

as far as to these rigorous Calvinist terms themselves. I follow Harth's original thought that 'we might easily suspect that Mandeville's intention was satirical and that he merely pretends to accept rigorism in order to expose the impossibility of its demands when viewed in the stern light of experience and common sense' (Harth, 'Satiric Purpose', 335). The satire is not directed *for the sake* of moral rigorism; the satire is directed *at* moral rigorism. This Mandeville is one of those whom, as David Wootton has put it, 'deliberately masqueraded as Calvinists' (Wootton, *Power, Pleasure, and Profit*, 3); that is, they professed strong standards of morality in the spirit of undermining not just our ability to meet those standards, but the very standards themselves—see also Colman's 'Bernard Mandeville'. There is no doubt much to say still in favour of differing interpretations. For a helpful recent critique of Mandeville's account of virtue: Douglass, 'Origins of Virtue'; for a defence: Welchman, 'Who Rebutted Bernard Mandeville?'

44. For the concept of moral virtue in eighteenth-century philosophy: Fate Norton and Kuehn, 'Foundations of Morality'; Garrett and Heydt, 'Moral Philosophy'; Heydt, 'Practical Ethics'; Kail, 'Moral Judgment'; Perinetti, 'Nature of Virtue'.

45. Mandeville, *Fable of the Bees*, 2:270, sixth dialogue.

46. Mandeville, 1:41,'Enquiry into the Origin of Moral Virtue'. For a helpful overview of the problem of self-interest in the period, see Maurer's 'Self-Interest and Sociability', and for a fuller study, Force's *Self-Interest before Adam Smith*.

47. Mandeville, *Fable of the Bees*, 1:42, 'Enquiry into the Origin of Moral Virtue'.

48. Mandeville, 1:42.

49. Mandeville, 1:43.

50. Mandeville, 1:43.

51. Mandeville, 1:45.

52. Mandeville, 1:48–49.

53. Mandeville, 1:51.

54. Mandeville, 1:47.

55. It is, of course, always possible that Mandeville sincerely believed all this, and that he is writing as a Pierre Nicole transported to London, shocked not at the vice around him but at the complacency with which Londoners believe virtue to be achievable and compatible with their ordinary lifestyles. To take this reading, however, requires a gymnastic account of the role of irony in Mandeville's writings. Few deny irony is present in his writings, yet one would have to claim it is present only in some analyses and entirely absent in others. It is also worth stating, however, that there is still room, even on the anti-Christian interpretation I argue for here, that Mandeville had some sort of religious commitment, possibly deistic, left over after his rejection of Christian doctrine had been completed.

56. Mandeville, *Free Thoughts on Religion*, 22, ch. 2, 'On Religion'.

57. For a helpful discussion of the extent of atheism in early modern times, see Wootton's 'Unbelief'.

58. Mandeville, *Fable of the Bees*, 1:230, remark T.

59. Dario Castiglione connects this point with how Mandeville had Philopirio argue against the coherence of an immaterial soul in the *Treatise* (Castiglione, 'Considering Things Minutely', 486–87).

60. Bayle, *Various Thoughts*, 139, seventh letter (July 9, 1681), sec. 108.

61. Mandeville, *Fable of the Bees*, 1:124, remark M.

62. Rochester, *Poems*, 89–90. For a discussion of some of the paradoxical elements of Rochester's 'Satyr': I. White, '"So Great a Disproportion"'.

63. Abbadie, *Art of Knowing One-Self*, 229–30.

64. Law, *Remarks upon a Late Book*, 9.

65. Erasmus, *Praise of Folly*, 23.

66. Bayle, *Various Thoughts*, 168, eighth letter (July 29, 1681), sec. 136.

67. Mandeville, *Fable of the Bees*, 1:168, remark O.

68. Mandeville, 1:168, remark O.

Chapter 7

1. What follows in this chapter is an account of some of the political context of works already discussed, to demonstrate how they can be viewed as responses to the particular political scene. I don't offer here a complete account of Mandeville's political philosophy, which would have to include a more comprehensive account of his *Free Thoughts* and *Enquiry into the Origin of Honour*. For a work that directly engages with Mandeville's writings considered as political and social philosophy, see Douglass's *Mandeville's Fable*.

2. For the social and political context of Mandeville's writings in general: Burtt, *Virtue Transformed*, esp. ch. 7; Dickinson, *Liberty and Property*, chs 1–3; Goldsmith, *Private Vices, Public Benefits*, chs 1 and 4; Hoppit, *Land of Liberty?*, esp. chs 2, 5, 9, and 10; Horne, *Social Thought*, ch. 1, and 'Envy and Commercial Society'; Hundert, *Enlightenment's Fable*, ch. 1; Jones, *Country and Court*; Kenyon, *Revolution Principles*, ch. 7; I Kramnick, *Bolingbroke and His Circle*; J. Kramnick, 'Unwilling to Be Short'; O'Gorman, *Long Eighteenth Century*, ch. 2; Plumb, *Growth of Political Stability*; Pocock, *Machiavellian Moment*; Prior, *Mandeville and Augustan Ideass*; Speck, *Tory and Whig* and 'Bernard Mandeville'.

3. For a single interesting example, see Peltonen's 'Politeness and Whiggism' for a discussion of the differing views among Whig factions on the strategic importance of politeness as a standard within the new commercial society. For the role of politeness in eighteenth-century philosophy, see Klein's *Shaftesbury*.

4. For these details, see H. Cook's 'Bernard Mandeville'.

5. Kaye, introduction to Mandeville, *Fable of the Bees*, 1:xx.

6. Horne, *Social Thought*, 66.

7. Browning, *Political and Constitutional Ideas*, 12.

8. I. Kramnick, *Bolingbroke and His Circle*.

9. Anonymous, *Reflexions upon the Moral State*, 2.

10. Harrington, *Commonwealth of Oceana*, 196–97.

11. Davenant, *Essays* 1, 'Balance of Power, 1.

12. Davenant, 2.

13. Davenant, 5–6.

14. Davenant, 'Essay on Public Virtue' (1696), quoted in Dickinson, *Liberty and Property*, 110–11.

15. Davenant, *Essays* 1, 'Balance of Power', 4.

16. Davenant, 'Essay on Public Virtue' (1696), quoted in Dickinson, *Liberty and Property*, 111.

17. Fénelon, *Telemachus*, bk. 10, 163.

18. A good overview of the scene as it related to Mandeville in particular can be found in chapter 4 of Horne's *Social Thought*. For some useful analyses on these themes: Bick, 'Bernard Mandeville'; R. Cook, *Bernard Mandeville*, ch. 6; Hundert, *Enlightenment's Fable*, ch. 4; Landreth, 'Economic Thought'.

19. O'Gorman, *Long Eighteenth Century*, 39.

20. J. White, *London in the 18th Century*, 178–79.

21. Coward and Gaunt, *Stuart Age*, 516.

22. Coward and Gaunt, 527.

23. Porter, *English Society*, 220.

24. O'Gorman, *Long Eighteenth Century*, 23.

25. Mandeville, *Free Thoughts on Religion*, 176.

26. Jonathan Swift, *Examiner* no. 14 (1) (October 26 to November 2, 1710), quoted in Damrosch, *Jonathan Swift*, 170.

27. Mandeville, *Pamphleteers: A Satyr*, 5.

28. Mandeville, 6.

29. Mandeville, 8.

30. Mandeville, *Free Thoughts on Religion*, 187.

31. For a historical perspective on austerity that makes use of Mandeville and Voltaire, see Schui's *Austerity : The Great Failure*, chapter 2.

32. Mandeville, *Grumbling Hive*, in *Fable of the Bees*, 1:36.

33. *Tatler* no.183 (June 10, 1710), in Bond, *Tatler*, 493.

34. For Mandeville's contributions to the *Female Tatler*, see the fine introduction by Goldsmith to Mandeville's *By a Society of Ladies*, as well as chapter 2 of Goldsmith's *Private Vices, Public Benefits*; see also Anderson's 'Splendor out of Scandal' and chapter 1 of Branchi's *Pride, Manners, and Morals*.

35. *Female Tatler* no. 80, in Mandeville, *By a Society of Ladies*, 152.

36. The prevalence of the ideology of civic virtue across the parties is well documented in chapter 1 of Goldsmith's *Private Vices, Public Benefits*.

37. Swift, *Advancement of Religion*, 18.

38. For this attribution, see Moore's '*Groans of Great Britain*'.

39. Gildon, *Groans of Great Britain*, preface.

40. Gildon, 6.

41. Gildon, 10. For the Fénelon-like claims regarding luxury, see pages 10, 15, 18, 19, 28, 50, and 90.

42. Gildon, 10.

43. Gildon, 15.

44. Gildon, 23.

45. This is not to say that Gildon was alone in this form of rhetoric—as Goldsmith points out, the theme had been explored in pamphlets by various writers from the time of the Glorious Revolution and, as has been mentioned in chapter 1, was a regular theme in Steele's *Tatler*—for discussion, see chapter 1 of Goldsmith's *Private Vices, Public Benefits*.

46. Gildon, *Groans of Great Britain*, 19.

47. Mandeville, *Fable of the Bees*, 1:57, 'Enquiry into the Origin of Moral Virtue'.

48. The point is not often made but is central to understanding Mandeville's motives. One meritorious exception is Burtt, in *Virtue Transformed*, 133n17.

49. As recounted by Samuel Johnson in his treatment of Addison in *Lives of the English Poets* (48).

50. Mandeville, *Mischiefs* 6.

51. Mandeville, *Fable of the Bees*, 1:232–33, remark T.

52. Mandeville, *Free Thoughts on Religion*, ch. 11, 'Of Government'.

53. Mandeville, *Mischiefs*, 38.

54. For an overview of the South Sea Bubble scandal, see Balen's *Very English Deceit*; for a corrective to some popular misconceptions on the Bubble, see Hoppit's 'Myths'.

55. Trenchard and Gordon, *Cato's Letters*, 1:161, 'Reflections upon Libeling', no. 32 (June 10, 1721).

56. Trenchard and Gordon, *Cato's Letters*, 1:158, 'Considerations on the Weakness and Inconsistencies of Human Nature', no. 31 (May 27, 1721).

57. Mandeville, *Fable of the Bees*, 1:335, 'Search into the Nature of Society'.

58. Mandeville, 1:335.

59. Mandeville, 1:268, 'Essay on Charity, and Charity Schools'.

60. Mandeville, 1:269.

61. Trenchard and Gordon, *Cato's Letters*, 2:126, 'Of Charity, and Charity-Schools', no. 133 (June 15, 1723).

62. See Speck, 'Bernard Mandeville'.

63. Mandeville, *Fable of the Bees*, 1:385, 'Vindication of the Book'.

64. That Mandeville's thought is of an inherently conservative cast is claimed by Lamprecht in '*Fable of the Bees*'.

65. Mandeville, *Fable of the Bees*, 1:270, 'Essay on Charity, and Charity Schools'.

66. Mandeville, 1:286–87.

67. Mandeville, 1:288.

68. J.-J. Rousseau, 'Discourse on the Moral Effects of the Arts and Sciences', in *Discourses*, 18–24. For discussion of the influence of Mandeville: Kow, 'Rousseau's Mandevillean Conception'.

69. Mandeville, *Fable of the Bees*, 1:287, 'Essay on Charity, and Charity Schools'.

70. Mandeville, 1:307.

71. Mandeville, 1:310.

72. Mandeville, 1:310.

73. Mandeville, *Free Thoughts on Religion*, 186.

74. Mandeville, 186–87.

75. For this anecdote, I am indebted to Wahrman's excellent *Making of the Modern Self*. Allen, in 'Burning the *Fable*', also notes the relevance of Mandeville's contrast with Warder.

76. Warder, *True Amazons*, v–vi.

Chapter 8

1. There are many other works that deal with his economic thinking in more detail, and I have in this chapter drawn upon the following: Backhouse, *Penguin History of Economics*; Barnett, 'Keynes, Animal Spirits'; Biddle, Davis, and Samuels, *History of Economic Thought*; Chalk, 'Mandeville's *Fable*'; Goldsmith, 'Mandeville and the Spirit'; Landreth, 'Economic Thought'; Prendergast, 'Bernard Mandeville' and 'Jonathan Swift's Critique'; Roncaglia, *Wealth of Ideas*; Screpanti and Zamagni, *History of Economic Thought*; Turner, 'Mandeville against Luxury'; Vaggi and Groenewegen, *Concise History*; Viner, 'Introduction to Bernard Mandeville'.

2. Hayek, *Dr. Bernard Mandeville*, 74–75.

3. Keynes, *General Theory of Employment*, 319–22.

4. Keynes, 319–22.

5. Coward and Gaunt, *Stuart Age*, 519. For general discussions, see chapters 10 and 11 of Hoppit's *Land of Liberty?*.

6. Shaftesbury, *Characteristics of Men*, 214.

7. As Brandon Turner notes, Mandeville does think that luxury can be bad at the individual level, as when the moneyed Misomedon in the *Treatise* leads a life of luxury that eventually leads to his melancholia and depression (Turner, 'Mandeville against Luxury').

8. Harris, 'Maxims'—I'm deeply indebted to Harris's work here and this chapter is an attempt to extend the type of contextual analysis he puts forward in this paper. For important work on the Dutch context of Mandeville's economic thinking: Bick, 'Bernard Mandeville'; Blom, 'Decay'; Dekker, 'Private Vices, Public Virtues'; Stapelbroek, 'Dutch Decline'.

9. Temple, *Observations* 143–44.

10. The opposition is clearly set out in chapter 2 of Jack's *Corruption and Progress*.

11. For a discussion of the Dutch background, with particular reference to the influence of the brothers De la Court to Mandeville's thinking, see Verburg's 'Dutch Background'. For a full length study of the thought of the brothers De la Court, see Weststeijn's *Commercial Republicanism*, where the influence upon Mandeville is discussed in the conclusion.

12. Temple, *Observations*, 142.

13. Temple, 142.

14. Mandeville rarely puts things this way himself since, on my reading, his aim is to maintain a exoteric allegiance to Christian providence while maintaining an esoteric commitment to a naturalistic alternative. I explore this theme more fully in the following chapter.

15. For discussion with regard to Mandeville, see R. Cook's *Bernard Mandeville*, 105–8.

16. Mandeville, *Executions at Tyburn*, 13.

17. Mandeville, 12.

18. Mandeville, 11.

19. Mandeville, *Modest Defence*, 84.

20. Mandeville, 60.

21. Mandeville, 61.

22. Mandeville, 88.

23. Mandeville, 87.

24. Nacol, 'Beehive and the Stew'; Rosenthal, *Infamous Commerce*, ch. 2.

25. Mandeville, *Modest Defence*, 56.

26. Mandeville, 56.

27. For an extended discussion of Mandeville' arguments against charity schools: J. Kramnick, 'Unwilling to Be Short'; Pongiglione and Tolonen, 'Mandeville on Charity Schools'.

28. Mandeville, *Fable of the Bees*, 1:301.

29. Mandeville, 1:301–2.

30. This is the spirit of the work according to Dew in 'Spurs to Industry' and 'Damn'd to Sythes'.

31. Mandeville, *Fable of the Bees*, 1:311.

32. A point importantly stressed by Mitchell in 'Character'.

33. Mandeville, *Virgin Unmask'd*, 163.

34. Mandeville, 164–65.

35. Mandeville, 167.

36. Temple, *Observations*, 131.

37. Temple, 131.

38. Mandeville, *Fable of the Bees*, 1:240.

39. Mandeville, 1:356–57. For a general discussion of Mandeville's influence upon Smith's thought: Pongiglione, 'Bernard Mandeville's Influence'. For discussion of Mandeville on the division of labour in its evolutionary context: Prendergast, 'Knowledge, Innovation and Emulation'.

40. Mandeville, *Fable of the Bees*, 1:359.

41. Mandeville, 1:366.

42. Mandeville, 1:367.

43. Mandeville, 1:63. The point of the reference to the Christian 'golden rule' is noted by Prendergast in 'Bernard Mandeville', 114.

44. For Mandeville's contested relationship to the doctrine of laissez-faire: Prendergast, 'Bernard Mandeville'; Rashid, 'Mandeville's Fable'; Viner, 'Introduction to Bernard Mandeville'.

45. Mandeville, *Fable of the Bees*, 1:116.

46. Mandeville, 1:116.

47. A helpful overview on the role of satire here can be found in Viner's 'Satire and Economics'.

48. Swift, *Answer to a Paper*, in *Irish Political Writings*, 34–35.

49. Swift, 35.

50. For a discussion of this relevance, see Bartlett's 'Jonathan Swift'.

51. Swift, *Modest Proposal*, in *Irish Political Writings*, 149–50.

52. Swift, 155.

53. Swift, 159.

54. For discussion of Swift's satire in relation to consequentialist reading, see Prendergast's 'Jonathan Swift's Critique'.

55. For helpful discussions of this context: Prendergast, 'Bernard Mandeville'; Rashid, 'Mandeville's Fable'.

56. Hayek, *Trend of Economic Thinking*, 76.

57. Hayek, 79.

58. This point is well argued for in Heath's 'Carrying Matters Too Far?'

59. Goffman, *Presentation of Self*, 241.

Chapter 9

1. Henceforth I'll refer to these texts as *Fable II* and *Enquiry* respectively. While there is much important work in the *Enquiry*, I focus in this chapter upon the core of the theory as it is presented in *Fable II*. For work that makes a fuller examination of the *Enquiry*, see Branchi's *Pride, Manners, and Morals* and Douglass's *Mandeville's Fable*. Branchi's work seeks to show that honour is the unifying concept that ties Mandeville's works together.

2. Mandeville, *Origin of Honour*, 139, third dialogue.

3. Some notable exceptions: Branchi, *Pride, Manners, and Morals*; Douglass, *Mandeville's Fable*; Hundert, *Enlightenment's Fable*; Tolonen, *Mandeville and Hume*.

4. Mandeville, *Fable of the Bees*, 2:21, preface.

5. As John Robertson notes, there is a work by Gassendi—*Disquisitio metaphysica seu dubitationes et instantiae adversus Renati Cartesii Metaphysicam et responsa* (1644)—that, although not exactly a dialogue, involves a point–counterpoint structure between Gassendi and his intended opponent, Descartes (Robertson, *Case for the Enlightenment*, 271n25). For an account of Gassendi's ethical thought, see Sarasohn' *Gassendi's Ethics*.

6. Mandeville, *Fable of the Bees*, 2:186, 207, fourth dialogue.

7. Dykstal's 'Commerce, Conversation, and Contradiction' offers a sensitive exploration of the role of dialogue and conversation in Mandeville's thought.

8. For discussion of self-liking: Berkovski, 'Mandeville on Self-Liking'; Colman, 'Bernard Mandeville'; Heath, 'Mandeville's Bewitching Engine' and 'Carrying Matters Too Far?'; Hundert, *Enlightenment's Fable*, 53–55, 137–39; Simonazzi, 'Bernard Mandeville on Hypochondria'.

9. There are dangers in conflating Mandeville's appeal to the emergence of rational order and Hayek's later appropriation of it as the notion of spontaneous order—for discussion, see Douglass's *Mandeville's Fable* (175–79).

10. The generality of Mandeville's evolutionary thinking is well noted in Prendergast's 'Knowledge, Innovation and Emulation'.

11. The especial importance of Shaftesbury for Mandeville's later thought is noted by many authors, though particularly helpful discussions can be found in Stuart-Buttle's *From Moral Theology* and chapter 3 of Douglass's *Mandeville's Fable*.

12. Shaftesbury, *Characteristics of Men*, 167. The *Inquiry* was first published in 1699, but we can imagine that it came properly to Mandeville's attention only after it was published as part of Shaftesbury's *Characteristics of Men, Manners, Opinions, Times*, published in 1711.

13. Shaftesbury, *Characteristics of Men*, 169.

14. Shaftesbury, 191.

15. For a discussion of the importance of Mandeville for Law's thought, see Maxwell's 'Ethics and Politics', Nieli's 'Commercial Society', and especially Starkie's 'William Law'.

16. For discussion of some of these critics, see Welchman's 'Who Rebutted Bernard Mandeville?' Another important critic, Archibald Campbell, is discussed in Maurer's 'What Can an Egoist Say'.

17. Law, *Remarks upon a Late Book*, 12. I quote here from the first edition of Law's *Remarks*, being the edition Mandeville was mostly likely responding to.

18. Law, 16.

19. Law, 17.

20. Law, 19–20.

21. Coleridge, *Table Talk*, 242, July 1, 1833.

22. A long-standing question is whether Mandeville's idea of morality, whereby something is moral if self-interest is entirely removed from the equation, is in fact far too demanding. The most recent exploration of the topic can be found in Douglass's 'Origins of Virtue' and *Mandeville's Fable*. A helpful overview of objections to Mandeville—with some possible responses—can be found in Welchman's 'Who Rebutted Bernard Mandeville?'

23. Hutcheson, *Inquiry into the Original*, treatise 2, sec. 5, 148. For a helpful discussion: Sheridan, 'Parental Affection and Self-Interest'. For the antagonistic relationship between Hutcheson and Mandeville: Broussois, 'Francis Hutcheson on Luxury'; McKee, 'Francis Hutcheson'.

24. J. Butler, *Fifteen Sermons*, sermon 1, 23n2.

25. Hume, *Principles of Morals*, appendix 2, 298. For further discussion of Hume's critique: Luban, 'Bernard Mandeville as Moralist'; Welchman, 'Who Rebutted Bernard Mandeville?'

26. Law, *Remarks upon a Late Book*, 8–9.

27. Law, 10–11.

28. Mandeville, *Fable of the Bees*, 2:308, sixth dialogue.

29. Mandeville, 2:310, sixth dialogue.

30. Mandeville, 2:252, fifth dialogue.

31. My discussion here and throughout argues the case for Mandeville's atheism. Yet it is crucial to Mandeville's exoteric dialectic that he can claim to be arguing against his opponents on behalf of Christianity, and in particular against those who would claim that religion can be grasped purely by rational means and without the aid of revelation. For this reason, it is always open to one to read Mandeville as being more Christian than many Christians, and that his sceptical attacks are only ever directed towards an insistence upon the necessity of revealed religion. This ambiguity similarly stalks any interpretation of Bayle's theological commitments. My point of view hinges on the ideas that Mandeville's defence of revelation is necessary as a rhetorical ploy anyway, that he alludes to his Epicureanism throughout *Fable II*, and that as a matter of fact he seemed to hold views—e.g., regarding the poor, prostitution, and sexual and social mores—that don't look particularly Christian.

32. The point is explored well in chapter 2 of Jack's *Corruption and Progress*. For a detailed account of Mandeville's 'historical turn', see chapter 4 of Douglass's *Mandeville's Fable*.

33. Mandeville, *Fable of the Bees*, 2:251, fifth dialogue.

34. Mandeville, 2:130–31, third dialogue.

35. My reading here is indebted to Heath in 'Carrying Matters Too Far?', who also gives an account of how Mandeville's theory of self-liking is offered to provide an evolutionary account of moral value, and develops an account first set out in Heath's 'Mandeville's Bewitching Engine'. Heath's account stresses the role of self-liking in fostering group inclusivity, which it seems to me stresses the social human manifestation of it. Here I suggest that the more fundamental manifestation of self-liking is as a simple manifestation of attractiveness, or strength, etc., as a display to others for biological purposes. Mandeville's theory of the origin of society, too complex to fully analyse here, receives very interesting discussions in Knott's 'Mandeville on Governability' and chapter 4 of Douglass's *Mandeville's Fable*.

36. Mandeville, *Fable of the Bees*, 2:130, third dialogue.

37. Mandeville, 2:133–34.

38. Mandeville, 2:134.

39. Mandeville, 2:80–81, second dialogue.

40. Mandeville, 2:128, third dialogue.

41. Mandeville, 2:128, third dialogue.

42. Lucretius, *Nature of Things*, bk. 5, lines 1447–57, pp. 207–8.

43. Lucretius, bk. 2, lines 1090–92, p. 94.

44. Mandeville, *Fable of the Bees*, 2:141, third dialogue.

45. Mandeville, 2:142.

46. Mandeville, 2:145.

47. For an important discussion of how the development of Mandeville's theory related to the fate of eighteenth-century conjectural history, see chapter 1 of Palmeri's *State of Nature*.

48. Mandeville, *Fable of the Bees*, 2:139, third dialogue.

49. There are thus far more complex connotations to 'nature' in Mandeville's thinking than are frequently noted by commentators, such as Skarsten in 'Nature in Mandeville'.

50. For a critical evaluation of the idea, see Luban's 'What Is Spontaneous Order?'

51. Smith, *Wealth of Nations*, bk. 4, ch. 2, 456.

52. Ferguson, *History of Civil Society*, pt 3, sec. 2, 119.

53. Mandeville, *Fable of the Bees*, 1:91, remark G.

54. Lucretius, *Nature of Things*, bk. 4, lines 823–40, p. 153.

55. Mandeville, *Fable of the Bees*, 2:188–89, fourth dialogue.

56. Mandeville, 2:175.

57. Mandeville, 2:259, fifth dialogue.

Chapter 10

1. *Spectator* no. 425 (July 8, 1712), in Bond, *Spectator*, 3:593.

2. Pope, Epistle to Bathurst, 'Of the Uses of Riches'(1733), in *Major Works*, 257.

3. *Tatler* no. 89 (November 1709), in Addison and Steele, *Selections from the 'Tatler'*, 128.

4. *Tatler* no. 89, 128.

5. *Female Tatler* no. 109 (March 1710), in Mandeville, *By a Society of Ladies*, 233.

6. *Female Tatler* no. 109, 233.

7. Ricoeur, *Freud and Philosophy*, 32.

8. Heinlein, *Gulf*, in *Assignment in Eternity*, 542.

9. Mandeville, *Fable of the Bees*, 2:39, first dialogue.

10. Mandeville, *Letter to Dion*, 8.

11. Pocock, *Machiavellian Moment*, 466.

12. Habermas, 'Entwinement of Myth', 13.

13. I am far from the first to think of Mandeville in relation to an incipient—if perhaps a necessarily ill-defined—'modernity'. For fascinating discussions on this theme: Allen, 'Burning the *Fable*'; Hjort, 'Mandeville's Ambivalent Modernity'; Hundert, 'Satire of Self-Disclosure' and 'Bernard Mandeville'.

14. *Female Tatler* no. 109 (March 1710), in Mandeville, *By a Society of Ladies*, 234–35.

15. Pocock, *Machiavellian Moment*, 465.

16. Mandeville, *Fable of the Bees*, 1:145, remark N.

17. Swift, letter to Pope, September 29, 1725, in *Essential Writings*, 676.

18. Swift, *Tale of a Tub*, in *Essential Writings*, 75.

19. As Tim Stuart-Buttle notes, Mandeville understood himself as opposing the inevitable misanthropy of Shaftesbury's high moral standards in his works (Stuart-Buttle, *From Moral Theology*, 121–22).

20. Mandeville, *Fable of the Bees*, 2:19.

21. Mandeville, 2:18.

22. Mandeville, *Hypochondriack and Hysterick Diseases*, 174, third dialogue.

23. Mandeville, *Free Thoughts on Religion*, 189.

24. Mandeville, 189.

25. Quoted in Kaye, introduction to Mandeville, *Fable of the Bees*, 1:xxii.

26. Franklin, *Autobiography*, 44.

27. Reproduced on an unnumbered page between pages xxvi and xxvii of Kaye's introduction to Mandeville, *Fable of the Bees*, vol. 1.

28. *B. Berrington's Evening Post*, January 23, 1733, 3, reprinted in Kaye, introduction to Mandeville, *Fable of the Bees*, 1:xxix–xxxn6.

Primary Sources

Abbadie, Jacques. *The Art of Knowing One-Self, or, An Enquiry into the Sources of Morality.* London, 1698.

Addison, Joseph, and Richard Steele. *Selections from the 'Tatler' and the 'Spectator' of Steele and Addison.* Edited by Angus Ross. Harmondsworth, UK: Penguin Books, 1982.

Á Kempis, Thomas. *The Imitation of Christ.* 1441. Edited and translated by Leo Sherley-Price. Harmondsworth, UK: Penguin Books, 1965.

Anonymous. *Aesop at Islington.* 1699.

——. *The Character of the Times Delineated. In Two Parts. I. Containing a Description of the Most Flagrant Enormities. II. A Detail of the Most Remarkable Blemishes in the Professors of Virtue and Religion. Design'd for the Use of Those Who Mourn in Secret for the Iniquities of the Nation, and Are Convinc'd by Sad Experience, that Private Vices Are Publick and Real Mischiefs.* London: printed for J. Wilford, at the Three Flower de Luces, behind the Chapter-House, in St. Paul's Church-Yard, 1732.

——. *Reflexions upon the Moral State of the Nation: With an Offer at Some Amendments Therein. To a Member of Parliament.* Matt. Wotton, 1701.

Baglivi, Giorgio. *The Practice of Physick: Reduc'd to the Ancient Way of Observations: Containing a Just Parallel between the Wisdom and Experience of the Ancients, and the Hypothesis of Modern Physicians: Intermix'd with Many Practical Remarks upon Most Distempers: Together with Several New and Curious Dissertations, Particularly of the Tarantella, and the Nature of Its Poison: Of the Use and Abuse of Blistering Plasters: Of Epidemical Apoplexies, &c.* London: printed for D. Midwinter . . . [et al.], 1723.

Bayle, Pierre. *Various Thoughts on the Occasion of a Comet.* 1682. Translated by Robert C. Bartlett. Albany: State University of New York Press, 2000.

Bluett, T. *An Enquiry whether a General Practice of Virtue Tends to the Wealth or Poverty, Benefit or Disadvantage of a People?: In Which the Pleas Offered by the Author of 'The Fable of the Bees, Or Private Vices Publick Benefits', for the Usefulness of Vice and Roguery Are Considered: With Some Thoughts Concerning a Toleration of Publick Stews.* R. Wilkin at the King's Head in St. Paul's Church-yard, 1725.

Bond, Donald, ed. *The Spectator.* Vol. 3. Oxford: Oxford University Press, 2014.

——. *The Tatler.* Vol. 2. Oxford: Clarendon, 1987.

Burrow, R. *Civil Society and Government Vindicated from the Charge of Being Founded on, and Preserv'd by, Dishonest Arts: In a Sermon Preached before the . . . Lord-Mayor; . . . at the Guild-Hall Chappel, on Sept. 28, 1723.* . . . . . John and Barham Clark, 1723.

Butler, Joseph. *Fifteen Sermons Preached at the Rolls Chapel: And Other Writings on Ethics.* 1726. Reprint, Oxford: Oxford University Press, 2017.

Butler, Samuel. *Characters and Passages from Note-Books.* Edited by A. R. Waller. Cambridge: Cambridge University Press, 1908.

——. *Hudibras.* Dublin: S. Powell, 1732.

Calvin, John. *Institutes of the Christian Religion.* 1559. Translated by Henry Beveridge. 2 vols. Grand Rapids, MI: Eerdmans, 1975.

Campbell, Archibald, and Alexander Innes. *Arete-Logia, or, An Enquiry into the Original of Moral Virtue; Wherein the False Notions of Machiavel, Hobbes, Spinoza, and Mr. Bayle, as They Are Collected and Digested by the Author of 'The Fable of the Bees', Are Examin'd and Confuted; . . . To Which Is Prefix'd, a Prefatory Introduction, in a Letter to That Author. By*

Alexander Innes, ... Westminster: Printed by J. Cluer and A. Campbell, for B. Creake: Sold by J. Hazard near Ludgate; and by B. Barker, 1728.

Coleridge, Samuel Taylor. *Specimens of the Table Talk of Samuel Taylor Coleridge.* Edited by W. H. Deverel. London: John Murray, 1836.

Davenant, Charles. *Essays.* 1, 'Essay on the Balance of Power', and 2, 'Essay on the Right of Making War, Peace and Alliances'. [Printed] for James Knapton, at the Crown in St. Paul's Church-yard, 1701.

Dennis, J. *Vice and Luxury Publick Mischiefs: Or, Remarks on a Book Entitled 'The Fable of the Bees; Or, Private Vices Publick Benefits'* . . . . W. Mears, 1724.

Descartes, René. *Philosophical Essays and Correspondence.* Edited by Roger Ariew. Indianapolis: Hackett, 2000.

———.*The Philosophical Writings of Descartes.* Vol. 1. Edited by John Cottingham, Dugald Murdoch, and Robert Stoothoff. Cambridge: Cambridge University Press, 1985.

———. *The Philosophical Writings of Descartes.* Vol. 3. Edited by John. Cottingham. Cambridge: Cambridge University Press, 1991.

Du Châtelet, E. *Selected Philosophical and Scientific Writings.* Edited by J. P. Zinsser and I. Bour. Chicago: University of Chicago Press, 2009.

Erasmus, Desiderius. *'The Praise of Folly' and Other Writings.* Edited by Robert M. Adams. New York: Norton, 1989.

Fénelon, François de Salignac de La Mothe-. *Telemachus.* 1699. Edited by Patrick Riley. Cambridge: Cambridge University Press, 1994.

Ferguson, Adam. *Essay on the History of Civil Society.* 1767. Edited by Fania Oz-Salzberger, Cambridge: Cambridge University Press, 2001.

Fiddes, R. *A General Treatise of Morality, Form'd upon the Principles of Natural Reason Only.* Billingsley, 1724.

Fielding, Henry. *The Miscellaneous Works of Henry Fielding.* Vol. 3, *Amelia.* H. W. Derby, 1861.

Franklin, Benjamin. *Benjamin Franklin's Autobiography: An Authoritative Text, Contexts, Criticism.* Edited by Joyce E. Chaplin. New York: W. W. Norton, 2012.

Gildon, Charles. *Les Soupirs de La Grand Britaigne, Or, The Groans of Great Britain: Being the Second Part to The Groans of Europe.* John Baker, at the Black Boy in Pater-Noster-Row, 1713.

Harrington, James. *The Commonwealth of Oceana.* 1656. Edited by J.G.A. Pocock. Cambridge: Cambridge University Press, 2008.

Hendley, W. *A Defence of the Charity-Schools: Wherein the Many False, Scandalous and Malicious Objections of Those Advocates for Ignorance and Irreligion, the Author of 'The Fable of the Bees', and 'Cato's Letter' in the 'British Journal', June 15. 1723. Are Fully and Distinctly Answer'd; . . . To Which Is Added by Way of Appendix, the Presentment of the Grand Jury of the 'British Journal', . . . 1723.* . . . . English Short Title Catalogue Eighteenth Century Collection. W. Mears, 1725.

Hobbes, Thomas. *Leviathan.* 1651. Edited by Richard Tuck. Cambridge: Cambridge University Press, 1996.

Hume, David. *An Enquiry concerning the Principles of Morals.* 1751. Edited by Tom Beauchamp. Oxford: Oxford University Press, 1998.

———.*A Treatise of Human Nature.* 1739–40. Edited by David Fate Norton and Mary J. Norton. Oxford: Oxford University Press, 2007.

Hutcheson, Francis. *An Inquiry into the Original of Our Ideas of Beauty and Virtue.* 1726. Edited by Wolfgang Leidhold. Indianapolis: Liberty Fund, 2004.

Johnson, Samuel. *The Lives of the English Poets; and a Criticism on Their Works.* Vol. 2. Dublin: Whitestone, 1779.

Kant, Immanuel. *Critique of Practical Reason.* 1788. Edited by Andrews Reath and translated by Mary Gregor. Cambridge: Cambridge University Press, 2015.

La Rochefoucauld, François. *Collected Maxims and Other Reflections.* 1678. Translated by E. H. Blackmore, Francine Giguère, and A. M. Blackmore. Oxford: Oxford University Press, 2008.

Law, William. *Remarks upon a Late Book, Entitled the 'Fable of the Bees, or Private Vices, Publick Benefits', in a Letter to the Author: To Which Is Added, a Postscript, Containing an Observation or Two upon Mr. Bayle*. London, 1724.

Locke, John. *An Essay concerning Human Understanding*. 1689. Edited by P. H. Nidditch. Oxford: Clarendon, 1975.

———. *'Some Thoughts concerning Education' and, 'Of the Conduct of the Understanding'*. Edited by Ruth Weissbourd Grant. Indianapolis: Hackett, 1998.

Lucretius, Titus. *On the Nature of Things*. Translated by Martin Ferguson Smith. London: Sphere Books, 1969.

Machiavelli, Niccolo. *The Prince*. 1532. Translated by Peter Bondanella. Oxford: Oxford University Press, 2008.

Mandeville, Bernard. *Aesop Dress'd, or A Collection of Fables Writ in Familiar Verse*. London: Richard Wellington, 1704.

———. *Bernard Mandeville's 'A Modest Defence of Publick Stews': Prostitution and Its Discontents in Early Georgian England*. 1724. Edited by Irwin Primer. New York: Palgrave Macmillan, 2006.

———. *By a Society of Ladies: Essays in 'The Female Tatler'*. 1709–10. Edited and with an introduction by M. M. Goldsmith. Bristol, UK: Thoemmes, 1999.

———. *An Enquiry into the Causes of the Frequent Executions at Tyburn*. 1725. Edited by Malvin R. Zirker. Los Angeles: University of California, 1964.

———. *An Enquiry into the Origin of Honour and the Usefulness of Christianity in War*. 1732. Reprint, London: Frank Cas, 1971.

———. *The Fable of the Bees*. 1732. Edited and with an introduction by F. B. Kaye. 2 vols. 1924. Reprint, Indianapolis: Liberty, 1988.

———. *Free Thoughts on Religion, the Church, and National Happiness*. 1720. Edited by Irwin Primer. London: Routledge, 2018.

———. *A Letter to Dion*. 1732. Edited by Bonamy Dobree. Liverpool: University of Liverpool Press, 1954.

———. *The Mischiefs That Ought Justly to Be Apprehended from a Whig-Government*. London: J. Roberts, 1714.

———. *The Pamphleteers: A Satyr*. London, 1703.

———. *A Treatise of the Hypochondriack and Hysterick Diseases*. 1730. Translated and with an introduction by Sylvie Kleiman-Lafon. Cham, Switzerland: Springer, 2017.

———. *Typhon: Or the Wars between the Gods and Giants*. London: J. Pero, 1704.

———. *The Virgin Unmask'd*. London: J. Morphew and J. Woodward, 1709.

———. *Wishes to a Godson, with Other Miscellany Poems*. London: J. Baker, 1712.

Milton, John. *Paradise Lost*. 1674. Edited by John Leonard. London: Penguin Books, 2003.

Montaigne, Michel de. *Essays*. Translated by M. A. Screech. London: Penguin Books, 2003.

More, Thomas. *Utopia*. 1516. Edited by George M. Logan and Robert Merrihew Adams. Cambridge: Cambridge University Press, 1989.

Nicole, Pierre. *Moral Essayes*. 4 vols. 1674. Reprint, London: Samuel Manship, 1696.

———. *Essais de morale*. Vol. 6. Paris: Guillaume Desprez and Jean Dessesartz, 1714.

Pope, Alexander. *The Dunciad, in Four Books. Printed according to the Complete Copy Found in the Year 1742. . . . To Which Are Added Several Notes Now First Publish'd, the Hypercritics of Aristarchus, and His Dissertation on the Hero of the Poem*. M. Cooper, 1743.

———. *The Major Works: Including 'The Rape of the Lock' and the 'Dunciad'*. Edited by Pat Rogers. Oxford: Oxford University Press, 2008.

———. *The Works of the English Poets, with Prefaces, Biographical and Critical by Samuel Johnson*. Vol. 34. London: W. and A. Strahan, 1779.

Robinson, H. C., and T. Sadler. *Diary, Reminiscences, and Correspondence of Henry Crabb Robinson: . . .* Vol. 1. Fields, Osgood, 1870.

Rochester, 2nd Earl of (John Wilmot). *John Wilmot, Earl of Rochester: The Poems and 'Lucina's Rape'*. Edited by Keith Walker and Nicholas Fisher. Chichester, UK: Wiley-Blackwell, 2010.

Rousseau, Jean-Jacques. *The Discourses and Other Early Political Writings*. Edited by Victor Gourevitch. Cambridge: Cambridge University Press, 2008.

Shaftesbury, 1st Earl of (Anthony Ashley Cooper). *Characteristics of Men, Manners, Opinions, Times*. 1711. Reprint, Cambridge: Cambridge University Press, 1999.

Smith, Adam. *An Inquiry into the Nature and Causes of the Wealth of Nations*. 1776. Edited by R. H. Campbell and Andrew S. Skinner. Oxford: Oxford University Press, 1976.

———. *The Theory of Moral Sentiments*. Edited by Ryan Patrick Hanley. New York: Penguin Books, 2009.

Stone, Oliver, director. *Wall Street*. 20th Century Fox, 1987.

Swift, Jonathan. *The Essential Writings of Jonathan Swift*. Edited by Claude Rawson and Ian Higgins. New York: W. W. Norton, 2010.

———. *Irish Political Writings after 1725: 'A Modest Proposal' and Other Works*. Edited by David Hayton and Adam Rounce. Cambridge: Cambridge University Press, 2018.

———. *Miscellanies in Prose and Verse. The Third Volume. To Which Are Added Several Poems, and Other Curious Tracts Not in the English Edition*. 2nd ed. [Dublin]: London printed, and re-printed in Dublin, by and for Sam. Fairbrother, at the King's-Arms in Skinner-Row, opposite to the Tholsel, 1733.

———. *A Project for the Advancement of Religion, and the Reformation of Manners*. H. Hills, in Black-fryars, near the Water-side. For the benefite of the poor, 1709.

———. *A Tale of a Tub and Other Works*. Edited by Marcus Walsh. Cambridge: Cambridge University Press, 2018.

Sydenham, Thomas. *The Works of Thomas Sydenham M.D.* 1685. Edited by R. G. Latham. Vol. 2. London: Sydenham Society, 1850.

Temple, Sir William. *Observations upon the United Provinces of the Netherlands*. 1687. Reprint, Cambridge: Cambridge University Press, 1932.

Trenchard, John, and Thomas Gordon. *Cato's Letters or Essays on Liberty, Civil and Religious, and Other Important Subjects*. 2 vols. Edited by Ronald Hamowy. Vol. 1. Indianapolis: Liberty Fund, 2007.

Trollope, Anthony. *The Way We Live Now*. Edited by Frances O'Gorman. Oxford: Oxford University Press, 2020.

Voltaire. *The Works of Voltaire: A Contemporary Version*. Vol. 10. Translated by W. F. Fleming, with notes by T. Smollett. New York: St. Hubert Guild, 1901.

Walker, George. *The Necessity and Advantages of an Early Piety: In a Sermon Preach'd February 11, 1727-8. in Twickenham-Chapel, in the County of Middlesex. By the Reverend Mr. Walker, Curate There*. London: printed for Bernard Lintot, at the Cross-Keys between the Temple-Gates, 1728.

Warburton, W. *The Divine Legation of Moses Demonstrated: In Nine Books*. Vol. 1. A. Millar . . . and J. and R. Tonson, 1765.

Warder, Joseph. *The True Amazons: or, The Monarchy of Bees: Being a New Discovery and Improvement of Those Wonderful Creatures . . . : Also How to Make the English Wine or Mead, Equal, if Not Superior to the Best of Other Wines*. J. Pemberton and W. Taylor, 1713.

Wesley, John. *The Journal of the Rev. John Wesley, M.A., Sometime Fellow of Lincoln College, Oxford: To Which Is Prefixed an Account of His Early Life, Christian Experience, Death, and Character, and Biographical Sketches of His Family*. Edited by John Bennett and Andrew Dickson White. 1837.

Willis, T. *Two Discourses concerning the Soul of Brutes: Which Is That of the Vital and Sensitive of Man*. 1672. Edited and translated by S. Pordage. 1683. Reprint, History of Psychology Series. Gainesville, FL: Scholars' Facsimiles and Reprints. 1971.

Secondary Sources

Allen, Danielle. 'Burning the *Fable of the Bees*: The Incendiary Authority of Nature'. In *The Moral Authority of Nature*, edited by Lorraine Daston and Fernando Vidal, 74–99. Chicago: University of Chicago Press, 2004.

Alter, Stephen G. 'Mandeville's Ship: Theistic Design and Philosophical History in Charles Darwin's Vision of Natural Selection'. *Journal of the History of Ideas* 69, no. 3 (2008): 441–65.

Anderson, Paul Bunyan. 'Bernard Mandeville on Gin'. *PMLA* 54, no. 3 (1939): 775–84.

———. 'Splendor out of Scandal: The Lucinda-Artesia Papers in *The Female Tatler*'. *Philological Quarterly* 15 (1936): 286–300.

Backhouse, R. E. *The Penguin History of Economics*. London: Penguin Adult, 2002.

Balen, Malcolm. *A Very English Deceit: The Secret History of the South Sea Bubble and the First Great Financial Scandal*. London: Fourth Estate, 2008.

Barnett, Vincent. 'Keynes, Animal Spirits, and Instinct: Reason Plus Intuition Is Better than Rational'. *Journal of the History of Economic Thought* 39, no. 3 (2017): 381–99.

Bartlett, Bruce. 'Jonathan Swift: Father of Supply-Side Economics?' *History of Political Economy* 24, no. 3 (1992): 745–48.

Berkovski, Sandy. 'Mandeville on Self-Liking, Morality, and Hypocrisy'. *Intellectual History Review* 32, no. 1 (2022): 157–78.

Bick, Alexander. 'Bernard Mandeville and the "Economy" of the Dutch'. *Erasmus Journal for Philosophy and Economics* 1, no. 1 (2008): 87–106.

Biddle, Jeff E., John Bryan Davis, and Warren J. Samuels. *A Companion to the History of Economic Thought*. Malden, MA: Blackwell, 2009.

Biro, John. 'Hume's New Science of the Mind'. In *The Cambridge Companion to Hume*, edited by David Fate Norton and Jacqueline Taylor, 2nd ed., 40–69. Cambridge: Cambridge University Press, 2008.

Blom, Hans. 'Decay and the Political Gestalt of Decline in Bernard Mandeville and His Dutch Contemporaries'. In 'Dutch Decline in Eighteenth-Century Europe', edited by Koen Stapelbroek, special issue, *History of European Ideas* 36, no. 2 (2010): 153–66.

Bouwsma, William J. *John Calvin: A Sixteenth-Century Portrait*. Oxford: Oxford University Press, 1989.

Branchi, Andrea. *Pride, Manners, and Morals: Bernard Mandeville's Anatomy of Honour*. Madrid: Brill, 2021.

Broussois, Lisa. 'Francis Hutcheson on Luxury and Intemperance: The Mandeville Threat'. *History of European Ideas* 41, no. 8 (2015): 1093–106.

Browning, Reed. *Political and Constitutional Ideas of the Court Whigs*. Baton Rouge: Louisiana State University Press, 1982.

Burtt, Shelley G. *Virtue Transformed: Political Argument in England, 1688–1740*. Cambridge: Cambridge University Press, 1992.

Castiglione, Dario. 'Considering Things Minutely: Reflections on Mandeville and the Eighteenth-Century Science of Man'. *History of Political Thought* 7, no. 3 (1986): 463–88.

Çeşmeli, Işıl. 'Is Adam Smith Heir of Bernard Mandeville?' In *Bernard de Mandeville's Tropology of Paradoxes: Morals, Politics, Economics, and Therapy*, edited by Edmundo Balsemão Pires and Joaquim Braga, 113–24. Studies in History and Philosophy of Science. Cham, Switzerland: Springer International, 2015.

Chalk, Alfred F. 'Mandeville's *Fable of the Bees*: A Reappraisal'. *Southern Economic Journal* 33, no. 1 (1966): 1–16.

Clarke, Desmond M. *Descartes's Theory of Mind*. Oxford: Clarendon, 2005.

Colie, Rosalie Littell. *Paradoxia Epidemica: The Renaissance Tradition of Paradox*. Princeton, NJ: Princeton University Press, 2015.

Collins, R. A. 'Private Vices, Public Benefits: Dr. Mandeville and the Body Politic'. PhD thesis, University of Oxford, 1988.

Colman, John. 'Bernard Mandeville and the Reality of Virtue'. *Philosophy* 47, no. 180 (1972): 125–39.

Cook, Harold J. 'Bernard Mandeville'. In *A Companion to Early Modern Philosophy*, edited by Steven M. Nadler, 469–82. Malden, MA: Blackwell, 2002.

———. 'Bernard Mandeville and the Therapy of "The Clever Politician"'. *Journal of the History of Ideas* 60, no. 1 (1999): 101.

——. *Matters of Exchange: Commerce, Medicine, and Science in the Dutch Golden Age*. New Haven, CT: Yale University Press, 2007.

——. 'Treating of Bodies Medical and Political: Dr. Mandeville's Materialism'. *Erasmus Journal for Philosophy and Economics* 9, no. 1 (2016): 1.

Cook, R. I. *Bernard Mandeville*. New York: Twayne, 1974.

Cottingham, John. '"A Brute to the Brutes?": Descartes' Treatment of Animals'. *Philosophy* 53, no. 206 (1978): 551–59.

Coward, Barry, and Peter Gaunt. *The Stuart Age: England, 1603–1714*. London: Routledge, 2017.

Crisp, Roger. 'Mandeville: Morality after the Fall'. In *Sacrifice Regained: Morality and Self-Interest in British Moral Philosophy from Hobbes to Bentham*, 60–73. Oxford: Oxford University Press, 2019.

Damrosch, Leopold. *Jonathan Swift: His Life and His World*. New Haven, CT: Yale University Press, 2015.

Daniel, Stephen H. 'Myth and Rationality in Mandeville'. *Journal of the History of Ideas* 47, no. 4 (1986): 595–609.

——. 'Political and Philosophical Uses of Fables in Eighteenth-Century England'. *Eighteenth Century* 23, no. 2 (1982): 151–71.

Dawson, Hannah. 'Shame in Early Modern Thought: From Sin to Sociability'. *History of European Ideas* 45, no. 3 (2019): 377–98.

Dekker, Rudolf. 'Private Vices, Public Virtues Revisited: The Dutch Background of Bernard Mandeville'. *History of European Ideas* 14, no. 4 (1992): 481–98.

Demeter, Tamás. 'The Science in Hume's Science of Man'. *Journal of Scottish Philosophy* 18, no. 3 (2020): 257–71.

Dew, Ben. '"Damn'd to Sythes and Spades": Labour and Wealth Creation in the Writing of Bernard Mandeville'. *Intellectual History Review* 23, no. 2 (2013): 187–205.

——. 'Spurs to Industry in Bernard Mandeville's *Fable of the Bees*'. *Journal for Eighteenth-Century Studies* 28, no. 2 (2005): 151–65.

Dickinson, H. T. *Liberty and Property: Political Ideology in Eighteenth-Century Britain*. London: Weidenfeld and Nicolson, 1977.

Douglass, Robin. 'The Dark Side of Recognition: Bernard Mandeville and the Morality of Pride'. *British Journal for the History of Philosophy*, October 11, 2021.

——. 'Mandeville on the Origins of Virtue'. *British Journal for the History of Philosophy* 28, no. 2 (2019): 276–95.

——. *Mandeville's Fable: Pride, Hypocrisy, and Sociability*. Princeton, NJ: Princeton University Press, 2023.

——. 'Morality and Sociability in Commercial Society: Smith, Rousseau—and Mandeville'. *Review of Politics* 79, no. 4 (2017): 597–620.

Dumont, Louis. *From Mandeville to Marx: The Genesis and Triumph of Economic Ideology*. Chicago: University of Chicago Press, 1977.

Dykstal, Timothy. 'Commerce, Conversation, and Contradiction in Mandeville's *Fable*'. *Studies in Eighteenth-Century Culture* 23, no. 1 (1994): 93–110.

Enders, Giulia. *Gut: The Inside Story of Our Body's Most Underrated Organ*. Translated by David Shaw. Melbourne: Scribe, 2015.

Farrell, William J. 'The Role of Mandeville's Bee Analogy in *The Grumbling Hive*'. *Studies in English Literature, 1500–1900* 25, no. 3 (1985): 511–27.

Fate Norton, David, and Manfred Kuehn. 'The Foundations of Morality'. In *The Cambridge History of Eighteenth-Century Philosophy*, edited by Knud Haakonssen, 1:939–86. Cambridge: Cambridge University Press, 2006.

Force, Pierre. *Self-Interest before Adam Smith: A Genealogy of Economic Science*. Cambridge: Cambridge University Press, 2007.

Garrett, Aaron. 'Anthropology: The "Original" of Human Nature'. In *The Cambridge Companion to the Scottish Enlightenment*, edited by Alexander Broadie, 79–93. Cambridge: Cambridge University Press, 2003.

———. 'Human Nature'. In *The Cambridge History of Eighteenth-Century Philosophy*, edited by Knud Haakonssen, 1:160–233. Cambridge: Cambridge University Press, 2006.

———. 'Women in the Science of Man' (pdf). Unpublished MS. n.d. https://www.academia.edu /9191324/Women_in_the_Science_of_Man.

Garrett, Aaron, and Colin Heydt. 'Moral Philosophy: Practical and Speculative'. In *Scottish Philosophy in the Eighteenth Century*, vol. 1, *Morals, Politics, Art, Religion*, edited by Garrett and James A. Harris, 77–130. Oxford: Oxford University Press, 2015.

Gaston, Sean. 'The Fables of Pity: Rousseau, Mandeville and the Animal-Fable'. *Derrida Today* 5, no. 1 (2012): 21–38.

Gladwell, Malcolm. *Blink: The Power of Thinking without Thinking*. New York: Little, Brown, 2005.

Goffman, Erving. *The Presentation of Self in Everyday Life*. London: Penguin Books, 1990.

Goldsmith, M. M. 'Mandeville and the Spirit of Capitalism'. *Journal of British Studies* 17, no. 1 (1977): 63–81.

———. *Private Vices, Public Benefits: Bernard Mandeville's Social and Political Thought*. Rev. ed. Christchurch: Cybereditions, 2001.

Haas, Guenther H. 'Calvin's Ethics'. In *The Cambridge Companion to John Calvin*, edited by Donald K. McKim, 93–105. Cambridge: Cambridge University Press, 2004.

Habermas, Jürgen. 'The Entwinement of Myth and Enlightenment: Re-reading Dialectic of Enlightenment'. Translated by Thomas Y. Levin. *New German Critique*, no. 26 (1982): 13–30.

Harris, James, '"Maxims to Make a People Great and Flourishing": *The Fable of the Bees* in Political Context' (pdf). Unpublished MS. n.d. Author's private papers.

Harth, Phillip. 'The Satiric Purpose of *The Fable of the Bees*'. *Eighteenth-Century Studies* 2, no. 4 (1969): 321–40.

Hawkins, J. *The Life of Samuel Johnson, LL.D.* Chambers, 1787.

Hayek, Friedrich August von. *Dr. Bernard Mandeville*. London: Oxford University Press, 1967.

———. *The Trend of Economic Thinking: Essays on Political Economists and Economic History*. Edited by William Warren Bartley and Stephen Kresge. Indianapolis: Liberty Fund, 2009.

Heath, Eugene. 'Carrying Matters Too Far? Mandeville and the Eighteenth-Century Scots on the Evolution of Morals'. *Journal of Scottish Philosophy* 12, no. 1 (2014): 95–119.

———. 'Mandeville's Bewitching Engine of Praise'. *History of Philosophy Quarterly* 15, no. 2 (1998): 205–26.

Heinlein, Robert A. *Assignment in Eternity: Four Long Science Fiction Stories*. London: Museum Press, 1955.

Heydt, Colin. 'Practical Ethics'. In *The Oxford Handbook of British Philosophy in the Eighteenth Century*, edited by James Harris, 369–89. Oxford: Oxford University Press, 2013.

Hilton, Phillip. *Bitter Honey: Recuperating the Medical and Scientific Context of Bernard Mandeville*. Bern, Switzerland: Peter Lang, 2010.

Hjort, Anne Mette. 'Mandeville's Ambivalent Modernity'. *Modern Language Notes* 106, no. 5 (1991): 951–66.

Hoppit, Julian. *A Land of Liberty? England, 1689–1727*. Oxford: Oxford University Press, 2000.

———. 'The Myths of the South Sea Bubble'. *Transactions of the Royal Historical Society* 12 (2002): 141–65.

Horne, Thomas A. 'Envy and Commercial Society: Mandeville and Smith on "Private Vices, Public Benefits"'. *Political Theory* 9, no. 4 (1981): 551–69.

———. *The Social Thought of Bernard Mandeville: Virtue and Commerce in Early Eighteenth Century England*. London: Macmillan, 1978.

Hundert, E. J. 'Bernard Mandeville and the Enlightenment's Maxims of Modernity'. *Journal of the History of Ideas* 56, no. 4 (1995): 577–93.

——. *The Enlightenment's Fable: Bernard Mandeville and the Discovery of Society*. Cambridge: Cambridge University Press, 1994.

——. 'A Satire of Self-Disclosure: From Hegel through Rameau to the Augustans'. *Journal of the History of Ideas* 47, no. 2 (1986): 235–48.

Hurtado Prieto, Jimena. 'Bernard Mandeville's Heir: Adam Smith or Jean Jacques Rousseau on the Possibility of Economic Analysis'. *European Journal of the History of Economic Thought* 11, no. 1 (2004): 1–31.

Jack, Malcolm. *Corruption and Progress: The Eighteenth-Century Debate*. New York: AMS, 1989.

——. 'One State of Nature: Mandeville and Rousseau'. *Journal of the History of Ideas* 39, no. 1 (1978): 119–24.

Jones, J. R. *Country and Court: England, 1658-1714*. Cambridge, MA: Harvard University Press, 1979.

Kail, Peter J. E. 'Moral Judgment'. In *The Oxford Handbook of British Philosophy in the Eighteenth Century*, edited by James Harris, 315–32. Oxford: Oxford University Press, 2013.

Karras, Ruth Mazo. 'The Regulation of Brothels in Later Medieval England'. *Signs* 14, no. 2 (1989): 399–433.

Kenyon, John P. *Revolution Principles: The Politics of Party, 1689-1720*. Cambridge: Cambridge University Press, 1977.

Kerkhof, Bert. 'A Fatal Attraction? Smith's *Theory of Moral Sentiments* and Mandeville's *Fable*'. *History of Political Thought* 16, no. 2 (1995): 219–33.

Keynes, John Maynard. *The General Theory of Employment, Interest and Money*. New York: Harcourt, Brace, 1936.

Kleiman-Lafon, Sylvie. 'The Healing Power of Words: Medicine as Literature in Bernard Mandeville's *Treatise of the Hypochondriack and Hysterick Diseases*'. In *Medicine and Narration in the Eighteenth Century*, edited by Sophie Vasset, 161–81. Oxford: Voltaire Foundation, 2013.

Klein, Lawrence Eliot. *Shaftesbury and the Culture of Politeness: Moral Discourse and Cultural Politics in Early Eighteenth-Century England*. Cambridge: Cambridge University Press, 2004.

Knott, Martin Otero. 'Mandeville on Governability'. *Journal of Scottish Philosophy* 12, no. 1 (2014): 19–49.

Kow, Simon. 'Rousseau's Mandevillean Conception of Desire and Modern Society'. In *Rousseau and Desire*, edited by Kow, Mark Blackell, and John Duncan, 62–82. Toronto: University of Toronto Press, 2009.

Kramnick, Isaac. *Bolingbroke and His Circle: The Politics of Nostalgia in the Age of Walpole*. Ithaca, NY: Cornell University Press, 1992.

Kramnick, Jonathan Brody. '"Unwilling to Be Short, or Plain, in Any Thing Concerning Gain": Bernard Mandeville and the Dialectic of Charity'. *Eighteenth Century* 33, no. 2 (1992): 148–75.

Lamprecht, Sterling P. '*The Fable of the Bees*'. *Journal of Philosophy* 23, no. 21 (1926): 561–79.

Landreth, H. 'The Economic Thought of Bernard Mandeville'. *History of Political Economy* 7, no. 2 (1975): 193–208.

Leyburn, Ellen Douglass. '*Hudibras* Considered as Satiric Allegory'. *Huntington Library Quarterly* 16, no. 2 (1953): 141–60.

Lovejoy, Arthur O. '"Pride" in Eighteenth-Century Thought'. *Modern Language Notes* 36, no. 1 (1921): 31–37.

Loveridge, Mark. *A History of Augustan Fable*. Cambridge: Cambridge University Press, 2006.

Luban, Daniel. 'Bernard Mandeville as Moralist and Materialist'. *History of European Ideas* 41, no. 7 (2015): 831–57.

——. 'What Is Spontaneous Order?' *American Political Science Review* 114, no. 1 (2020): 68–80.

Marx, Karl. *Karl Marx: A Reader*. Edited by Jon Elster. Cambridge: Press Syndicate of the University of Cambridge, 1986.

Maurer, Christian. 'Self-Interest and Sociability'. In *The Oxford Handbook of British Philosophy in the Eighteenth Century*, edited by James Harris, 291–314. Oxford: Oxford University Press, 2013.

———. 'What Can an Egoist Say against an Egoist? On Archibald Campbell's Criticisms of Bernard Mandeville'. *Journal of Scottish Philosophy* 12, no. 1 (2014): 1–18.

Maxwell, J. C. 'Ethics and Politics in Mandeville'. *Philosophy* 26, no. 98 (1951): 242–52.

McKee, Francis. 'An Anatomy of Power: The Early Works of Bernard Mandeville'. PhD thesis, University of Glasgow, 1991.

———. 'Francis Hutcheson and Bernard Mandeville'. *Eighteenth-Century Ireland/Iris an Dá Chultúr* 3 (1988): 123–32.

Melehy, Hassan. 'Silencing the Animals: Montaigne, Descartes, and the Hyperbole of Reason'. *Symplokē* 13, no. 1/2 (2005): 263–82.

Miller, Henry Knight. 'The Paradoxical Encomium with Special Reference to Its Vogue in England, 1600–1800'. *Modern Philology* 53, no. 3 (1956): 145–78.

Mitchell, Annie. 'Character of an Independent Whig—"Cato" and Bernard Mandeville'. *History of European Ideas* 29, no. 3 (2003): 291–311.

Monro, D. H. *The Ambivalence of Bernard Mandeville*. Oxford: Clarendon, 1975.

Moore, John Robert. 'The Groans of Great Britain: An Unassigned Tract by Charles Gildon'. *Papers of the Bibliographical Society of America* 40, no. 1 (1946): 22–31.

Moriarty, Michael. *Disguised Vices: Theories of Virtue in Early Modern French Thought*. Oxford: Oxford University Press, 2011.

———. *Fallen Nature, Fallen Selves: Early Modern French Thought II*. Oxford: Oxford University Press, 2006.

Muceni, Elena. 'Mandeville and France: The Reception of the *Fable of the Bees* and Its Influence on the French Enlightenment'. *French Studies* 69, no. 4 (2015): 449–61.

Nacol, Emily C. 'The Beehive and the Stew: Prostitution and the Politics of Risk in Bernard Mandeville's Political Thought'. *Polity* 47, no. 1 (2015): 61–83.

Nakhimovsky, Isaac. 'The Enlightened Epicureanism of Jacques Abbadie: *L'Art de Se Connoître Soi-Même* and the Morality of Self-Interest'. *History of European Ideas* 29, no. 1 (2003): 1–14.

Nieli, Russell. 'Commercial Society and Christian Virtue: The Mandeville–Law Dispute'. *Review of Politics* 51, no. 4 (1989): 581–610.

Noel, Thomas. *Theories of the Fable in the Eighteenth Century*. New York: Columbia University Press, 1975.

O'Brien, Karen. *Women and Enlightenment in Eighteenth-Century Britain*. Cambridge: Cambridge University Press, 2010.

O'Gorman, Frank. *The Long Eighteenth Century: British Political and Social History, 1688–1832*. London: Arnold, 1997.

Oliveira, Luís. 'Mandeville and Smith on the Problem of Moral Order'. In *Bernard de Mandeville's Tropology of Paradoxes: Morals, Politics, Economics, and Therapy*, edited by Edmundo Balsemão Pires and Joaquim Braga, 213–20. Studies in History and Philosophy of Science. Cham, Switzerland: Springer International, 2015.

Olsthoorn, Peter. 'Bernard Mandeville on Honor, Hypocrisy, and War'. *Heythrop Journal* 60, no. 2 (2019): 205–18.

Palmeri, Frank. *State of Nature, Stages of Society: Enlightenment Conjectural History and Modern Social Discourse*. New York: Columbia University Press, 2016.

Peltonen, Markku. 'Politeness and Whiggism, 1688–1732'. *Historical Journal* 48, no. 2 (2005): 391–414.

Perinetti, Darío. 'The Nature of Virtue'. In *The Oxford Handbook of British Philosophy in the Eighteenth Century*, edited by James Harris, 333–68. Oxford: Oxford University Press, 2013.

Plumb, J. H. *The Growth of Political Stability in England, 1675–1725*. London: Macmillan, 1967.

Pocock, J.G.A. *The Machiavellian Moment: Florentine Political Thought and the Atlantic Republican Tradition*. Princeton, NJ: Princeton University Press, 1975.

Pongiglione, Francesca. 'Bernard Mandeville's Influence on Adam Smith's *Wealth of Nations*'. *I castelli di Yale online*, 2019.

Pongiglione, Francesca, and Mikko Tolonen. 'Mandeville on Charity Schools: Happiness, Social Order and the Psychology of Poverty'. *Erasmus Journal for Philosophy and Economics* 9, no. 1 (2016): 82–100.

Porter, Roy. *English Society in the Eighteenth Century*. Harmondsworth, UK: Penguin Books, 1984.

Prendergast, Renee. 'Bernard Mandeville and the Doctrine of Laissez-Faire'. *Erasmus Journal for Philosophy and Economics* 9, no. 1 (2016): 101–23.

———. 'Jonathan Swift's Critique of Consequentialism?' *Cambridge Journal of Economics* 39, no. 1 (2015): 281–97.

———. 'Knowledge, Innovation and Emulation in the Evolutionary Thought of Bernard Mandeville'. *Cambridge Journal of Economics* 38, no. 1 (2014): 87–107.

Primer, I. 'Erasmus and Bernard Mandeville: A Reconsideration.' *Philological Quarterly* 73, no. 3 (1993): 313–35.

———, ed. *Mandeville Studies: New Explorations in the Art and Thought of Dr. Bernard Mandeville (1670-1733)*. International Archives of the History of Ideas. Dordrecht: Springer Netherlands, 1975.

Prior, Charles W. A. *Mandeville and Augustan Ideas: New Essays*. Victoria, BC: University of Victoria, 2000.

Rashid, Salim. 'Mandeville's *Fable*: Laissez-Faire or Libertinism?' *Eighteenth-Century Studies* 18, no. 3 (1985): 313–30.

Ricoeur, Paul. *Freud and Philosophy: An Essay on Interpretation*. Translated by Denis Savage. New Haven, CT: Yale University Press, 1970.

Robertson, John. *The Case for the Enlightenment: Scotland and Naples, 1680-1760*. Cambridge: Cambridge University Press, 2005.

Romão, Rui. 'Mandeville as a Sceptical and Medical Philosopher'. In *Bernard de Mandeville's Tropology of Paradoxes*, edited by Edmundo Balsemão Pires and Joaquim Braga, 105–112. Studies in History and Philosophy of Science. Cham, Switzerland: Springer International, 2015.

Roncaglia, Alessandro. *The Wealth of Ideas: A History of Economic Thought*. Cambridge: Cambridge University Press, 2009.

Rosenberg, Nathan. 'Mandeville and Laissez-Faire'. *Journal of the History of Ideas* 24, no. 2 (1963): 183–96.

Rosenthal, Laura J. *Infamous Commerce: Prostitution in Eighteenth-Century British Literature and Culture*. Ithaca, NY: Cornell University Press, 2006.

Rousseau, G. S. 'Mandeville and Europe: Medicine and Philosophy'. In *Mandeville Studies*, edited by I. Primer, 11–21. 1975.

Runciman, David. *Political Hypocrisy: The Mask of Power, from Hobbes to Orwell and Beyond*. Rev. ed. Princeton, NJ: Princeton University Press Princeton, 2018.

Sagar, Paul. *The Opinion of Mankind: Sociability and the Theory of the State from Hobbes to Smith*. Princeton, NJ: Princeton University Press, 2018.

———. 'Smith and Rousseau, after Hume and Mandeville'. *Political Theory* 46, no. 1 (2018): 29–58.

Sarasohn, Lisa T. *Gassendi's Ethics: Freedom in a Mechanistic Universe*. Ithaca, NY: Cornell University Press, 1996.

Schneider, Louis. *Paradox and Society: The Work of Bernard Mandeville*. New Brunswick, NJ: Transaction Books, 1987.

Schui, Florian. *Austerity: The Great Failure*. New Haven, CT: Yale University Press, 2015.

Scott, Kyle. 'Mandeville's Paradox as Satire: The Moral Consequences of Being a Good Citizen in a Commercial Society'. *Politics and Policy* 37, no. 2 (2009): 369–94.

Screpanti, Ernesto, and Stefano Zamagni. *An Outline of the History of Economic Thought*. Oxford: Oxford University Press, 2010.

Sheridan, Patricia. 'Parental Affection and Self-Interest: Mandeville, Hutcheson, and the Question of Natural Benevolence'. *History of Philosophy Quarterly* 24, no. 4 (2007): 377–92.

Simonazzi, Mauro. 'Bernard Mandeville on Hypochondria and Self-Liking'. *Erasmus Journal for Philosophy and Economics* 9, no. 1 (2016): 62–81.

Skarsten, A. Keith. 'Nature in Mandeville'. *Journal of English and Germanic Philology* 53, no. 4 (1954): 562–68.

Speck, W. A. 'Bernard Mandeville and the Middlesex Grand Jury'. *Eighteenth-Century Studies* 11, no. 3 (1978): 362–74.

———. *Tory and Whig : The Struggle in the Constituencies, 1701–1715*. London: Macmillan, 1970.

Spiegel, Henry William. *The Growth of Economic Thought*. Durham, NC: Duke University Press, 2004.

Stafford, John Martin. *Private Vices, Public Benefits? The Contemporary Reception of Bernard Mandeville*. Solihull, UK: Ismeron, 1997.

Stapelbroek, Koen. 'Dutch Decline as a European Phenomenon'. *History of European Ideas* 36, no. 2 (2010): 139–52.

Starkie, Andrew. 'William Law and *The Fable of the Bees*'. *Journal for Eighteenth-Century Studies* 32, no. 3 (2009): 307–19.

Stuart-Buttle, Tim. *From Moral Theology to Moral Philosophy: Cicero and Visions of Humanity from Locke to Hume*. Oxford: Oxford University Press, 2019.

Tolonen, Mikko. *Mandeville and Hume: Anatomists of Civil Society*. Oxford: Voltaire Foundation, 2013.

Turner, Brandon P. 'Mandeville against Luxury'. *Political Theory* 44, no. 1 (2016): 26–52.

Vaggi, Gianni, and Peter D. Groenewegen. *A Concise History of Economic Thought: From Mercantilism to Monetarism*. London: Palgrave Macmillan, 2014.

Van der Lugt, Mara. *Dark Matters: Pessimism and the Problem of Suffering*. Princeton, NJ: Princeton University Press Princeton, 2021.

Verburg, Rudi. 'Bernard Mandeville's Vision of the Social Utility of Pride and Greed'. *European Journal of the History of Economic Thought* 22, no. 4 (2015): 662–91.

———. 'The Dutch Background of Bernard Mandeville's Thought: Escaping the Procrustean Bed of Neo-Augustinianism'. *Erasmus Journal for Philosophy and Economics* 9, no. 1 (2016): 32–61.

Vichert, Gordon S. 'Bernard Mandeville's *The Virgin Unmask'd*'. In *Mandeville Studies: New Explorations in the Art and Thought of Dr. Bernard Mandeville (1670–1733)*, edited by Irwin Primer, 1–10. International Archives of the History of Ideas. Dordrecht: Springer Netherlands, 1975.

Viner, Jacob. *Essays on the Intellectual History of Economics*. Edited by D. A. Irwin. Princeton Legacy Library. Princeton, NJ: Princeton University Press, 1991.

———. 'Introduction to Bernard Mandeville, *A Letter to Dion* (1732)'. In *Essays on the Intellectual History of Economics*, edited by Douglas A. Irwin, 176–88. Princeton, NJ: Princeton University Press, 1991.

———. *The Role of Providence in the Social Order: An Essay in Intellectual History*, Princeton, NJ: Princeton University Press, 2016.

———. 'Satire and Economics in the Augustan Age of Satire'. In *Essays on the Intellectual History of Economics*, edited by Douglas A. Irwin, 303–24. Princeton, NJ: Princeton University Press, 1991.

Wahrman, Dror. *The Making of the Modern Self: Identity and Culture in Eighteenth-Century England*. New Haven, CT: Yale University Press, 2007.

Welchman, Jennifer. 'Who Rebutted Bernard Mandeville?' *History of Philosophy Quarterly* 24, no. 1 (2007): 57–74.

Weststeijn, Arthur. *Commercial Republicanism in the Dutch Golden Age: The Political Thought of Johan and Pieter de La Court*. Leiden: Brill, 2012.

White, Isabelle. '"So Great a Disproportion": Paradox and Structure in Rochester's "A Satyr against Reason and Mankind"'. *Restoration: Studies in English Literary Culture, 1660–1700* 8, no. 2 (1984): 47–55.

White, Jerry. *London in the 18th Century: A Great and Monstrous Thing*. London: Vintage, 2013.

Wootton, David. 'Pierre Bayle, Libertine?' In *Studies in Seventeenth-Century European Philosophy*, edited by M. A. Stewart, ch. 8. Oxford: Clarendon, 1997.

———. *Power, Pleasure, and Profit: Insatiable Appetites from Machiavelli to Madison*. Cambridge, MA: Belknapp Press of Harvard University Press, 2018.

———. 'Unbelief in Early Modern Europe'. *History Workshop*, no. 20 (1985): 82–100.

Young, James Dean. 'Mandeville: A Popularizer of Hobbes'. *Modern Language Notes* 74, no. 1 (1959): 10–13.

INDEX

Abbadie, Jacques, 17, 129, 149–50
abortion, 220. *See also* infanticide
Act of Settlement (1701), 159, 172
Act of Union (1707), 165
Adages (Erasmus), 54
Adam and Eve, 119, 239, 240
Addison, Joseph, 171, 174, 176, 266
Aesop at Amsterdam, 103
Aesop at Bath, 103
Aesop at Epsom, 103
Aesop at Islington, 103, 156
Aesop at Tunbridge, 103
Aesop at Whitehall, 103
Aesop Dress'd (Mandeville), 103–6, 108, 124
Aesop's Fables (Aesop), 98, 99, 102
afterlife, theological element of belief in, 32
Alciphron (Berkeley), 16
Amelia (Fielding), 16
An Answer to a Paper, Called 'A Memorial of the Poor Inhabitants, Tradesmen and Labourers of the Kingdom of Ireland' (Swift), 218
Anglican Church, 154
animals, 28–38. 144–45; anatomies, 39; behaviour of, 31, 36, 39; human beings vs., 32–34; suffering of, 37; topic of minds of, 35–36
animal spirits: movement of, 128; role of, 44; theory of, 40–41, 65–66
Anne, Queen of Great Britain, 106, 168, 170, 175, 191, 196
Antichrist, 15
'Apology for Raymond Sebond' (Montaigne), 109
Aquinas, St. Thomas, 266
Arete-Logica, or, An Enquiry into the Original of Moral Virtue (Campbell), 14
Aristotle, 89, 110, 266
Atterbury Plot, 179, 181
Augustine, 129, 134–35

Bacon, Francis, 42
Baglivi, Giorgio, 42–44, 47
Bank of England, 164
Battle of Blenheim (1704), 170
Bayle, 4, 24–25, 27, 35, 68, 129, 148, 151, 177
bees: description of, 110–12; tale of, 1–3
Berkeley, George, 16, 225
Bickerstaff, Isaac, 89
Bible, 162, 215
Bluet, George, 12
Bolingbroke, Henry St. John, 171–72
British Journal (journal), 10, 199
British society, degradation of, 12
Bruyère, Jean de La, 17
Burrow, Robert, 10
Butler, Joseph, 237
Butler, Samuel, 101–2

Calvinist Church, 189; standards, 190; theology, 129
Calvin, John, 129, 134–35, 140, 141, 144, 151, 189–90
Campbell, Archibald, 14
Catholic/Catholicism, 158; Church, 155, 168; French king, 163; movement, 134; Protestant and, 4; threat, 190; tyranny and intolerance of, on throne 106, 111–12
Catiline, 162
Cato, 180–83
Cato, a Tragedy (Addison), 180
Cato's Letters (Trenchard and Gordon), 179
Character of the Times Delineated, The (anonymous), 15
charity, 136–37, 237; charity schools, 182–88, 205–6
Charles II ,154
childbirth, dangers for women, 88–89
child development, pleasures, 139
Christianity, 11, 135–36, 147–48, 151, 241
Christians, 238–39; divine grace, 135–36; ethics, 241–42; morality, 147; sincerity, 133; theology of existence of pain, 36–37

Mandeville, Bernard: background of, 24;
death of, 274–75; education of, 25–26;
father Michael and, 27
marriage, 77, 78, 94; value of, 80
Marx, Karl, 2, 19, 264
Maslow, Abraham, 195
'Master Minds' lectures, Hayek, 19
materialism, 6, 131
mathematics, 44, 65, 249–50
Maxims (La Rochefoucauld), 5, 23, 46, 71,
98, 125, 129, 132, 192, 225, 260
medical practice: competitor model of, 61;
motives driving practitioners, 55–57;
obstacles to, 43; solving for symptoms,
65
medical theories: Galen, 58–59, 64;
Mandeville's, 127–28
medicine: doctor-patient relationship,
47–50; Mandeville's view of true, 57–58;
Mandeville's theory of practice, 131;
obstacles to practice of, 43; pursuit of,
56–57
Meditations on First Philosophy (Descartes), 34, 228
men, political domination over women,
89–90
Middlesex County Court, 178, 183
military, 8, 111, 113–14, 132, 167, 170, 179–80
Miscellanies (Swift), 15
*Mischiefs That Ought Justly to Be Appre-
hended from a Whig Government, The*
(Mandeville), 176, 178
moderation: Calvinist model of, 144–45;
Calvinist recommendation, 140–41;
human beings, 134; self-denial and, 151
Modest Defence of Publick Stews, A
(Mandeville), 79, 91, 93–94, 202, 225
*Modest Proposal for Preventing the
Children of Poor People from Being a
Burden to Their Parents, or Country,
and for Making Them Beneficial to the
Public* (Swift), 101, 219
Montaigne, Michel de, 4, 29–33, 43, 60,
68, 109–10, 140, 148, 259
morality: abstract reality, 258; debunking
of, 176, 189–90; economics and, 9–10;
foundations of virtue and, 10; religious
virtue, 137–38; social control, 150;

unnatural explanation of, 233; very
idea of, 12
moral philosophy, Kant's, 258
moral psychology, 95, 226; pride and
shame, 138
moral virtue: human artifice, 257; origin
of, 150–51
More, Thomas, 32–33, 100–101, 122
Moriae Encomium (Erasmus), 99–100

Nacol, Emily, 203
nature: knowledge of, 42–43; theories, 43
Noah, 238–39
Nicole, Pierre, 129, 136–39, 259
Nietzsche, Friedrich, 64, 264

*Observations upon the United Provinces
of the Netherlands* (Temple), 196
Oceana (Harrington), 160
Old Pretender, 181, 182
original sin, 29, 37

pain existence, Christian theology on,
36–37
Pamphleteers, The (Mandeville), 106,
167–70
paradox, 99, 102, 123, 129, 136, 257, 266,
267
Parker, Thomas, Earl Of Macclesfield,
176, 273–74
Parliament, Tory and Whig factions, 154
passions, 127
passive obedience, 154, 177–78, 189
physicians, ancient, 58–59
Pilkington, Matthew, 18
Plato, 227, 266
Pocock, J.G.A., 266, 269
political situation: constitutional monarchy,
105; government and consequences of
change, 104–5; immigration, 103; making changes, 105–6; morals of, 103–4
politics of nostalgia, 159
Pope, Alexander, 16, 18, 260–61
Poverty, 205–208
Practice of Physick, The (Baglivi), 42
Praise of Folly, The (Erasmus), 99–100,
112–13, 123, 136, 151
pregnancy, 88, 205, 220

A NOTE ON THE TYPE

———◆———

THIS BOOK has been composed in Miller, a Scotch Roman typeface designed by Matthew Carter and first released by Font Bureau in 1997. It resembles Monticello, the typeface developed for The Papers of Thomas Jefferson in the 1940s by C. H. Griffith and P. J. Conkwright and reinterpreted in digital form by Carter in 2003.

Pleasant Jefferson ("P. J.") Conkwright (1905–1986) was Typographer at Princeton University Press from 1939 to 1970. He was an acclaimed book designer and AIGA Medalist.